MW00803058

Alexis de Tocqueville and the Art of Democratic Statesmanship

Alexis de Tocqueville and the Art of Democratic Statesmanship

Edited by Brian Danoff and L. Joseph Hebert, Jr.

LEXINGTON BOOKS
A division of
ROWMAN & LITTLEFIELD PUBLISHERS, INC.
Lanham • Boulder • New York • Toronto • Plymouth, UK

Published by Lexington Books
A division of Rowman & Littlefield Publishers, Inc.
A wholly owned subsidiary of The Rowman & Littlefield Publishing Group, Inc.
4501 Forbes Boulevard, Suite 200, Lanham, Maryland 20706
http://www.lexingtonbooks.com

Estover Road, Plymouth PL6 7PY, United Kingdom

Copyright © 2011 by Lexington Books

All rights reserved. No part of this book may be reproduced in any form or by any
electronic or mechanical means, including information storage and retrieval systems,
without written permission from the publisher, except by a reviewer who may quote
passages in a review.

British Library Cataloguing in Publication Information Available

Library of Congress Cataloging-in-Publication Data
Alexis de Tocqueville and the art of democratic statesmanship / edited by Brian Danoff
and L. Joseph Hebert.
    p. cm.
  Includes index.
  ISBN 978-0-7391-4529-6 (cloth : alk. paper) — ISBN 978-0-7391-4530-2 (pbk. : alk.
paper)
  1. Tocqueville, Alexis de, 1805–1859.—Political and social views. 2. Democracy. 3.
Political leadership. 4. Political science—Philosophy—History—19th century. I.
Danoff, Brian. II. Hebert, L. Joseph (Louie Joseph), 1975–
  JC229.T8A425 2011
  321.8—dc22   2010039838

♾™ The paper used in this publication meets the minimum requirements of American
National Standard for Information Sciences—Permanence of Paper for Printed Library
Materials, ANSI/NISO Z39.48-1992.

Printed in the United States of America

Contents

Acknowledgments

We are deeply grateful to the contributors for their generous and spirited efforts. Thanks are also due to Joseph Parry, Jana Wilson, Erin Walpole, Amy King, Patricia Stevenson, and others at Lexington Books for embracing this project and for ushering us through the publication process so ably.

Brian Danoff is indebted to his wife and son for their love and support. He dedicates this volume to his parents, with gratitude for all that they have taught him.

Joe Hebert would like to thank Brian Danoff for conceiving this project and for his patience and diligence in seeing it through. He dedicates this volume to his beloved wife, Elena.

Chapter 15 of this volume originally appeared as "De Tweeledige uitdaging van een democratische cultuur in onze tijd," trans. Henny Vlot, *Nexus* 40 (2004): 73-85, and is reprinted here with kind permission of the Nexus Institute.

Introduction[1]

Brian Danoff

Harvey Mansfield and Delba Winthrop have written that *"Democracy in America* is at once the best book ever written on democracy and the best book ever written on America."[2] The editors of this volume concur with this assessment, and aim to advance a related claim: it is our contention that a key part of what makes Tocqueville's masterpiece the best book ever written on democracy is that it is the best book ever written on *democratic statesmanship.*

What, though, is democratic statesmanship?

Democratic statesmen are those leaders who have the wisdom and the prudence to successfully guide and shape their polities during the modern era, an era marked by widespread equality of conditions.

But how do we know when a statesman has been successful? Toward what ends should statesmen guide and shape their polities? At the end of *Democracy in America*, Tocqueville provides us with an answer to this, for he writes, "The nations of our day cannot prevent conditions of equality from spreading in their midst. But it depends upon themselves whether equality is to lead to servitude or freedom, knowledge or barbarism, prosperity or wretchedness."[3] The *successful* democratic statesman is thus a leader who helps steer his or her fellow citizens towards knowledge, prosperity, and—above all else—towards freedom. The democratic statesman helps nations achieve Tocqueville's greatest hopes for political life in democratic times, while avoiding the dangers that Tocqueville fears.

Tocqueville feared that in the modern era, democratic peoples would revel in the easy pleasures of equality, but neglect the hard work that is necessary to maintain political freedom.[4] In short, he feared that democratic peoples would one day succumb to an "equality of servitude."[5] Tocqueville suggests that this loss of freedom will be the sorry fate of democratic nations which do not succeed in keeping the problem of "individualism" at bay. By "individualism," Tocqueville refers to, "a calm and considered feeling which disposes each citizen to isolate himself from the mass of his fellows and withdraw into the circle of family and friends; with this little

1

society formed to his taste, he gladly leaves the greater society to look after itself."[6] For Tocqueville, "individualism" is a problem that only arises in the modern democratic era; during the age of aristocracy, individualism did not emerge, because people were connected, by law and custom, to both their contemporaries and to past and future generations. As Tocqueville puts it, "Aristocracy links everybody, from peasant to king, in one long chain."[7] But in the era of democracy, the ties that bind are cut, resulting in the danger that each person will focus solely on his or her own self, and ignore the political community. Tocqueville suggests that in a nation of individualists people will be equal to one another, but they will not be free, for real freedom demands participation in political life.[8] It is thus Tocqueville's hope that statesmen will be able to keep the individualism to which democratic nations are prone in check, so that people in the democratic era will gain not only equality, but freedom as well.

The task of democratic statesmanship is well described by Tocqueville in the Introduction to *Democracy in America*, wherein Tocqueville declares that·"The first duty imposed on those who now direct society is to educate democracy; to put, if possible, new life into its beliefs; to purify its mores; to control its actions; gradually to substitute understanding of statecraft for present inexperience and knowledge of its true interests for blind instincts; to adapt government to the needs of time and place; and to modify it as men and circumstances require."[9]

In this passage, Tocqueville articulates a conception of statesmanship that is close, in some respects, to that of the ancients. In his *Politics*, Aristotle insisted that "It is a mistake to believe that the 'statesman' is the same as the monarch of a kingdom or the manager of a household, or the master of a number of slaves."[10] This is mistaken because the goal of the genuine statesman is not to dominate or manipulate; instead, the goal of the statesman is to *educate* the citizenry, to make them virtuous so that they are fit for free government—fit, that is, for ruling and being ruled in turn.

Like Aristotle, Tocqueville maintains that a key task—indeed, *the* key task—of statesmanship is to educate citizens and shape their character.[11] But in contrast to Aristotle, Tocqueville faced a world in which "equality of conditions" is the "basic fact."[12] Unlike Aristotle, Tocqueville asked: In the age of equality—that is, in the era of what Tocqueville calls the democratic "social state"—what are the special problems, challenges, and possibilities that statesmen must confront?[13]

Taken as a whole, the contributors to this volume suggest that Tocqueville thought more searchingly—and more fruitfully—about this question than any other modern political theorist. The contributors also suggest that Tocqueville's analysis of democratic statesmanship remains highly relevant today. To be sure, not all of the contributors concur with every one of Tocqueville's ideas; however, the contributors all suggest that thinking *with* Tocqueville remains indispensable for those who want to understand the proper place and role of statesmanship in democratic times, and this includes, of course, our *own* time.

In 1835, Tocqueville famously called for "a new political science" that could address the problems and possibilities of a "world itself quite new."[14] It was Tocqueville's hope that this new political science could then be put into practice by statesmen and other concerned citizens, so that the promise of the democratic world could be realized, and its pitfalls avoided. For Tocqueville, then, the democratic world needed not just a new political science, but also new arts of statesmanship and leadership. In the years that followed, Tocqueville strove to further both the art of statesmanship—for example, through his actions as French foreign minister—and the science of politics. In his 1852 address to the annual meeting of the Academy of Moral and Political Sciences, Tocqueville provided a particularly lucid account of the nature of and connections among political philosophy, political science, and the political art, an account that sheds light on his own words and actions elsewhere, and on the challenges facing democratic statesmen today. A fresh translation of Tocqueville's 1852 speech appears as chapter 1 of this volume.

The speech to the Academy of Moral and Political Sciences contains Tocqueville's most sustained reflections on the relationship between theory and practice—or, to put it another way, the relationship between political science, on the one hand, and political leadership, on the other. In this speech, Tocqueville maintains that politicians who dismiss political science are wrong to do so. Politicians, Tocqueville suggests, too often assume that political science offers only theoretical abstractions that are not useful in the real world of political life. Politicians suppose that because they must respond to a constantly changing and always unpredictable political landscape, the theories of political scientists can do little to help them learn how to govern. In the view of most political actors, "simple good sense" is more helpful for learning how to rule than the "theories and maxims" that come from "studying philosophy and history."[15]

Tocqueville concedes that the practitioner of politics here touches on a partial truth, for Tocqueville agrees with the politicians that writing "fine books . . . on politics . . . prepares one quite poorly for the government of men and the management of affairs." But if Tocqueville concedes that political scientists do not necessarily themselves make good rulers, he insists that those practitioners of politics who dismiss political science as useless and irrelevant are "greatly in the wrong."[16]

For according to Tocqueville, the political sciences shape how people *think* about politics, and, eventually, this shapes how people *practice* politics. As Tocqueville puts it,

> among all civilized peoples, the political sciences give birth to, or at least form, those general ideas from which then emerge the particular facts in whose midst men of politics busy themselves, and the laws they believe they invent; these ideas form around each society something like a sort of intellectual atmosphere breathed by the spirit of both governed and governors, and from which the former as well as the latter draw, often without knowing it, sometimes without wanting it, the principles of their conduct.[17]

This passage can be fruitfully compared to Abraham Lincoln's observation that "he who molds public sentiment, goes deeper than he who enacts statutes or pronounces decisions. He makes statutes and decisions possible or impossible to be executed."[18] Just as Lincoln believed that it is the molder of "public sentiment" who determines whether particular "statutes" are enacted or not, so, too, did Tocqueville believe that it is the political sciences which form the "intellectual atmosphere" out of which grow a nation's laws.

For Tocqueville, then, the political theories espoused by political scientists have a profound impact on political practice. Moreover, it should be noted that Tocqueville's discussion points toward the idea that the political scientist is potentially a type of *statesman*, for Tocqueville suggests that the ideas and theories of political scientists can end up shaping and guiding actual political life in fundamental respects.

As an example of how the ideas of political thinkers can decisively shape the destiny of nations, Tocqueville cites the French Revolution. "The great artisans of this fearsome revolution were precisely the only men of those times who had never taken the least part in public affairs. It was authors of whom no one is ignorant, it was the most abstract science that deposited in the spirit of our fathers those seeds of novelties from which sprouted suddenly so many political institutions and civil laws unknown to their ancestors." For Tocqueville, then, it was the ideas and visions of French political thinkers which led to the French Revolution, a revolution which "changed the face of the world"; practical politicians who try to dismiss the efficacy or power of political theory are thus very much mistaken, according to Tocqueville.[19]

Tocqueville's example of the French Revolution is no doubt intended to be at least in part a kind of cautionary tale regarding the potentially *dangerous* power of political theory. For as readers of *The Old Regime and the French Revolution* well know, while Tocqueville may have praised the grand and freedom-loving spirit of 1789, he was also highly critical of the ways in which the French Revolutionaries eventually centralized power and thus wiped out local freedoms. Moreover, in the *Old Regime*, Tocqueville places the blame for the negative aspects of the French Revolution in large part on the political thinkers known as the *philosophes*. The *philosophes*, according to Tocqueville, promoted an "abstract, literary politics" as they foolishly sought "to remold society on entirely new lines, traced by each thinker in the sole light of reason."[20]

Tocqueville thus suggests that the political sciences can have a damaging influence on political life, particularly if political scientists lack any practical experience with political action. Just as Lincoln believed that the words and ideas of leaders mold "public sentiment" in ways that tend to promote the preservation of virtue, on the one hand, or corruption, on the other, Tocqueville believed that the political sciences "secretly and slowly" impart "general ideas" that either harm or improve the political and moral life of a nation.[21]

In Tocqueville's view, the *philosophes* were unstatesmanlike in their desire to impose their abstract political ideals onto political practice; however, Tocqueville thinks that it *is* possible for political scientists to act successfully as statesmen who can help educate and guide their polities. Tocqueville himself aspired to be precisely this kind of statesmanlike political scientist, for he hoped that his "new political science," as he put it in *Democracy*, would be able to help steer humanity (particularly the French people) towards enlightenment, prosperity, and freedom.

The claim that Tocqueville's "new political science" was statesmanlike in its aspirations might at first seem to contradict Tocqueville's insistence in his 1852 speech that "political science and the art of governing are two very distinct things."[22] For if the "science" (theory) and the "art" (practice) of politics are so different, then is a statesmanlike political science not an impossibility?

At first glance, Tocqueville does seem to suggest that the theory and the practice of politics are entirely different matters. In the 1852 speech, he states that "There are two parts of politics that must not be confused, one fixed and the other in motion." The "fixed" aspect of politics is "founded on the very nature of man, on his interests, on his faculties, on his needs as revealed by philosophy and history, on his instincts, which change their objects according to the times without changing their nature, and which are as immortal as his race." In short, this fixed part of politics "teaches us what laws are best adapted to the general and permanent condition of humanity. All this is the science [of politics.]"[23] As Sheldon Wolin has noted, by "science of politics," then, Tocqueville does not mean the kind of knowledge sought by positivist practitioners of social science who model their enterprise along the lines of the natural sciences. Instead, by "science of politics," Tocqueville refers to the quest for wisdom about political things that is characteristic of the classical political theorists.[24]

Whereas the "science" of politics seeks to find eternal, or "fixed" truths about the nature of political life, Tocqueville states that the "art of government" is instead concerned with the flux of current political matters. The practitioner of the "art of government" does not focus on transcendent truths, but rather must grapple with the "the difficulties of each day" and "the passing needs of the moment" in a political landscape marked by an ever-changing "variety of incidents."[25]

After defining both the "science" and "art" of politics, Tocqueville then emphasizes that the "art assuredly differs from the science";[26] however, the speech also suggests—as does his *oeuvre* as a whole—that a fusion of science and art (that is, a fusion of theory and practice) is not only possible, but also highly desirable. For Tocqueville, it is precisely statesmen (including statesmanlike political theorists) who successfully fuse the theory ("science") and the practice ("art") of politics.

Tocqueville suggests that to practice the "art of government" is to grapple with the flux of constantly changing political affairs. However, Tocqueville also notes that "Barbarians are the only ones who recognize in politics nothing but practice."[27] This means that while some politicians may (foolishly) disdain theory, a true statesman must honor theory and have at least some knowledge of it. Unlike a mere politician, a true statesman is guided, at least in part, by his or her knowledge of the "nature of man." Like the mere politician, the true statesman is concerned with "the difficulties of each day" and the always changing "variety of incidents"; however, the true statesman, unlike the mere politician, considers these difficulties and incidents in the light of the wisdom provided by the study of "philosophy and history."[28] The true statesman, then, must not ignore theory as he or she practices the art of government.

By the same token, Tocqueville believes that the true political theorist (as opposed to a mere abstract philosopher) must not ignore practice as he or she theorizes. Hence, just as Tocqueville condemns "barbarians" for practicing politics without knowledge of theory, so, too, does he condemn the *philosophes* for engaging in theory without any knowledge of practice. Because they lived under a centralized system that denied them the political education that can only come from political participation and political responsibility, the theoretical vision of the *philosophes* was completely uninformed by political practice. As Tocqueville puts it in *The Old Regime*:

> Their very way of living led these writers to indulge in abstract theories and genera-lizations regarding the nature of government, and to place a blind confidence in these. For living as they did, quite out of touch with practical politics, they lacked the experience which might have tempered their enthusiasm. Thus they completely failed to perceive the very real obstacles in the way of even the most praiseworthy reforms, and to gauge the perils involved in even the most salutary revolutions.[29]

For Tocqueville, then, just as the statesman must have some knowledge of political theory, a statesmanlike political theorist must have some knowledge of political practice.

To be sure, Tocqueville thinks that political theorists must retain a healthy in-dependence from the vagaries of practical party politics. (In the same vein, he famously insists in *Democracy* that religion must remain independent from the state.) Hence, in his 1852 speech, Tocqueville declares that "We ought never to forget . . . that we are a learned society and not a political body; the security and the dignity of our labors depend upon it."[30] But if Tocqueville wants to ensure that political scien-tists are not co-opted by political elites, this does not mean, as we have seen, that he thinks political theory and political practice must remain completely separate from one another.

Indeed, in the *Old Regime*, Tocqueville explicitly praises eighteenth century England for the way in which it fused theory and practice. Tocqueville writes that,

> In England writers on the theory of government and those who actually   governed co-operated with each other, the former setting forth their new theories, the latter amending or circumscribing these in the light of practical experience. In France, however, precept and practice were kept quite distinct and remained in the hands of two quite independent groups. One of these carried on the actual administration while the other set forth the abstract principles on which good government should, they said, be based; one took the routine measures appropriate to the needs of the moment, the other propounded general laws without a thought for their practical ap-plication.[31]

In France, a total separation of theory and practice led to disaster; in England, on the other hand, those who practiced the "science" of politics and those who practiced the "art" of politics were in dialogue with one another and were hence able to educate one another. In short, Tocqueville suggests that while the "art" and the "science" of politics are distinct activities, the great statesmen—and the great statesmanlike pol-itical theorists—to some degree always combine the two.

In chapter 2 of this volume, Susan McWilliams argues that Tocqueville was himself a statesmanlike political theorist of the highest order. McWilliams demonstrates that Tocqueville acted much like the ancient Greek *theoros*—theorist—who would visit strange and distant lands in order to gain insights that could be of benefit to his home city-state. Tocqueville thus engaged in what McWilliams calls "leading by leaving." Using Tocqueville as her example *par excellence*, McWilliams goes on to suggest that in the democratic age—an age of flux and uncertainty—the leave-taker, or stranger, is uniquely equipped to carry out the perennially important tasks of statesmanship.

Chapters 3-6 each compare and contrast Tocqueville's understanding of statesmanship with the understanding of statesmanship held by another major political philosopher. Through this comparative approach, the contours of Tocqueville's theory of democratic statesmanship come into sharper focus. In chapter 3, Aristide Tessitore suggests that in many (but by no means all) respects, Tocqueville's "new political science" represents a return to Aristotelian thought. While Tessitore assiduously notes key differences between the ideas of Aristotle and Tocqueville, he demonstrates that there are important affinities: both Aristotle and Tocqueville eschew abstract theorizing and instead give careful attention to the context of political life; both are concerned with the ways in which politics and the soul affect one another; and both believe in the enduring need for statesmen who can give the citizenry an "education relative to the regime," as Aristotle put it, so that the goods specific to a particular regime can shine forth, and its ills can be minimized.

In chapter 4, Khalil Habib explores Tocqueville's and Machiavelli's differing assessments of the "People" and the "Great," to put it in Machiavelli's terms. Whereas Machiavelli argues that founding-statesmen should found their states on the people—on the grounds that they are more decent than the ambitious and domineering "Great"—Tocqueville warns that founding a government on the people can lead to a highly destructive "tyranny of the majority." The task of the democratic statesman, then, is to ward off democratic despotism. Whereas Machiavelli disdained Christianity, Tocqueville's democratic statesman believes that nurturing Christianity is one of the most important ways to reduce the danger that a stultifying "new despotism" will arise in democratic times.

Like Habib, F. Flagg Taylor IV also explores Tocqueville's argument that democracy can lead to tyranny as easily as it can lead to freedom. In chapter 5, Taylor demonstrates that while Montesquieu and Tocqueville had a similar understanding of the relationship between laws, institutions, and mores, Tocqueville departed from Montesquieu insofar as Tocqueville thought that democratic mores could promote servitude rather than liberty. To avoid this fate, the democratic statesman must give careful attention to the mores of the citizenry, even in the liberal age. That is, what Montesquieu had said of ancient republics—that their sustenance depends on society's action on itself—Tocqueville suggests continues to be true of the liberal republic of the United States.

In chapter 6, Richard Boyd and Conor Williams compare Tocqueville's ideas on statesmanship to the ideas of a much more recent political theorist, namely, Michael Oakeshott. Boyd and Williams demonstrate that for both Tocqueville and Oakeshott, the theoretical knowledge of the philosopher cannot on its own possibly prepare one for statesmanship, for statesmanship requires practical political knowledge. Boyd and Williams go on to suggest that while both Tocqueville and Oakeshott make a similar epistemological distinction between theoretical and practical knowledge, the two theorists differ in their understanding of the political implications of this distinction. Whereas the distinction between theoretical and practical knowledge is used by Oakeshott in the service of "conservative," or anti-democratic arguments, Tocqueville uses this same distinction to make a pro-democratic argument: for Tocqueville, ordinary citizens are capable of ruling themselves in a statesmanlike way, as long as they have the practical political knowledge that results from ongoing democratic participation and civic engagement.

The next three chapters explore Tocqueville's ideas on the ways in which democratic leaders can act as statesmen within the channels of government. In chapter 7, William Parsons carefully elucidates Tocqueville's hopes and fears about the American presidency. Tocqueville hoped for statesmanlike presidents who would have the courage to sometimes defy—and ultimately educate—popular opinion, as President Washington did. Tocqueville feared, though, that most presidents would simply follow the passions of the people, as President Jackson did. Tocqueville also feared that one day, when America took a more active role on the world stage, the powers of the presidency would expand in ways that pose a threat to republican liberty. Parsons argues that Tocqueville's fears were prescient: the massive federal bureaucracy which today is headed by the president has produced something akin to the administrative despotism that Tocqueville dreaded. Parsons maintains that the only solution to this problem is virtue in the people; however, the modern bureaucratic state itself tends to sap this virtue. For Parsons, then, Tocqueville's analysis suggests that it highly difficult—although not utterly impossible—for an American president to exercise genuine statesmanship.

In chapter 8, Thad Williamson also warns against investing too much hope in the notion that a particular president can somehow single-handedly revitalize American democracy. Williamson offers a Tocquevillian analysis of Obama's presidential campaign and of his first year in office. Williamson notes that Obama's presidential campaign excited many neo-Tocquevillian political theorists of a civic republican bent, precisely because Obama seemed to give voice to themes often neglected by liberal or "progressive" politicians: an emphasis on the importance of citizens taking responsibility both in their personal lives and for the good of the community, an emphasis on direct citizen engagement in political activity, and a claim that citizens have the ability to re-shape the meaning and substance of American democracy. While Obama has continued to deploy the rhetoric of the would-be transformational leader, Williamson argues that the rhetoric has not in fact been lent substance (to date) by the way the Obama administration has governed. In contrast to the almost unconstrained pessimism of analysts such as Sheldon Wolin, however, Williamson argues that there are limited but important steps the Obama administration could make to encourage a long-term shift in American political culture, consonant with Stephen Elkin's ideas about a reconstructed commercial republic. Above all, Obama must try to encourage local political participation, in order to help foster a political culture in which citizens take responsibility for their own political problems.

Like Williamson, Albert Dzur emphasizes that ordinary citizens today need to be given more civic and political responsibility; in Dzur's view, the justice system is an important governmental arena in which this increased empowerment of the citizenry should take place. Motivated in part by his concerns over the high level of incarceration in the U.S., Dzur considers in chapter 9 an approach toward both encouraging and moderating citizen participation in the justice system suggested by Alexis de Tocqueville and further elaborated by John Stuart Mill. Tocqueville's argument rests on a "civic schoolhouse" account of jury trials as sites of socialization and legitimation. Dzur suggests that Tocqueville and Mill believed jury socialization operated hierarchically, through lay deference to the judge's professional knowledge in civil and criminal trials. While keeping core features of Tocqueville's framework intact, Dzur posits a more democratic account of how juries socialize and create legitimacy that stresses the distinct capabilities and experiences of lay citizens as they work together in the courtroom. A major leadership task for reform-minded court professionals is thus to create more rather than less popular participation and responsibility in the criminal justice process.

One element that makes this book true to the spirit of Tocqueville is that it does not focus solely on leaders in government. For both implicitly and explicitly, Tocqueville suggests that it is not just political leaders who need to guide and to "educate democracy," but also philosophers, moralists, poets, historians, religious leaders, and others. In part 4 of the volume, therefore, the essays examine Tocqueville's ideas on statesmanship conducted outside of the usual channels of government.

In chapter 10, Derek Barker notes a parallel between Tocqueville's celebration of nineteenth century associational life as a locus of civic habit-formation and recent hopes that nongovernmental associations (NGOs) might provide modern-day citizens with spaces in which they can govern their own affairs. Drawing carefully on Tocqueville's political theory, Barker argues that thus far such hopes have been misplaced, as NGOs have taken on many of the same bureaucratic features that distance citizens from modern government. Barker explains that for Tocqueville, associations are crucial for democracies because they can play the civic leadership role that was once played by aristocrats. But whereas Tocquevillian associations once helped to provide citizens with opportunities to engage in collective action, today's NGOs are so professionalized and specialized that they rarely help develop people's civic capacities. Barker concludes by suggesting some methods that today's organizations might use to strengthen rather than erode democratic citizenship.

In chapter 11, Jon Schaff compares Willa Cather's treatment of the paradox of modern democratic progress in *My Àntonia* to Tocqueville's analysis of the same issue in *Democracy in America*. Both Cather and Tocqueville appreciate the benefits of scientific and political advances while noting the dangers of an ideological fixation on a supposedly unlimited progress that ignores the ways change can erode stability, virtue, family, and community. Although Cather's analysis is tragic, insofar as she suggests that the conflict between progress and traditional virtues is ultimately irreconcilable, her writing exhibits Tocquevillian statesmanship in that it seeks to educate the democratic soul about goods it is all too prone to ignore, and thereby to mitigate the extent to which democratic progress will trample on such goods.

In chapter 12, L. Joseph Hebert, Jr. examines the application of Tocqueville's political art to contemporary religious leadership. Tocqueville sees religious authority as both compatible with genuine democratic liberty and essential to the formation and preservation of the mores that allow liberal democracy to flourish. Yet Tocqueville also holds that democracy poses a threat to religion. Religious leaders must therefore practice the art of democratic statesmanship in order to preserve what is essential in religion while adapting prudently to democratic proclivities where possible. Relying upon Tocqueville's own treatment of Christianity in general and Catholicism in particular, Hebert analyzes the strengths and weaknesses of the Second Vatican Council, the Catholic Church's most concerted attempt to engage in the kind of democratic statesmanship for which Tocqueville calls. Hebert finds a remarkable resemblance between the aims of Vatican II and the advice Tocqueville gives to modern religious leaders. At the same time, Hebert suggests that the actual effects of the Council have often diverged from these original aims. Hebert then uses Tocqueville's ideas to explore the reasons behind—as well as possible solutions for—the discrepancies between the intentions and the results (thus far) of Vatican II.

In chapter 13, Peter Augustine Lawler expands upon the need for a religious dimension to contemporary democratic statesmanship. If democratic statesmen today are to follow Tocqueville's advice and "apply themselves relentlessly to raising up souls," then they must help Americans remember, understand, and honor their Puritan legacy, for rather than being enemies of freedom and equality (as many falsely assume today), the Puritans provide us with the ideas that undergird egalitarianism and freedom, properly understood. As Lawler discusses, Tocqueville himself was a great admirer of the Puritans; indeed, for Tocqueville, the local-political and religious antidotes to individualism are rooted in Puritanism. To properly appreciate the Puritan contribution to America, Lawler suggests that we should turn not only to Tocqueville, but also to the novelist/theologian Marilynne Robinson. Taken together, Lawler suggests, Tocqueville and Robinson can teach us that the Puritans were correct to insist that the spirit of liberty requires the spirit of religion.

For Tocqueville, the art of politics applies as much to foreign affairs as to domestic, although it cannot apply in precisely the same way. For one thing, Tocqueville was too aware of the influence of mores and other variables influencing political life to believe that the same policies could be best—or even practicable—in different societies. For another, he noted that the "society of nations of which each people is a citizen [is] a society that is always rather barbarous, even in the most civilized centuries, whatever effort is made to soften and regulate the relations of those who compose it."[32] While an application of Tocqueville's insights in *Democracy* to international relations and comparative government is possible, therefore, it must tackle exceedingly difficult questions about the degree and kind of justice or goodness that can be achieved in complicated circumstances. This is the theme of part 5 of our volume.

In chapter 14, Paul Carrese confronts some of the difficult questions posed by international relations to the democratic political art. He examines the controversy stirred by Tocqueville's own treatment of French foreign affairs, both in his writings and during his brief stint as French foreign minister. Does Tocqueville's support—however qualified—for French colonialism and American expansion contradict his liberal principles? By carefully examining both the immediate circumstances in which Tocqueville acted and spoke, and the philosophic premises of Tocqueville and his critics, Carrese argues that Tocqueville sought a prudent blend of realism and liberalism on international affairs, one that aims at heeding liberal principles where possible, while finding the least-worst departure from them where a departure is necessary.

In the final chapter of our volume, Thomas Pangle applies Tocqueville's classic analysis of democracy to the challenges facing European leaders today. (One reason that this is a very worthwhile and appropriate endeavor, of course, is that Tocqueville himself wrote *Democracy* with the hope that European leaders would draw crucial lessons from its pages.) Noting Tocqueville's warning that democracy can lead upward, to an unprecedentedly broad culture of human dignity and even nobility, or drift downward, toward an unprecedentedly pervasive civic degradation, Pangle selects from Tocqueville's rich cabinet of remedies two that seem especially worth pondering in contemporary Europe: a strenuous commitment to governmental decentralization and reliance upon voluntary associations wherever possible; and, a welcoming and exploitation of crises that call whole democratic peoples to greatness. Pangle also recommends a renewed focus on leisure, or serious pleasures transcending both work and recreation, while warning those who will lead such efforts against a simplistic and dangerous contempt for the inevitably practical and popularized culture of modern democracy.

As we have seen, Tocqueville declared that "The first duty imposed on those who now direct society is to educate democracy." The contributors to this volume seek not only to understand this statement, but also ultimately to exemplify it. That is, the volume's authors not only seek to analyze Tocqueville's ideas on how democracy can best be educated by statesmen; in addition, the authors, inspired by Tocqueville, all seek to offer their *own* advice on how democracy can best be educated today. It is the highest hope of the editors that this book can contribute not only to a better understanding of Tocqueville for its own sake, but also, in at least some small way, to a better understanding of how to achieve the highest possibilities—and how to avoid the perils—of democratic life in our own day.

Notes

1. I thank Joseph Hebert for his very helpful suggestions and comments on this introductory essay.

2. Harvey C. Mansfield and Delba Winthrop, "Editors' Introduction," in Alexis de Tocqueville, *Democracy in America*, ed. Mansfield and Winthrop (University of Chicago Press, 2000), xvii.

3. Alexis de Tocqueville, *Democracy in America*, ed. J.P. Mayer and trans. George Lawrence (New York: Harper & Row, 1988), 705.

4. Ibid., 503-506.

5. Ibid., 57.

6. Ibid., 506.

7. Ibid., 508.

8. That for Tocqueville freedom demands participation in politics is evident from such passages as the following: "It is possible to imagine an extreme point at which freedom and equality would meet and blend. Let us suppose that all the citizens take a part in the government and that each of them has an equal right to do so. Then, no man is different from his fellows, and nobody can wield tyrannical power; men will be perfectly free because they are entirely equal, and they will be perfectly equal because they are entirely free." See *Democracy*, 503. It is clear from this passage that "tak[ing] a part in the government" is a crucial aspect of freedom for Tocqueville.

9. Tocqueville, *Democracy*, 12.

10. Aristotle, *Politics*, trans. Ernest Barker (Oxford: Oxford University Press, 1958), 1.

11. For my own extended analysis of Tocqueville's ideas on how leaders can best "educate" their fellow citizens, see Brian Danoff, *Educating Democracy: Alexis de Tocqueville and Leadership in America* (Albany, NY: State University of New York Press, 2010). For another recent analysis of Tocqueville's understanding of democratic statesmanship, see L. Joseph Hebert, Jr., *More than Kings and Less than Men: Tocqueville on the Promise and Perils of Democratic Individualism* (Lanham, MD: Lexington Books, 2010), especially chapter 6.

12. Tocqueville, *Democracy*, 9.

13. Tocqueville uses the term "social state" throughout *Democracy*. A key discussion of the democratic "social state" comes in volume I, part 1, chapter 3. See *Democracy*, 50-57.

14. Tocqueville, *Democracy*, 12.

15. Alexis de Tocqueville, "Speech Given to the Annual Public Meeting of the Academy of Moral and Political Sciences on April 3, 1852." This speech appears as chapter 1 of this volume, in a translation by L. Joseph Hebert, Jr. The quotations are from p. 17 of this volume.

16. Ibid., 18.

17. Ibid., 20.

18. Abraham Lincoln, *Speeches and Writings 1832-1858* (New York: Library of America, 1989), 525.

19. Tocqueville, "Speech Given to the Academy of Moral and Political Sciences," 20.

20. Alexis de Tocqueville, *The Old Regime and the French Revolution*, trans. Stuart Gilbert (New York: Anchor Books, 1955), 139, 140.

21. Tocqueville, "Speech Given to the Academy of Moral and Political Sciences," 20.

22. Ibid., 19.

23. Ibid., 18.

24. Sheldon Wolin, *Tocqueville between Two Worlds: The Making of a Political and Theoretical Life* (Princeton, NJ: Princeton University Press, 2001), 519.

25. Tocqueville, "Speech Given to the Academy of Moral and Political Sciences," 18.

26. Ibid.

27. Ibid., 20.

28. Ibid., 18. Notably, Tocqueville also states that "political men" are "the very ones who ought naturally to practice [the] science [of politics]." Ibid., 17.

29. Tocqueville, *The Old Regime*, 140.

30. Tocqueville, "Speech Given to the Academy of Moral and Political Sciences," 28.

31. Tocqueville, *The Old Regime*, 145-146. In his speech to the Academy, Tocqueville makes a somewhat similar argument about the relationship between "commentators" (defined as "those who interpret and clarify existing institutions, treaties, constitutions, and laws") and "publicists" (political philosophers such as Plato, Machiavelli, Montesquieu, and Rousseau). As Tocqueville puts it, "There is not a commentator who has not often supported himself on the abstract and general truths that the publicists have found, and the latter constantly need to found their theory on the particular facts and the institutions of our experience that the commentators have revealed or described." See Tocqueville, "Speech Given to the Academy of Moral and Political Sciences," 19-20.

32. Tocqueville, "Speech Given to the Academy of Moral and Political Sciences," 19.

Part I
Statesmanship and Political Philosophy

Chapter 1

Speech Given to the Annual Public Meeting of the Academy of Moral and Political Sciences on April 3, 1852[1]

Alexis de Tocqueville, President of the Academy

Translated by L. Joseph Hebert, Jr.

Gentlemen,

The academy in whose name I have the honor of speaking today has been exposed from birth to strange judgments; her very reason for being has been contested. It is willingly admitted that the actions of the private man ought to be subject to a permanent rule, and that morality is a science. But is it the same for those collections of men one calls societies? Is there a science of politics? It has hitherto been denied, and, oddly enough, it has generally been political men, that is to say, the very ones who ought naturally to practice this science, who have taken such liberties with it. They have sometimes permitted themselves to call it chimerical or at least vain.

There is something rather puerile, they have said, in imagining that there is a particular art that teaches one to govern. The field of politics is too varied and volatile to permit one to place there the foundations of a science. The facts[2] that would constitute its matter never have anything but a false and deceptive resemblance to one another. The epoch in which they take place, the condition of the peoples in which one observes them, the character of the men who produce them or who submit to them renders them so profoundly dissimilar that it can only be useful to consider each of them separately. The prince who tried to govern his people with the aid of theories and maxims formed[3] while studying philosophy and history would turn out very poorly; it is to be believed that simple good sense would have been of greater use to him.

17

Such is the rather condescending language I have sometimes heard used by political men regarding the sciences whose subject is politics and regarding those who cultivate them.

I have always found them to be greatly in the wrong.[4]

There are two parts of politics that must not be confused, one fixed and the other in motion.

The first, founded on the very nature of man, on his interests, on his faculties, on his needs as revealed by philosophy and history, on his instincts, which change their objects according to the times without changing their nature, and which are as immortal as his race; the first, I say, teaches us what laws are best adapted to the general and permanent condition of humanity.

All this is the science.

And then there is a practical and militant politics that struggles against the difficulties of each day, adapting to the variety of incidents, providing for the passing needs of the moment, and calling to its aid the ephemeral passions of contemporaries.

This is the art of government.

The art assuredly differs from the science, practice is often removed from theory, I do not deny it; I would go even farther, if desired, and make this concession, admitting that, in my judgment, to excel at one is no reason at all to succeed in the other. I do not know, gentlemen, whether, in a country that has counted among its great publicists and its great writers so many eminent statesmen, it is even permitted to say that to make fine books, even on politics or things connected to it, prepares one quite poorly for the government of men and the management of affairs. I permit myself, however, to believe and to think that these eminent writers who showed themselves to be at the same time statesmen have shone in affairs not because they were illustrious authors, but despite being so.

Indeed, the art of writing suggests, to those who have practiced it for a long time, habits of mind hardly favorable to the conduct of affairs. It enslaves them to the logic of ideas, when the crowd never obeys any logic save that of the passions. It gives them the taste for the fine, the delicate, the ingenious, the original, when it is coarse commonplaces that lead the world.

Even the study of history, which often enlightens the field of present facts, sometimes obscures it. How many men would one not encounter among us who, with minds surrounded by a learned darkness, saw 1640 in 1789 and 1688 in 1830,[5] and, always behind by one revolution, wanted to apply to the second the remedy for the first, like those medical doctors who, completely up to date on previous maladies of the human body, but always ignorant of the particular and new ill from which their patient suffers, hardly fail to kill him with erudition! I have sometimes heard it regretted that Montesquieu lived in a time when he could not experiment with the politics whose science he advanced so much. I have always found much indiscretion in these regrets; perhaps the rather subtle finesse of his mind would often have made him miss in practice precisely that point by which the success of affairs is decided; he might well have been able to succeed at becoming the rarest of publicists, while being a rather poor minister, a thing that is very common.

We recognize therefore, gentlemen, that political science and the art of governing are two very distinct things. But does it follow that political science does not exist or that it is vain?

If I seek for what prevents certain minds from perceiving this science, I find that it is its very grandeur. The science that treats of the conduct of societies covers, indeed, an immense space extending from philosophy to the elementary studies of civil justice. Being almost without limits, it forms but a single object to the view. One confuses it with all the knowledge connected directly or indirectly to man, and in this immensity one loses sight of it.

But when we apply ourselves to the attentive consideration of this great science, when we remove whatever touches it without adhering to it, then the diverse parts that really compose it appear, and we finish by forming (*se faire*) a clear idea of the whole. We then see that this science descends by degrees from the general to the particular, and from pure theory to written laws and to facts.

For those who consider it in this way, the authors who are famous for cultivating it cease to form a confused crowd; they are divided into very distinct groups each of which can be examined separately. Some, with the aid of detailed accounts of history, or the abstract study of man, seek out the natural rights belonging to the body social and the rights exercised by the individual, what laws best fit societies according to the forms these have received from birth or adopted, and what systems of government are applicable according to the case, the place, the time. These are the publicists: Plato, Aristotle, Machiavelli, Montesquieu, Rousseau, to cite but a few brilliant names.

Others attempt the same labor with respect to that society of nations of which each people is a citizen, a society that is always rather barbarous, even in the most civilized centuries, whatever effort is made to soften and regulate the relations of those who compose it. They discover and indicate what international law is, beyond particular treaties. This is the work of Grotius and Pufendorf.

Others still, while preserving the general and theoretical character of political science, confine themselves to a single part of the vast subject they embrace: this is Beccaria establishing what the rules of criminal justice ought to be among all peoples; this is Adam Smith attempting to find the foundation of the wealth of nations.

Thus we arrive, always constricting our sphere, at the jurists and great commentators: Cujas, Domat, Pothier, and all those who interpret and clarify existing institutions, treaties, constitutions, and laws.

To the extent that we have descended from ideas to facts, the field of political science narrows and becomes firmer; but it is always the same science. One can be convinced of this if one compares all the authors who occupied themselves with the different matters we have just indicated, and if one remarks that, however far they seem to be from one another, they nonetheless lend one another a hand and aid one another constantly. There is not a commentator who has not often supported himself on the abstract and general truths that the publicists have found, and the latter constantly need to found their theory on the particular facts and the institutions of our experience that the commentators have revealed or described.

But I am astonished, gentlemen, to have to demonstrate the existence of the political sciences in a country where their power shines forth in every direction. You deny the political sciences and what they are capable of doing? Look around you: see these monuments, see these ruins! Who raised the former, who made (*a fait*) the latter? Who has changed the face of the world of our day to the point that, if your grandfather could be born again, he would recognize neither the laws, nor the mores, nor the ideas, nor the customs, nor the usages that he knew; and hardly the language that he spoke? Who, in a word, has produced this French Revolution, the greatest event in history? I say the greatest and not the most useful, for this revolution still endures, and I await its last effect in order to characterize it with such a word; but finally, who has produced it? Was it the political men of the eighteenth century, the princes, the ministers, the great lords? We need neither bless nor curse them; we must instead pity them, for they have almost always done other than they wanted to do, and finished by achieving a result they detested. The great artisans of this fearsome revolution were precisely the only men of those times who had never taken the least part in public affairs. It was authors of whom no one is ignorant, it was the most abstract science that deposited in the spirit of our fathers those seeds of novelties from which sprouted suddenly so many political institutions and civil laws unknown to their ancestors.

And note that whatever the political sciences have done here with such irresistible power and such marvelous brilliance, they do everywhere and always, though more secretly and slowly; among all civilized peoples, the political sciences give birth to, or at least form[6], those general ideas from which then emerge the particular facts in whose midst men of politics busy themselves, and the laws they believe they invent; these ideas form around each society something like a sort of intellectual atmosphere breathed by the spirit of both governed and governors, and from which the former as well as the latter draw, often without knowing it, sometimes without wanting it, the principles of their conduct. Barbarians are the only ones who recognize in politics nothing but practice.

Our Academy, gentlemen, has for her mission the furnishing to these sciences, so necessary and so fearsome, of a hearth and a rule.[7] She ought to cultivate them in full liberty, but never to depart from them, reminding herself always that she is a learned society, and not a political body. The dignity of her labors depends on it.

This is anyhow what she has always done, and one asks nothing of her now but that she remain in agreement with herself. Always the Academy has taken care to hold herself at a distance from parties, in that serene region of pure theory and abstract science. Not only has she enclosed herself there, but she has made a constant effort to attract and retain there those spirits whom the passions of the moment and the clamor of affairs would constantly have distracted. The subjects she has proposed for her contests attest to this, and the contest itself that we are going to judge today succeeds in proving it.

The first question she proposed was this: "Compare the moral and political philosophy of Plato and Aristotle with the doctrines of the greatest modern philosophers on the same matters. Appraise what is temporary and false, and what is true and immortal in these different systems."

The path thus opened is immense; it contains almost the entire history of the moral and political sciences; now, of all the sciences, it is these with which the human spirit is most immediately and most constantly occupied. A study so old and so sustained must have produced an almost infinite number of different notions and diverse systems. To summarize this immense labor of the intelligence and to judge it seems a work that not only surpasses the limits of an article, but also those of a book. Indeed, the enterprise is difficult; yet it is not impracticable.

There is this great difference, among many others, between the physical sciences and the moral sciences: that the field of the first is almost without boundaries, since it has no boundaries save those of nature, while the latter sciences are contained within the study of a single subject, man; and as much as this unique object changes a great deal in aspect according to the individual and the times, and while the half-darkness that always surrounds it also lends itself to all sorts of illusions and errors, nonetheless the number of mother-ideas these sciences have produced is not as great as one might think, considering all those who have been occupied with them.

It is incredible how often moral and political systems have been successively found, forgotten, found again, forgotten once more only to reappear a little later, always charming or surprising the world as if they were new, attesting to the ignorance of men, and not to the fecundity of the human spirit.

Perhaps it is permissible to apply to the moral and political sciences what Mme de Sévigné said so agreeably of love, that *"il est un grand recommenceur."*[8] Indeed, it often happens that they repeat what they had already said in another manner. They offer a small number of truths that are not very old, and few errors that do not appear decrepit if one knows the date of their birth. Thus these makers of social theories whom we see in our day, and who seem to us, with reason, to be so dangerous, would appear all the more boring had we more erudition and more memory.

It is therefore possible, in studying the most illustrious authors that have treated of the moral and political sciences in different centuries, to find out what are in these matters the principal ideas that have had currency among humankind, to reduce them into a rather small number of systems, and then to compare them to each other and judge them. In any case, the difficulty of this task appears to have frightened the spirit of the contestants. One alone has presented himself: his work has attracted the serious attention of the Academy, and merits it; nonetheless he has not been able to induce her to award the prize this year.

She hopes that new contestants will present themselves, and above all that the author of the only article that has been entrusted to her can himself perfect the already remarkable work he has submitted. She therefore remits the question to the competition of 1853. All those who cultivate these noble studies whose object is man and society shall doubtlessly think, the Academy hopes, that if there are few subjects as difficult to treat as that which she has proposed, there is none more grand and more beautiful.

The section on legislation has likewise posed this question: "What are, from the juridical and philosophic points of view, the reforms to which our civil procedure is open?"

You see here, gentlemen, that the horizon is contracting. This latter subject is as particular as the former was general. It is concerned not with the man, but with the litigant.

Procedure, we must recall, is not in high honor with the public; we often permit ourselves to confuse it with chicanery. It would be better nonetheless were it revered, and we are wrong to judge it by the abuses made of it; for without procedure the judge and the litigant act without rule in all that precedes and follows judgment, and the domain of law remains, in the best case, an empire of the arbitrary. Now, arbitrary justice is the very stamp of barbarism; thus civilized peoples have always attached a great importance to the rules of procedure.

Free peoples, above all, have always been great proceduralists; they have drawn in good part from forms for the defense of their liberty, and one has seen them oppose power more advantageously with the thousand little formalities procedure furnishes than with the general rights guaranteed by the constitution, just as it often happens that neighbors of the sea succeed better at preventing its ravages by sowing reeds upon its banks, with whose aid they divide and slow down its surges, than by raising high dikes to contain it. This part of the laws, so important, has nonetheless remained the most imperfect.

Those innovators who, for the last sixty years, have transformed everything in France, have, despite their longings, hardly modified the laws relative to the administration of civil justice. Napoleon himself ran aground here. All efforts combined have ended only by changing the position, but not the nature, of the laws. We have done nothing with the ordinances of our ancient kings but transport them into our codes. Thus I have always thought it a slight exaggeration to say that among us nothing is free from revolutions, since civil procedure has been; it is to be believed that it will retain this rare privilege until some great writer does for it what Filangieri and Beccaria did for criminal procedure, drawing it from the dust and the obscurity of the studies and the court offices, exposing it to the light of day, and succeeding at removing it from the prejudiced interests of practice and submitting it to the general notions of philosophy and good sense.

This is what the Academy has tried to do in posing the questions indicated, and ten contestants have responded to her appeal.

Three articles have merited her praise; the goal has been approached, but it has not yet been reached, and the Academy judges, by the articles that have been transmitted to her, by the importance of the subject, and by the hope that one must conceive of the utility of the labors she has provoked, that it is best to remit the question to the contest of 1853.

Three prizes were proposed for this year. The Academy regrets that she must refuse the first two. She is pleased to be able to award the third.

This prize has been obtained by M. Bodin, doctor of law, advocate for the Paris Court of Appeal. The question that prompted M. Bodin's article, or rather his book—for the work of which we will speak has the extent and the merit of a great treatise on its subject—was this: "Seek the origin of judicial order[9] in France, tracing its history and shedding light upon the principles of its current organization."

All peoples, gentlemen, ought to be interested in the history and the constitution of justice; for the judicial power is possibly, all things considered, the one with the most influence on the daily conditions of each citizen.

But do we not have, as Frenchmen, particular reasons to inquire into what justice has been among us? When I seek for the two classes of men who have most contributed to forming the traits of our national character, I find that they are writers and magistrates.

The first have given to the French spirit that temperament at once vigorous and delicate that we see in ourselves, that nature so curious, audacious, restive, often factious and always intractable, which acts incessantly in Europe and in our own midst. The second have bequeathed to us judicial mores, a certain respect for individual independence, and a persevering taste for forms and judicial guarantees, which we follow even in the midst of the disorders of revolutions and the indifference that succeeds them.

To make a history of literature and justice in France is to seek the origins of ourselves.

M. Bodin has acquitted himself very remarkably of this task in all that concerns justice. He traces for us the vicissitudes of judicial order in France from the Romans to our day. The details, perhaps a bit numerous, which fill this vast tableau, do not in any case impede us from grasping the ensemble, and the general view here is imposing. The historical part of this article is therefore very worthy of our praise. The philosophical portion of the work is not equal to the other and harms it slightly. It is much easier indeed to describe well than to judge well. The Academy would also have liked to find more brilliance in the thought and more color in the style. It seems that the author is a better draftsman than grand painter. But his work remains nonetheless a noble (*beau*) one that gives honor as much to the one who produced it as to the learned body that inspired it.

After having judged the articles that competed in 1851, the Academy has had to occupy herself with choosing new subjects. Two are indicated by her this year. The first has been furnished by the section on philosophy: it concerns one of the most mysterious phenomena that can be presented by this being so full of mysteries that one calls man.

What is sleep? What essential difference is there between dreaming and thinking? Does artificial sleepwalking, which so to speak is nothing but the perfection or utilization of dreaming, exist? What is this singular state during which
several faculties of the human spirit seem rather enlarged than restrained, save
the first of them all: the will, which here remains blind or subordinated? Can
one account for these phenomena according to the rules of a sound philosophical method?

The second question posed this year interests at once the family and society.
The Academy asks us to examine from a moral and economic point of view the
best regime to which marriage contracts can be submitted.

You know, gentlemen, that M. le Baron Félix de Beaujour has established a
quinquennial prize for the author of the best book on the relief of poverty.

The book that the Academy demands of contestants this year is a manual of
morals and political economy for the use of the working classes.

All times have seen laborers and the poor; but what seems peculiar to our
own is the opinion, so widespread in our day, that there exists somewhere a remedy for this hereditary and incurable sickness of poverty and labor, and that
with a little good will governors might easily succeed at discovering it. We are
prepared to accord to each power that is born a reasonable time to find and apply
this new medicine, and, if it fails, we are ever ready to chase this practitioner out
and call upon another doctor. Experiments follow and generations succeed one
another without this error dissipating, and we have come to believe that the same
chimera will always traverse the same ruins.

The Academy, in posing the question I am going to announce, has had for
her end the combating of this false idea from which evils flow. She desires, to
this effect, that the contestants apply themselves to spreading among the working classes to whom they address themselves some of the most elementary and
certain notions of political economy; that they make it well understood, for example, that there is something permanent and necessary in the economic laws
that govern the rates of wages; why these laws, being in some sense of divine
right, since they emerge from the nature of man and the very structure of society, are placed beyond the reach of revolutions; and that the government cannot
make wages rise when the demand for labor diminishes, just as no one can prevent water from spilling over the rim of a leaning glass.

But what the Academy desires above all is that the different authors she
provokes set in light this truth: that the principle remedy of poverty is found in
the poor man himself, in his activity, his frugality, his forward-thinking; in the
good and intelligent employment of his faculties, far more than those of others;
and finally that, if man owes his well-being somewhat to the laws, he owes it far
more to himself; moreover, one could say that to himself alone is he beholden,
for as much as the citizen is worth, so much is the law worth.

Is it not strange, gentlemen, that a truth so simple and so clear has ceaselessly needed to be restored, and that it seems so obscure in our times and
among our lights? Alas! It is easy to say the cause: mathematical truths for their

demonstration require only observations and facts; but to grasp and believe moral truths it is necessary to have [good] mores.

The Academy asks of its contestants not a treatise but a manual, which is to say that she invites them to make a work that is short, practical, and within the reach of all; in fine, one which is written for the people, yet without the pretense of reproducing the language of the people, a kind of affectation contrary to any diffusion of the truth among the inferior classes that could be sought by a noble (*bel*) spirit. The importance that she attaches to this little book is manifested by the prize of ten thousand francs she promises to him who shall be its author. But she announces in advance that she will award this prize only if there emerges from the contest a work that is remarkable and suited to fulfill the need she has conceived.

I stop here, gentlemen; it is time to cede the floor to the permanent secretary, who is going to speak to us of one of our colleagues whose loss we regret and whose memory we venerate, M. Droz. To praise his writings and retrace his actions is neither to emerge from the circle of our studies nor to fail in our grand mission; for honesty shows itself better by example than by precept, and the best course in morals—and I beg the pardon of my colleagues in the section on philosophy—shall always be the life of a good man retraced by a historian who understands and makes known the love of virtue.

Appendix

Our Academy, gentlemen, has this for her mission: to be the hearth and regulator of these necessary and fearsome sciences; this is her glory, but it is also her peril.

Governments are generally indifferent enough to what happens in the bosom of academies, and even, in ordinary times, in the world of ideas. When we are occupied with nothing but literature, philosophy, science, and even with religion, they willingly believe that these do not touch on anything else. But as soon as we speak of politics in any of its parts, they become very attentive. They imagine that we do not act upon politics except when we speak about it. Yet do not believe, gentlemen, that this is merely the failing of those petty souls who generally lead human affairs. The most noble (*beaux*) geniuses have fallen here. There are philosophic or religious opinions that have changed the face of empires and that were born beside the greatest men without their having taken any notice. It is to be believed that if these same princes had heard their subjects discussing a question of communal roads they would have been all eyes and ears.

An academy of moral and political sciences is therefore not, it is necessary to recognize, equally appropriate to every country and to every time. Her place is hardly anywhere but in free countries and places where the discussion of everything is permitted. These are conditions of existence with which we are honored, gentlemen; let us not contest them.

The *ancien régime*, which treated the moral and political sciences like an ingenious and respectable occupation of the human spirit, never permitted those who cultivated them to unite in an academy. The revolutionary dictatorship, which of all dictatorships is the greatest enemy of liberty, stifled these sciences, and, as the sole efficacious means of preventing writings treating of them, suppressed as much as possible their authors: almost all that remained of the old eighteenth century school, Bailly, Condorcet, Malesherbes, perished by its hands. One may believe that the same fate would have befallen Montesquieu, Voltaire, Turgot, and Rousseau himself, had they then lived. Happily for them, they were dead before they could see the frightening times for which one holds them responsible. But scarcely had the Terror ceased when the moral and political sciences immediately returned to great honor, and were, it must be said, the object of an unjust preference; for in the creation of the Institute which then took place, a separate division was made for them, while one was refused to *belles-lettres*: strange ingratitude of a generation that literature had nourished and conducted into power!

The revolution continued on its course, but liberty soon returned to the rear: for revolution and liberty are two words it is necessary to hold carefully apart in history. The First Consul—who personified and continued the French Revolution in his own manner, but who was nothing less than the greatest adversary liberty has yet encountered in the world—this First Consul did not delay in casting a very evil eye upon the Academy, or, as it was then called, the Division of Moral and Political Sciences. The Academy was then composed, it is true, almost exclusively of political men who had played various roles in the preceding events. One counted there Cabanis, Daunou, Merlin de Douai, Dupont de Nemours, Cessac, Roederer, Sieyès, Talleyrand, Lebrun (later Duke of Plaisance), and Destutt-Tracey. She had for a foreign associate the illustrious Jefferson, then president of the United States of America, which was no great title of recommendation with the First Magistrate of the Republic of France. Yet despite being composed of famous persons, she tended only to make herself forgotten; seeing the spirit of her master, which was no longer contained by the spirit of the times, she withdrew voluntarily into the obscurity of her own sphere; one sees this well in perusing her final works.

In philosophic history, she was occupied with the government of France under the first two dynasties; this did not seem bound to compromise her. Nonetheless, for more innocence yet, she believed it necessary to go back even to the Pharaohs; one finds her employing her last meetings to listen to M. de Volney, who, according to the minutes, was charged with sharing interesting information about the tunics of Egyptian mummies.

In morals, M. Dupont de Nemours read his articles on instinct, which, being common to beast and man, could hardly disquiet the government.

In political economy, the Academy was occupied with the daily growth and diminution of the Seine.

And in politics properly so-called, she was occupied with nothing.

The public treated the Academy a bit like it treated itself: she no longer attracted serious ideas from outside or acted upon them within her own bosom. One sees nothing in her final minutes other than the title of a single work of some length to which she paid homage: *Course on Morals for the Use of Young Ladies*, by Citizen Almaric.

None of this could appear fearsome, and yet the First Consul became preoccupied with her. The Academy had rendered herself very small, but the eye of Napoleon perceived her despite the darkness into which she had cast herself.

When Napoleon had effaced the last vestiges of public liberty—or, as he put it, abolished government by lawyers—he wanted to close the last asylum of free thinkers—or ideologues as he called them, forgetting that without these ideologues, who had prepared the ruin of the *ancien régime*, and without these lawyers who had consummated its ruin, he would never have become the master of France and of Europe, but would doubtless have remained, despite his genius, an obscure and petty gentleman, lost in the thousand inferior ranks of the hierarchy they had destroyed.

I have searched very attentively in many diverse documents, and notably in the administrative documents deposited in the national archives, seeking just how this destruction of the division on moral and political sciences took place; I have found nothing worthy of consideration. By reading these documents one sees only that it is not in parliamentary governments alone that those who lead affairs give themselves the trouble of hiding their true thoughts in a multiplicity of words. However all-powerful they proclaim themselves to be, despotic governments dispense no more than others with this ruse. They condescend at other times to the use of deception. In the report of the minister of the interior, Chaptal, the report preceding the decree, a copy of which I found corrected by the hand of the minister himself, not a single word is said on the reasons for suppressing the Division of Moral and Political Sciences. No critique, no insinuations against her: it is not even said that she is being suppressed; all that is contemplated is the reform of the Institute in accordance with a better plan and the introduction within her of a division of labor more favorable to the interests of letters and of the sciences. In reading the considerations behind this decree, it seems that no thought has even been given to us. In reading the decree itself, one perceives that we no longer exist, and that we have been killed gently through omission.

Likewise, one sees in the report that the original idea of the minister was, purely and simply, to return to the old academic organization, not only as to things, but also as to names; in one word, to do in 1803 what Louis XVIII did in 1816: to re-fasten the chains of time, as he himself later said. The First Consul accepted the thing, but rejected the words. M. de Fontanes, who remained very much in love with the past, and who was, to use the modern jargon, a great reactionary, pressed him to give again to these sections the name Academy; we are assured that he responded to him, "No! Not the Academy! That would be too Bourbon!"

Thus ended the Division of Moral and Political Sciences. She was buried, like all other public liberties, wrapped in the flag of Marengo. At least it was a glorious shroud.

One does not see her reborn until the French once again become free.

Even in the most favorable times, the Academy is placed between two reefs. She must equally fear going beyond her sphere and remaining inactive within it.

We ought never to forget, gentlemen, that we are a learned society and not a political body: the security and the dignity of our labors depend upon it.

This line of demarcation between theory and practice is, one must admit, easier to trace than to hold. A question that at first glance seems purely theoretical can, in response to the passions of the moment, turn easily into a question of facts and an instrument of parties; for we are a reasoning and noble-spirited (*bel esprit*) people among whom one willingly makes the most subtle theories serve for the satisfaction of the most coarse appetites, and often wraps rather villainous actions in the most noble (*beaux*) words. There are political matters that naturally pertain to practice and others that are occasionally drawn toward it; the Academy has known how to avoid, with a reserve that does her honor, both the one and the other. She has held firm to the sphere of theory. She has done more: she has striven to draw spirits there; if she has not always succeeded, there is no need to be astonished.

One might believe that in a time when all men take part in governing, the abstract science of government will be cultivated most and best. The contrary would be closer to the truth. The greatest publicists who have appeared in the world have preceded or followed ages of public liberty. Aristotle wrote of the republic from the court of Alexander; *The Spirit of the Laws* and *The Social Contract* were composed under absolute monarchy. These books have made (*fait*) us what we are, but we would probably be incapable of making them today. Facts incessantly depart from ideas and practice from science, and politics ends by being nothing but a game of chance: one in which the dice are loaded.

It is with the end of attracting toward speculative politics those spirits who would be distracted by the clamor of parties and the care of affairs that the Academy has established contests and distributed annual prizes to those writers who distinguish themselves therein. To judge these contests, and distribute these prizes, is the object that has united us today.

Notes

1. Previously published, in a translation by J. P. Mayer, as "The Art & Science of Politics: An Unpublished Speech," in *Encounter* 36:1 (January, 1971). The present translation is based on the speech proper as presented in the first volume of Tocqueville's *Oeuvres*, Edition Pléade, A. Jardin (Paris: Gallimard, 1991), 1215-1226; and on the Appendix included in volume IX of Gustave de Beaumont's edition of Tocqueville's *Oeu-*

vres (Paris: Michel-Lévy Frères, 1866), 643-647. I have striven to render Tocqueville's French as literally as possible while employing English that is grammatically correct and stylistically tolerable. Brian Danoff and Elena Hebert assisted me in improving this translation; any remaining deficiencies are mine.

2. Here and throughout the text, "fact" translates the French *"fait,"* which can mean either "fact" or "act." The latter meaning should not be dismissed, since the facts upon which political science focuses concern the actions (*les actions*) of men.

3. Here and elsewhere, the verb "form" is *"se faire,"* containing the root of *"fait"* (see note 2 above). One of the actions of men—in their public or governing as well as private capacity—is to theorize about human action; political science must therefore study itself.

4. Tocqueville's expression, *"avoir grand tort,"* is suggestive of both error and injury.

5. Tocqueville refers to the English Civil War, the French Revolution, the "Glorious" Revolution in England, and the July Revolution in France, respectively.

6. The word "form," used twice in this paragraph, translates *"donnent la forme aux"* and *"forment,"* respectively.

7. Here Tocqueville omitted to read a portion of his speech, which is reproduced in the Appendix below. Four months earlier, Louis Napoleon had staged a successful *coup d'état*.

8. "It is a great beginner-again."

9. *"L'ordre judiciaire"* refers to courts in the normal order of procedure.

Chapter 2

Leading By Leaving

Susan McWilliams

In *Crito*, Socrates refuses to leave Athens. He refuses to leave even though the city's assembly has sentenced him to death, and staying in Athens guarantees his execution. Crito, who with some others had arranged for Socrates' escape, is confused by his teacher's decision and asks for an explanation. Socrates tells Crito to imagine a conversation with the laws of Athens. The laws, Socrates says, would recount the many ways they have taken care of him—legitimating his parents' marriage, providing his education, setting the terms of his children's upbringing—and would only ask for some amount of care in return. To leave Athens would be to reject its laws and to show a lack of care for the city. In other words, Socrates suggests, if you care for the laws of a place, and if you care for the place itself, you should not leave it.

Socrates underscores this analysis by reminding Crito that he has never travelled beyond the city limits, except for military service. Unlike many of his fellow citizens, he has not gone out to festivals in the countryside or shown any desire to acquaint himself with another city-state.[1] (Indeed, in the only Platonic dialogue where we see Socrates travel beyond the Athenian walls, *Phaedrus*, he is basically tricked into doing so—and once he is in the countryside, he loses much of his usual composure.)[2] He says this is the best evidence of his love of Athens and its laws. Socrates associates his care for Athens with his physical presence in it. As a citizen, he demonstrates his commitment to the city in the same way he demonstrated his commitment as a soldier: by standing his ground, quite literally speaking.[3] The ultimate proof that he cares for Athens, and that his teachings are meant to serve rather than undermine Athens, Socrates says, is that he will not leave Athens.

Socrates offers a compelling vision of political commitment on these terms, one that the historian Garry Willis has argued is a model of intellectual leadership in a democratic context.[4] Socrates suggests, prefiguring Michael Walzer,

31

that it is necessary to be deeply "connected" to a place and a people if you want to raise challenging political questions and have those questions taken serious-ly.[5] The most obvious way to cultivate your connection to a place is to stay in it; the most obvious way to cultivate your connection to a people is to stay with them. Democratic leaders, as the Antifederalists would contend many centuries later, need to be as close to the citizenry as possible.[6] This is particularly the case for intellectual leaders, who in democratic times need to be able to con-vince their fellows to see outside conventional wisdom, need to have the trust of those fellows to do so—at least if they want their ideas to be heeded. To gain that trust, perhaps the clearest strategy is to remain within the community you wish to serve, never leaving and in doing so putting your loyalties in doubt, or risking the perception that you have been corrupted by foreign ways of thinking.

In the light of that argument, the success of Alexis de Tocqueville seems hard to explain. Tocqueville, after all, was good at leaving. He left his native France when he was in his early twenties, though his life was not in danger, his family had established professional plans for him, his country had demonstrable political needs, and at least some of his friends were begging him not to go.[7] In the United States, he became well enough acquainted with American political culture to write a book about it, but he did not stay. He left and returned to France. Tocqueville was not, like Socrates, moored exclusively in one political place. He was not even really moored in two political places or "worlds," as Sheldon Wolin says, but between them.[8] Yet to this day Tocqueville is heralded both in France and in the United States as a political visionary and intellectual leader. He has been quoted by every American president since Dwight Eisen-hower, and his words frequently appear in Supreme Court decisions.[9] In France he has reached similar prominence; his name is invoked during almost all major political discussions, and some pundits there have proclaimed that all of France is Tocquevillian.[10] No one seems to doubt the fact that Tocqueville raises chal-lenging questions about democratic life in both France and America, yet no one seems to doubt that he intended to serve democratic life in France and Ameri-ca—and to guide modern democracy more generally to a better place. He thus seems to resist the loosely Socratic notion that an intellectual gadfly or critic should, to attain some following among a democratic citizenry, remain among or with the citizens he means to serve. In fact, most people would probably credit his double departure—first from France and then from America—as the source of his wisdom and eminence. It is hard to imagine valorizing Tocqueville if he had *not* left France to go to America, or if he had *not* left America to go back to France in turn. Tocqueville demonstrates that leaving can in fact be a crucial part of, or a step toward, leading.

By no means is Tocqueville the only person of his kind in this regard. But his case provides us with a clear opportunity to explore the questions: On what terms may *leaving*—a polity, a place, a set of comrades or constituents—come to be regarded as an act of leadership or statesmanship? What is it about Tocqueville that has inspired so much trust and confidence among people who lived (and live) in the very places that he was willing to leave? How do you persuade others that you care for a place when you not only recommend changes in the rules of that place—but also have elected, at least for a time, to leave it? Might Tocqueville provide a model of leading by leaving?

I think that he does, at least in the context of modern democratic politics. Briefly put, Tocqueville makes a sustained and clever argument, throughout *Democracy in America* in particular, that leave-takers know *more* about a given polity than anyone else. He also marshals the universalizing tendencies of democracy in his favor, essentially contending that they eviscerate the political boundaries that he might be faulted for crossing in the first place. Most importantly, though, he taps into (and takes advantage of) the estranging character of modern democratic life. Modern democracy, he argues, is itself constantly in motion and perpetually in danger of losing its grounding; the modern democratic state is an unsettled thing. The vagaries of modern democratic life render self-understanding almost impossible, and in such a context all leaders must be, to a certain extent, people who depart from the normal operation of things. In such a context, the leave-taker is not so much someone who unsettles or disturbs the city but someone who helps the city to see itself more clearly. But before turning to his example, I first want to underscore the extent and endurance of the problem of leave-taking and political leadership, a problem that dates back at least to the beginning of what we tend to identify as Western political thought. It is a problem that finds embodiment in two characters: the *theoros* and the foreign-founder.

In the West, political theory actually has its origins in a tradition of leave-taking: the word "theory" itself derives from the ancient Greek word *theoria* (θεωρία), and *theoria* signified a particular form of travel beyond the bounds of a political community. Specifically, many of the ancient Greek city-states employed a *theoros* (θεορός)—a theorist—whose job it was to travel to visit foreign city-states or religious oracles.[11] The *theoros* was expected to return to his home city and report on what he had seen, to give a full account, especially with regard to the essentials or principles that lay behind specific foreign conventions. His reports would be used to inform and structure subsequent political practice. The ancient Greeks promoted the activity of the *theoros* in the general belief that cross-border travel leads to a particular kind of political wisdom. The *theoros* left the city-state in order to serve the city-state.

At bottom, the Greeks justified the association between leaving the city-state and giving political wisdom to the city-state in terms of worldly experience. In Plato's *Laws,* for instance, the Athenian Stranger convinces his interlocutors to let him lead their discussion about politics because he is the most widely traveled. He has seen more, so he can be said to know more. Of various political customs, he tells Kleinias and Megillus, "you two will answer that you have never seen them at all, because they are not customary or lawful in your country." By contrast, he says, "I have come across many of them in many different places, and moreover I have made enquiries about them wherever I went." Kleinias admits right away his and Megillus' "inexperience in such matters."

And due to their inexperience, Kleinias continues, they "might very likely not know, even if they came in our way, what was right or wrong in such societies."[12] Since the Athenian Stranger has had exposure to the greatest diversity of political customs, he can claim to have the clearest understanding of the range of possibilities in the world, not to mention the clearest understanding of what makes some political customs better or worse than others.

The very word *theoria* reflects this understanding: it has two possible derivations within ancient Greek, both of which underscore this association between a literal seeing of the world and gaining deep insight. First, it might derive from the root words *théa* (θέᾱ) and *horao* ('οράω)—*théa* meaning "a view, a thing seen, a sight, or a spectacle" and *horao* meaning "to see, look deeply, perceive, be aware of, or discern." In this telling, *theoria* means to learn things from looking at the world. Alternatively, it might derive from the root words *theá* (θεά) and *ora* ('ώρα), where *theá* means "goddess" and *ora* means "to pay heed or regard to a thing." In this rendering, *theoria* means to pay attention to things in service to the divine.[13] What is important is that in either case, there is a link between the apprehension of things that are seen in the world and a deeper form of knowledge, knowledge that goes beneath the surfaces of what is seen. The *theoros*, by leaving on a mission where his job is to see new and diverse things in the world, stands to learn a great deal. His experience of seeing much will allow him to claim a kind of superior knowledge.

But as the Greeks well knew, even if it is easy to accept this relationship between worldly experience and political knowledge in the abstract, the relationship between the *theoros* and his city was not always so simple. In practice, the *theoros* was likely to struggle, when he returned to his city-state, in order to convince his fellows that he still had their best interests at heart. Such was not an easy task; we might call this the traveler-city problem, and it appears frequently in Greek political thought. Herodotus tells the story of Anacharsis the Scythian, who returns from *theoria* and tries to introduce a Greek cult into his home city— and gets killed for what is perceived as treason.[14] Thucydides blames the desire for *theoria* among young Athenians for their poor judgment about how best to defend and serve their city, suggesting the degree of suspicion that was often directed at people who went past the city walls.[15] The conviction that someone who leaves the city has special trouble proving he loves the city is evident in Socrates' argument in *Crito* as well. Throughout Greek writing, there is a general worry about the potential for travelers to become aimless wanderers, distanced from the human life of the *polis*, living the "vagrant life" that Odysseus decries as unfit for mortals.[16] Even the Athenian stranger is uncertain about how a city ought to treat its *theoroi*, emphasizing the extent to which travel beyond the city's limits is an invitation to political corruption or obsession with political "novelties."[17] To leave a city, even temporarily, is to detach oneself from that city's social matrix and values.[18] That detachment may end up becoming profound, and in almost every conceivable dimension the *theoros* might come to care less for his home city.

The Athenian Stranger mulls over this problem extensively and ends up deciding, to quote Seth Benardete, that if people like the *theoroi* are going to expose themselves to the corruptions of strangers, they will subsequently have to "prove whether they have withstood the intoxication of freedom from supervision and the lure of foreign ways" in front of an assembly of lawmakers.[19] In this model, the *theoros* is not given the benefit of the doubt; the onus is on him to prove to his city that although he left for a time, his loyalty to the city has not wavered. And if the *theoros* cannot prove his loyalty to the lawmakers, the punishment is severe: "if on his return home he appears to have been corrupted, pretending to be wise when he is not," his fellow citizens are to have no communication with him. They are to hold him in disgrace and, if he tries to influence education or the laws, indict him in court.[20]

To the extent that he offers details, it seems that in trying to mitigate the risk attendant to those leave-taking *theoroi*, the Athenian Stranger effectively neuters them. In his vision, the *theoros* is allowed to say anything that a group of elders deems supportive or loyal, but not allowed to say anything that would be regarded as a serious challenge to the status quo. But this limitation robs the *theoros* of any critical voice—except, perhaps, in very minor matters. (As Sara Monoson says, on these terms the *theoros* is only allowed to come back more confident of the city's excellence or "more or less the same" as when he left.)[21] The Athenian Stranger's rules thus undermine the very reason that a public-minded *theoros* might want to leave the city in the first place: to learn from other communities, to see if there are elements of conventional life that might be made better. In fact, his rules would, in a great twist of Platonic irony, result in the punishment of not only the Athenian Stranger himself but also the two young men with whom he has been having this conversation. After all, they are all travelers who have left their home cities and, having left, are considering customs that might be superior to those demanded by their own respective traditions.

On one level, then, the Athenian Stranger is warning Kleinias and Megillus that they should be cautious about what they say and how they say it when they return to their home cities. In particular, he signals that they need to think carefully about how they discuss the conversation they have just had—or whether they should tell their fellows that they engaged in this kind of conversation at all. The Athenian Stranger indicates to the young *theoroi* that when they return to their own cities, having left, their fellow citizens will have little reason to trust them. It may even be good that their fellows are so suspicious: if they are trying to protect a city that they love, they should be wary of people who come in, peddling foreign novelties that might as well be imagined cities in speech. On those terms, the kind of conversation that takes places in *Laws* is deeply threatening. It is natural for the city to be wary of those people who would choose to leave it, even if only for a time.

In *Democracy and the Foreigner*, Bonnie Honig arrives at a similar formulation of the problem of leave-taking and political leadership—though she reaches it by approaching from a different direction. She focuses in that book on the phenomenon of the "foreign-founder," an archetypal character who has long been celebrated, in everything from the biblical story of Moses to the popular storylines of *Shane* and *The Wizard of Oz*. Such figures arrive almost mystically, coming from outside into a regime dominated by suffering or corruption. They then work to refound or restore that regime on more just terms. Moses leads the Israelites out of Egypt and brings them new laws; Shane saves a town from corrupt hooligans; Dorothy unmasks the Wizard and ends a reign of bureaucratic terror. But the critical part of all these stories, Honig notes, is that the foreign-founder, having established a more just political order, *leaves*. Moses dies; Shane rides off into the sunset; Dorothy clicks her sequined shoes and heads back to Kansas. They thus leave open, in their wake, the possibility for democratic self-governance. Further, their ultimate leave-taking is what justifies placing faith in a foreign-founder: the idea that a foreigner is able to "discover the best rules for society, see all of men's passions yet experience none of them; have no relationship at all to our nature yet know it thoroughly and, perhaps most important of all, have a happiness that is independent of us." For all of that to be true, and thus for trust in the foreign-founder to be deserved, that foreigner must not remain within the new regime he has created. Leaving, in such stories, is posited as perhaps the supreme virtue of statesmanship.

Yet Honig is well aware that "there is surely something too neat about this script."[22] For one thing, if a basically democratic society has a story about its own founding in which the people were impotent until the arrival of an almost godlike foreign-founder, does that not undermine democratic self-confidence, or the society's sense of its own unity? Even if the foreign-founder leaves in body, he might forever haunt the populace in spirit. In fact, for any one of a number of reasons, his leave-taking might generate more confusion than it avoids. He might hurt many of the people he has left behind; Honig returns to the movie *Shane* to draw attention to the little boy who, having developed a father-and-son relationship with Shane, spends the last moments of the movie screaming for his hero to come back. The foreign-founder's departure might even, in the end, leave people angry at him enough to reject the rules he made and thus reject him as a statesman.

Moreover, we might ask why a people should trust a foreigner with the task of founding from the outset, since they can have no guarantee that their foreign-founder will leave after instantiating a new form of rule. Take Dorothy: her life in Oz, and the post-Wizard Oz in particular, has many things to recommend it over the injustices of life in Kansas. Rather than return to her aunt and uncle's house, a wind-torn farm where the creepy Miss Gulch is always threatening her dog, Dorothy just as easily might have gotten over her homesickness and stayed in the full-color landscape she helped to improve. It would be hard to fault her for doing so. In fact, we might regard as suspicious any person who does *not* want to live under laws of his own making. Nor would it be unreasonable to distrust someone whose final promise is that he will leave you. Even Jean-Jacques Rousseau, whose foreign lawgiver in *The Social Contract* presents an idealized picture of a foreign-founder, a man who operationalizes the general will then proves his true greatness by leaving, suggests elsewhere in his writing that people will only trust a leader who promises to stay with them, in the physical as well as the spiritual sense, for the rest of his life.[23]

In her analysis, Honig rightly identifies this messiness in foreign-founder stories as reflecting what she terms the "undecidability" of the foreigner in democratic life.[24] But it is just as apt to see that messiness as indicative of something else: a deep and unsettled ambivalence about the relationship between leading and leaving. These foreign-founder stories depend on the idea that leaving is the ultimate virtue of statesmanship, yet they invite us to wonder why anyone would trust something so important—the creation of laws—to someone who only promises to leave us (and the rules he brought into being) behind.

The stories of these two figures—the *theoros* and the foreign-founder—are revealing in their shared anxiety about the relationship between leading and leaving. Each figure gives us a model of leadership in which the act of leaving a people behind is central. In both types of stories, there is an underlying acknowledgement that leaving a place can serve a critical political purpose. In the case of the *theoros*, the idea is that leaving a place will force an encounter with a wide variety of customs and conventions, exposing the person who leaves to a fuller range of human possibilities and, in doing so, imbuing him with wisdom that he can bring back to his city-state. In the foreign-founder stories, leaving is posited as an act of almost divine self-restraint that is necessary in order to allow for true communal self-governance. The foreign-founder, like the *theoros*, is also understood to have a kind of wisdom that inheres from exposure to more than one set of political rules and conventions. But both kinds of stories have a sharp double edge. They both point to the significant concern that someone who leaves a place might not, in some critical terms, be trusted to care for it enough to govern it well. Both kinds of stories indicate that there is a natural tension between the city and the leave-taker.

Therefore, any leave-taker who aspires to have a say in the governance of a particular place—to be heard and heeded—somehow has to overcome that tension. And it is clear that Alexis de Tocqueville overcame that tension many times over. He gained not only the trust but also the devotion of people in two different countries, both of which he left. Although he has functioned something like a *theoros* in his relationship to France, and something like a foreign-founder in his relationship to the United States, he and his intentions are rarely questioned. He seems to have avoided, or somehow conquered, the natural skepticism that might be directed at his endeavors. His success on these terms seems to demand some reflection.

The easy thing to do might just be to say that Tocqueville naturally overcame any concerns that Frenchmen or Americans might have had about him because he was such a genius. Tocqueville was smart, and he said things that proved, over time, to be insightful—and therefore his work demonstrated that he was worthy of trust. Doubtless, there is some truth to that argument. For well over a century, political thinkers have been arguing that, in one writer's words,

he "deserves to rank among the immortal few."[25] But that kind of justification
falls somewhat short. First of all, it fails to consider the fact that Tocqueville's
work was popular as soon as it was published—long before it would have been
possible to "prove" the predictive wisdom of what he said. Second, and more
importantly, it neglects the extent to which, in his writing, Tocqueville relentlessly makes the argument on behalf of the value of leave-taking. As we shall
see, throughout *Democracy in America*, and throughout his many other letters
and notebooks and essays about traveling, Tocqueville develops an aggressive
case for leading by leaving. In fact, the argument itself might be a critical element of Tocqueville's genius. He argues, both explicitly and implicitly, that his
work has special and particular use *because* of his leave-taking.

To be sure, Tocqueville may have felt that he had to make this argument.
Although he was by most accounts confident in the merits of his work, Tocqueville did worry about being able to attract an audience given the questions that
might be raised about his political loyalties. As his biographer Hugh Brogan
describes, he was particularly concerned about the difficulties attendant to writing about America in a France where most of his friends and family were legitimists; Brogan even describes Tocqueville's writing, at times, as designed more
to manipulate the opinions of the legitimists than to tell them what he really
thought.[26] Tocqueville also worried that American audiences would not receive
the book warmly.[27] He knew that in both places he would have to overcome a
kind of natural suspicion that people were likely to bring to his writing, an understanding he reveals early in *Democracy in America*: "I am aware," he writes,
"that, notwithstanding my care, nothing will be easier than to criticize this book
should anyone care to do so."[28] He was aware, in other words, that people might
be skeptical of what he had to say, which explains why he spends so much energy trying to undercut the grounds of that skepticism.

Early in *Democracy in America*, Tocqueville argues that "a stranger frequently hears important truths at the fireside of his host, which the latter would
perhaps conceal from the ear of friendship." The host "consoles himself with his
guest for the silence to which he is restricted, and the shortness of the traveler's
stay takes away all fear of an indiscretion."[29] In other words, people are more
likely to be honest with someone they know is going to leave. It is a point he
repeats later in the book:

> A stranger does, indeed, sometimes meet with Americans who dissent from the
> rigor of these formulas, with men who deplore the defects of the laws, the mu-
> tability and the ignorance of democracy, who even go so far as to observe the
> evil tendencies as it might be possible to apply; but no one is there to hear them
> except yourself, and who, to whom these secret reflections are confided, are a
> stranger and a bird of passage. They are very ready to communicate truths
> which are useless to you, but they hold a different language in public.[30]

Tocqueville asserts more than once that being a "bird of passage," being someone who is going to leave, gets you a kind of access to the truth that you would never have otherwise. People are more honest with outsiders than insiders, more apt to speak the truth—especially when the truth is difficult—to someone who will not stick around and to whom they have only a temporary, private connection.

Of course, there is a serious problem with this argument. Though it certainly holds true some of the time, this argument ignores the fact that the opposite may be true as well: it is often much easier to tell lies to a stranger. (There are great examples of this in the history of political thought; for instance, one of the great errors in Herodotus' *History*—his assertion that an inscription on the pyramid of Cheops lists the amount of money the pyramid-builders spent on radishes—almost surely owes to a native translator who lied to the Greek stranger, doubtless with some glee.)[31] It is easy to lie to someone who you think you will never see again: because your lie is not likely to come back to haunt you, and because your lie is less likely to be exposed. You are less likely to be caught in the lie, and it is less likely to matter if you are. There is likely to be less social sanction for lying to strangers than there is for lying to close fellows. Indeed, psychologists have determined that while almost all cultural groups consider telling lies within the community unacceptable, in many cultural groups lying to strangers is socially acceptable.[32]

Tocqueville was not unaware of this argument, nor did he disagree with it. In fact, in private, it was an argument he made himself! As a young man, almost a decade before he went to America, he wrote to his boyhood friend Eugène Stoffels, counseling him that to avoid "injustice and deceit" it is necessary to deal almost exclusively with people you already know well. One must, he writes, "restrict oneself to a certain circle of friends, outside of that to expect only coldness and indifference hidden or open, and to keep oneself on one's guard."[33] In other words, Tocqueville knew that people are happy to lie to strangers, that deception is always a risk. There are good reasons for telling secrets only to your close friends and being circumspect with strangers.

And without question, Tocqueville knew he had had conversations in which Americans were withholding the truth from him to some degree. When he met former President John Quincy Adams, for instance, Tocqueville asked him about the possibility of a sectional dispute between the North and the South. Adams had just written at length on the problem of nullification to John C. Calhoun and Alexander Everett, the latter of whom was sitting at the table when Tocqueville raised the issue. But Adams refused to answer Tocqueville's question—George Wilson Pierson hypothesizes that he was "too depressed to want to say anything about it to a stranger"—and Everett did not volunteer any information about Adams' position. Although Tocqueville could not know the extent to which Adams was withholding his considered opinions on the subject, he did know that Adams was holding back, a fact he recorded in his notebook.[34]

How, then, do we explain the fact that, although Tocqueville knew the ease with which strangers deceive strangers, and knew that Americans had at times withheld the truth from him, he portrays that relationship in *Democracy in*

America as one of unalloyed honesty? The answer seems to me obvious. It is a calculated argument, designed not to tell the whole truth but to persuade and to set the terms by which people encounter his work. Coming at the beginning of the book, it undercuts the argument that elements of Tocqueville's report are untrustworthy before that argument can be made. It is a savvy rhetorical move, a statement of partial truth, more than it is a statement of total conviction. And it begins to suggest the extent to which Tocqueville's arguments about leave-taking should be understood as a persuasive endeavor.

Tellingly, Tocqueville reinforces his claim with a brash assertion. Having just said that people will confide things to strangers that they will not say to fellows, he writes, "If these lines are ever read in America, I am well assured of two things: in the first place, that all who peruse them will raise their voices to condemn me; and, in the second place, that many of them will acquit me at the bottom of their conscience."[35] On this count, Tocqueville's argument bears a striking resemblance to the famous argument made by President Richard Nixon, when that embattled leader claimed in the face of vocal public opposition to have the support of a "silent majority." He claims access to a truth so secret that it is not likely to be spoken in public. This claim reinforces the notion that public speech among fellows may often be deceitful—"even if they know I'm right, they will not say it to others"—and dishonest. Tocqueville reframes possible objections to his work, even before they are raised, as belonging to a public sphere where insincere speech is common currency. This is in contrast to the things people say to "birds of passage" like himself, which he continues to posit as the epitome of candor. He tries to undermine the natural doubts about the veracity of his work, in short, by calling into question the veracity of what members of a community tell each other every day, especially when they speak to each other in public.

Now, Tocqueville's assertion on this point has force because it has some truth to it. Of course people are sometimes careful about the things they say in public, and of course they may sometimes hold the truth closer to home. The trick in Tocqueville's depiction of things is that, having established that sometimes people do not say what they really think in the public sphere, he locates himself—the stranger, the leave-taker—in the most intimate of spaces. In his picture, the leave-taker does not stand in the public space or even outside it, as a kind of distant and detached observer on the model of the *theoros*. Rather, he locates the leave-taker in the most cozy of domestic scenes: "at the fireside," in the homestead where, he argues, people say what they really think. The image is both clear and subtle, as well as deeply evocative. Quite marvelously, Tocqueville manages to transform the outsider, the transient and leave-taker, into the ultimate insider. In his telling, the stranger has access to spaces, both literal and figurative, that even people within a given society do not. He draws a picture in which the leave-taker is the person who is not just the furthest inside a society but also closest to the truth. As he has framed the situation, he leaves us almost no choice but to take his word for it. Much like Niccolo Machiavelli begins *The Prince* by telling Lorenzo d'Medici that common people understand princeship better than any prince, Tocqueville begins *Democracy in America* by telling his readers that strangers understand a society better than the people in it. (Joshua Mitchell has quipped that in Tocqueville's writing, the Delphic injunction to "know thyself" seems not to apply.)[36]

It should be clear that in no way are Tocqueville's general contentions about the value of leave-taking unassailable in rational or argumentative terms. Though they do have a rhetorical power, they are easily debatable, and by themselves, they are not enough to explain his ability to gain the trust of both Americans and Frenchmen. They are only an entrée into the real argument by which Tocqueville justifies his leave-taking, which is his argument about the nature of modern democracy. In order to fully transform the standard image of the leave-taker, Tocqueville must also transform the standard image of the city from which leave may be taken.

"In America I saw more than America," writes Tocqueville. "I sought there the image of democracy itself, with its inclinations, its character, its prejudices, and its passions, in order to learn what we have to fear or to hope from its progress." Perhaps the most evident theme in the introduction to *Democracy in America* is the idea that democracy has a providential character in the world, that democracy is an "irresistible revolution which has advanced for centuries in spite of every obstacle and which is still advancing in the midst of the ruins it has caused." Democracy is "universal, it is lasting, it constantly eludes all human interference, and all events as well as all men contribute to its progress." Almost more often than it is possible to count, Tocqueville tells his readers—particularly his French readers—that as goes America, so goes their world. He stresses that he has not traveled to America "merely to satisfy a curiosity" but "to find there instruction by which we may ourselves profit," since "sooner or later, we shall arrive, like the Americans, at an almost complete equality of condition."[37]

When combined with Tocqueville's assertions about the insight that leave-takers may have into a society, this argument allows him to be able to make an astonishing and substantial claim—that is, if as a stranger in America Tocqueville was able to see to the heart of America, and if America represents the future of France, he can claim to see better than anyone else into the heart of France's future. By leaving France, he contends, he gained the ability to know France on terms that are unrivaled by people who have spent their entire lives there and never left. His arguments suggest that by estranging himself somewhat from both France and America, he has come to know them both more intimately. Far from describing his own perspective as one of intellectual distance or objectivity, as some scholars in his position might do, Tocqueville describes his own perspective as located in the heart of things. Essentially, he says that as a leave-taker he has come closer to home than people who have stayed at home. Because of the universalizing nature of modern democracy, in leaving France—even in embracing certain political institutions and practices that are not accepted in France!—Tocqueville can declare that he has come closer to France, closer to the soul of the modern world.

But something bigger is at stake here. Tocqueville's understanding of the nature of democracy, as a phenomenon that is both inevitable and internationalizing, leads him to the conclusion that political borders are in general ceasing to matter as much as they have in the past. In his telling, the modern world is moving toward a political convergence:

> Variety is disappearing from the human race; the same ways of acting, thinking, and feeling are to be met with all over the world. This is not only because nations work more upon each other and copy each other more faithfully, but as the men of each country relinquish more and more the peculiar opinions and feelings of a caste, a profession, or a family, they simultaneously arrive at something nearer to the constitution of man, which is everywhere the same. Thus they become more alike, even without having imitated each other.

For Tocqueville, democracy presages a world in which the old political identities and borders are going to apply less and less. What he calls the "boundless" quality of American existence prefigures a more boundless world. In democratic times, he says, when you talk about politics the "whole civilized world" is at stake, not just one country or even two.[38]

If that is indeed the case, as Tocqueville argues, then it is also reasonable to understand that thinking in terms of the political boundary between, say, France and the United States is largely an irrelevant way of thinking. And if it is generally irrelevant to speak about the political differences between France and the United States, there is less intellectual reason than ever to question the loyalty of the would-be political leader who shuttles between them. In a world where political borders matter less and less, it is hard to accuse anyone of being a political leaver in the first place, much less to associate that leave-taking with potential disloyalty. Now, Tocqueville does not go so far as to make the argument that modern democracy will destroy political boundaries altogether—he does indicate that democracy may manifest itself differently in different places—but he does not need to do so, at least as far as his argument speaks to the relationship between leading and leaving. He merely needs to suggest, as he does both by word and example, that the world is entering an age in which the boundaries between nations no longer represent boundaries between incommensurate political systems. In such an age, crossing a political border cannot be regarded as the gesture of political abandonment that it might once have been. Given what Tocqueville says about the universalizing tendencies of democracy, his writing about America can be understood, in his words, to involve a "perpetual silent reference" to France, and vice versa.[39] In other words, the nature of modern democracy itself helps to lessen the distinctions between what had long seemed to be distinct political societies. In modern democratic times, then, people who travel between different nations are in critical ways not leave-takers at all.

Tocqueville even goes so far as to argue that the inevitable internationalization of modern democracy effectively turns the entire human race into "travelers scattered about some large wood." That is to say, modern democratic life encourages a way of thinking that draws attention to what is uniform among people—"not any particular man, but Man himself"—and thus over time lessens particularist allegiances and loyalties.[40] In this way, in *Democracy in America* Tocqueville argues that the world is turning into a place where the kind of leave-taking in which he has been engaged will no longer be the exception but the rule. Thus, his own exercises in leave-taking make him a paradigmatic creature of modern democratic life, well positioned to understand the nature of that life—and understand it from the inside.

But that is not the only argument that Tocqueville makes about modern democracy in terms that justify his own leave-taking. He also frames his leave-taking as working counter to one of the great threats inherent to modern democratic existence: the tyranny of the majority. As it is well known, Tocqueville argues that perhaps the greatest force and danger in democratic life is the tyranny of the majority, which may hold sway over not merely laws and behavior, but also thought. The "omnipotence of the majority," or the "moral power of the majority," as Tocqueville depicts it, casts a formidable shadow over all public discussion in democratic society. The tyranny of the majority may have many ill effects, Tocqueville thinks, but perhaps no effect more deleterious than the effect of congratulatory self-delusion. It is easy for a democratic society to become too satisfied with itself, with little institutional or informal counterweight against the hubris of the majority. So, Tocqueville says, in democratic times, when the tyranny of the majority and such self-delusion are always a threat, outside perspectives are required for moderation and clarity. He posits his own trip to America in precisely those terms. Because in the United States "the majority lives in the perpetual utterance of self-applause," he writes, "there are certain truths which the Americans can learn only from strangers or from experience."[41] In this formulation, Tocqueville suggests that as a leave-taker he is able to articulate the nature and limits of democratic life because his leave-taking puts him in critical ways on the outside. Not subject to the sway of the majority, the leave-taker can speak truth to its power.

Notably, both these arguments that justify leave-taking in terms of democracy—one dependent on the idea of an increasingly boundless world and the other dependent on the tyranny of the majority—are premised on the idea that the modern democratic world is a deeply strange and estranging one. The first argument relies on the notion that democracy is undoing everything that came before it, and the second argument relies on the notion that democracy is unleashing new and dangerous powers in the world. Throughout *Democracy in America*, Tocqueville emphasizes the estranging features of democratic life and argues that coming to terms with democracy is about learning to live with discontinuity.[42] As democracy spreads, he says, "society changes its forms, humanity its condition," and "new destinies are impending." He claims that "a new science of politics is needed for a new world."[43] The world itself, under democratic rule, is becoming a place that is unrecognizable to everyone, to one degree or another.

This emphasis on the strangeness of the modern democratic world is important, for it provides a key to Tocqueville's ability to leave and lead. Because Tocqueville posits the world that he and his readers inhabit as one that is so overwhelming in its scope and so strange in its machinations, he is able to portray his own leave-taking as a project of relative familiarity. His own position as a leave-taker, in the context of such strange and estranging conditions, comes across as just a variation on the common project of coming to terms with the modern world. There is an important psychological dynamic at work here: if the world itself is one of estrangements that are beyond your control, then leave-taking—a kind of intentional estrangement—may almost paradoxically be a way of coming to feel more at home in the world. (Along these lines, we might recall Hannah Arendt's judgment that at the heart of political understanding is the project of trying to be at home in a world that is not of our own making, "for every single person needs to be reconciled to a world into which he was born a stranger and in which, to the extent of his distinct uniqueness, he always remains a stranger.")[44] But in any case, what comes across as most strange in Tocqueville's writing is the world itself—not the man who chooses to estrange himself, for a time, from his fellows. Tocqueville might even resist the depiction of his own actions as estrangements at all; in general, he tended to resist the idea that estrangement was a political or intellectual virtue.[45]

We might even say that Tocqueville works to undercut his readers' likely skepticism about him by undercutting their confidence in their own position. That is, his emphasis on the speed and scope and permanence of democratic change helps to unsettle whatever confidence his readers might have about the ground on which they stand. Without question, he plays up the instabilities and uncertainties of the modern political world they inhabit. It is a political world where, as he describes it, everything is "agitated, disputed, and uncertain."[46] He tells his readers, to borrow an image from Martin Zetterbaum, that they are patients without a clear prognosis.[47] In such a strange and estranging world the leave-taker comes across as less of an outlier than he would in more stable political times. In a world that we are made to understand is strange and estranging, the kind of leave-taking in which Tocqueville is engaged seems relatively homebound, or at least relatively recognizable.

In *Democracy in America*, Tocqueville turns our traditional image of the leave-taker on its head. In his telling, the person who leaves a place is not becoming an outsider, but becoming the consummate insider. The person who leaves does not merit distrust but total trust. The person who leaves is not estranging himself from his fellows but trying to help his fellows build a home in an estranging world. In representing the act of leave-taking this way, Tocqueville undercuts skepticism about his trustworthiness before that skepticism has time to emerge. Part of what is new about the "new world" of democratic life, Tocqueville suggests, is that it is a world in which we must reassess our classical ambivalence about the leave-taker.

Not all of Tocqueville's arguments toward this end are iron-clad, as I have suggested. But his case has been persuasive largely, I think, because he recognizes (and takes advantage of) the relative instabilities of modern democratic life. Contrary to Socrates' description of a relatively fixed democratic community, a community with a deep sense of its own settledness, Tocqueville sees in his own era the emergence of democratic communities that are not stable in terms of their size, their membership, their internal ranks, their institutions, or their opinions. In *Crito*, Socrates can assume a basically stable set of laws and a basically stable and coherent community. But Tocqueville argues that modern democratic citizens can make no such assumption. He describes a world in which laws are constantly up for revision, and the community itself changes all the time. The age of mass democracy, he says, is an age of restlessness and motion and turbulence—an age in which decent self-understanding is made difficult at both the individual and communal level.[48] The experience of living in the age of mass democracy is at bottom an experience of estrangement. That is, Tocqueville is able to turn the traditional image of the leave-taker on its head in part because he is able to turn the traditional image of the city on its head.

To the extent that Tocqueville really does establish "a new science of politics," as he claims, this transformation is at its heart. As Tocqueville tells it, the modern democratic community is not the stable and fixed thing that is assumed in the stories of the *theoros* and the foreign-founder. Rather, it is itself in flux in virtually every dimension. In the modern democratic context, then, leave-taking cannot be regarded as an unusually unsettling activity. Because the coherence of the city is weak, the man who leaves the city is able to seem stronger than he has ever seemed before.

In the United States, recent experience seems to support Tocqueville's analysis. As at least some commentators noticed, the 2008 presidential election was notable in part because of the background shared by its two major contenders, John McCain and Barack Obama. Specifically, as Peggy Noonan told it, "Obama and McCain aren't 'from' anywhere."[49] Both men had itinerant childhoods, spent at least part of their lives living outside the continental United States, and had gotten elected to the Senate in states where they had not lived for long.[50] In classical terms, they would both be regarded as leave-takers, but for the most part voters did not question the patriotism or loyalty of the candidates on those grounds.[51] And they elected Obama, the more globe-trotting of the candidates—the candidate, moreover, who spoke often about his long and restless journey toward self-understanding, in terms straight out of *Democracy in America*. Americans, as some pundits said, seemed to admire Obama's ability to "walk between worlds" rather than to be suspicious of it.[52] Although to many the 2008 election seemed on those terms to represent a new phenomenon in American politics, it was a phenomenon that Tocqueville seems to have seen more than a century and a half earlier.

With that in mind the old notion that in democratic times a leader must cultivate his or her connection to a people is worth revisiting, since it is clear that in a funny way that is exactly what Tocqueville did. He locates himself as a leave-taker in a world dominated by comings and goings, a man of motion in a world dominated by restlessness. Modern democratic life, in all its difficult uncertainties, gives a kind of opportunity for leave-takers to lead that they have never had in such scope and measure before. In an era dominated by the politics of estrangement, what could be more familiar than a stranger?

Notes

1. Plato, "Crito," in *The Last Days of Socrates*, trans. Hugh Tredenick and Harold Tarrant (New York: Penguin Books, 2003), 93 [52b].

2. Alexander Nehemas, *Virtues of Authenticity: Essays on Plato and Socrates* (Princeton: Princeton University Press, 1999), 329-330. Of course, the discussion in Plato's *Republic* takes place in Piraeus, a few miles from the center of Athens, but Piraeus was at the time physically joined to Athens by the Long Walls. To get there, then, "Socrates need not leave the urban megalopolis" or venture outside the walled city. See Josiah Ober, *Political Dissent in Democratic Athens: Intellectual Critics of Popular Rule* (Princeton: Princeton University Press, 1998), 215 n108.

3. Plato, "Laches," in *The Dialogues of Plato, Volume 3*, trans. R. E. Allen (New Haven: Yale University Press, 1998), 63 [181b].

4. Garry Willis, *Certain Trumpets: The Nature of Leadership* (New York: Simon and Schuster, 1994), 163.

5. Michael Walzer, *Interpretation and Social Criticism* (Cambridge: Harvard University Press, 1993), 39.

6. Herbert J. Storing, *What the Anti-Federalists Were For: The Political Thought of the Opponents of the Constitution* (Chicago: The University of Chicago Press, 1981), vol. 2, 43-44.

7. George Wilson Pierson, *Tocqueville in America* (Baltimore: Johns Hopkins University Press, 1996), 32.

8. Sheldon S. Wolin, *Tocqueville Between Two Worlds: The Making of a Political and Theoretical Life* (Princeton: Princeton University Press, 2003).

9. Harvey Mansfield and Delba Winthrop, "What Tocqueville Says to Liberals and Conservatives Today," in *Democracy and Its Friendly Critics: Tocqueville and Political Life Today*, ed. Peter Augustine Lawler (Lanham, MD: Lexington Books, 2004), 1.

10. Seymour Drescher, foreword to *Tocqueville and the French* by Françoise Mélonio (Charlottesville: University of Virginia Press, 1998), viii.

11. See J. Peter Euben, *The Tragedy of Political Theory: The Road Not Taken* (Princeton: Princeton University Press, 1990), 232-233. See also Dante Germino, "The Revival of Political Theory," *The Journal of Politics* 25, no. 3 (August 1963): 437-460.

12. Plato, *Laws*, trans. Benjamin Jowett (Amherst, NY: Prometheus Books, 2000), 23 [639].

13. Most people who study *theoria* rely on the first set of root words that I have provided. Peter Gould offers the latter possibility in his article "Letting the Data Speak for Themselves," *Annals of the Association of American Geographers* 71, no. 2 (June 1981): 173. The latter is also the etymology given in Henry George Liddell and Robert Scott's *Greek-English Lexicon*; they indicate that *theoros* (θεορός) derives from *theos*

(θεός), the word meaning "god" and *ora* ('ὥρα). (Oxford: Oxford University Press, 2003), 317.

14. Herodotus, *The History*, trans. David Grene (Chicago: The University of Chicago Press, 1987), 308 [4.76].

15. Thucydides, *The Landmark Thucydides: A Comprehensive Guide to the Peloponnesian War*, ed. Robert B. Strassler (New York: The Free Press, 1996), 375 [6.24].

16. Silvia Montiglio, *Wandering in Ancient Greek Culture* (Chicago: University of Chicago Press, 2005), 2ff. See also Homer, *The Odyssey*, trans. Richard Lattimore (New York: Harper and Row, 1967), 234 [15.353].

17. Plato, *Laws*, 286 [949e].

18. Eric J. Leed, *The Mind of the Traveler: From Gilgamesh to Global Tourism* (New York: Basic Books, 1991), 29.

19. Seth Benardete, *Plato's "Laws": The Discovery of Being* (Chicago: The University of Chicago Press, 2000), 336.

20. Plato, *Laws*, 286-290 [950-953].

21. S. Sara Monoson, *Plato's Democratic Entanglements: Athenian Politics and the Practice of Philosophy* (Princeton: Princeton University Press, 2000), 231.

22. Bonnie Honig, *Democracy and the Foreigner* (Princeton: Princeton University Press, 2001), 21; 23.

23. Emile's tutor must pledge his life to him. Otherwise, Emile will not be able to trust him, worrying endlessly about the moment when the tutor will choose to leave. "As soon as they envisage from afar their separation, as soon as they foresee the moment which is going to make them strangers to one another, they are already strangers." See Jean-Jacques Rousseau, *Emile: Or, On Education*, trans. Allan Bloom (New York: Basic Books, 1979), 53.

24. Honig, *Democracy and the Foreigner*, 32.

25. John Bigelow, introduction to *Democracy in America* by Alexis de Tocqueville, trans. Henry Reeve (New York: D. Appleton and Company, 1904), xxvii.

26. Hugh Brogan, *Alexis de Tocqueville: A Life* (New Haven: Yale University Press, 2006), 263.

27. Matthew J. Mancini, *Alexis de Tocqueville and American Intellectuals: From His Times to Ours* (Lanham, MD: Lexington Books, 2006), 3-4.

28. Alexis de Tocqueville, *Democracy in America*, ed. Phillips Bradley (New York, Vintage Books, 1990), Vol. I, 16.

29. Ibid., I, 15-16.

30. Ibid., I, 267.

31. Leslie Greener, *The Discovery of Egypt* (New York: Viking Press, 1967), 10. See also Herodotus, *The History*, 186 [2.125].

32. Charles F. Bond, Jr. and Adnan Omar Atoum, "International Deception," *Personality and Social Psychology Bulletin* 26, no. 3 (2000): 385-395.

33. Alexis de Tocqueville, "To Eugène Stoffels (Amiens, September 16, 1823)" in *Selected Letters on Politics and Society*, ed. Roger Boesche, trans. James Toupin and Roger Boesche (Berkeley: University of California Press, 1985), 29-30.

34. Pierson, *Tocqueville in America*, 420-421.

35. Tocqueville, *Democracy in America*, I, 267.

36. Joshua Mitchell, *The Fragility of Freedom: Tocqueville on Religion, Democracy, and the American Future* (Chicago: University of Chicago Press, 1999), 1.

37. Tocqueville, *Democracy in America*, I, 14; 6; 14.

38. Ibid., I, 14; II, 229; II, 236; I, xx.

39. Alexis de Tocqueville, "To Louis de Kergorlay (Clairoix, October 19, 1843)," in *Memoir, Letters, and Remains*, trans. unknown (Boston: Ticknor and Fields, 1862), 342.

40. Tocqueville, *Democracy in America*, II, 229.

41. Ibid., I, 255-256; I, 265.

42. See Wolin, *Tocqueville Between Two Worlds*, 130.

43. Tocqueville, *Democracy in America*, I, xix; I, 7.

44. Hannah Arendt, "Understanding and Politics," in *Essays in Understanding 1930-1954*, ed. Jerome Kohn (New York: Harcourt Brace & Company), 308.

45. Dick Pels, *The Intellectual as Stranger: Studies in Spokespersonship* (New York: Routledge, 2000), 222.

46. Tocqueville, *Democracy in America*, I, 44.

47. Marvin Zetterbaum, *Tocqueville and the Problem of Democracy* (Stanford: Stanford University Press, 1967), 43.

48. Matthew Sitman and Brian Smith, "The Rift in the Modern Mind: Tocqueville and Percy on the Rise of the Cartesian Self," in *Democracy Reconsidered* (Lanham, MD: Lexington Books, 2009), 102.

49. Peggy Noonan, "The End of Placeness," *The Wall Street Journal*, 15 August 2008, A11.

50. Tellingly, their "foreign" provenance did not make McCain or Obama unusual within the United States Senate. More than a decade before, the portion of Senators born outside the state they represented reached 40 percent. See Jamie Stiehm, "For 38 Senators, 'Carpetbagging' Is Not a Pejorative Term," *The Hill*, May 24, 1995.

51. To be fair, a so-called "birther" movement emerged to raise questions about whether or not Obama had really been born in the United States, as he claimed. And others wondered whether or not McCain's birth in the Panama Canal Zone disqualified his candidacy. These questions got some attention during and after the campaign, but they were largely fringe movements, dismissed by the vast majority of Americans. See Brian Stelter, "A Dispute Over Obama's Birth Lives on in the Media," *The New York Times*, July 25, 2009, B2; and Carl Hulse, "McCain's Canal Zone Birth Prompts Queries About Whether That Rules Him Out," *The New York Times*, February 28, 2008, A21.

52. Sharon Cohen, "Barack Obama Straddles Different Worlds," *Associated Press Online*, December 14, 2007.

Chapter 3

Aristotle and Tocqueville on Statesmanship

Aristide Tessitore

At first blush Aristotle and Tocqueville seem strange bedfellows, each occupying a niche in a galaxy of political thinkers at an almost infinite remove from the other. This can be made apparent by even the briefest of inventories. Aristotle belongs to a distant constellation comprised of those inhabitants of the ancient and pre-biblical world who gave birth to Western philosophy. In sharp contrast, Tocqueville comes of age in a European world still convulsed by the effort to cast off its biblical (especially Christian) heritage, and reshape itself under the guiding star of emphatically modern philosophic principles. Aristotle was a philosopher of the first rank, writing on virtually every aspect of human experience from physics to politics to metaphysics, one who perhaps more than any other single person contributed to a conception of science and nature that has dominated the Western world well into the twentieth century. Tocqueville, on the other hand, was primarily a student of politics, someone who suffered from what might be called a chronic condition of "philosophic malaise," from which he sought to find refuge by immersing himself in the life of political action.[1] Although Tocqueville's analyses have proven to possess continuing relevance, he is more apt to be considered a sociologist or thoughtful observer of politics than a philosopher.[2]

Even if we restrict the scope of this comparison to their common interest in politics, the differences separating Aristotle and Tocqueville are substantial. Aristotle's study of politics aspires to be comprehensive in a fundamental sense, that is, he attempts to offer a consideration of the full range of possible political configurations, as well as to provide a measure or standard by which they can be distinguished and evaluated. Tocqueville's more limited goal was to understand the new and emerging world of modern liberal democracy, and his major books focus on its most advanced expression in America and considerably more violent French and European trajectory. Moreover, the aristocratic leaning of Aristotle's political teaching, central importance assigned to virtue, inattention to religion or piety, and explicit subordination of politics to theoretical excellence, are directly at odds with central components in Tocqueville's "new political science." Tocqueville embraces democratic politics, yields central place to the principle of self-interest well-understood, gives careful attention to the complex interaction between religion and politics, and seems to assign greater weight to political practice than he does to the theoretical and philosophic concerns that arise from political inquiry.

Whether one takes as a measure their stature as political philosophers, enduring influence on the tradition of political thought, or the specific content of their teachings, the chasm separating Aristotle and Tocqueville is both wide and deep. Without in any way denying these differences, I would, however, maintain that there exists an important affinity between them. Both Aristotle and Tocqueville emphasize the enduring need for statesmanship and, more generally, the inescapable importance of prudence or practical wisdom in politics. This important agreement is made possible by two others: a deeply anti-utopian awareness of both the inescapability and limitations of politics, and an important similarity in the way in which both Aristotle and Tocqueville approach the study of politics itself.

Although this essay will emphasize important similarities between Aristotle and Tocqueville, I want to make clear at the outset that I am not suggesting that Tocqueville viewed himself as a student of Aristotle, or even that he was deeply familiar with the full scope of Aristotle's political teaching. Indeed, among classical political philosophers, Tocqueville seems to give first place to Plato, about whom he writes, "he will live as long as there are men; he will carry along even those who only half-understand him, and he will always be an enormous figure in the world of intellects."[3] It is of course one thing to recognize Plato's greatness and quite another to take one's bearings from his teaching. Insofar as Plato was primarily concerned to portray and defend the philosophic life, this preoccupation is not at the center of Tocqueville's own work. I hasten to add, however, that Tocqueville's writing is informed by respect and appreciation for the importance of political philosophy, as we shall see in his speech on the nature of political science (considered below). Although Plato's writing encourages readers to look beyond politics to the life of philosophy, the emphatically political horizon within which Plato places his investigation, together with the unparalleled range and seriousness with which the Platonic Socrates engages and illuminates it,[4] lies closer to the center of Tocqueville's own political concerns.

The far greater affinity between Tocqueville and Plato's greatest student is due to the fact that Aristotle is the first political philosopher to give his full attention to the nature, scope and limits of politics *on its own terms*. Although I would argue that Aristotle's political works share to a greater degree than is generally recognized Plato's central preoccupation with the political vulnerability of the philosophic life,[5] it is clearly the case that Aristotle's study of politics is animated by a concern to preserve and improve the quality of political life itself. If Aristotle is concerned to make the city safe for philosophy, he attempts to do so by both clarifying and enlarging the understanding of politics from the perspective of those most fully engaged in its activities, namely those citizens and statesmen who are both shaped by and give form to the distinctive character of political life. Aristotle's "philosophy of human affairs," as he calls it, is characterized by an unprecedented (philosophic) attentiveness to political things—not only as a means to philosophy, but as a sphere of activity pursued for its own sake. To a far greater degree than his teacher, Aristotle establishes a framework that allows those most engaged in politics to understand their own activity, especially as their activity bears on the kind of decency, excellence, and happiness which politics makes available for those who are not themselves given over to the philosophic way of life. Notwithstanding the profoundly changed circumstances of the modern world, Tocqueville also approaches the study of politics with an overriding concern to understand both the possibilities and dangers that attend to the quality of human life in the newly emerging democratic order. Moreover, like Aristotle, his written work attempts to enlarge the possibilities for human flourishing. He does so in large part by calling attention to often hidden obstacles which threaten human life, as they have begun to emerge in the dawning world of democratic politics.

In what follows I develop with greater specificity the general affinity between the teachings of Tocqueville and Aristotle, especially as they bear on the need for and importance of statesmanship. I do so by focusing especially on the way in which they approach the study of politics; their shared concern for what might be called the politics of the human soul; and their common recognition of the limits of politics. I conclude by showing how these similarities lead both authors to an appreciation for the enduring need for statesmanship.

Aristotle and Tocqueville on the Study of Politics

Aristotle is traditionally regarded as the founder of political science, understood as one discipline among others. Tocqueville, on the other hand, is best known for his claim that a "new political science" is needed for a new, distinctively modern world.[6] Although the differences separating classical and modern political science rightly call attention to substantive differences between these authors, I maintain that an important dimension of what is most distinctive about Tocqueville's way of approaching the study of politics—his "new political science"—is precisely that which resembles crucial aspects of classical, specifically Aristotelian, political science. As a way of beginning to defend this claim, it is first important to locate the distinctive contributions of Aristotle and Tocqueville within the larger historical context provided by the tradition of political philosophy.

Aristotle's Study of Politics in Context

Neither Aristotle nor Tocqueville originates the tradition of the political philosophy within which they develop their distinctive and influential approaches to the study of politics. In the case of Aristotle, it is obviously a tradition that he inherited from Plato, who had in turn taken it over from Socrates. Socrates is said to have been the first to turn philosophy to a study of the political things. If both the historical Socrates and the Platonic Socrates were most responsible for providing an initial context for the tradition of political philosophy, Aristotle's greatest innovation was his attention to and development of a political science that sought to enlarge, refine and educate the views of those most fully engaged in the activities of politics.[7] Although, like Socrates and Plato before him, Aristotle's analysis of politics takes its bearings from the highest and in some sense trans-political activity of philosophy, he is rightly considered the originator of the discipline of political science as it is typically understood today, that is, as a comprehensive study that can be understood on its own terms.

One way to begin to see what is most distinctive about Aristotle's own approach to the study of politics is to recall his critique of those who had written about politics before him. In addition to his critical review of Plato, Aristotle singles out the work of Phaleas and Hippodamus, two authors who, like Aristotle, were interested in preserving and improving the quality of political life. Aristotle's fundamental critique of these authors appears to be that neither was sufficiently attentive to the distinctive character of the political association, and that as a consequence, each offered prescriptions that failed to get to the heart of the particular problems they were attempting to ameliorate.

Phaleas sought to minimize political conflict by equalizing property, but his preoccupation with this "external good" led him to underestimate the importance of other goods sought by those who comprise the political association (*Politics* 2.7). Aristotle remarks that although "many" would welcome an effort to equalize property, a significant minority, consisting of those especially concerned with honor, would resist it. Moreover, Aristotle contends that such resistance is likely to prompt the most ambitious among them to establish a tyranny, something that would destroy the political partnership altogether. The underlying problem in Phaleas' reform derives from the fact that he gave insufficient attention to the nature of human desire itself. Whereas his proposal might rectify some "minor injustices," Phaleas' single-minded focus on property equalization blinds him to the essentially *ine*galitarian and *un*limited nature of human desire and ambition. This deeper and more persistent source of political conflict—one capable of turning the political partnership into a tyranny—is not only unaddressed by Phaleas, but inadvertently rendered more acute by his proposed reform.

The case of Hippodamus is even more instructive. Apparently the first town-planner, Hippodamus sought to rationalize politics by approaching it in the same way that one might approach the other sciences or arts (*Politics* 2.8). As part of his effort to rationalize politics, Hippodamus proposed a mathematical schema of organization (dividing every aspect of the city into three), and came up with a way to insure ongoing and progressive development within the city by providing citizens with incentives to improve the laws. Although Aristotle is sympathetic to the aim of this latter reform, he observes that Hippodamus' seemingly attractive proposal for improving the quality of political life inadvertently undermines political authority and jeopardizes political security. Not only does Hippodamus fail to appreciate the essential but precarious nature of legal authority, which is necessarily weakened by easily and frequently changing laws (2.8.1269a12-24), he is also insufficiently attentive to the exigencies of political security. As Aristotle later notes, the same orderly layout of roads that is "pleasing" in peacetime, renders the city more vulnerable to foreign attack during periods of political conflict (7.11.1330b21-27; cf. Lord p. 250 n. 52). Hippodamus' attempt to invest the study of politics with the level of precision and rationality characteristic of natural science and the human arts, fails to take into account both the distinctive nature and peculiar requirements of political life.

Unlike his predecessors, Aristotle's study of politics does not take its bearings from a single principle or issue, as does Phaleas; nor does he, like Hippodamus, seek to impose an inappropriate level of mathematical or rational precision upon his subject matter, something that could unintentionally distort the very phenomena under investigation. Rather, in writing about politics, Aristotle takes seriously the perspective of citizens and statesmen (in much the same way that he looks to the normative standards of "morally serious" and "prudent" human being in his study of ethics). By attempting to view politics from a civic perspective, Aristotle is able to take his bearings from the phenomena of politics as they are actually lived and understood. This means that his articulation and assessment of political problems often reflect the level of precision characteristic of citizens and statesmen.[8] Although this is not the only perspective that informs Aristotle's study, it furnishes the most consistent horizon within which he develops his political writings and constitutes an essential feature of his approach to the study of politics. Aristotle consistently draws both the *substance* and *form* of his political science from the political phenomena under investigation (especially the perspective of those most fully engaged in it), rather than attempting to deduce its fundamental principles from some Archimedean vantage point, on the basis of an *a priori* commitment or paradigm of inquiry.

Aristotle on the Peculiar Character of the Political

Aristotle famously begins Book III of the *Politics* by reopening a question initially undertaken in Book I: "Whatever is a polis?" (3.1.1274b31-33). This time the question is taken up from the point of view of those citizens who compose the civic association. The book that provides Aristotle's most theoretical examination of the problem of justice in the *Politics* is not introduced from the vantage point of the philosopher, but from the vantage point of the citizen. Aristotle's consideration of the civic viewpoint characteristically includes analyses of those evaluative beliefs which are inseparable from the practice of politics—such as the particular understanding(s) of justice or happiness explicitly or implicitly sanctioned and promoted by every actual regime. His standard procedure in undertaking a normative or evaluative analysis is to examine those opinions which are most in evidence, those which are held in highest regard (*endoxa*), as well as the views of those reputed to be wise. We will consider Aristotle's analysis of the conflicting understandings of justice in the final section of this essay. At present it suffices to note that conflicting perceptions of justice or the different objects with which human beings attempt to satisfy their common longing for happiness cannot be easily or fully reconciled, much less reduced to a set of consistent abstract formulas. It is the inevitably messy and contested character of politics (one might say of human life itself) that, as we have seen, led Aristotle to reject political reforms based on excessively rational or mathematical models. The political partnership may be composed of those who are open to the promptings of reason, but these same citizens (and their leaders) are also deeply influenced by less than fully rational forces, such as habit, tradition, and authority.[9] For Aristotle the peculiar nature of the political association must be taken into account to determine the most appropriate way to study it.[10]

Tocqueville's New Political Science in Context

Tocqueville's call for a new science of politics echoes the language of Alexander Hamilton in the *Federalist Papers*.[11] Hamilton argues that the American experiment in popular government was far more likely to succeed than the fitful democracies of ancient Greece, because it was grounded in "wholly new discoveries" in the science of politics (*Federalist Papers* 9). The novelty of the American experience was acknowledged by Tocqueville himself, who writes that the American Constitution rests "on an entirely new theory, a theory that should be hailed as one of the great discoveries of political science in our age" (*Democracy*, 156). The "new theory" in question was itself the product of modern political philosophy, a tradition of political thought that encompasses such disparate figures as Machiavelli, Bacon, Hobbes, Locke, Spinoza, and Montesquieu (among others). It is important to situate Tocqueville's new science of politics within the larger context of modern political thought in order to ascertain the most direct philosophic influences on Tocqueville's own work.[12] More important for purposes of this study, awareness of this context reveals that Tocqueville's call for a *new* science of politics in *Democracy in America* is at the same time a critique of the (earlier) new tradition of political science relied upon and interpreted by the Founders of the American experiment, and, to an even greater degree, appropriated by the philosophic architects of the French revolution.[13]

In order to understand the critical dimension of Tocqueville's new political science, it is necessary to provide a very brief summary of the "new" political science that preceded it. One hundred and fifty years before the publication of *Democracy in America*, Thomas Hobbes had inaugurated a new political science, one sometimes considered to be the forerunner of contemporary "rational choice theory." Rejecting classical approaches to the study of politics, Hobbes, like his contemporary Descartes, sought to model his new science on mathematics (especially geometry), which he considered to be the only true science.[14] Beginning with precise and methodical definitions, Hobbes wanted to avoid the "absurd" teachings of earlier and still-authoritative philosophers, and in so doing, establish a firm foundation for future progress. Also like Descartes, Hobbes ridicules his contemporaries for their slavish adherence to ancient authorities.[15] Instead of turning to ancient and medieval authors with their seemingly unscientific and certainly shifting standards of ethical evaluation, Hobbes anchors his study of politics on the firm and reliable ground furnished by the various passions that actually motivate human actions. He attempts to cut through the various conventions that constrain and skew a true understanding of the human animal with a vivid depiction of human nature as it would appear in an original, pre-political "state of nature" (*Leviathan*, chapter 13). Building upon the most fundamental passion of all, the desire of all living beings for self-preservation, Hobbes deduces a series of natural laws—or, more properly, "conclusions or theorems"—which, he maintains, constitute the "true moral philosophy" and provide a basis for a genuinely scientific understanding of politics (*Leviathan*, 100).

Hobbes' new science of politics is comprised of a series of rational calculations arising from the fundamental desire for self-preservation (and "commodius living"), as well as the institutional forms most likely to secure them. Although John Locke, writing a generation later, explicitly rejects the kind of absolute monarchy advocated by Hobbes (and lacks as well the latter's deference to the authority of mathematics), his more liberal political teaching resembles that of Hobbes insofar as Locke also grounds his teaching on the dependable human preoccupation with self-preservation and desire to acquire property, which he also depicts with reference to an original, pre-political "state of nature" (*Second Treatise of Government*, chapter 2). Unlike Hobbes, however, Locke advocates a division of powers among self-interested individuals (rather than the absolute power of the sovereign) as the best and most rational way to effect these goods. It was a version of this low but solid theory of modern politics that found expression in the American Constitution, which organized American government on the now familiar principles of "separation of powers" and "checks and balances." In Madison's famous words, "this policy of supplying by opposite and rival interest, the defect of better motives, might be traced through the whole system of human affairs, private as well as public" (*Federalist* 51).[16] It was precisely this new theory of government and, more generally, the tradition of modern political thought from which it arose, that Tocqueville at one and the same time admired and found insufficient.

Whatever one might say about the new political science exhibited in Tocqueville's works, one would be hard pressed to understand it on the basis of a mathematical model, theoretical paradigm about the "state of nature," or institutional system of checks and balances. Rather, Tocqueville's approach to the study of politics appears to be closer to that of Aristotle, not only in its resistance to the mathematical, abstract and reductive tendencies of the new science of politics that began to gain theoretical and political traction in the seventeenth and eighteenth centuries, but, as we shall have occasion to consider, in Tocqueville's preoccupation with the effect of these new theories and the political arrangements to which they gave rise on the "quality of life" of those living within them.

Tocqueville and the Nature of Political Science

Tocqueville's most comprehensive statement about the nature of political science was given at a pivotal moment in his career, after leaving political office and before undertaking his final book on the *Old Regime and the Revolution*. Tocqueville set out his understanding of the "art" and "science" of politics in a speech delivered to the *Académie des Sciences Morales et Politiques* in 1852.[17] He maintains that, while the aims and purposes of human beings undoubtedly change over time, the same is not true of human nature. It is this latter fact that provides the fixed basis for a "science" of politics. On the other hand, the practical dimension of politics takes its bearings from "a variety of incidents . . . passing needs . . . and . . . ephemeral passions," which in turn give rise to the "art" of government. For Tocqueville, the science of politics and the art of ruling are not only distinct, but also require and develop different qualities on the part of their practitioners. Whereas those seeking to develop a science of politics become adept at following the logic of ideas and tend to develop a taste for the subtle and ingenious, practitioners of politics, especially in a democratic age, are necessarily constrained by the promptings of passion and compelled to take their bearings from the most obvious and widely accepted opinions.[18] Excellence as a writer on the subject of politics is not necessarily or even typically good preparation for the art of governing.

Despite the different qualities needed to excel in either the art or science of politics, Tocqueville insists on the existence of a single, comprehensive science ordered from the general to the particular, one that moves from the realm of pure theory to written laws and facts. At the top of the pyramid, Tocqueville places the "publicists" and names Plato, Aristotle, Machiavelli, Montesquieu, and Rousseau as its most famous exemplars. The greatest publicists are able to base theories of right, law and regime on both an understanding of human nature and the varying conditions, places and times in which human beings find themselves. Other contributors to the science of politics, such as Grotius and Pufendorf, focus especially on relations between nations. Still others specialize on particular topics, such as Beccaria's study of criminal justice or Adam Smith's work on political economy. Yet more limited in scope are the studies of legal experts who interpret already existing institutions, treaties, constitutions, and laws.

Tocqueville's speech delimits a single science of politics in which each area or part is inextricably linked to the others. The practitioners of political science (especially the publicists) create or at least shape "general ideas" from which arise many of the specific problems with which politicians struggle, as well as the "laws" that they (with the sometimes not altogether conscious help of publicists) create.[19] Tocqueville explains that the science of politics gives rise to "a sort of intellectual atmosphere breathed by the spirit of both governed and governors, and from which the former as well as the latter draw, often without knowing it, sometimes without wanting it, the principles of their conduct."[20] For Tocqueville, as for both Plato and Aristotle, the "art" of governing is explicitly or implicitly circumscribed by the discoveries of those who have contributed most to the development of the science of politics.[21] We should note as well that Tocqueville's delineation of the hierarchy of influence in politics bespeaks his appreciation for the crucial importance of philosophy for a proper understanding of political life.

Like Aristotle, Tocqueville distinguishes the art or practice of politics from the scientific effort to comprehend politics as a whole, and also like Aristotle, he subordinates the former to the latter. As we shall see, although Tocqueville recognizes the power of "general ideas" to shape politics, he is at the same time critical of that power, especially as it bears on the development of modern politics. To state this in a slightly different way, political theorists ("publicists" in Tocqueville's language) are capable of shaping the realities of political life for *both* good and ill. While he believes that some of the greatest publicists have contributed in important ways to both the development of political science and the practice of politics, this is not always the case. If those writing about politics become excessively captivated by the logic of ideas or fall prey to the charms of subtlety and ingenuity, they can easily lose sight of those contingencies that simultaneously challenge and limit the political activities of citizens and statesmen. A science of politics that loses touch with the art of governing is not only bad science, it is also politically dangerous. Ideas that may seem compelling on paper can prove disastrous in practice, as Aristotle had observed in cautioning against Hippodamus' seemingly sensible and certainly attractive desire to insure enlightened laws.

For Tocqueville, the most relevant example of the capacity of well-intentioned and apparently compelling political theories to adversely and dangerously impact the practice of politics was close to hand. It was precisely this problem that gave rise to the excesses accompanying the French Revolution and its aftermath, to which Tocqueville devoted his final book. For Tocqueville, the French Revolution was a key event in the ongoing and irresistible revolution that was taking place "in all the Christian universe," one in which aristocratic society was giving way to a new democratic order (*Democracy*, 6-7). Whereas Tocque-

ville championed the greater justice afforded by the new and still-emerging dis-
pensation (*Democracy*, 675), he was at the same time critical of the extreme and
violent character with which this shift was taking place in France. In the *Old
Regime and the Revolution*, Tocqueville maintains not only that the central
"ideas" of this revolution, but also its "temperament and disposition" were due
to the influence of the leading intellectuals and political philosophers of the
eighteenth century (*Old Regime*, 195-202, esp. 201, 196). Whereas the American Revolution had "astonished" the rest of Europe, in France the American
example seemed only to confirm what the French *philosophes* believed they
already knew (and about which they had written). Tocqueville maintains that the
proof or assurance given to the leading French intellectuals by the example of
the American Revolution triggered a genuinely new situation—not only in
France, but in all of human history. He explains this unprecedented circumstance as one in which "the entire political education of a great nation was completely shaped by men of letters." It was, moreover, to this peculiar situation that
Tocqueville traces the unique character of the Revolution, writing that it im-
parted to "the French Revolution its particular spirit, and made it lead to what
we see today" (*Old Regime*, 201).

Not unlike Phaleas and Hippodamus, leading publicists and intellectuals of
the eighteenth century were confronted by the "spectacle of . . . many abusive or
ridiculous privileges" and "many bizarre and irregular institutions." Also like
their ancient Greek counterparts, the sight engendered "a disgust for old things
and for tradition," while igniting a desire to rebuild society "according to an
entirely new plan" drawn from "the inspiration of . . . reason alone" (*Old Regime*, 196-97). While Tocqueville's book analyzes the various social, economic,
administrative, and political factors that conspired to bring about the violent
excesses accompanying the French Revolution and its aftermath, he emphasizes
the almost complete blindness of the most influential political writers of the age
to the distinctive exigencies of the world of political action. Not only were they
without any direct experience of politics themselves, but, as Tocqueville points
out, they had no appreciation for the kind of obstacles that "existing facts might
place before even the most desirable reforms," nor did they understand the serious "dangers which always accompany even the most necessary revolutions"
(*Old Regime*, 197). Like Phaleas and Hippodamus centuries earlier, their well-
meaning and seemingly rational ideas were uninformed by an appreciation for
the inescapable limitations accompanying any and every practical political
reform.

In sharp contrast, both Aristotle and Tocqueville share a deep appreciation
for the twofold character of political science. Political science is not and can
never be a purely theoretical science like mathematics, because it is inescapably
practical. While it is true that political science can lead to an increase of knowledge, it is first and foremost directed to the benefit of human life or action. As
Aristotle writes in the first part of his study of politics, "the end of this kind of
study is not knowledge but action" (*NE* 1.3.1095a4-6; cf. 2.2.1103b26-30).[22] For
Tocqueville, as for Aristotle, the distinctive character of political science arises

in part from the natural variability of human actions, geographic conditions, and historical circumstances that contribute to the particular possibilities and limitations of political life. It is also the case, however, that, unlike physics or mathematics, political science requires its practitioners to take into account the perspective of citizens and statesmen, those who are actively engaged in the "art" or "practice"—rather than "science"—of politics. Indeed, Aristotle's notion of *politikē*, which can be appropriately translated as "political art" *or* "political science," reflects the same double character of politics that Tocqueville emphasizes in his speech before the Academy. What is distinctive about Tocqueville's political science is not that he jettisons theory, but that he deploys an older understanding of theory, one that takes into account the particular demands of political practice. Tocqueville develops his political science with a keen awareness of the way in which practical contingencies invariably defeat abstract political principles. It was precisely the absence of any appreciation for the peculiar character of political science that he decried in the hubristic philosophies of the Enlightenment, and to which he attributed the most dangerous and violent excesses spawned by the French Revolution.

Politics and the Human Soul

Aristotle on the Politics of the Human Soul

As Aristotle describes it, the political association encompasses both families and villages because it aims at "a complete and self-sufficient life." Whereas this is clear enough with respect to those things that human beings require to live, such as food, shelter, clothing, and security, Aristotle maintains that a human life is neither complete nor self-sufficient without some consideration and provision for that which makes life worth living for a human being. He explains that since human beings desire "to live happily and finely" (*to zēn eudaimonōs kai kalōs*), the political association cannot be fully understood simply in terms of the desire to live together, but exists for the purpose of making possible those noble actions which are capable of giving meaning or purpose to human life (*Politics* 3.9. esp. 1280b29-81a7 and 1.2. esp. 1252b27-30). For Aristotle the political association aims at a distinctive combination of goods: it seeks to secure at one and the same time the requirements of life and a good quality of life. Consequently, any political society that represses, thwarts or destroys those activities essential for happiness or noble deeds, is regarded by Aristotle as a deficient or defective political association. In much the same way, Aristotle would judge deficient any attempt to develop a political science that leaves out, suspends, or cuts off consideration of the seemingly-subjective and always-contested goods bearing directly on the quality of political life. Aristotle's study of politics, as well as that of the classical tradition generally, necessarily encompass and integrate both the empirical and normative spheres of political life, especially as they exert influence upon the actions and behaviors of citizens and statesmen.

For example, Aristotle's political science contains a description and analysis of the various kinds of democracy and oligarchy to which he had access (esp. *Politics* 6) as well as an exhaustive catalogue of known or extant constitutions (in the *Athenian Constitution*)—both of which would be regarded as components of the empirical dimension of the discipline today. However, he also takes up disputes about the nature of political justice (esp. *Politics* 3) and, as we have already noted, conflicting understandings of the best regime (esp. *Politics* 2 and 7-8), both of which are part of his effort to articulate a normative standard by which the variety of political regimes or constitutions can be evaluated. From an Aristotelian point of view, it is simply impossible to understand conflicts surrounding the question, "Who should rule?" or the sadly enduring realities of war, while restricting oneself to a study of empirical facts. The most persistent tensions at the very center of politics—both those that call forth and draw upon the human capacity for courage, prudence, and greatness of soul, as well as those that have given rise to the innumerable cruelties with which political history is filled—result from different and conflicting normative beliefs. As is all too evident to students of contemporary politics, contested normative beliefs are no less capable of moving the human soul in the twenty-first century than they were in fourth B.C.E.[23] As Plato's Socrates once pointed out in his typically understated manner, people do not fight because of differences in opinion that can be empirically resolved, but because they hold and are moved by different understandings about what is just or unjust, good or evil, fine or base (*Euthyphro* 7b-d). The most explosive and revealing dimension of politics is utterly unintelligible without undertaking a serious and critical examination of those opinions (what we tend to refer to today as "values") that animate political action, whether on the part of citizens, subjects, or political leaders.

It is in part for this reason that Aristotle begins his study of politics with the *Nicomachean Ethics*, a book that attempts to clarify the deepest longings of the human soul for happiness.[24] In it, Aristotle considers a range of external and internal goods that are thought by most people or by the wise to satisfy those longings, insofar as it is possible for human beings. In the course of his study, Aristotle examines both the nature and limits attaching to the human desire for happiness, giving particular prominence to the qualities of mind and character that bear most directly on the possibility of its realization. Aristotle considers the study of ethics to be part of the study of politics, not only because our beliefs about happiness influence in a decisive way our actions in the political arena, but also and perhaps especially because the particular character and arrangement of the political association within which we find ourselves, profoundly influences our beliefs about happiness, as well as our understanding of those qualities and activities most likely to facilitate its enjoyment. The reciprocal influence of politics and the human soul on each other was for Aristotle, and the classical tradition of political science more generally, an inescapable fact of political life.

Tocqueville and the Politics of the Human Soul

In sharp contrast to the new science of politics that had given rise to the ingenious Constitutional arrangements defended in the *Federalist Papers* and admired by Tocqueville, one of the most distinctive dimensions of Tocqueville's
new science of politics is his preoccupation with the effect of the dawning democratic age on the "souls" of citizens. Despite the range of problems associated
with the notion of "soul" in the modern era, Tocqueville does not hesitate to use
it. His usage resembles the way in which Aristotle deploys the word in his political writings, notwithstanding some important differences. The usage of "soul"
in Aristotle and Tocqueville overlap when the word is used to describe the distinctive animating spirit or life of a given individual or people, especially as it
bears on character; a particular and characteristic human mode of acting, thinking or feeling; or as the locus for beliefs that sustain distinctively human activities.[25] Tocqueville's political science is concerned with something more than the
particular institutional arrangements that secure or jeopardize republican forms
of government in the modern world (although he is deeply concerned with this
dimension of political science as well). He is especially preoccupied with the
effect that new institutional forms derived from the "wholly new discoveries" of
modern politics will have on the character, mind, and heart—in a word, the
"soul"—of those destined to live increasingly under their influence.

Tocqueville's focus on the reciprocal relationship between politics and the
human soul is especially evident in the attention he gives to "mores" throughout
Democracy in America. In fact, Tocqueville indicates that he understands the
expression *moeurs* "in the sense the ancients attached to the word," as applying
to the "whole moral and intellectual state of a people." For Tocqueville, the term
encompasses not only "habits of the heart," but also the particular notions, opinions and ideas that give rise to the distinctive "habits of the mind" characteristic of peoples or individuals (*Democracy*, 275). In Tocqueville's expansive
usage, *moeurs* seem to describe that complex interaction between more or less
conscious movements of the heart and mind that provide the springs of human
action and identity. Mores are both a means of shaping and an expression of the
soul of any given individual or people.

Tocqueville warns that one of the challenges confronting current and future
political leaders concerns the possibility that Americans (and more generally,
members of increasingly democratic societies) might surrender their belief in the
existence of the human soul altogether. Whereas Tocqueville considered the
desire for well-being to be both natural and legitimate, he is also cognizant of
the dangerous excesses to which it is prone in democratic societies. The democratic social state, unlike the aristocratic one, naturally inclines democratic
peoples to perfect the useful arts, and in so doing it renders life easier, milder
and more comfortable (*Democracy*, 518). While Tocqueville seems to admire

the energy, creativity and dynamism with which Americans characteristically seek to improve the material conditions of life, he also regrets and expresses concern about the mediocre character of their ambition (*Democracy*, 601). Tocqueville attributes the pervasive love of well-being that has taken hold in America to the influence of the democratic social condition that prevails there. He explains that the human heart is far less attached to the peaceful possession of an object, than it is to the imperfectly satisfied desire to possess it and incessant fear of losing it (*Democracy*, 506-507). It is this psychological truth, one that weighs heavily upon the democratic soul, which has given rise to a situation in which a pervasive and often-frenetic love of material gain has become the national and dominant taste in America. If anything, Tocqueville's nineteenth century observation seems even more relevant to America at the dawn of the twenty-first century.

Tocqueville maintains that the tendency to become absorbed in the pursuit of material enjoyments renders democratic peoples especially susceptible to the philosophic doctrine of materialism. A philosophic teaching that reduces everything to matter and motion comports very well with the already existing American preoccupation with material goods. The time, energy and intensity which Americans devote to the pursuit of those goods, together with the simplicity of a doctrine that reduces everything to that which already most engages their attention, Tocqueville believed, would only increase the appeal of philosophic materialism over time (*Democracy*, 519). Although he did not think it inevitable, Tocqueville considered philosophic materialism a grave threat to both individual and political health in the newly emerging democratic order. About those destined to live in the enlightened and free democratic societies of the future, Tocqueville writes, "it is to be feared that [they] will finally lose the use of [their] most sublime faculties, and that by wishing to improve everything around [them], [they] will finally degrade [themselves]" (*Democracy*, 519).

It is within this context that Tocqueville speaks of the value of religious belief in a democratic society, notwithstanding his own personal doubts about religion. Tocqueville's published works do not engage in a direct way philosophic questions about the truth of religious claims, or the possibility of divine revelation. Rather, he is primarily interested in understanding the "truth" about those citizens destined to live in modern democratic societies. The great political advantage of most religions, as Tocqueville understands it, is that they provide "general, simple, and practical means of teaching the immortality of the soul" (*Democracy*, 519). Tocqueville maintains that even metempsychosis is preferable to philosophic materialism, since belief in some kind of immaterial and immortal principle is far more conducive to the full development of human greatness than this temptingly simple philosophic doctrine. Consistently understood, philosophic materialism deprives human beings of any distinctive dignity by reducing them to accidental expressions of a material universe comprised exclusively of temporary and constantly shifting configurations of atoms. While Tocqueville's political science concerns itself with the institutions, mechanisms and processes most conducive to the security and well-being of citizens in the emerging democratic order, he attaches far greater importance to the influence exerted by the novel empirical realities of modern political societies on the souls of those destined to live under their influence.

Not only do both Aristotle and Tocqueville find it necessary to include empirical and normative considerations in their study of politics, they are also acutely sensitive to and especially concerned about the pervasive power of political and social institutions to shape the less visible but more revealing locus of individual human identity. Notwithstanding the comparative neglect of the soul characteristic of early modern political philosophers such as Machiavelli, Hobbes, and Locke, Tocqueville is especially preoccupied with the effects of the ongoing democratic revolution on the souls of those who will live increasingly within its orbit. For Tocqueville, as for Aristotle, an awareness of the reciprocal influence that politics and the human soul exert upon each other is an inescapable fact of political life, one that must figure prominently in any fully adequate study of politics.

The Limits of Politics and Enduring Need for Statesmanship

Classical and especially Aristotelian political science seeks not only to clarify the phenomenon of politics, but also to enlarge the horizon of its participants. It is characteristic of Aristotle's political science, that he directs readers to an understanding of human and political excellence which takes its bearings from a given political regime, while at the same time pointing beyond it to a higher possibility. This twofold character of classical and especially Aristotelian political science directs the attention of readers to both the highest possibilities of the political association, as well as its inevitable limitations. Moreover, it is distinguished by the conviction that human development reaches its pinnacle only in and through the political association while, at the same time, retaining a characteristically keen awareness of the persistent tension between the requirements of the civic association and those of the best human life.[26] It is precisely this awareness of the limits of politics—that is, the impossibility of fully resolving or satisfying the needs and aspirations to which the political association gives voice—that points to the enduring need for statesmanship. Although political leaders and even founders are unable to harmonize the full range of legitimate needs and aspirations that come to the fore in the political association, they are in a position to enhance or diminish those possibilities in significant ways. If Aristotle's teaching on the limits of politics directs some to a life of philosophy in a way that Tocqueville's does not, that same teaching shares with Tocqueville a concern to enlarge the horizon of present and future political leaders. Both Aristotle and Tocqueville seek to equip current and future statesmen with an understanding that allows them to draw out the highest possibilities and offset the most debilitating weaknesses of the regime within which they find themselves.

Aristotle on the Limits of Justice and Education Relative to the Regime

Aristotle's careful and complex treatment of the various claims to citizenship in Book 3 of the *Politics* gives way to a consideration of the different and competing claims to rule at the center of politics (esp. *Politics* 3.9-18). It is characteristic of Aristotle's analysis that he attempts to adjudicate this conflict by entering into the distinctive and competing perspectives of each of the rival claimants to power within the political association. As he considers, analyzes, and even provides arguments for the different claims to rule advanced by the many, the rich, the virtuous, the one best of all, and the law, Aristotle introduces and renders visible the importance of the "regime" (*politeia*) for understanding political life.

The nature of the regime is determined by nothing so much as the constitution of the governing body, that individual or group possessing final authority (*Politics* 3.6.1278b8-11). The sovereign body advances a particular view of justice which is comprised of two key elements. The first involves some standard or measure of equality and inequality, while the second puts forward a specific understanding about which, among the many goods that comprise a self-sufficient polity, counts most. Aristotle explains that the view of justice advanced by democratic citizens insists on the centrality of equality, based on their belief that maintaining the status of a free man constitutes the fundamental good of the political partnership. Whereas both oligarchic and aristocratic conceptions of justice emphasize the centrality of inequality (or a principle of proportional equality that results in inequality), each grounds this claim on a different foundation. Oligarchs believe that because wealth is the life-blood of politics, those who contribute most to the economic well-being of the city and are most capable of managing large sums of money should, in justice, possess the lion's share of the rule. Aristocrats, on the other hand, maintain their claim to rule on the basis of their superior excellence or political virtue. Although oligarchs and aristocrats agree that both free birth and money are necessary to bring the political association into existence, aristocrats point out that the highest purpose or aim of politics is to encourage and develop excellence, that is, the capacity for noble actions on the part of citizens. Since this is best done by those who themselves embody the excellence in question, aristocrats maintain that they, among all contenders, possess the strongest and most just claim to sovereign power.

Whereas Aristotle's articulation of the conflicting claims to rule advanced by each of the groups constituting the political association would seem to favor the aristocratic claim, his attempt to adjudicate the conflict at the very center of political justice proves unsuccessful. Aristotle shows that the arguments of oligarchs and aristocrats can be used against them by the many, in their collective rather than individual capacity. Although individually inferior in wealth or virtue to any given oligarch or aristocrat, they may in their collective capacity possess greater wealth than the ruling group of oligarchs or a greater array of virtues than the particular aristocrats sharing sovereign authority. The claims of the rich and virtuous may also be superseded in certain cases by the possession of extraordinary wealth or superlative virtue by a single individual or family, in which case justice would seem to require voluntary submission to the rule of one. This, however, would destroy the kind of equality which is a hallmark of the political association or partnership, turning it instead into a household (*Politics* 3.14.1285b29-33). Neither can the rule of law offer any fully satisfactory way of resolving the problem. This is because laws are always made by human beings and, as a consequence, invariably favor the interests of one of these groups to the detriment of the others. Aristotle even considers the possibility of establishing a proportional value for each of the goods necessary to sustain political life, but concludes that it is not possible (esp. *Politics* 3.12). On what basis could one assign a numerical measure to goods as necessary and incommensurable as free birth, wealth, military virtue, excellence of character, and practical or political wisdom? The result of Aristotle's effort to resolve the conflict among different and legitimate claims to rule leads to the conclusion that each of these claims is partial at best (including rule by those who are superior in virtue), and that there is no principle of commensurability capable of harmonizing them into a single whole (esp. *Politics* 3.9.1281a8-10 and context; 3.10; 3:12.1283a14-22 and context; and 3.13.1283b27-30).

The most relevant point for our consideration is that Aristotle's fullest treatment of the problem of political justice in the *Politics* fails.[27] Indeed, the absence of any fully adequate solution to this problem helps to explain the less than perfectly just arrangement characteristic of Aristotle's proposed best regime (a regime that "one might pray for") in the final books of the *Politics*.[28] The essentially problematic or limited character of political justice is not, however, presented by Aristotle as something tragic; it is rather, offered as an essential and useful component in the education of political leaders. The teaching is not tragic for two reasons. First, Aristotle shows how the deepest human longings for justice and the noble point beyond themselves to the life of philosophy for those who possess the requisite inclinations, abilities and opportunities (esp. *NE* 10.7-8). Secondly, the impossibility of perfect political justice underscores the dignity of and persistent need for statesmanship. Aristotle's political teaching is in the first place emphatically anti-utopian; he attempts to foster in future statesmen a kind of moderation that would protect politics from its most dangerous extremes—especially the kind of crises precipitated by those who embrace a partial view of justice with the unwavering conviction that their understanding or cause is absolutely right and alternative views inexorably wrong.

If keen awareness of the limits of political justice fortifies political leaders against the sometimes attractive but usually destructive simplicity of the political ideologue, it also proves indispensable in the effort to elicit for any given polity the degree of security and justice of which it admits. Aristotle argues that the "greatest" of all measures for regime longevity resides in the ability of statesmen (and political philosophers) to provide citizens with an "education relative to the regime" (*to paideuesthai pros tas politeias*). Aristotle's expression refers to an education that to some degree counteracts the dominant tendencies of the regime (*Politics* 5.9.1309b18-35 and 1310a12-22 and context). Since every regime embraces a partial vision of justice, it necessarily disenfranchises some of its members with inevitably destabilizing results over time. If, on the other hand, a statesman understands the partial character of justice in the regime in which he happens to live, he is in a position to make laws or enact policies that can mitigate its deficiencies while at the same time building upon its strengths. Without changing the fundamental character of the regime, Aristotle encourages statesmen, in the measure possible, to incorporate the claims of those individuals or groups who contribute something essential to the existence or health of the political community, but who are disenfranchised by the partial character of justice that prevails in this (and every) existing political order. Aristotle's emphasis on the importance of education relative to the regime is not an attempt to weaken, but rather to enlarge the understanding and practice of justice in any given political context. Far from subverting the existing political order, Aristotle maintains that political leaders capable of exercising this ability are the greatest guarantors of regime longevity for their political communities.

Tocqueville on the Limits of Justice

Although Tocqueville's thematic treatment of the nature and limits of justice is less comprehensive in scope than that of Aristotle, he shares with Aristotle a fundamental appreciation for both the inescapable importance of political justice as well as its essentially limited character.[29] This understanding of politics animates not only several of Tocqueville's specific suggestions, but, more importantly, his enterprise as a whole. It is most clearly seen in the persistent contrast between democratic and aristocratic societies that inform *Democracy in America*. As Tocqueville contemplates "the great democratic revolution" that is taking place, he confesses that the entire book was written "under the pressure of a sort of religious terror . . . produced by the sight of this irresistible revolution," one that has defeated every obstacle in its path over the course of the last seven hundred years (*Democracy*, 6, cf. 3). Why should Tocqueville feel something akin to religious terror when contemplating a revolution that was bringing into being a new form of politics which he himself believed to be characterized by greater justice than the aristocratic order it was in the process of displacing?

While Tocqueville's sense of religious dread clearly has something to do with the still uncertain fate of freedom in the newly emerging world, it also results from Tocqueville's own ambivalence about the costs involved in the transition. Notwithstanding his own unwavering commitment to the new order because of its greater justice (*Democracy*, 675), Tocqueville also regrets the loss of those social goods characteristic of aristocracy (among which he numbers its propensity to greater brilliance, high achievements in art and science, instinctive appreciation for glory, and ability to elicit and develop some of the most sublime capacities of the human soul—at least for some). Both democratic and aristocratic regimes cultivate important attributes essential for human and political flourishing, but neither nurtures the development of all of them. Indeed, so great is his ambivalence that although Tocqueville accepts this revolution as an accomplished fact, he has not presumed to judge whether it will be "advantageous or fatal to humanity" (*Democracy*, 13).

Like Aristotle, Tocqueville does not believe it is possible to reconcile in a fully adequate way the expressions of nobility characteristic of aristocratic societies at their best, with the promise of greater justice accompanying the new democratic order. Even with respect to democracy, the superior justice of which, Tocqueville maintains, constitutes "its greatness and its beauty" (*Democracy*, 675), Tocqueville also brings to light its susceptibility to tyranny of the majority (*Democracy*, 240ff.), as well as its tendency to devolve into a mild form of despotism (*Democracy*, esp. 661-665). Although some believe they can conceive a perfectly just regime, one capable of satisfying the basic human longings for the good, the just, and the noble, Tocqueville is not among them. Instead, he includes himself among "those who believe that there is almost never any *absolute good* in the laws" (*Democracy*, 13, emphasis added). The best that one can do is to minimize the ills and foster the goods that characterize a given political regime, something that points to the persistent need for statesmanship in politics.

Tocqueville on Statesmanship as Education Relative to the Regime

Tocqueville does not use the word "statesman" in his study of America, but refers instead to the "legislator," which appears to be its functional equivalent. The "whole art of the legislator," Tocqueville writes, "consists in discerning well and in advance" the "natural inclinations of human societies," so as to know when to "aid the efforts of citizens and when . . . to slow them down" (*Democracy*, 518). In terms of Tocqueville's comprehensive understanding of the science of politics considered earlier, whereas "publicists" contribute to the development of the *science* of politics, "legislators" practice the *art* of government; the latter apply the discoveries of the publicists to the unique conditions, circumstances and character of the people with whom they live.

This is of course precisely what the Founders of the American Constitution did, something that leads Tocqueville to praise the remarkable enlightenment and patriotism of the "legislators of the Union" (*Democracy*, 143). Tocqueville observes that "each government brings with it a natural vice that seems attached to the very principle of its life," and that "the genius of the legislator consists in discerning it well" (*Democracy*, 129). He explains that whereas the ruin of monarchy lies in the unlimited and unreasonable extension of royal power, the danger in democratic countries comes from laws that make the action of the people increasingly prompt and irresistible. The "greatest merit of the American legislators" was to have discerned this potentially fatal danger, and to have created powers that, while they are not completely independent of the people, provide "a rather large degree of freedom in their own sphere." The admirable result of the foresight and courage of the American founders was that while they were "forced to obey the permanent direction of the majority, they could nevertheless struggle against its caprices and refuse its dangerous demands" (*Democracy*, 129, cf. 486-87).

The action of the Founders in fashioning the fundamental law of the American nation would seem to exemplify in a precise way Aristotle's teaching on the need for legislators to provide citizens with an education relative to the regime. The *Constitution* both respects and asserts the sovereignty of the people, while at the same time establishing a schema of government that systematically attempts to counteract the most dangerous excesses to which a sovereign people are prone. One need only consider Madison's explanation and defense of the need in a democratic society to weaken the legislative power by severing it into two distinct branches (*Federalist* 51). Or one could recall Hamilton's insistence on the need for an independent Supreme Court and his defense of judicial review as a bulwark against legislative encroachments (*Federalist* 81 and 78). Tocqueville admires the work of the American founders precisely because they accurately diagnosed the "natural vice" attached to "the very principle . . . of life" in America (*Democracy*, 129), while implementing a series of antidotes that did not subvert, but strengthen the newly emerging order.

The *art of the legislator* as it was practiced by the founding generation is given a preeminent status in Tocqueville's analysis of America, in much the same way that Tocqueville ranks Machiavelli, Montesquieu and Rousseau among the greatest practitioners of the *science of politics* in his speech before the Academy. The need for statesmanship, however, does not cease with the Founding generation. In fact, Tocqueville maintains that as the consequences of the democratic revolution increasingly suffuse the modern world, the need for legislators will become increasingly acute. Tocqueville is especially concerned that the gradual erosion of social, economic and familial bonds, together with the greater importance of and preoccupation with material well-being, is likely to isolate citizens and render them inattentive to politics. Indeed, withdrawal from politics and retreat within the cocoon of "individualism" was one of the tendencies he most feared (*Democracy*, 482-485). If the emerging democratic order was all but inevitable for Tocqueville, he warns that it is compatible with *either* freedom *or* servitude. The great challenge for future legislators will be to discover ways to strengthen the natural love of liberty characteristic of citizens living in democratic societies, while at the same time helping them to resist their powerful inclination to accept a benign form of servitude (compatible with the outward forms of freedom), as they immerse themselves in an increasingly frenetic pursuit of security, comfort and material well-being (*Democracy*, 661-665 and 666-673). It seems entirely appropriate to think of Tocqueville's master-work on the dawning democratic age, as an effort to provide present and future citizens and statesmen with an education relative to a new and still-emerging regime—one intended to help them compensate for its hidden weaknesses, while discovering and drawing upon its strengths.

Conclusion

Tocqueville by no means urges a return to the pre-liberal configurations of the ancient polity; nor does he explicitly affirm the classical position regarding the priority of the theoretical life. He does, however, give important and perhaps novel expression to other aspects of the classical approach as he applies himself to the study of a deeply changed world. Tocqueville's "new political science" proves to have something in common with an older approach to the study of politics; it can be identified with neither the new political science that preceded it, nor the positive science that follows. Like many great publicists in the tradition of political thought, Tocqueville's writing combines an awareness of the distinctive character of the study of politics, preoccupation with the effects of different regimes on the human soul, profound appreciation for both the importance and limits of politics, and a keen understanding of the enduring need for the art of statesmanship. It is the distinctive synthesis of these elements and their application to a new political world built upon the ruins of the *ancien régime* that most accounts for the novelty of Tocqueville's political science. Ironically, its newness does not, in the manner of Hobbes, entail a radical break with the past, but exhibits—to some extent at least—an appropriation of it. Whether fully conscious or not, Tocqueville succeeds in bringing something of the broad horizon of classical and especially Aristotelian political science to bear on some of the most distinctive features and challenges of the modern world.

Notes

1. Consider Tocqueville's letters to Sophie Swetchine on February 11 and 26, 1857 (among others) in *Correspondance d'Alexis de Tocqueville et Madame Swetchine*, ed. Pierre Gilbert. In *Tocqueville: Oeuvres Complète*. Vol. XV, ed. J.-P. Mayer (Paris: Librairie Gallimard, 1983), 308-310 and 313-316. See also the analysis of Peter Lawler in *The Restless Mind: Alexis de Tocqueville on the Origin and Perpetuation of Human Liberty* (Lanham MD: Rowman and Littlefield, 1993): esp. 106-108, and "Was Tocqueville a Philosopher?" in *Interpretation: A Journal of Political Philosophy* 17 (1990): 401-414.

2. J. S. Mill is a notable exception. In his review of *Democracy in America*, he referred to it as "the first philosophic book written on Democracy." In "De Tocqueville on Democracy in America (II)," in *The Collected Works of John Stuart Mill*, Vol. 18: *Essays on Politics and Society*, ed. J. M. Robson (Toronto and Buffalo: University of Toronto Press, [1840] 1977), 156.

3. *Selected Letters on Politics and Society*, ed. Roger Boesche, trans. Roger Boesche and James Taupin (Berkeley and Los Angeles: University of California Press, 1985).

4. Although Plato is in fact critical of political life—even at times dismissively so (e.g. *Republic* 496c-e)—the serious attention given to politics is especially visible when the Platonic corpus is viewed in light of the philosophic tradition that preceded it. Unlike the pre-Socratic philosophers, all of whom are characterized by the absence of any serious consideration of politics, the problematic relationship between philosophy and the city is an enduring and central component of Platonic political philosophy.

5. For an argument regarding the overlapping concern of both Plato and Aristotle for the precarious political status of the philosophic life as it emerges in the *Nicomachean Ethics*, see Aristide Tessitore "Making the City Safe for Philosophy," *American Political Science Review* 84, no. 4 (December 1990): 1251-61 and *Reading Aristotle's Ethics* (Albany: State University of New York Press, 1996).

6. Alexis de Tocqueville, *Democracy in America*, ed. and trans. by Harvey C. Mansfield and Delba Winthrop (Chicago and London: University of Chicago Press, [1835 & 1840] 2000), 7.

7. This perspective was also shared to some extent by Xenophon, a contemporary of Plato. Xenophon's Socratic writings defend the goodness and nobility of Socrates' philosophic way of life, especially (but not exclusively) for those who not primarily philosophers.

8. In his discussion of political science in the *Nicomachean Ethics* (hereafter *NE*), Aristotle discusses the level of precision appropriate to this inquiry. Owing to the variability of its subject matter, Aristotle indicates that its conclusions will hold "for the most part," but not in every single case. He also suggests that the study of political science should be characterized by a level of precision that is greater than the kind of persuasiveness that makes for good rhetoric, but less than the precision of mathematics. This is due in large part to the fact that political science is a practical rather than theoretical science, as we shall have occasion to see below. See *NE* 1.3.1094b11-1095a2.

9. It is in part for this reason that Aristotle rejects the adequacy of Hippodamus' mathematical and excessively rational approach to the study of politics (*Politics* 2.8.1267b21-69a27).

10. In sharp contrast to the approach to political science taken by Aristotle and, more generally, the classical tradition, it is significant that the new tradition of modern political science begun by Hobbes takes its bearings, less from the peculiar nature of the political association, and more from the pre-political condition of human beings in the "state of nature." Cf. Hobbes, *Leviathan*, chapter 13, Locke, *Second Treatise on Government*, chapter 2, and Rousseau's *Discourse on the Origin and Foundations of Inequality Among Men*.

11. Sheldon Wolin maintains that Tocqueville's new political science, as well as the term itself, was inspired by the *Federalist Papers*. See *Tocqueville Between Two Worlds: The Making of a Political and Theoretical Life* (Princeton: Princeton University Press, 2001), 189ff.

12. In 1836, while working on the second volume of *Democracy in America*, Tocqueville wrote to his friend, Louis de Kergorlay, that he worked in the daily company of Pascal, Montesquieu and Rousseau. See *Correspondance D'Alexis de Tocqueville et de Louis de Kergolay* (Paris: Gallimard, 1977), 418.

13. See *The Old Regime and the French Revolution*, ed. François Furet and Françoise Mélonio and trans. Alan S. Kahan (London and Chicago: University of Chicago Press [1856] 1998) esp. 195-202.

14. See Thomas Hobbes, *Leviathan*, ed. Edwin Curley (Indianapolis: Hackett Publishing, [1668] 1994), 19, 24, 100 and René Descartes, *Discourse on Method*, trans. Donald A. Cress. Indianapolis and Cambridge: Hackett Publishing, [1637] 1980), 4, 11-12, 19-20.

15. Hobbes likens those who take their bearings from classic texts to birds "fluttering over their books." After entering a room by the chimney, they "flutter at the false light of a glass window, for want of wit to consider which way they came in" (*Leviathan*, 19). Descartes paints a similarly unflattering picture of those who take their bearings from ancient authorities: "They are like ivy that tends to climb no higher than the trees supporting it, and even which often tends downward again after it has reached the top" (*Discourse on Method*, 37).

16. It should be noted that Madison also recognized the insufficiency of this institutional solution. See especially the conclusion to *Federalist* 55.

17. Alexis de Tocqueville, Speech Given to the Annual Public Meeting of the Academy of Moral and Political Sciences on April 3, 1852. This speech appears as chapter 1 of this volume, in a translation by L. Joseph Hebert, Jr.

18. Tocqueville, Speech Given to the Academy of Moral and Political Sciences, 18.

19. Ibid., 20.

20. Ibid.

21. The view of political science described here bears more than passing resemblance to Plato's famous image of the cave, in which "philosopher-kings" are called upon to shape political reality for mostly unsuspecting citizen inhabitants of the cave-like political association (*Republic* 7.514a-518d; cf. Aristotle *NE* 7.11.1152b1-3).

22. In speaking about the foundations of political science, Carnes Lord writes, "The human sciences are preeminently "practical" (*praktikai*) sciences whose express purpose is not simply to increase knowledge but rather to benefit human life or human action (*praxis*)." *Essays on the Foundations of Aristotelian Science*, ed. by Carnes Lord and David K. O'Connor (Berkeley, Los Angeles, Oxford: University of California Press, 1991), 2.

23. The problem of terrorism and the continuing conflict between America and China on human rights are among the most pressing and serious global challenges at the beginning of the twenty-first century—both are rooted in the persistence of different and conflicting normative beliefs.

24. For an excellent discussion of happiness in the opening book of the *Nicomachean Ethics*, and its importance for understanding the book as a whole, see Robert Bartlett, "Aristotle's Introduction to the Problem of Happiness: On Book I of the *Nicomachean Ethics*" in *American Journal of Political Science* 52, no. 3 (July 2008): 677-687.

25. Although Tocqueville's understanding of "soul" resembles that of Aristotle in the sense indicated, it is also significantly different. It carries nothing of Aristotle's application of the term to all living beings or his more precise definition of soul as the form of the body. Moreover, unlike Aristotle, Tocqueville does emphasize the importance of a belief in "the immortality of the soul," although he does not necessarily link it to the orthodox Christian view of rewards or punishment after death (cf. *Democracy*, 519-20).

26. With respect to enlarging the horizon of citizens, the inescapable importance of politics, and the persistent tension between politics and the best human life, consider Aristotle's distinction between the best citizen and the best human being (*Politics* 3.4.1277b33-1278b5) and his discussion of the best way of life (*Politics* 7.1-3). One might also think of Socrates' claim to be the only Athenian to teach the true political art

in the *Gorgias* (521d-e), or his refusal to leave Athens to avoid execution during and after his trial (*Apology* 29c-30c, and *Crito*).

27. This teaching on the limits of political justice in the *Politics* is mirrored in Aristotle's account of justice in the *Nicomachean Ethics*. Whereas Aristotle's treatment of justice in Book V of the *Nicomachean Ethics* emphasizes law-abidingness, he also articulates and clarifies in an unprecedented way the perspective of morally serious persons who take their bearings from the noble. Susan Collins points to the problematic relationship between these two standards by bringing to light an irreducible tension between the requirements of the common good to which laws direct citizens, and the natural desire to seek the good for oneself, which, in the most admirable case, expresses itself in the human longing for the noble. The problem is given its sharpest expression in the case of those who dutifully and knowingly forfeit their lives in defense of country. See *Aristotle and the Rediscovery of Citizenship* (Cambridge and New York: Cambridge University Press, 2006).

28. Aristotle's endorsement of slavery to secure the leisure necessary for citizens to engage the always difficult and time-consuming issues involved in political deliberation, violates his earlier critique of conventional slavery, implicit in his definition of the "natural slave." Cf. *Politics* 7.9.1329a24-26 and 7.10.1330a25-33 with 1.4-7, esp. 1.5.1254b16-26.

29. Whereas Aristotle purports, at least in principle, to consider the full range of alternative political configurations, Tocqueville's treatment of the nature and limits of justice revolves around the two regimes of aristocracy and democracy, and within these two, especially the latter. Notwithstanding this difference in scope, both Tocqueville and Aristotle insist on the fundamental point—the inescapable importance and necessarily limited character of political justice.

Chapter 4

Machiavelli and Tocqueville on Majority Tyranny

Khalil M. Habib

Niccolo Machiavelli is famous for being the first political philosopher in the West to expound the virtues of republican government based upon the "decency of the people" and to praise the role of a mixed government in shaping citizens towards law and order and successful political and economic stability.[1] Alexis de Tocqueville, several centuries later, is among the first observers to offer a thoughtful critique of modern democracy and to contemplate its implications. This chapter seeks to understand the limits of Machiavelli's analysis of the "people" and a mixed republic through Tocqueville's critique of "majority tyranny" and the latter's views on the insufficiency of political institutions to guide and educate citizens towards responsible freedom.

This chapter is divided into four main parts. The first lays out Machiavelli's view of the "great" and the "people" and the manner in which he describes the underlying passions, driven by what he calls "humors," that make each class behave in its own predictable manner. The people, he teaches us, possess an innate desire to be left alone by tyrannizing and ambitious rulers, whereas the "great" (the nobles, patricians, or aristocrats) seek to oppress and dominate. Machiavelli recommends founding a regime on the decency of the "people" and their love of liberty. Political instability, Machiavelli claims, generally grows out of the ambitions of the ruling "great," along with a government's inability to restrain them. The second section continues the theme of liberty and provides an examination of both thinkers' views on the effects Christianity has had on freedom. Machiavelli sees Christianity, with its emphasis on the afterlife, as a debilitating force, stripping citizens of their natural inclination toward political action and freedom. Tocqueville is more sympathetic to Christianity, attributing to it a moralizing sense of commitment to community and liberty, an influence that

guards against falling into isolating individualism and majority tyranny. The
next section turns to Machiavelli's discussion of a mixed regime and uses ancient Rome as an example of the problem of ambition and its relationship to
political liberty. According to Machiavelli, Rome was best as a mixed republic
when citizens were free to exercise their liberty and to restrain their rulers. By
declaring himself a god, however, the emperor destroyed the republic and transformed citizens into enervated subjects. The Roman republic collapsed into tyranny because it was incapable of restraining the ambitions of the "great." Machiavelli advises readers to look critically at the political ambitions of the
"great" in order to avoid future destruction of the conditions for freedom. Machiavelli's suggestions for avoiding tyranny require an active citizenry with an
obstinate love of liberty and institutional checks on the ambitions of rulers. The
fourth and final section turns to Tocqueville and examines his views on tyranny
perpetrated by the majority (the "people"), the conditions that bring it about, and
the reasons why he rejects the ability of a mixed regime to thwart it.

My connection between Machiavelli and Tocqueville revolves around the
following set of questions: What happens to a democratic government when its
people no longer possess the love of individual liberty? Do Tocqueville's reflections on the insufficiency of political institutions for the maintenance of healthy
government and the need for moral and civic education point to serious difficulties in Machiavelli's endorsement of a mixed regime? Could citizens' passion
for equality along with a large tutelary state bring citizens and their leaders to
ignore the value of civic participation and therewith destroy the conditions for
liberty?[2]

Machiavelli on the "Great" and the "People"

In the *Discourses*, the *Prince,* and the *Florentine Histories*, Machiavelli divides
all human beings into two contrasting but not always dissimilar types, the
"great" and the "people." Each type possesses a unique pattern of behavior that
is motivated by a powerful underlying passion or "humor." The great desire to
dominate and oppress, and the people desire not to *be* dominated or oppressed.
According to Machiavelli, the great seek glory by dominating both their political
rivals and the people. By contrast, the people possess, by nature, a love of liberty; they seek to be free from their tyrannizing rulers. As he puts it in the *Discourses*, the "great" are a small minority of ambitious individuals who desire "to
be free so as to command," whereas the people "desire freedom so as to live
secure" (*DL* I.16, 46).[3] Something close to the same formulation is found in the
Prince. Machiavelli here argues that the people "desire neither to be commanded
nor oppressed by the great," and that the great "desire to command and oppress
the people."[4] The parallel passage in the *Florentine Histories* states that the
"grave and natural enmities . . . between the men of the people and the nobles,
caused by the wish of the latter to command and the former not to obey, are the

cause of all evils that arise in cities. For from this diversity of humors all other things that agitate republics take their nourishment."[5] According to Machiavelli, the people are much better guardians of freedom than the great because the people are less able to seize freedom for themselves, and are generally on guard against those who threaten their liberty. As he puts it:

> If one considers the end of the nobles and of the ignoble [the "people"], one will see great desire to dominate in the former, and in the latter only desire not to be dominated; and, in consequence, a greater will to be free, being less able to hope to usurp it [freedom] than are the great. So when those who are popular are posted as the guard of freedom, it is reasonable that they have more care for it, and since they are not able to seize it, they do not permit others to seize it (*DL* I. 5, 18).

Although both the great and the people desire freedom, each possesses its own understanding of it. For the great politics exists to satisfy their desire for glory and thirst to dominate, whereas the people desire not to *be* dominated and are, as Machiavelli states, better guards of freedom and are instinctively on the lookout for tyranny. For the people politics exists to serve man's freedom or security. In order to achieve this aim, Machiavelli must structure government in such a way as to manage those political men who are attracted to politics by power and glory in whatever way is necessary to create a civil society which will serve security and order.

According to Machiavelli, the people and the great also share two powerful passions: fear and greed. "Nature has created men so that they are able to desire everything and are unable to attain everything." Herein lies the problem, however: "the result is discontent with what one possesses and a lack of satisfaction with it," motivating all "to enmities and to war" (*DL* 1.37, 78). Here Machiavelli cites his Roman example: "it was not enough for the Roman plebs to secure itself against the nobles by the creation of the tribunes, to which desire it was constrained by necessity, for having obtained [its security], it began to engage in combat through ambition, and to wish to share honors and belongings with the nobility as the thing esteemed most by men" (ibid.). According to Machiavelli, even the people can become a cause of unrest and tension, if they can attain power or cease to fear the great.

It appears, then, that Machiavelli has blurred the distinction between the people and great. At times Machiavelli portrays the people as innocuous, at times as rapacious. Yet, throughout his work, Machiavelli insists on a sharp distinction between the freedom loving character of the people and the rapacious nature of the great. How can these two conflicting accounts of their humors be reconciled? In his book, *Machiavelli's Romans: Liberty and Greatness in the Discourses on Livy*, Patrick Coby offers several plausible answers.[6] The first is the necessity imposed by nature on all human beings. Most people simply lack the natural talent and imagination to exploit opportunities provided by wealth or political circumstances, Coby observes. Most live in poverty, limited to mundane necessities, such as food, clothing, and shelter, or they often lack the political means or desire to be rapacious. The second reason Coby gives is that by "the great" Machiavelli refers to both a psychological type and the social classes consisting of rulers, patricians, and the nobility. But not all of the great are born into a noble caste. Some, such as Agathocles, for example, whose story is retold vividly in chapter 8 of the *Prince*, worked their way up from the lower classes. In other words, not all the great are born into, or live among, their kind. Since ambition is necessitated by nature, rather than class only, Machiavelli extends (but not always) the qualities of the great to some plebeians. This allows Machiavelli to view ambition as widespread while retaining the view that the "humors" of classes differ, and that the differences depend on the situation and nature of the individual and available resources. Hence Machiavelli's famous advice to "presuppose that all men are bad" when designing government (*DL* I.3, 15). Simply put, "some men [the great], acquire always and on their own initiative while others [the people] acquire intermittently and out of self-defense."[7] The ambitious or rapacious among the people are the exceptions rather than the rule.

Consider, for example, Machiavelli's criticism of Titus Livy's view that "nothing is more vain and inconsistent than the multitude" (*DL* I. 58, 115), or of the classical tradition of political philosophy that claims "that peoples, when they are princes, are varying, mutable, and ungrateful." Machiavelli retorts:

> these sins are not otherwise in them than in particular princes. Someone accusing peoples and princes together might be able to say the truth, but in excepting princes, he would be deceived; for a people that commands and is well ordered will be stable, prudent, and grateful no otherwise than a prince, or better than a prince, even one esteemed wise (*DL* I. 58, 117).

Moreover, a prince or ruler "unshackled from the laws will be more ungrateful, varying, and more imprudent than a people" (*DL* I.58, 117). According to Machiavelli, this disparity arises not "from a diverse nature," because all are potentially (but not always) ambitious, rapacious, or ungrateful, given success, but rather from a greater respect for the laws on the part of the people, and less respect from the great (ibid..).

Why do the people generally show a greater respect for the laws than their rulers? In order to understand this, Machiavelli invites us to consider the behavior of the great and the people first within society regulated by laws, and then "unshackled from the laws." Once no longer obligated by law, the great can act freely. They are naturally superior types. The laws serve to protect the weaker, the people. These same laws constrain the strong. Nietzsche understands this point very well: the unshackled great, without laws, become, in his words, "not much better than uncaged beasts of prey in the world outside . . . There they enjoy freedom from every social constraint, in the wilderness they compensate for the tension which is caused by being closed in and fenced in by the peace of the community for so long, they *return* to the innocent conscience of the wild beast, as exultant monsters."[8] The people, by contrast, cannot succeed or thrive without the protection of laws because they have no guarantee for their security nor protection against being taken advantage of or oppressed by their superiors; it is to the advantage of the people to promote respect for the laws that guard their freedom. The people's decency stems from the great fear of a war of all against all, and from their need for security and their desire not to *be* oppressed. Machiavelli points out that in a condition in which the people and the great are unshackled by the laws, the badness or rapaciousness of the great far exceeds the goodness of the people.[9]

In other words, the desire to command and the desire not to *be* dominated are both expressions of the desire for liberty, or as Machiavelli himself puts it, "one mode in all" (*DL* I.58, 117). In society regulated by laws and social constraints, however, the desire for freedom manifests itself for the people in a liberty conceived as security and freedom from tyranny, and for the great in a liberty conceived as power to dominate. These opposed concepts of freedom "emerge as different humors in society, visibly apart, because [the people and the great] want different and opposite things."[10] The people believe themselves to be free when they are governed by laws that serve their security and freedom from oppression and when those laws are observed by authorities (*DL* I.16, 46). In other words, Machiavelli anticipates Montesquieu's view that "less virtue is needed in a monarchy [or despotism], where the one who sees to the execution of the laws judges himself *above the laws*, than in a popular government, where the one who sees to the execution of the laws feels that he is *subject to them himself and that he will bear their weight*."[11] The great, by contrast, believe themselves to be free when they are able to dominate and seek glory through their political actions. Hence Machiavelli's view that once unshackled from the law, "if there is advantage of good, it is in the people," and not in the rulers. Indeed, Machiavelli insists that "a people is more prudent, more stable, and of better judgment than a prince." He goes so far as to claim that "*Not without cause may the voice of a people be likened to that of God*" (emphasis added, *DL* I. 58, 117-18).

A freedom-loving people can be brought to understand that their love of liberty and self-government depend on personal self-restraint, as self-government requires that each individual can govern himself. Self-government, Machiavelli suggests, depends on a virtuous citizenry governing together with civic habits of self-restraint. Although the people can appreciate the value of ordered liberty and the necessity for law and order, the same cannot be said of the great: "there is no one who can speak to a wicked prince, nor is there any remedy other than steel." Indeed, the great are the problem and are far more at fault: "if to cure the illness of the people words are enough . . . for the prince's steel is needed, [so] there will never be anyone who will not judge that where a greater cure is needed there are greater errors" (*DL* I. 58, 119). And errors must be held in check. The virtuous presence of the people as a security-seeking class is needed as a counter balance to the ambitions of rulers.

For Machiavelli, the struggle for domination and freedom is the core of politics. The enmity between those who seek glory and freedom through domination and those who desire not to *be* dominated creates a perpetual dynamic between the great and the people, between glory and fear, as ambitious rulers are insatiable in their lust for domination and the people fear losing their freedom and their lives. It appears that no common good can be reached between these two types, hence Machiavelli's insistence on a mixed republic to manage, as much as possible, their differences through some form of checks and balances.

Machiavelli and Tocqueville on Liberty and Religion

According to Machiavelli, liberty (as understood by "the people") is the essence of a strong government and the key to its security and prosperity, "for it is seen through experience that cities have never expanded either in dominion or in riches if they have not been in freedom" (*DL* II.2, 129).[12] The love of freedom is also the greatest defense against foreign and domestic tyranny, as "nothing made it more laborious for the Romans to overcome the peoples nearby and parts of the distant provinces than the love that many peoples in those times had for freedom; they defended it so obstinately that they would never have been subjugated if not by excessive virtue" (ibid.). As much as the people's love of freedom is the greatest defense against tyranny and the key to prosperity, servitude threatens both freedom and prosperity (ibid.). According to Machiavelli, freedom is not only threatened by the ambitions of the great, but it is also endangered by Christianity. In this section, we turn briefly to Machiavelli's views of the latter, as he is of the opinion that Christianity is also a force which undermines the love of political liberty.[13] For Machiavelli, the love of freedom and virtue, rather than reliance upon fortune or divine providence, underlies political success.

Machiavelli faults Christianity for holding up a universal brotherhood in the afterlife over the love of political liberty in this life. Christians lack an obstinate love of liberty because Christianity teaches citizens to "esteem less the honor of the world, whereas the [non-Christians], esteeming it very much and having placed the highest good in it, were more ferocious in their actions" (*DL* II.2, 131). Since Machiavelli argues that freedom is natural and necessary for healthy government, he clearly prefers what he considers to be the natural, pre-Christian love of political freedom to the Christian love of God and humility which, according to him, has made the world weak. He implies that Christianity has corrupted human nature and politics and, in doing so, has turned the political world upside down:

> Our religion has glorified humble and contemplative more than active men. It has then placed the highest good in humility, abjectness, and contempt of things human. . . . And if our religion asks that you have strength in yourself, it wishes you to be capable more of suffering than of doing something strong. This mode

of life thus seems to have rendered the world weak and given it in prey to criminal men, who can manage it securely, seeing that the collectivity of men, so as
to go to paradise, think more of enduring their beatings than of avenging them.
And although the world appears to be made effeminate and heaven disarmed, it
arises without doubt more from the cowardice of the men who have interpreted
our religion according to idleness and not according to virtue (*DL* II.2, 131-32).

Virtue, for Machiavelli, is both the obstinate love of liberty and the ability
to succeed through one's own arms rather than the arms of others, particularly
God's.[14] Christianity teaches the opposite of Machiavelli's understanding of
virtue, namely to bear the sufferings of this world, to abhor material gain, and to
submit humbly to God's authority and will. For these reasons Machiavelli
claims that Christianity is in conflict with politics and human nature, rather than
representing their fulfillment or perfection. Although Christianity offers an alternative in the afterlife to strife on this earth, Machiavelli places his emphasis
on seeking a solution to partisanship in this life. In revisiting and praising the
mixed regime of the ancient Roman republic that predates the existence of
Christianity, Machiavelli seeks to restore the love of liberty among the people
who have forgotten their natural, worldly virtue. By encouraging human beings
to concentrate their attention on worldly acquisitions and freedom, Machiavelli
teaches his readers to focus on this life rather than on salvation in the afterlife.

Whereas Machiavelli draws attention to the tension between liberty and religion, Tocqueville praises the role of religion in democracy and the manner in
which the spirit of liberty and the spirit of religion may coexist and nourish each
other (*DIM*, 47).[15] Among other things, Tocqueville recommends civic participation and religion to aid democratic statesmanship. Although religion and the
state coexist in separate realms, religion contributes to the maintenance of the
law.[16] Tocqueville observes that "Liberty regards religion as its companion in all
its battles and its triumphs . . . it considers religion as the safeguard of morality,
and morality as the best security of law and the surest pledge of the duration of
freedom."[17] He concludes that "Despotism may be able to do without faith, but
freedom cannot" (*DIM*, 294).

Tocqueville is sympathetic to religion in democratic society as a means of
preserving the conditions, especially the ethical beliefs, necessary to maintain
political life and for establishing and maintaining not only moral but also liberal
and civic education. In this case, Tocqueville shares Nietzsche's revulsion
against the "last man," a being for whom no striving for excellence, or commitment to anything beyond materialism and comfortable self-preservation, exists
to inform one's inner life. This unwillingness to sacrifice anything beyond our
immediate material gratification drains human existence of its higher callings,
Tocqueville warns. It can also weaken democratic society, causing a drift toward
majority tyranny, as life ceases to offer any alternatives to mindless entertainment and conformism. Religion heads off the dangerous effects of materialism
and individualism, while also satisfying the human quest for meaning beyond
trivial daily concerns. Thus, for Machiavelli, Christianity poses only dangers to

liberty, while for Tocqueville, the results of religious beliefs in a democracy can produce salutary results, as the demands placed on human passions by religion help to prepare citizens for self-restraint and self-governance.

Machiavelli and Tocqueville on the Mixed Republic

In this section we turn to Machiavelli's discussion of a mixed regime and examine his treatment of ancient Rome as an example of the problem of ambition and its relationship to political liberty. According to Machiavelli, Rome reached its political peak as a mixed republic when citizens were free to exercise their liberty and to restrain their rulers, and declined when the emperor destroyed the republic and transformed citizens into enervated subjects. The Roman republic failed the cause of liberty because it was incapable of restraining the ambitions of the "great." In order to avoid future destruction of the conditions for freedom, Machiavelli advises readers to look critically at the political ambitions of the "great" and suggests that liberty requires an active citizenry with an obstinate love of liberty and institutional checks on the ambitions of rulers.

According to Machiavelli, liberty thrived under the Roman republic; however, the transition from republic to empire destroyed the conditions for political liberty by eliminating "all civic ways of life." As he explains,

> I believe [the cause of the loss of liberty . . .] to be rather that the Roman Empire, with its arms and its greatness, eliminated all republics and all civil ways of life. And although that empire was dissolved, the cities still have not been able to put themselves back together or reorder themselves for civil life except in very few places of that empire. However that may be, in every least part of the world the Romans found a conspiracy of republics very armed and very obstinate in defense of their freedom. This shows that without a rare and extreme virtue, the Roman people would never have been able to overcome them (*DL* II.2, 132).

Machiavelli judges that Rome was best as a mixed republic, but it lost its taste for liberty under its emperor, who destroyed the republic by declaring himself a God on earth. He was able to ascend by taking up the cause of the plebeians against the patricians. In so doing, Caesar prepared the multitude under his rule to accept his tyranny, the rule of one man over the entire known world (*DL* I. 10-12). According to Vickie Sullivan, the Roman republic failed to restrain the ambitions of its "great" and collapsed into tyranny because it was "vulnerable to its great men's attempts to attain sole rule."[18] Having discovered the cause for the Roman Republic's descent into tyranny, Machiavelli advises us to take "the dimmest possible view of" the political ambitions of the "great" in order to avoid future collapse, as the great could turn against their own republic to satisfy their ambitions.[19]

As Sullivan notes, Machiavelli, therefore, "teaches the prospective founder that a republic cannot countenance any insolence towards its laws and that, as a result, it must maintain the utmost suspicion towards its leading men" by properly channeling "the ambitions of the great," while skillfully managing the more "decent" needs and desires of the people.[20] The solution to tyranny is found in Machiavelli's understanding of a mixed republic and the manner in which institutional designs will both discourage the concentration of power and frustrate tyranny.

Machiavelli begins his reflections on republics by recasting the traditional survey of the forms of government that were articulated by ancient thinkers such as Aristotle[21] and Polybius:[22] "There are," Machiavelli instructs, "six types of government, of which three [tyranny, oligarchy and democracy] are the worst; . . . three others [princedom, aristocracy and popular government] are . . . easily corrupted [so] that they too come to be pernicious" (*DL* I.2, 11).[23] Consequently, "the principality easily becomes tyrannical, the aristocrats with ease become a state of the few; the popular is without difficulty converted into the licentious" (*DL* I.2, 11).

Yet, what specifically makes a regime "good" and why are the "good" regimes so easily corrupted? According to Aristotle, a regime is good when its rulers are good, and a regime becomes bad when its leaders become corrupt and cease to be good.[24] All regimes, therefore, reflect the moral character of the rulers, who in turn influence the character of citizens. Machiavelli, on the other hand, is of the opinion that "men never work any good unless through necessity" (*DL* I.3, 15). According to him, rulers only "appear" to be good when they cannot act wickedly. To illustrate this point, Machiavelli turns to political life under the Tarquins, where the appearance of a unity or common good between the nobles and the plebs was built upon a "deception . . . concealed" from sight— fear, not moral character, was the cause of its being "good"—"nor did one see the cause of [this unity] while the Tarquins lived. Fearing them, and having fear that if the plebs were treated badly it would not take their side, the nobility behaved humanely toward [the plebs]." With the fear of the Tarquins removed, however, the so-called nobility "began to spit out that poison against the plebs that they had held in their breast, and they offended it in all the modes they could." Once the check against the nobles disappeared, civil life was "full of confusion and disorder" (*DL* I.3, 15).

From Machiavelli's perspective, those like Aristotle mistake a "good regime" for qualities of soul in rulers because they fail to see that beneath all "good qualities" lies a hidden a cause, such as fear, keeping the so-called "noble" or "good" in check. "Good" nobles are but a chimera. Indeed, according to Machiavelli, "he who wishes to make a republic where there are very many gentlemen"—that is, those lords who live from their "castles and possessions"— "cannot do it unless he first eliminates all of them" (*DL* I. 55, 112). By lowering our opinion of the great and by counterbalancing vice rather than empowering virtue, a system of checks and balances would, according to Machiavelli, "have the same effect as the Tarquins had when they were alive" (*DL* I.3, 15). Since no social group living under a mixed republic is permitted to dominate the entire republic or hold all instruments of government, a mixed regime can resolve, or at least moderate, the natural antagonism between groups through the medium of the law and the instruments of government.

Drawing from history to support the dispersing of the powers of government, Machiavelli praises Lycurgus, "who in Sparta ordered his laws so as to give their roles to the kings, the aristocrats, and the people and made a state that lasted more than eight hundred years, achieving the highest praise for himself and quiet in that city" (*DL* I.2, 13). By contrast, Solon of Athens erred when he ordered the laws of Athens around only the popular state, which resulted in a short life; hence, "before [Lycurgus] died he saw the tyranny of Pisistratus" (*DL* I.2, 13).

The perfection of the Roman model, on the other hand, rested on the skillful management of "the disunion of the plebs and the senate," through a system of Consuls, Senate, and Tribunes (representatives of the people). The Roman republic "never took away all authority from kingly qualities so as to give authority to the aristocrats, nor did it diminish the authority of the aristocrats altogether so as to give it to the people. But remaining mixed, it made a perfect republic" (*DL* I.2, 14). According to Machiavelli, however, the checks that led to Rome's "perfection" emerged by accident or by chance (*DL* 1.2, 14). Machiavelli advises that what emerged by chance can, nevertheless, be consciously recreated by an enlightened founder or lawgiver.

A mixed republic with a strong system of checks could, therefore, remedy the problem of political instability and end "the cycle of regimes." Without these checks each of the so-called "good" regimes will inevitably drift towards its bad counterpart, Machiavelli believes, as moral virtue is too weak and ineffectual to prevent political decline. He observes that when a founder "of a republic orders one of those three states in a city [without institutional checks], he orders it there for a short time; for no remedy can be applied there to prevent it from slipping into its contrary because of the likeness that the virtue and the vice have in this case" (*DL* I.2, 11).

Tocqueville, who lived through the French Revolution, is less confident than Machiavelli that it is inherently wise to build government on the people, and Tocqueville also rejects Machiavelli's belief in the possibility of a genuine mixed regime: "I have always considered what is called a mixed government to be a chimera. There is in truth no such thing as a mixed government, since in any society one finds in the end some principle of action that dominates all the others" (*DIM*, 251). The principle of modern democracy is the sovereignty of the people and, Tocqueville asks,

> What is a majority, in its collective capacity, if not an individual with opinions, and usually with interests, contrary to those of another individual, called the minority? Now, if you admit that a man vested with omnipotence can abuse it against his adversaries, why not admit the same concerning a majority? Have men, by joining together, changed their character? By becoming stronger, have

they become more patient of obstacles? For my part, I cannot believe that, and I will never grant to several that power to do everything which I refuse to a single man (*DIM*, 251).

In a striking passage that recalls Machiavelli's distinction between the "people" and the "great," Tocqueville states that the mistaken notion that a mixed regime can remedy tyranny "is due to those who, constantly seeing the interests of the great in conflict with those of the people, have thought only about the struggle and have not paid attention to the result thereof, which was more important. When a society really does have a mixed government . . . one equally shared between contrary principles, either a revolution breaks out or that society breaks up" (*DIM*, 251).

For Tocqueville, the people in a democratic republic possess political and institutional omnipotence, which "in itself" is a "bad and dangerous thing." Again, in a passage that recalls Machiavelli's view that "the voice of a people be likened to that of God,"[25] Tocqueville says that the people in their freedom are omnipotent and that their "exercise is beyond man's strength, whoever he be, and that only God can be omnipotent without danger because His wisdom and justice are always equal to His power. So there is no power on earth in itself so worthy of respect or vested with such a sacred right that I would wish to let it act without control and dominate without obstacles . . . the germ of tyranny is there" (*DIM*, 252). Indeed, according to Tocqueville, the "greatest complaint against democratic government . . . is not . . . its weakness, but rather its irresistible strength. What I find most repulsive in America is not the extreme freedom reigning there but the shortage of guarantees against tyranny" (*DIM*, 252). The tyranny to which Tocqueville refers is not the tyranny of aristocracy, monarchy, or oligarchy, but the tyranny of the majority, a tyranny of the people. Tocqueville's reflections on majority tyranny challenge Machiavelli's belief in a mixed regime as a viable remedy to despotism.

Tocqueville on the Dangers of Democratic Despotism and the Tyranny of the Majority

In the previous section we examined how for Machiavelli avoiding the tyranny of the great requires an active citizenry with an obstinate love of liberty and institutional checks on the ambitions of rulers. In this section we turn to Tocqueville and examine his views on tyranny perpetrated by the majority (the "people"), the conditions that bring it about, and the reasons why he rejects the ability of a mixed regime to thwart it.

Three hundred years after Machiavelli, Tocqueville sees his own democratic age as part of an inevitable process: "the gradual progress of equality is something fated . . . [the] effort to halt democracy appears as a fight against God Himself, and nations have no alternative but to acquiesce in the social state imposed by Providence" (*DIM*, 12). And so Tocqueville finds it his duty to assist this new age from the vantage point of the victory of a democratic republic. The people's passion for equality, according to Tocqueville, accompanies the desire to overcome any perceived or real inequalities by seeking to democratize all things, even if this means majority tyranny in the name of equality: "One must admit that equality, while it brings great benefits to mankind, opens the door . . . to very dangerous instincts" (*DIM*, 444).

Throughout his work, Tocqueville refers to two particular threats to a healthy republic and individual liberty that distinguish his thought from Machiavelli's. The one Tocqueville calls the "tyranny of the majority." The other he labels "administrative despotism," a form of oppression he describes in terms of a tutelary state that "does not break men's will, but softens, bends, and guides it . . . so that in the end each [citizen] . . . is no more than a . . . timid and hardworking [animal] and the government [his] shepherd" (*DIM*, 692).

Majority tyranny and administrative despotism both threaten individual liberty. Tocqueville fears that under a centralized administrative "tutelary" power, citizens will further withdraw from civic participation and cease asserting their liberty and dignity as citizens. Indeed, according to Tocqueville, a society of atomized individuals leads to a weak body of citizens who "can do hardly anything for themselves, and none of them is in a position to force his fellows to help him. If the inhabitants of democratic countries had neither the right nor the taste for uniting for political objects, their independence would run great risks." He warns that "tyranny would be bound to increase . . . . [in] a people in which individuals had lost the power of carrying through great enterprises by themselves," and he adds that "without acquiring the faculty of doing them together, [a civilized people] would soon fall back into barbarism" (*DIM*, 513-15).

Just as life under the ancient Roman emperor destroyed the conditions of liberty, Tocqueville believes that an overpowering and tutelary government "once established in [a democracy] would not only oppress men but would, in the end, strip each man there of several of the chief attributes of humanity." Perhaps Machiavelli did not anticipate the possibility of an administrative despotism within a republic, but it is administrative despotism that Tocqueville believes "is particularly to be feared in ages of democracy" (*DIM*, 694). The centralization of government downplays the strength of the individual and "thus . . . daily makes the exercise of free choice less useful and rarer, restricts the activity of free will within a narrower compass, and little by little robs each citizen of the proper use of his own faculties." Tocqueville faults the pursuit of equality for this unacceptable lethargy, where deluded citizens "endure it and often even regard it as beneficial" (*DIM*, 692).

Democracy's drift toward egalitarian tyranny gathers strength from the equality of conditions and the indifference to a loss of political liberty and civic participation. Moreover, according to Tocqueville, "the absolute sovereignty of the will of the majority" is "the essence of democratic government," and he adds that within "democracy there is nothing outside the majority capable of resisting it. Many American constitutions have sought further artificially to increase this natural strength of the majority" (*DIM*, 246). This is why he regarded the trend toward equality as "not only predominant but irresistible" (*DIM*, 247).

Although, in general, the majority within a democracy possesses neither taste nor time nor patience for the cultivation of the mind and intellectual matters, the majority does claim a moral superiority over the few. This sense of superiority is derived principally from the idea of equality, which seems to assume "that there is more enlightenment and wisdom in a numerous assembly than in a single man, and the number of the legislators is more important than their quality" (*DIM*, 247). Tocqueville describes this democratic attitude as the "doctrine of equality applied to brains" (*DIM*, 247), a moral doctrine which he suggests constitutes an attack on the independence of the human mind, "the last asylum of human pride" (ibid.). The idea of equality applied to brains places the majority, for the first time in history, in a position to preside over public opinion as a kind of democratic divinity; as Marvin Zetterbaum notes, the majority forces conformity on itself and also precludes arguments outside its own imposed orthodoxy.[26]

This leads Tocqueville to conclude that "the majority in the United States has immense actual power and a power of opinion which is almost as great. When once it has made its mind up on any question, there are, so to say, no other obstacles which can retard, much less halt, its progress and give it time to hear the wails of those it crushes as it passes" (*DIM*, 248). Once public opinion becomes an omnipotent God, the public sphere becomes the sacred ground upon which no dissent is tolerated. Only opinions that further or flatter equality are permitted. Hence we read that Tocqueville knows "no country in which, speaking generally, there is less independence of mind and true freedom of discussion than in America" (*DIM*, 254-55).

Under the rule of majority tyranny, American democracy has become a mass without a head. The problem with such a headless herd is compounded by the fact that there are no independent classes within America to combat or challenge the will of the majority, which transforms a mass or majority of "equal" individuals into an omnipotent authority over all. As noted above, Tocqueville explicitly denies the benefits of the mixed regime Machiavelli favors. As Harvey Mansfield notes, "there is potential for tyranny wherever unmixed authority is found, which is everywhere; and tyranny becomes actual where this authority meets no formidable obstacle."[27] Where there is no check by any opposing social class to democratic dogma, Tocqueville wonders,

> [w]hen a man or a party suffers an injustice in the United States, to whom can he turn? To public opinion? That is what forms the majority. To the legislative body? It represents the majority and obeys it blindly. To the executive power? It is appointed by the majority and serves as its passive instrument. To the police? They are nothing but majority under arms. A jury? The jury is the majority vested with the right to pronounce judgment; even the judges in certain states are elected by the majority. So, however iniquitous or unreasonable the measure which hurts you, you must submit (*DIM*, 252).

By contrast, the monarchies of the past, Tocqueville assures us, allowed a greater range of intellectual honesty, and open debate was tolerated and even encouraged by some kings, who were clearly more confident in their superiority than the people in theirs. "In the proudest nations of the Old World," according to Tocqueville, works faithfully portraying the vices and absurdities of monarchs and political leaders were published and often tolerated by ruling elites: "Bruyere," for instance, "lived in Louis XIV's palace while he wrote his chapter on the great, and Moliere criticized the court in plays acted before the courtiers." In the United States, by contrast, Tocqueville observes that the majority which dominates "does not understand being mocked at like that. The least reproach offends it, and the slightest sting of truth turns it fierce." The only option available is to flatter democracy: "and one must praise everything, from the turn of its phrases to its most robust virtues. No writer, no matter how famous, can escape from this obligation to sprinkle incense over his fellow citizens. Hence the majority lives in a state of perpetual self-adoration; only strangers or experience may be able to bring certain truths to the Americans' attention" (*DIM*, 256).

Tocqueville's point here is not that all European feudal monarchs were generous and benign, but rather that the egalitarian tyrant is a humorless despot, unlike those proud and confident monarchs of the past; the democratic tyranny cannot withstand the slightest criticism and, consequently, its punitive nature reduces human beings to groveling flatterers and courtiers of equality. Its omnipotent and "absolute and irresistible sway" toward equality forces one to "renounce one's rights as a citizen and . . . [one's] status as a man when one wants to diverge from the path it has marked out" (*DIM*, 258).

Tocqueville's observations on the effect of this tyranny on genuine independence of mind are chilling:

> In America the majority has enclosed thought within a formidable fence. A writer is free inside that area, but woe to the man who goes beyond it. Not that he stands in fear of an *auto-da-fe*, but he must face all kinds of unpleasantness and everyday persecution. A career in politics is closed to him, for he has offended the only power that holds the keys. He is denied everything, including renown. Before he goes into print, he believes he has supporters; but he feels that he has them no more once he stands revealed to all, for those who condemn him express their views loudly, while those who think as he does, but without his courage, retreat into silence as if ashamed of having told the truth (*DIM*, 255).

Like the Christian calumniators described in Machiavelli's *Discourses*,[28] the tyrants of egalitarianism during Tocqueville's time seek inner conformity to equality and will punish those who do not bow before it. Although they do not openly persecute, they have devised clever means to punish nonbelievers. The dehumanizing consequences of thinking outside the dogmas of, or holding opinions contrary to, equality sap the spirit of liberty, as dissenting opinion is shouted down, slandered, or simply ignored by public opinion and the press. Only egalitarian views are tolerated and rewarded, while opposing opinions are censored through political correctness. In denying a standard of excellence or perspective beyond egalitarianism, the intellectual probity derived from an independent mind is declared invalid on the ground of equality. The denial of a genuine standard for knowledge or truth outside of majority opinion spells the end of philosophy and affirms only mass society and public opinion.

The great danger of this form of tyranny is that it appears to act like democracy: "the orderly, gentle, peaceful slavery . . . might be combined with some of the external forms of freedom, and . . . there is a possibility of its getting itself established even under [the pretence] of the sovereignty of the people" (*DIM*, 692-93). Tocqueville also warns that "there is nothing as irresistible as a tyrannical power commanding in the name of the people," because its will is the moral authority of the people; it "acts . . . with the speed and tenacity of a single man" (*DIM*, 222).

Tocqueville, therefore, helps us to see that equality is not always democratic, nor is it always a defense against tyranny, but an invitation for a majority to deprive the few of their individual liberty and independence of mind: "The chief . . . condition necessary in order to succeed in centralizing the supreme power in a democratic community is to love equality or to make men believe that you do so. Thus the art of despotism, once so complicated, has been simplified; one may almost say that it has been reduced to a single principle" (*DIM*, 678-79).

Although this new soft despotism does not physically harm its detractors, Tocqueville believes that it is nevertheless as dangerous as the violent tyrannies of the past: "Formerly tyranny used the clumsy weapons of chains and hangman; nowadays even despotism, though it seemed to have nothing more to learn, has been perfected by civilization" (*DIM*, 255). Tocqueville explains:

> Princes made violence a physical thing, but our contemporary democratic republics have turned it into something as intellectual as the human will it is intended to constrain. Under the absolute government of a single man, despotism, to reach the soul, clumsily struck at the body, and the soul, escaping from such blows, rose gloriously above it; but in democratic republics that is not at all how tyranny behaves; it leaves the body alone and goes straight for the soul (*DIM*, 255-56).

Democratic despotism is more insidious and less obvious than earlier violent tyrannies in its insatiable appetite for control and domination; it is more difficult to recognize and restrain and, for these reasons, much deadlier to the spirit than bodily violence. A despotic king seeks but cannot take the life of all those who oppose him. Egalitarian despotism by contrast leaves the body alone, yet manages to insinuate its authority over all in the name of equality and is unlimited in its claim to be *the* authority over the mind.[29]

Tocqueville warns that in an age of majority tyranny and excessive equality, any attempt to restore strong individual leadership in an effort to educate, guide, and improve democracy, will be difficult—even as such conditions invite theoretical reflection upon the most fundamental questions of human life and politics. Tocqueville laments that

> there is now no ruler so skillful and so strong that he can establish . . . permanent distinctions between his subjects. Nor is there any legislator, however wise or powerful, who could maintain free institutions without making equality his first principle and watchword. Therefore all those who now wish to establish or secure the independence and dignity of their fellow men must show themselves friends of equality; and the only worthy means of appearing such is to be so; upon this depends the success of their holy enterprise (*DIM*, 695).

Nevertheless, Tocqueville invites supporters of democracy to play a leadership role in educating and leading their fellow citizens toward liberty. For Tocqueville, genuine leadership is required to educate democracy toward responsible freedom, precisely because the challenges to freedom within democracy are so great. But majority tyranny thwarts the ability of genuine leaders to rise. By articulating the character of the menace undermining freedom within democracy, Tocqueville provides the framework for thinking more carefully about freedom and democracy. This is the source of the claim that he is a friendly critic of democracy, and not its enemy.[30]

Conclusion

Both Machiavelli and Tocqueville are concerned with tyranny. Both seek remedies for it. Both consider it to be the greatest threat to a healthy republic. Whereas Machiavelli looks back to the Roman republic in order to show how one ambitious man destroyed the republic when he propelled himself to divine ruler, Tocqueville examines democracy in practice in the United States and warns against the extremes to which equality could be taken in the hands of an overzealous multitude. Whereas Rome was vulnerable to the few who sought to rule over all, and later to Christianity which weakened politics, democracy in America is vulnerable to the people and its whims. According to Machiavelli, Rome's greatness and perfection consisted in its mixed government, but the conditions for its liberty were ruined by the ambition of a "great" who destroyed the republic by taking up the cause of the people against the nobles and the patricians.[31] In destroying the republic, Caesar destroyed the taste for liberty among the citizens. This momentous occasion laid the ground for Christianity by preparing the multitude under Caesar to accept and learn to live with the rule of one man. Although Machiavelli recognizes the foibles of the people, he nevertheless trusts them in politics more than he trusts the great, who he argues could be skillfully managed through institutional means and a mixed government.

Tocqueville does not share Machiavelli's confidence that the problem of politics is the opposition between the people and a few "great," nor does he believe that a mixed regime is a viable remedy to tyranny. Tocqueville fears a majority tyranny and he is equally concerned with the prospect for liberty, which he does not believe will fare well in the new democratic age. For Tocqueville, gaining an all-powerful centralized government is not worth losing the conditions for individual liberty, especially if the result is disconnected and atomized individuals who are dominated by majority tyranny. Without a thoughtful response to egalitarian excesses, "democratic citizens" may very well "press for increasing the power of the majority without being able to assure its wisdom or justice."[32] The dangers menacing republics concern both these thinkers. It is in the assessment of their causes and the recommendations for their solutions that Machiavelli and Tocqueville disagree.

Notes

1. I wish to acknowledge the helpful comments of Brian Danoff and Joe Hebert on earlier drafts of this chapter.

2. Whether or not Tocqueville has Machiavelli in mind when he examines majority tyranny and a mixed republic is not my concern. My intention is to bring these two thinkers together in a dialogue, in order that such a comparison may help to shed light on each thinker and on the theoretical foundations of democratic government.

3. Niccolo Machiavelli, *The Discourses on Livy*, trans. Harvey C. Mansfield and Nathan Tarcov (Chicago: University of Chicago Press, 1996), 46. References in this chapter to Machiavelli's *Discourses on Livy* (DL) are included parenthetically in the text by book, chapter, and page. All references to the *Discourses on Livy* are to this edition, unless otherwise noted. With the exception of Alexis de Tocqueville's *Democracy in America*, all references are documented in the endnotes.

4. Niccolo Machiavelli, *The Prince*, trans. Harvey C. Mansfield (Chicago: University of Chicago Press, 1985), 39.

5. Niccolo Machiavelli, *Florentine Histories*, trans. Laura F. Banfield and Harvey C. Mansfield with an introduction by Harvey C. Mansfield (Princeton: Princeton University Press, 1990), 105.

6. Patrick Coby, *Machiavelli's Romans: Liberty and Greatness in the Discourses on Livy* (Lanham, MD: Lexington Press, 1999), 96.

7. Ibid., 93.

8. Friedrich Nietzsche, *On the Genealogy of Morality*, trans. Carol Diethe and edited by Keith Ansell-Pearson (Cambridge: Cambridge University Press, 2007), 23.

9. Machiavelli's argument is strikingly similar to Glaucon's account of the origin of justice in Plato's *Republic*. See, for example, Book 2, 358e-359e.

10. Patrick Coby, *Machiavelli's Romans*, 94.

11. Charles de Montesquieu, *The Spirit of the Laws*, ed. and trans. Anne Cohler, Basia Miller, and Harold Stone (Cambridge: Cambridge University Press, 1989), 22.

12. See also chapters 5 and 9 of the *Prince*.

13. Harvey C. Mansfield, *Machiavelli's New Modes and Orders: A Study of the Discourses on Livy* (Chicago: University of Chicago Press, 2001), 192-206.

14. See also chapter 1 of the *Prince*.

15. I have used Alexis de Tocqueville's *Democracy in America*, ed, J.P. Mayer, trans. G. Lawrence (New York: Perennial Classics, 2000). All references to *Democracy*

in America are to this edition, unless otherwise noted, and will be cited parenthetically as (*DIM*), including page number.

16. For an analysis of Tocqueville's views on the relationship between Christianity and American democracy, see Sanford Kessler, *Tocqueville's Civil Religion: American Christianity and the Prospects for Freedom* (Albany: State University of New York Press, 1994).

17. Quoted in Michael A. Ledeen, *Tocqueville on American Character: Why Tocqueville's Brilliant Exploration of the American Spirit is as Vital and Important Today as it was Nearly Two Hundred Years Ago* (New York: St. Martin's Press, 2000), 70.

18. Vickie B. Sullivan, *Machiavelli, Hobbes, and the Formation of a Liberal Republicanism in England* (New York: Cambridge University Press, 2004), 31. The subtext of Machiavelli's discussion of ancient Rome is that the emperor is partly to blame for Rome's collapse and for the emergence of Christianity.

19. Ibid.

20. Ibid., 32.

21. *Politics* 1279, 1280 25-81 4, 1295 1-2, 1295; see also *Ethics* 1129 31-1130.

22. *Histories* VI 4 1-6. Although Machiavelli appears to follow Polybius's understanding of the constitution of the Roman republic carefully, the former subordinates the changes in government to self-preservation. See Mansfield, *Machiavelli's New Modes and Orders*, 34-40; and, for a different account of the relationship between Polybius and Machiavelli on this subject, see Gennare Sasso, *Studi su Machiavelli* (Naples: Marano, 1967), chapters 4 and 5.

23. Compare chapter 1, *Prince*.

24. *Politics* 1280a 25-81a 4, 1295b 1-2. Aristotle classifies regimes in light of the moral character of the rulers and or the degree to which the rulers pursue the public good of the whole, see especially 1279a.

25. I. 58, 117-18.

26. Marvin Zetterbaum, "Alexis de Tocqueville," in *History of Political Philosophy*, Leo Strauss and Joseph Cropsey, eds. (Chicago: University of Chicago Press, 1963), 770.

27. Alexis de Tocqueville, *Democracy in America,* trans. Harvey C. Mansfield, Jr., and Delba Winthrop (Chicago: University of Chicago Press, 2000), liii. In this context Mansfield is discussing Tocqueville's rejection of Aristotle's notion of a mixed regime, rather than Machiavelli's endorsement of such a possibility.

28. See, for example, *Discourses on Livy,* 1.8, 26-28.

29. Tocqueville appears much more sympathetic to philosophy and the life of the mind than Machiavelli. The latter reduces the quest to seek "the city in speech"—the Platonic standard of human perfection and happiness that establishes the conception of human excellence as the life of philosophy—to a futile and "imaginary" exercise of the mind. See, for example, chapter 15 of the *Prince*. Moreover, Tocqueville critiques majority tyranny in the name of moral and intellectual virtue, for the majority's "equality applied to brains" constitutes an attack on the necessary grounds for establishing and maintaining a noble ideal for the perfection of the human soul. Similarly, the inherent Cartesianism of American intellectual habits, to which Tocqueville draws our attention, focuses the mind's attention on the acquisition of power as a means to relieving the general human condition, resulting in the broad view that intellectual virtue is not an end in itself. Once reason is reduced to a means, the notion of human excellence as the best life is undermined.

30. For an excellent treatment of this theme, see *Democracy and Its Friendly Critics: Tocqueville and Political Life Today*, ed. Peter Augustine Lawler (Lanham, MD: Lexington Books, 2004).

31. See Vickie B. Sullivan, *Machiavelli, Hobbes, and the Formation of a Liberal Republicanism in England*. (New York: Cambridge University Press, 2004). Sullivan's treatment of Machiavelli's preference for and critique of ancient Rome is excellent.

32. *Democracy*, Mansfield's "Introduction," iv.

Chapter 5

Montesquieu, Tocqueville, and the Politics of Mores

F. Flagg Taylor IV

I am quite convinced that political societies are not what their laws make them, but what the sentiments, beliefs, ideas, habits of the heart, and the spirit of men who form them, prepare them in advance to be, as well as what nature and education have made them. If this truth does not emerge, at every turn, from my book, if it does not induce the readers to reflect, in this way, unceasingly on themselves, if it does not indicate at every instant, without ever having the pretense of instructing them, what are the sentiments, the ideas, the mores that alone can lead to public prosperity and liberty, what are the vices and errors that, on the other hand, divert them irresistibly from this, I will not have attained the principal and, as it were, unique goal that I have in view.
—Tocqueville to Claude-François de Corcelle, September 17, 1853[1]

The goal of all good statesmen is to encourage liberty and prevent tyranny. The statesman must have a special sort of political knowledge. Such knowledge includes an understanding of the nature of liberty and tyranny and the particular contexts in which the former may be secured and the latter prevented. Montesquieu and Tocqueville each reveal why and how the approach of tyranny is often slow and difficult to detect. Thus there is a direct link between the problem of tyranny and the problem of political self-knowledge. This is why their thought is of such immediate and enduring importance to statesmen. I will try to show how two preeminent French political philosophers sought to supply the knowledge crucial to statesmanship, and where they ultimately diverge on the problem of liberty in the liberal age.

Montesquieu and Tocqueville share a mode of analysis that has much to offer statesmen.[2] They are united in their singular devotion to evoking the subtle and crucial interplay between laws, institutions, and mores. Montesquieu's recourse to concepts such as "principle" and "general spirit" and Tocqueville's use of "social state" each suggests an attentiveness to the interpenetration of the political and what some would deem non-political realms.

Tocqueville is faithful to Montesquieu's analysis and categories up to a point, but his departures are crucial—and it is precisely these departures that make Tocqueville's analysis of more enduring importance for the democratic statesman. Montesquieu and Tocqueville each demonstrate the power of mores relative to laws. In his famous discussion of England, Montesquieu takes the measure of the modern transformation by noting the reversal of the priority of mores over laws there. Tocqueville, though faithful in many respects to his great teacher, thinks the modern transformation is both more and less radical than Montesquieu had thought. It is more radical in that the democratic revolution's effects on mores are more far reaching and likely to endure (hence Tocqueville's recourse to a new category, social state). But this revolution is also less radical in that mores themselves will always remain at the center of politics. Thus no political order, according to Tocqueville, can achieve the reversal of which Montesquieu speaks with respect to England.

Montesquieu: Nature and Principle

The key to the distinctiveness and value of Montesquieu's understanding of political corruption is the subtlety and suppleness of his categories of analysis. In Montesquieu's famous tripartite classification scheme republics and monarchies first appear as the choice-worthy alternatives to despotisms. Each regime is analyzed in terms of its "nature," or its formal political infrastructure, and its "principle," or the passions that animate the citizens and govern their attachment to the political order. The principle reveals itself in a variety of contexts in a regime—it is as much what we today would call a social principle as narrowly political. The perpetuation of a particular regime depends more on the vibrancy of the principle than anything else. Thus the statesman must attend to a much broader range of phenomena than the arrangement of institutions.

The principle of republics is virtue (or love of the homeland), honor the principle of monarchy, and fear that of despotism. A change of regimes from republic to monarchy or monarchy to republic he characterizes as a movement of moderate government to moderate government. The transformation of either regime to despotism is what must be avoided. Despotic government is the rule of one, without law, through fear. The atmosphere in such regimes is dismal. Tranquility is the end of the regime, but it is not a calm, self-assured peace, but a tense, apprehensive quiet. Montesquieu likens it to "the silence of the towns that the enemy is ready to occupy."[3] Passion and appetite run wild seemingly without direction or thought. There is no improvement. Nothing is cultivated or nurtured with thought for future generations.

Yet Montesquieu complicates this picture of the two moderate regimes standing opposed to immoderate despotism. Moderation is related to power being opposed by power—everyone who has power is led to abuse it. Moderation, Montesquieu suggests, is difficult to achieve in any context. A closer look at the operation of the principle in republics and monarchies is revealing.

The virtue characteristic of republics requires self-renunciation—a constraint of all other passions. All passions must somehow be repressed or channeled to this love of homeland. Virtue so understood must be inculcated with great care and constant attention. It is this passionate, unceasing devotion that binds people and institutions together. Moderation is difficult to achieve in a republic, for vibrancy of the principle depends upon constant surveillance of mores. And devotion will be heightened in a tense atmosphere where external threats loom.

In monarchy, the principle operates quite differently. It is the law (not honor) that replaces virtue. The law seeks to manage the vast corporate differentiation characteristic of monarchies. Institutions such as the nobility and the clergy are intermediate powers that may oppose or legitimize the will of the monarch. This fragmentation of authority transforms the nature and the extent of the political here. Whereas in a republic private crimes may be of public concern because mores are the test of the proper devotion to the public good, in monarchies the general good is an arrangement of laws and dependent upon relations between intermediate powers. So public crimes may in fact remain private to the extent they do not impact this overall relation.

Honor is the spring joined to the force of the law in monarchies. Honor is the "prejudice of each person and each condition" (*EL* III.6). It is, perhaps first and foremost, a principle of *social* differentiation. Yet because of the *nature* of monarchy, the fact that ranks and a hereditary nobility are essential components, honor is highly suited to it. Montesquieu argues that "honor has, in and of itself, a place in this government" (*EL* III.7). Its demand for distinction can fit quite well with the differentiated character of monarchy. Honor's fitness for monarchy resides in its potential to support its intermediary bodies, the keys to the mediation of power and hence to the overall moderation of the regime. These bodies, it has been argued, in turn support honor.[4] They provide outlets for the ambitious to exercise their talents—for although individual ambition can be harmful to republics, it can have salutary effects in monarchies. As Sharon Krause puts it, "Without honor the differentiated structure of monarchy would dissolve into the unopposed will of the sovereign."[5]

There is another important contrast between republics and monarchy with respect to education. Political virtue requires the subjection of the passions and their redirection toward the public good. Montesquieu calls this "a renunciation of oneself, which is always a very painful thing." By contrast, honor "is favored by the passions and favors them in turn" (*EL* IV.5). Honor, rather than being self-forgetting, requires constant self-awareness and self-assertion. It seeks not union with one's fellow citizens, but distinction from them.

Honor, though perhaps most often requiring obedience, appears more clearly through disobedience and refusal. Honor's tendency to infuse intermediate institutions with this ethic exerts a salutary influence in monarchy, since it encourages moderation by limiting power. It serves the monarchy by reconciling the authority and dignity of the nobility with the center of political and civil authority, the prince. Yet the precise terms of this reconciliation are left unclear. Michael Mosher puts it well, "Honor tempers sovereignty but not in any juridically comprehensible way."[6] The political inscription of honor is essential but ambiguous. Montesquieu heightens the problem with his articulation of one of honor's supreme rules. It seems that honor gains vibrancy or power by its contrast with the law. This is not to say that it automatically enjoins what the law does not, or prohibits what the law does not, only that its dictates gain force to the extent that these are at variance with the law. Honor, the principle of monarchy, the force which makes the government act, is also, so to speak, a social power. It cannot be simply identified with or reduced to the law, and even gains force when it departs from the law.[7] The singularity of monarchy lies in the disjunction between the circumscription of the public sphere (and fragmentary character of the political) and the broad scope of honor. In a sense, the vitality of monarchy depends on how this disjunction is negotiated. To use Diana Schaub's arresting image, monarchy's "political garment" does not always seem to fit its "social lining."[8]

The corruption of governments for Montesquieu begins with their principle. In republics, virtue is weakened most often by the spirit of extreme inequality. One no longer submits to being commanded by equals, but one objects to the very idea of being commanded at all. In monarchies, honor is undermined by the weakening and eventual obsolescence of intermediate powers. The monarch usurps powers which find their natural home elsewhere and reduces everything to his own person. Then the corrupt spirit of court appears where honor is associated with nothing other than gaining the favor of the prince.

Tocqueville and Social State: The Destruction of Aristocracy

Tocqueville's task would include encouraging people to think about politics partially in the terms Montesquieu had set. As Jean-Claude Lamberti puts it, both Montesquieu and Tocqueville "believed that between forms of society and forms of government there is an intelligible relation whose basis lies in the nature of reality, whereas neither accepted the view that social organization by itself can wholly determine the mode of government."[9] Both Frenchmen sought to reveal the interpenetration of the social and political realms—laws, mores, manners, and religion.[10]

Tocqueville goes even further than his predecessor in his respect for mores. He preserves and extends the dynamism implicit in Montesquieu's account of the relation between a regime's nature and principle. Indeed, his use of the concept "social state" points to his belief that one must always consider laws and mores together and how a change in one realm would affect the other. As Montesquieu emphasizes, the regime's principle holds the key to its preservation—as long as it manifests itself coherently and powerfully across the social body, corruption could be avoided and structural change tolerated. So with social state, Tocqueville explores how ideas, sentiments, and mores could lead a people toward freedom or servitude. Tocqueville's use of social state takes him beyond Montesquieu in this crucial respect: it allows him to lengthen his view, to see changes in mores and habits that persisted for centuries, and thus to make his case for a much more profound transformation of the political and social world than Montesquieu had seen.

With his usage of social state, Tocqueville subsumes under the category aristocracy what Montesquieu had rigorously distinguished—republics and monarchies. Why would Tocqueville put together what he no doubt knew to be such vastly different political orders? He does this for the sake of understanding the unprecedented nature of modern democracy. He wants his readers to look upon ancient republics and monarchies not as neutral arbiters between regimes, but as occupants of the emergent democratic social state. Such an occupant must feel the core claim of this democracy by witnessing the common denial of that claim by both the ancient republic and the feudal monarchy. That claim, the dogma of popular sovereignty—the assertion that every human being is good enough to govern himself in that which exclusively concerns himself, extending to all human relations—is denied in both regimes where command and obedience are legitimate and crucial.[11] As Pierre Manent points out, this dogma of the sovereignty of the people bears a striking resemblance to what Montesquieu calls the "spirit of extreme equality"—a spirit responsible for the corruption of the principle of republican government.[12] So according to Tocqueville the beginning of political wisdom is to recognize that what was taking place was not a change from one form of government to another, but a thorough-going, longstanding transformation that was changing the face of "almost all human institutions."[13]

Tocqueville knows well the moderate monarchy that Montesquieu evokes in the early pages of *The Spirit of the Laws*. The kings of feudal monarchy had "an almost boundless power" by right, but they seldom used it (*DA* I.ii.9). They were bounded by a host of intermediate powers—from nobility to clergy, from parlements to provincial privilege and usage. Yet something as powerful yet not as well known held kings in check according to Tocqueville: opinions and mores. Tocqueville writes, "Religion, love of subjects, the goodness of the prince, honor, the spirit of family, provincial prejudices, custom, and public opinion bounded the power of kings and confined their authority within an invisible circle. The constitutions of peoples then were despotic and their mores free" (*DA* I.ii.9). Montesquieu could see in his own time that aristocratic honor was coming under assault. The decline of these intermediate powers deprived honor of a stage and the growth of commerce and its effect on the nobility posed new challenges for an old ethic. Yet Montesquieu could still assert in his chapter on the possible corruption of monarchy, "Most European peoples are still governed by mores" (*EL* VIII.8). Tocqueville, writing eight decades later, would wonder, what mores? "Of the barriers that formerly stopped tyranny," he writes, "what remains to us today" (*DA* I.ii.9)? Religion had lost its authority, kings their prestige. The provincial privileges and self-consciousness had been undermined by uniformity in law and control by the central administration. Individual grandeur and self-assertion disappeared, replaced by common obscurity and weakness.

This transformation in opinions and mores was not the result of the self-conscious political will of the French revolutionaries of the 1780s and 1790s, but the product of an incessant and slow democratic revolution going back ten centuries. The post-revolutionary settlement actually preserved the dominant institutions and opinions that had stifled liberty in the era of absolute monarchy that preceded the revolution. One of the purposes of *The Old Regime and the Revolution* then is to reveal the transformation of the monarchy from its feudal to its absolute incarnation, the underlying cause being the maturation of the democratic social state.

This maturation could issue in either freedom or servitude. A democracy consistent with freedom would require attention to laws and mores, and the adaptation of one to the other. In the case of France, it would require laws and institutions that would favor the mores necessary to sustain freedom. As Tocqueville writes to his friend Eugène Stoffels, "I wish that the government would itself prepare mores and practices so that people would do without it in many cases in which its intervention is still necessary or invoked without necessity. . . . I conceive clearly the idea of a government that is not at all revolutionary or agitated beyond measure, and one which I believe possible to give our country. But on the other hand, I understand as well as anyone that such a government . . . in order to become established, requires mores, habits, laws that do not yet exist, and which can only be introduced slowly and with great precautions."[14]

Tocqueville's investigation then consists in part of an account of two processes: first, how laws and mores grew increasingly ill adapted to one another; and second, how a new conception of law and politics largely dispensed with attention to mores and the consequences of this. But one of Tocqueville's first objectives in the *Old Regime* is to resurrect an alternative to the present state of affairs. He evokes aristocracy's political incarnation in the feudal monarchy of the distant past. He is struck by the extension of a spirit and a similarity in laws and institutions all over Europe. "I think one may suggest that in the fourteenth century the social, political, administrative, judicial, economic, and literary institutions of Europe resembled each other perhaps even more than they do today, when civilization seems to have taken care to open all roads and break down all barriers."[15] As Delba Winthrop notes, Tocqueville seems intent upon presenting feudalism as a whole, that is, as a coherent and well-formed alternative to the secular, rational society of the revolutionaries.[16] He therefore questions their claims to theoretical sophistication and advancement. For what does it say if medieval practice beats their theory, at least on the ground of being a whole? As Tocqueville argues, a single spirit animated the feudal institutions—laws and mores formed a coherent whole—echoing Montesquieu's claim that honor seems highly suited to the differentiated structure of the French monarchy.

That spirit did not long remain untouched. The forms remained for a long time, but they were hollowed about by a new spirit, the spirit of equality, and new institutions introduced alongside the old. Tocqueville tells the story of the ancient causes of the revolution in book two of the *Old Regime*.

Tocqueville's analysis hinges on two long-standing causes transforming France, centralization and the transformation of the social body. The administrative centralization includes the gradual rise of new institutions with extensive powers that insinuate themselves into nearly every corner of provincial and local life. Tocqueville speaks of offices like the Royal Council, the Controller-General, and his agents in the provinces, the intendants. The central government penetrated many areas such as finance, commerce, public works, and public order. As the central government assumed more and more of these functions, it gradually displaced the local institutions that had once taken charge in these areas. The central government made its presence felt more and more in the lives of local populations—even forcing artisans to adopt preferred methods for their craft and ordering crops removed that had not been planted in sufficiently rich soil. The government was being transformed from a "sovereign" to a "guardian" (*OR* II.2).

Crucial to Tocqueville's argument here is that the nobles and local notables were always left with the mere shadow of self-government. Municipal assemblies and other local institutions were left in place, but hollowed out, left to rot as their functions were gradually usurped by central authorities. This mode of displacement proved effective in that the forms of freedom were preserved all the while freedom itself was disappearing.

While this bought the central authorities time and made this gradual usurpation more effectual, it also prepared the revolutionary spirit. Tocqueville argues that by the time of the Revolution France was the country where feudalism was weakest yet most hated. This hatred was a direct result of leaving the forms in place. It was apparent to anyone with eyes to see that these feudal institutions were contemptible. They served no real function any longer. The local nobility retained privileges, purchased from the central government, yet had no longer any ties of responsibility to their local communities.

The central government merely followed the instinct of all governments in extending its sphere of activity. The problem of the French bureaucracy, for Tocqueville, was not inactivity, but a frenzy of rules and regulations—always applied inconsistently, with seemingly limitless discretion. The law never seemed to guarantee the equal treatment one would expect. All of this resulted in contempt for the law as such.

As the central authorities extended their sphere and activity, they grew increasingly contemptuous of those individuals outside of the government that insisted on playing some role or having some voice in public affairs. The government was wise enough to see that some consolation must be offered. Tocqueville notes, "To console them for their servitude, the government permitted discussion of all kinds of general and abstract theories on questions of religion, philosophy, morals, even politics. It freely allowed attacks on the fundamental principles on which society was then based, and even allowed disputes about God himself, provided that its least agents were not criticized" (*OR* II.6).

The appearance of freedom then lingered under the old regime in two ways. First, the old forms remained—weak, a shadow of their former selves, to be sure, but there nonetheless. Second, an atmosphere of intense debate about politics and related matters emerged that would engage and help to create a new species: the intellectual. A new manner of thinking about politics emerged— highly abstract, speculative, and inclined toward universalist solutions.[17] In Tocqueville's mind, the most telling fact about the power of the new central government was that amidst all of the discussion, and with all of the dissatisfaction with the current state of affairs, all of the reformers recommended using this central authority as their agent of change. Nobody thought to question its existence or the range of objects under its purview. Only the power of the state was sufficient to accomplish whatever ends the reformers had in mind. As Tocqueville writes, "These ideas did not stay in books; they penetrated all minds, were mingled with mores, infused habits, and spread everywhere, even into everyday life. . . . No one seemed to suspect that behind the protector might hide the master" (*OR* II.6).

Now we turn to the striking impact this central authority had on the social body. For Tocqueville, on the eve of the Revolution, the French people present a strange spectacle. On the one hand he sees a people (speaking here about the upper and middle classes, not the peasants) who look increasingly similar. The bourgeois were rising, the nobles falling. Each were increasingly urbanized and subject to similar educations—ideas, habits, and mores were converging. And both were equal with respect to the central power, subjects, and nothing else. Yet Tocqueville also sees a people increasingly isolated—penned into microsocieties where each member looked outward with a mixture of contempt, anxiety, and fear. He refers to this state as a kind of "collective individualism" (*OR* II.9). How did this strange state of affairs come to pass?

During the old regime, as the Revolution approached, the nobility became less and less of an aristocracy and more and more of a caste. It was defined less as a ruling class and more by its particular privileges. With the disintegration of the manorial government of the lord, the bourgeois and noble had hardly any contact. The central authority had little use for the Estates-General and other such occasions for the classes to meet, and thus they became increasingly isolated. Yet the principle of isolation became narrower and narrower as privileges proliferated. The government sold titles of nobility to make money. Tax exemptions grew and became another means of differentiation. The gap between noble and bourgeois was closing, and the gap was relatively easy to cross, but the barrier that remained was fixed and visible. Thus, "The noble liked to console himself for the loss of his real power by the abuse of his conspicuous privileges"

(*OR* II.9). Vanity caused this caste to look outward with contempt and cling to the only things that constituted its difference—petty privileges.

For their part, the bourgeoisie found its own security in public employment and had its own benefits and exemptions. They had contempt for what they left behind and became objects of envy on the part of the masses and peasants. Differentiation through petty privilege was thus combined with political estrangement—the classes never met in the political fora that dominated feudal monarchy. So a cauldron of vanity and resentment was incessantly provoked by the central power. Everyone was increasingly subject to this power and increasingly alike in looking up to it. Differences were erased through urbanization and uniformity in law. Yet just as differences were erased, they were then reconstituted through the granting of privileges and exemptions. The needs of the state stoked the vanity of its subjects. Equality and inequalities were ceaselessly created, with no prospect for common deliberation.

What surfaced then as the avenue of reform was the abolition of privilege through the continued construction and intervention of an "immense social power" which would be the "product and the representative of everyone, and must make the rights of each bend before the will of all."[18] The physiocrats made democratic despotism the instrument and end of their reforms. This idea of government—an equally enlightened, identical people subject to one sovereign that they themselves had authorized to act in their name—would resurface again after the Revolution. Tocqueville thought these reformers were simply blind to the crucial interplay between mores and laws and the limits of what one could accomplish through laws. Montesquieu had explored precisely this topic in book nineteen of *The Spirit of the Laws*.

Montesquieu: The Problem of Tyranny and the General Spirit

Montesquieu has shown how crucial the principle is to the overall health of a regime. In the discussion of the general spirit in book nineteen Montesquieu abandons principle as a category. It appears that general spirit allows him to explore more fully why and how regimes become susceptible to corruption and what a statesman can to do prevent it. He pays particularly close attention to the relation between laws and mores, and how one must understand that relation across different regime types.

In this account the problem of tyranny is broader and deeper than the mere avoidance of despotic government. He opens a chapter entitled "On Tyranny" with this: "There are two sorts of tyranny: a real one, which consists in the violence of the government, and one of opinion, which is felt when those who govern establish things that run counter to a nation's way of thinking" (*EL* XIX.3). In the preceding chapter Montesquieu uses a number of examples to show how some political institutions and habits—even those associated with

free governments—will appear contemptible or ridiculous to those unaccus-
tomed to them. Tyranny of opinion, then, can be an obstacle to the reform of real
tyranny. That is, the continued experience of real tyranny will allow tyranny of
opinion to become so pervasive as to make free institutions dramatically unap-
pealing. Montesquieu thus raises the difficult problem of political reform. How
can a statesman introduce salutary political reform in the midst of a tyranny of
opinion that seems to blind a people to the very need for reform?

The chapter "On tyranny" allows Montesquieu to refine this analysis further. Here he draws a contrast between the early Romans who actually sought
liberty and the later Romans who merely claimed to do the same. The former
sought to avoid rule under a king because they feared his power. They feared
"real" tyranny. The latter were concerned with not suffering the "manners" of a
king. He explains: "For, although Ceasar, the triumvirs, and Augustus were real
kings, they had preserved the appearance of equality and in their private lives
they seemed opposed to the kingly pomp of that time; and when the Romans did
not want a king, this meant that they wanted to keep their own manners and not
take on those of African or Eastern peoples" (*EL* XIX.3). Not only can tyranny
of opinion be an obstacle to the reform of real tyranny, but the very absence of
tyranny of opinion can mask the approach of real tyranny. A people can even
feel the effects of tyranny of opinion more profoundly than the effects of real
tyranny. Montesquieu explains that Roman discontent under Augustus was great
due to the harshness of certain laws, but this discontent ceased when an actor,
Pylades, returned to Rome. "Such a people felt tyranny more vividly when a
buffoon was driven out than when all their laws were taken from them" (*EL*
XIX.3).

In the wake of these early chapters in book nineteen, Montesquieu introduces his concept of the "general spirit" of a people. This spirit is a compound of
particular causes which includes laws, maxims, mores, manners, religion, and
climate. The general spirit most reveals itself in mores and manners, even if
these are largely determined by another factor such as climate. The wise statesman must therefore attend most carefully to how these different elements of the
general spirit relate to one another. Stability and wise reform depend on such
understanding.

In the first place, Montesquieu counsels prudence and restraint. In a discussion of the French monarchy, he argues that one should not attempt to remedy
all vices. Some of these perceived defects might be closely aligned with the virtues of a people. Reform in one area might have the unintended effect of a fundamental alteration of the general spirit, which would overturn virtues as well as
vices. France's general spirit includes traits such as imprudence, indiscretion,
generosity, and a sociable humor—all of which are related to the liberation of
female vanity and commerce. One could try to correct the mores related to the
society of women and limit the luxury that forms taste, but one would lose the
virtues as well as the vices. So the preservation of the general spirit means accepting some of the good with the bad, or seeing the good effects of the bad.

Montesquieu appears to continue his counsel of restraint as the discussion proceeds, now with respect to despotisms. Here overturning mores and manners would have revolutionary effects. In despotic government, laws are never fixed, so mores and manners are the primary source of stability. But here Montesquieu departs quite starkly from his previous portrait of despotism. Tranquility is still the goal, but fear and appetite no longer dominate. And in a striking association, the "legislators" of China are spoken of in the same breath as Lycurgus, Moses, and the first Romans. The Chinese legislators "wanted men to have much respect for each other; they wanted each one to feel at every instant that he owed much to the others; they wanted every citizen to depend, in some respect, on another citizen. Therefore, they extended the rules of civility to a great many people" (*EL* XIX.16).

The Chinese legislators, like Lycurgus and the Spartans, accomplish this through "singular institutions"—that is, they intentionally confuse laws, mores, and manners. In China, the means for unity and respect is an elaborate system of rites that must be performed to show respect for fathers, elders, teachers, and the emperor. This is what Montesquieu calls "family government." "It is quite indifferent in itself, whether a daughter-in-law gets up every morning to perform such and such duties for a mother-in-law; but if one notes that these external practices constantly call one back to a feeling, which it is necessary to impress on all hearts, and which comes from all hearts to form the spirit that governs the empire, one will see that it is necessary for a certain particular action to be performed" (*EL* XIX.19). In China, this system confirmed the constant, overwhelming presence of hierarchy and the consequent duty to affirm it. The total subjection of the population ensured tranquility from household to emperor.

Montesquieu elsewhere addresses the "singular" Spartan institutions: "Lycurgus, mixing larceny with the spirit of justice, the harshest slavery with extreme liberty, the most heinous feelings with the greatest moderation, gave stability to his town. He seemed to remove all its resources, arts, commerce, silver, walls: one had ambition there without the expectation of bettering oneself; one had natural feelings but was neither child, husband or father" (*EL* IV.6). Thus every relation is reformed, even suppressed, in favor of love of homeland. Virtues are confused to favor the one virtue that matters—love of homeland.

Though the preservation of the general spirit is the goal in the cases of France on the one hand, and China and Sparta on the other, the stark contrast should now be apparent. Monarchy is the regime where laws and mores often disagree. The fragmentation of the political leads to moderation, and France's general spirit, though complex and not without faults, leads to numerous goods. The legislators of France should be aware of these benefits and not make the mistake of confusing moral vices with political vices. The complexity of human behavior and our participation in various social realms reveals that the legislator must not attempt to design a code which assimilates the demands of one realm to another. Hence, in a chapter called "How Laws Should Be Relative to the Mores and Manners," he explains that these things are "naturally separate," yet "closely related" (*EL* XIX.21). In China and Sparta, the total domination of a single cause, manners in the former case and mores in the latter, demands the deliberate confusion of things that are naturally separate. Sparta's "singular institutions" lead to a hyper-political order—total dedication to the public good. Montesquieu argues this total domination of the political disfigures other relations—thus Spartans mix larceny and justice, and extreme slavery and liberty. China is Sparta's mirror image. Here, constant participation in rites and ceremony means rule by manners. Paternal authority is omnipresent and is reinforced at all levels of society. If Sparta represents total politicization, China sanctions the disappearance of the political.

Montesquieu appears to warn his readers against revolutionary change. Overturning mores and manners in a despotic state, he has explained, would mean overturning everything. Yet this presents an opportunity. He argues that the natural way of changing the mores and manners of a nation is by introducing new mores and manners, or even better, inducing the people to change them themselves. For while laws are the particular institutions of a legislator, mores and manners are the general institutions of the nation. The examples Montesquieu provides here all have to do with the liberation of female vanity and commerce. Escaping despotic government requires encouraging communication between men and women—unleashing the desire to please and be pleased.

So just what are Montesquieu's recommendations to statesmen with respect to laws, mores, and the problem of corruption? First, changing or attempting to correct the general spirit is tricky business. Vices are bound up with virtues—not all moral vices are political vices. The prudent statesman must be alive to the interconnectedness of laws, mores, manners. Second, some statesmen achieve stability and avoid corruption by deliberately confusing laws, mores, and manners. Here we get the striking association of republican Sparta and despotic China. Third, insofar as laws are the particular institutions of the legislator and mores and manners are the general institutions of the nation, the best way to change the latter is through new mores and manners. Montesquieu reveals how undermining stifling despotic manners can occur through the liberation of female vanity and an end to enclosure. Fourth, this deliberate confusion of laws, mores, and manners through singular institutions leads to deeply unnatural consequences. So the prudent statesman must somehow acknowledge the separate realms but appreciate the relations between them. Montesquieu introduces Solon as the antidote to Lycurgus. Rather than designing the best laws in themselves, Solon gave the Athenians "the best laws they could endure" (*EL* XIX.21).

Yet this final solution to the problem of the relation between laws and mores is more apparent than real, and in the concluding chapters of book nineteen, Montesquieu reveals why this is so. For if laws are relative to mores to such a degree, then to what extent do they shape human behavior, or even provide a corrective function? Elsewhere he casts doubt on the ultimate utility of law and punishment with respect to mores. "Punishments will cast out of society a citizen who, having lost his mores, violates the laws, but if everyone loses his mores, will punishments reestablish them? Punishments will indeed check many consequences of the general evil, but they will not correct this evil" (*EL* XIX.17).[19] A mere two chapters after the chapter explaining that laws are *rela-*

tive to mores, he then explains "How the Laws *Follow* Mores" (emphasis added). This topic is treated in a series of meditations on the Romans, extending to the penultimate chapter of the book.

Together these chapters provide a sober lesson about the fundamental weakness of law in relation to mores. In his first example, mores are so offended by the crime of embezzlement, Roman opinion makes a minor punishment by law seem great. It is opinion that gives the law its force. Next, when mores become more corrupt, the law must consider things that it never had to before. The law began to punish crimes that mores themselves used to prevent. And finally, mores can become so corrupt that the law simply gives up. The law no longer recognizes corruption as corruption—it tolerates what mores have come to tolerate.

This series of chapters near the end of the book thus bring us back to the problem introduced at the beginning. The problem of two tyrannies was presented in the context of the corruption of Rome—now the book's conclusion treats the same topic from a different angle. Montesquieu argued in chapter three that the manipulation of opinion is essential to the introduction of real tyranny. We tend to feel tyranny more acutely when our mores are offended than when our laws are changed. We are susceptible to tyranny because mores are most often offended by a great spectacle. If this can be avoided, Montesquieu suggests we are easy prey. This analysis is supplemented by these concluding chapters. If the lack of offense to mores can distract us from changes in the law, it is also true that law seems powerless to prevent the degeneration of mores. Mores give the laws their force. Laws can punish abuses but not correct these same abuses; and eventually, the law will simply accommodate itself to the abuse by no longer recognizing it. Montesquieu's analysis of laws and mores in book nineteen has thus far not revealed a solution to the problem of the two tyrannies—it has shown rather the intractable nature of that problem.

Montesquieu: The English Solution

Montesquieu's analysis in this crucial book exhibits a profound pessimism regarding the possibility of fending off corruption in republics and monarchies. This pessimism is rooted in his understanding of the overall strength of mores relative to laws. Yet in the final chapter of book nineteen, Montesquieu turns to England to explore their solution to this problem. England is the place where mores follow laws. Space prevents a detailed consideration of this famous chapter. Three characteristics stand out and illustrate just how the English have achieved this novel and striking reversal of the priority of mores over laws.

First, the English have replaced the intermediate powers characteristic of feudal monarchy with an altogether different system. He writes, "Since in this state there would be two visible powers, legislative power and executive power, and as each citizen would have his own will and would value his independence according to his taste, most people would have more affection for one of these powers than for the other, as the multitude is ordinarily not fair or sensible enough to have equal affection for both of them" (*EL* XIX.27). We have then, on the one hand, the English constitution which separates powers, and on the other, the independence of the individual citizens.

In feudal monarchy intermediate powers place individuals in webs of dependence. Different bodies exert their will against and in conjunction with one another. Individual attachment to these bodies is not a matter of choice. Individual affections develop over time in the context of this web of relations. Independence here is found not at the level of individual wills, but in the mediation of authority—various relations of command and obedience demand acknowledgement from above and below.

Montesquieu argues that the English aim directly at liberty through their constitution—they separate powers into different institutions. Power is not checked by corporate bodies external to the government, but is limited rather through its internal division—a division related to a new understanding of the various functions of political power. The absence of intermediate powers means that the two "visible" powers are raised in prominence. Their very visibility is the result of the decline and abolition of intermediate powers. This abolition has another effect. It frees individuals from the webs of command and obedience that are the result of the presence of intermediate powers. In England citizens feel their own will—independence is palpable. In England, the feeling of independence does not preclude the existence of ranks. Montesquieu argues that in England, "The high positions that are a part of the fundamental constitution would be more fixed than elsewhere, but, on the other hand, the important men in this country of liberty would be closer to the people; therefore, ranks would be more separate and persons more confused" (*EL* XIX.27). Certain offices then would serve to reinforce the idea of ranks, yet the overall atmosphere would tend to discourage the automatic association of rank and power. People notice that the "important men" are not unlike themselves—the more this is so, the more individual citizens would sense their own wills.

Montesquieu's second crucial claim here is that the English have freed the passions. He does not identify a "principle" for England. In the context of this discussion about citizens' affection for one of the powers, he writes, "As all the passions are free there, hatred, envy, jealousy, and the ardor for enriching and distinguishing oneself would appear to their full extent, and if this were otherwise, the state would be like a man who, laid low by disease, has no passions because he has no strength" (*EL* XIX.27). The English regime gives scope to asocial passions like hatred and envy. The drive to enrich and distinguish themselves moves citizens to seek attachment to one of the two powers. In England, one does not see a principle, or a culmination of an authoritative shaping of the passions; rather, the constitution allows for a freeing of the passions. This is the manner in which mores follow laws.

Third, though there is this novel freeing of the passions, English mores do find a kind of stability. English mores are shaped and held in check by the spirit of party which forms around each of the two powers. Independent citizens would seek to attach themselves to one of the powers in order to secure their interests. However, valuing their independence, these individuals would also be wary of the potential dominance of one of these powers. Montesquieu argues that this ambivalence toward power would lead to a kind of equilibrium between the two powers. The new spirit of party leads partisans of one power to come to the aid of the other if it seems to be getting too weak. The unleashing of the passions and the independence of each citizen would, in effect, overcome the normal laws of affection characteristic of human beings. By following their "own caprices and fantasies," Englishmen would frequently change parties. He would have to leave his friends and join the company of his enemies, and thus to "forget both the laws of friendship and those of hatred" (*EL* XIX.27).

This last suggestion of Montesquieu's makes clear the radical nature of this new sort of attachment. The temporary nature of partisan loyalty is again rooted in individual "caprices and fantasies." If these preferences change, then partisan attachments are likely to as well. The English will also tend to wonder whether the attachments they have chosen are the proper vehicles to secure their interests. He writes, "One is afraid of seeing the escape of a good that one feels, that one scarcely knows, and that can be hidden from us; and fear always enlarges objects. The people would be uneasy about their situation and would believe themselves in danger even at the safest moments" (*EL* XIX.27). Thus transient desires and transient attachments result in an anxious people. The solid, stable affections of friendship have been displaced enough to render them ineffectual in countering this uneasiness. The spirit of party is quite different from how a common life of citizenship has been understood. The temporary attachments and anxious atmosphere cause the English to turn inward. "Each would regard himself as the monarch; the men in this nation would be confederates more than fellow citizens" (*EL* XIX.27). This weakened connection amongst individuals and the related uneasiness are not without their salutary effects. For if the English are uncertain about the goods they seek and maintaining those they have, they are also unsettled about what they fear. This counters the tendency toward withdrawal and isolation, for "if the terrors impressed on a people had no certain object, they would produce only empty clamors and insults and would even have the effect of stretching all the springs of the government and making all the citizens attentive" (*EL* XIX.27). If the English manage to steer clear of the timid, isolating, depoliticized atmosphere of despotism, they also avoid the strident, collective, hyper-political scene of republics. Here separated powers provide an obstacle, but perhaps more crucial is the device of representation. The agitations of the populace are moderated by the legislative body in England. The spirit of party draws the English people into collective life, but only in a limited way.

In Montesquieu's account, the principle of each regime is the seat of corruption. Particularly in republics, legislators design "singular institutions" that provide the stability in mores and manners. Elaborate means are required to maintain the self-renunciation evident in republics and in despotic government. In monarchy there seems to be more of a natural fit between honor and the diffe-

rentiated political structure. Honor can encourage the sort of self assertion that
allows power to oppose power. But in all of these cases, mores—constantly
threatened by corruption—must be animated by the principle. Only the English
seem to have discovered a radical solution to this problem.

Tocqueville: What is America?

As is well known, each of Montesquieu's two famous discussions of England
fall outside the regime-centered analysis of the first eight books of *The Spirit of
the Laws*. Montesquieu thus highlights by form what is also supported by the
content of his discussion: England presents something entirely new.[20] Pierre
Manent has given a particularly radical interpretation of Montesquieu's intent
with respect to his presentation of England and what it ultimately signifies. On
the one side are the regimes of law, including republics and monarchies; on the
other is England, the regime of liberty. Manent writes, "The classification of
political regimes according to their greater or lesser conformity to nature gives
way to the succession of the two regimes of law and liberty. To call these two
regimes political is anachronistic; it is much more appropriate to call them historical. History, and no longer Nature, is the umbrella under which the two regimes are joined in their succession and their incompatibility."[21]

Manent's claim with respect to Montesquieu provides a nice bridge to my
discussion of Tocqueville's analysis of this problem of the liberty, law, and
mores. Tocqueville's portrait of the decline of one social state, aristocracy, and
the ascendancy of another, democracy, would seem to be consistent with the
idea of the successive regimes of law and liberty. Tocqueville describes democracy as a providential fact whose coming is inevitable while aristocracy's disappearance is assured. Yet Tocqueville compares the incompatible and seemingly
incomparable incessantly with a great deal of care. Why?

First, Tocqueville understands democracy as a social state to be consistent
with two political possibilities, one free and one despotic. He dedicates himself
to sketching a new political science to be used by statesmen so they might better
understand what mores and laws would favor freedom. Second, he argues that
liberty is not peculiar to one social state (and was thus possible in an aristocracy)
and that tyranny is possible and probable in the democratic age. In his own day,
people were losing the very taste for liberty and they did not see the evil to
which they were tending. They failed to see the logic of their own political history and therefore did not understand the forces and decisions that made them
what they were. Tocqueville thus argues that what Montesquieu describes in his
chapter "On Tyranny" was a particularly acute problem in his own day and
would be for the foreseeable future. As he argues in the preface to *The Old Regime and the Revolution*, despotism enables base passions and vices to flourish
because it makes them nearly invisible. Conversely, liberty can "create the light
which allows one to see and judge the vices and virtues of men" (*OR* Preface).

But Tocqueville worries that the taste for liberty was nearly gone and the possible approach of a cunning, seemingly benign tyranny was hardly noticed. Tocqueville thus dedicates himself to supplying the political self-knowledge necessary for the self-understanding of the French people and to inculcating the proper appreciation of and taste for liberty.

But what would the political conditions where liberty might be secured and corruption avoided look like? How could a free people fend off the degeneration of mores? As an astute reader of Montesquieu, Tocqueville no doubt meditated on the problem presented in book nineteen and the striking presentation of England. A quotation from Tocqueville's preparatory notes to volume two of *Democracy in America*, brings us to the heart of his relationship to Montesquieu on the question of statesmanship and mores.

The Americans are not a virtuous people and yet they are free. This does not absolutely disprove that virtue, as Montesquieu thought, is essential to the existence of republics. It is not necessary to take Montesquieu's idea in a narrow sense. What this great man meant is that republics can survive only by the action of the society on itself. What he understood by virtue is the moral power that each individual exercises over himself and that prevents him from violating the rights of others. When this triumph of man over temptation is the result of the weakness of the temptation or of a calculation of personal interest, it does not constitute virtue in the eyes of the moralist; but it is included in the idea of Montesquieu who spoke much more of the result than of its cause. In America it is not virtue which is great, it is temptation which is small, which amounts to the same thing. It is not disinterestedness which is great, it is interest which is well-understood (*bien entendu*), which again almost amounts to the same thing. So Montesquieu was right even though he spoke of classical virtue, and what he said about the Greeks and Romans still applies to the Americans.[22]

What is interesting here is that one might expect Montesquieu's England to be the closest analogue, in Tocqueville's mind, for America. There are of course the constitutional similarities—a system of separated powers, with power checking power to prevent the dangerous accumulation in the hands of one branch. Like the English, Americans are not a virtuous people, yet free. Again like the English, their mores are less pure than those characteristic of the republics of antiquity.

Yet whereas Montesquieu nowhere points to a principle for the English regime and argues that the English nonetheless perpetuate their regime through a novel reversal of the priority of mores over laws, Tocqueville claims here that there is in fact something like a Montesquieuian principle at work in America, and that mores in America retain their priority over laws. Thus from the point of view of the statesman, who must attend to the perpetuation of America, America is more like an ancient republic than it is like England. Mores may in fact be less pure, but these mores do in fact allow an American to exercise a moral power over himself. Influences like love of material well-being, self-interest well understood, religion, a distaste for abstract ideas (to name a few) all exert a power over American mores that make Americans inclined toward certain actions and not others. Their mores, more than any other cause, is what holds the social body together and enables it to act politically. As Tocqueville notes near the end of volume one, "The importance of mores is a common truth to which study and experience constantly lead back. It seems to me that I have it placed in my mind as a central point; I perceive it at the end of all of my ideas. . . . If, in course of this work, I have not succeeded in making the reader feel the importance that I attribute to the practical experience of the Americans, to their habits, to their opinions—in a word, to their mores—in the maintenance of their laws, I have missed the principal goal that I proposed in writing it" (I.ii.9).[23]

Tocqueville's understanding of how the principle operates in America is crucial too. He says republics survive "only by the action of society on itself." This language shows up in two other places in *Democracy*—most important for present purposes is its occurrence in volume one, part one, chapter 4, "On the principle of the sovereignty of the people in America."[24] There he writes, "There are countries where a power in a way external to the social body acts on it and forces it to march on a certain track. There are others where force is divided, placed at once in society and outside it. Nothing like this is seen in the United States; *there society acts by itself and on itself. Power exists only within its bosom*; almost no one is encountered who dares to conceive and above all to express the idea of seeking it elsewhere" (I.i.4, emphasis added). Tocqueville here provides a typology of regimes.[25] The first type, where power is external to the social body, would include despotism and absolute monarchy. The second type, characterized by a mixture of internal and external power, would include what Montesquieu calls moderate monarchy and Tocqueville calls aristocracy. Republics fall into the last category.

Tocqueville's divisions here reflect Montesquieu's typology, but not for the explicit reasons Montesquieu provides. For Tocqueville as for Montesquieu, republican government requires that the principle fully animate the political and social relations. Mores must be infused with the principle so individuals will be disposed to love the whole and identify their interests with that whole. In despotic government power is imposed upon the populace. It obeys through fear and compulsion. In aristocracy, power is exercised by some whose social status gives them a claim to rule. Their privileges, lands, and offices entail certain obligations. They must administer justice in their lands and provide service to the king when required. For others, obedience will always be demanded. They will feel the weight of social and political power but never exercise it. Honor, as Montesquieu argues, is a principle of differentiation and hierarchy.

So here Tocqueville is faithful to the substance of Montesquieu's typology. But he differentiates them not according to who rules and whether that rule is exercised according to law, but according to the manner of the operation of the principle. Montesquieu encourages this line of thought when he argues that virtue in a republic is not "replaced" by honor in a monarchy, but by the law. What holds the social body together, strictly speaking, is not honor (which is a principle if differentiation), but the action of different social bodies drawn together and forced apart. Monarchy, he argues, is like the "system of the universe" (*EL* III.7).

Now if America and ancient republics are equally republics in this sense, then why does one belong to a social state called democracy and one belong to a social state called aristocracy? The difference lies in the content of the principle that animates each regime. In an ancient democratic republic, citizens were equal in their exercise of political authority. Social inequalities were accepted and legitimate. Further, the temporary relations of command and obedience were authorized by the recognition of excellence. For Tocqueville, democracy is defined by equality—but a sort of equality not limited to the political sphere. The "dogma of the sovereignty of the people" is at once a social and political principle. Equality reveals itself in other guises as well—in the sentiment of human likeness and in the power of public opinion. It reveals itself in the absence of the estates of the old regime or in equality of conditions. Tocqueville is somewhat imprecise in his use of the term democracy precisely because the equality it entails shows itself in so many different ways.[26] Democracy is a generative, providential, and revolutionary fact (*DA* Introduction).

Tocqueville: Liberty and Democracy

Appreciating the power of democracy requires seeing it operate in different contexts. Tocqueville watches democracy do its work in France, in the midst of an old, deeply rooted aristocracy; and in America, in the absence of an aristocratic past. Volume two of *Democracy* is strewn with comparisons between France and America—though Tocqueville seldom makes explicit mention of his homeland. As he writes to his friend Kergorlay, "Although I very rarely spoke of France in my book, I did not write one page of it without thinking about her and without having her, so to speak, before my eyes. And what above all I have sought to put in relief in relation to the United States and to have well understood, was less the complete picture of that foreign society than its contrasts and resemblances to our own. It is always either from opposition or from analogy with one that I set out to give a just and interesting idea of the other."[27] Democracy would reveal itself then in the continuities and contrasts. One crucial question Tocqueville sought to answer through comparison was the relation between democracy and revolution.[28] Was democracy revolutionary only in the context of doing its work in the midst of an aristocracy? Could one distinguish between the spirit of equality and the spirit of revolution? Tocqueville, I submit, came to the conclusion that democracy was not revolutionary only in the midst of an aristocracy. The age of democracy would require a new political science because democracy itself was potentially ceaselessly revolutionary. And further, this revolutionary aspect of democracy would show itself most powerfully in the realm of mores.

In America democracy came into being without having to combat aristocracy. In America the mores and laws together produced liberty. This is, broadly speaking, the lesson of volume one of *Democracy*. Yet Tocqueville was not convinced that the Americans had somehow solved the problem of democracy in any final way. They were free, but the struggle for liberty would always remain. The scope and trajectory of democratic mores convinced Tocqueville that liberty could find itself especially endangered in the age of democracy. So volume two of *Democracy* places less emphasis on Americans in particular and more on the logic of democracy itself.[29] For Tocqueville argues that the very vices toward which democratic peoples are naturally disposed also favor democratic despotism. One might say that just as Montesquieu saw a sort of natural fit between honor and moderate monarchy, so did Tocqueville see a natural fit between equality and democratic despotism. Volume two would require a more thorough-going analysis of democratic mores. In volume one of *Democracy* and elsewhere, Tocqueville used the word mores to "comprehend . . . the whole moral and intellectual state of a people" (*DA* I.ii.9). In volume two he would differentiate some of what he had subsumed under this broad usage. Part one would deal with the democratic mind, part two with sentiments (inner dispositions), and part three with "mores properly so-called" (dispositions toward others). What   Tocqueville here calls mores seems to correspond with Montesquieu's use of manners, while Tocqueville's use of sentiments seems to correspond with Montesquieu's use of mores.[30]

Tocqueville's shift in usage from volume one to two parallels Montesquieu's shift from his use of principle and nature in the first eight books of *The Spirit of the Laws* to his use of general spirit and laws, mores, and manners in book nineteen. In each case there is shift in categories that corresponds to a deepening of analysis. The vast scope of the analysis contained in volume two shows how far Tocqueville tried to take Montesquieu's approach in book nineteen.

Here I will select a few items that will provide some indication of the character and range of phenomena that a democratic statesman must confront. Tocqueville argues that democratic peoples seek both liberty and equality, but they seek the latter ardently and unceasingly (*DA* II.ii.1). This would incline them toward centralization and uniformity, each quite unfriendly to political liberty. Political liberty for Tocqueville depends upon influence and secondary powers. It depends upon peoples acting in common and acting upon one another. Liberty exists where some individuals attempt to move others to action and those same others are willing to be moved.

Volume two of *Democracy* seems to be, in part, a meditation on how democracy endangers these prerequisites for political liberty. Tocqueville worries that democracy encourages a certain narrowness of mind. A democratic citizen feels great pride in not submitting blindly to particular intellectual authorities. He knows he is the equal of every other, so why would he submit to such authority? Yet when he looks upon the mass of his fellow citizens, a group in which he sees his own likeness writ large, he cannot but feel his own weakness.

So he submits to common or mass opinion. And this opinion does not so much convince each individual, but imposes itself upon them. Near the end of this chapter, Tocqueville adds this: "Thus intellectual authority will be different, but it will not be less" (*DA* II.i.2). Part of the danger then is that democratic peoples will be inclined to think that they are not really submitting to any authority when they submit to common opinion. They will assert their sovereignty and turn away from particular intellectual authorities while being blind to their submission to common opinion. How will such a people be influenced, how will they be moved to act?

Tocqueville also explores a narrowness of heart. The objects of desire in a democracy will be dominated, so he argues, by the goods of this world. Such a people will never be idle. They will be in constant motion, driven by opportunity and the chance to rise. Desires will multiply as opportunities for their satisfaction increase. Tocqueville argues, "The instability of the social state comes to favor the natural instability of desires. Amid these perpetual fluctuations of fate the present grows large; it hides the future that is being effaced, and men want to think only of the next day" (*DA* II.ii.17). The statesman, as Tocqueville announces in the chapter title, must "move back the object of human actions." Desires must be encouraged to extend forward to goods realized by future generations and taught to expand upward, to goods of a higher order. Here the moralist must play a role too. True happiness will only emerge by a recognition that there is a hierarchy of desires in the human soul. The multitude of lower order desires must be denied by individuals in order for them to gain access to a fuller and deeper human flourishing.

Finally, in one of the more profound chapters in all of volume two, Tocqueville illustrates the nature of honor in a democracy.[31] He defines honor as "that particular rule, founded on a particular state, with the aid of which a people or class distributes blame or praise" (*DA* II.iii.18). Here Tocqueville evokes the honor of feudal monarchy in similar fashion to Montesquieu. He points to its emphasis on brilliance and audacity and its often strange prescriptions. Feudal honor lauded military virtue above all else, but its primary purpose was differentiation. Certain actions prohibited for a noble brought no shame upon a commoner. It demanded devotion to particular persons. Finally, and perhaps most importantly, it "ordered the forgetting of oneself" (*DA* II.iii.18).

Honor in democratic America takes on a decidedly different cast. Rather than being rooted in military virtue, honor here is centered around the peaceful virtues of commerce. Nothing is dishonored so much as idleness, and bankruptcy, usually the result of a kind of commercial audacity, brings one no shame.

So the particular prescriptions of honor change as one moves from one state to another. But Tocqueville argues that in democracy a more profound transformation occurs than the exchange of one set of rules for another. Honor in a democracy has trouble taking hold—everything is mobile, nothing is fixed. Honor is more powerful to the extent that its rules are more particular. It serves the needs of particular classes and nations. What happens when classes disappear and nations become increasingly similar? Tocqueville had already illustrated the extension of the sentiment of human likeness in his chapter on the mildness of democracy in part 3. He had further spoken of the democracy's dramatic re-working of the bond between master and servant—now defined only by "the temporary and free accord of their two wills" (*DA* II.iii.5). Neither master nor servant has mores of their own—and to the extent that real inequalities separate them, the imagination denies these same inequalities. Honor therefore cannot find a hold in the midst of constant motion and sameness. It finds no particulari-ty. Whereas what Tocqueville calls "simple virtue" is "satisfied with its own witness," honor needs a public. Honor demands recognition and distinction, but this is precisely what democratic peoples are disinclined to give one another. Montesquieu had argued that monarchy becomes corrupted when honors are opposed to honors and when a courtly servitude becomes a substitute for honor (*EL* VIII.7). What would happen in a regime if honor's rules were persistently unclear and people were inclined rather to assert their similarity?

Tocqueville's debts to Montesquieu are many and significant. He extends the thinking of his master as he seeks to take the measure of the phenomenon of democracy. To understand democracy is to understand democratic mores and how they might interact with certain laws to favor liberty. But ultimately the differences between these two great Frenchmen are profound. For Montesquieu republics require pure mores. Pure mores are no guarantee of liberty and even seem powerless in the face of the manifold possibilities for corruption. Montes-quieu looks to England and finds a reversal of the priority of mores over laws. Laws arrange powers and divide political loyalties. Mores are free and thus not susceptible to the sort of corruptions that doom republics.

Tocqueville sees no regime that would suggest a reversal of the priority of mores over laws. He even makes Montesquieu's republic the model for under-standing the operation of mores in that most modern regime, the United States of America. Whereas Montesquieu saw that the approach of tyranny might be cloaked by attention to manners and mores, Tocqueville saw that certain mores might make a people gradually and willingly embrace a new sort of tyranny. The vastness and depth of this new democracy, and its problematic disposition to-ward tyranny, led Tocqueville to see that mores must forever remain at the heart of the statesman's art.

Notes

1. In *Alexis de Tocqueville: Selected Letters on Politics and Society*, ed. Roger Boesche, trans. James Toupin and Roger Boesche (Berkeley: University of California Press, 1985), 294. This letter can also be found in *Tocqueville: Lettres choicies, Souve-nirs*, eds. François Mélonio and Laurence Guellec (Paris: Gallimard, 2003), 1080-1083.

2. See James Ceaser, *Liberal Democracy and Political Science* (Baltimore: Johns Hopkins University Press, 1990), chapter 3; Jean-Claude Lamberti, *Tocqueville and the Two Democracies*, trans. Arthur Goldhammer (Cambridge: Harvard University Press, 1989).

3. Montesquieu, *The Spirit of the Laws*, ed. A. Cohler, B. Miller, H. Stone (Cambridge: Cambridge University Press, 1989), V.13, 60. Subsequent references will be to this addition using book, chapter, and page numbers.

4. As Sharon Krause has argued, "Honor presupposes an institutional division of power, even as it supports such a division." See "The Politics of Distinction and Disobedience: Honor and the Defense of Liberty in Montesquieu," *Polity* 30, no. 3 (Spring 1999), 474.

5. Ibid., 475.

6. Michael Mosher, "Monarchy's Paradox: Honor in the Face of Sovereign Power," in *Montesquieu's Science of Politics*, eds. D. Carrithers, M. Mosher, and P. Rahe (Lanham, MD: Rowman and Littlefield, 2001), 217.

7. Rebecca Kingston makes a similar point, "Honour itself may serve the ends of public order, but in a way which is of its own dynamic and unrelated to the particular dispositions of the positive law." See her *Montesquieu and the Parlement of Bordeaux* (Geneva: Droz, 1996), 181.

8. Diana Schaub, *Erotic Liberalism: Women and Revolution in Montesquieu's* Persian Letters (Lanham, MD: Rowman and Littlefield, 1995), 16. See also Kingston, 152.

9. Lamberti, 18.

10. Each thinker also held that physical causes like climate and terrain had to be taken into account. See *The Spirit of the Laws*, books XIII-XVIII and *Democracy in America*, I.ii.9. Lamberti has a useful discussion comparing each thinker's use of these categories, see p 17-26. Melvin Richter discusses Tocqueville's debt to Montesquieu in the chapter in *Democracy* mentioned above. See his "The Uses of Theory: Tocqueville's Adaptation of Montesquieu", in *Essays in Theory and History*, ed. Melvin Richter (Cambridge: Harvard University Press, 1970), 74-102.

11. Pierre Manent, *Tocqueville and the Nature of Democracy*, trans. John Waggoner (Lanham, MD: Rowman and Littlefield, 1996), 20-21.

12. See *EL* VIII.3 and Pierre Manent, *Tocqueville and the Nature of Democracy*, 9.

13. Alexis de Tocqueville, *Democracy in America*, ed. and trans. Harvey Mansfield and Delba Winthrop (Chicago: University of Chicago Press, 2001), 53. Subsequent citations will be to this edition using volume, book and chapter numbers. I have consulted the French text available in the bilingual edition of *Democracy in America*, ed. Eduardo Nolla and trans. James Schleifer (Indianapolis: Liberty Fund, 2010), in four volumes.

14. Tocqueville to Stoffels, October 5, 1836, *Alexis de Tocqueville: Selected Letters on Politics and Society*, 114-115; *Tocqueville: Lettres choicies, Souvenirs*, 364-366.

15. Alexis de Tocqueville, *The Old Regime and the Revolution*, vol. I, ed. François Furet and Françoise Mélonio, trans. Alan S. Kahan (Chicago: University of Chicago Press, 1998), 88. Subsequent citations will be to this edition using book and chapter numbers. I have occasionally slightly altered the translation.

16. Delba Winthrop, "Tocqueville's *Old Regime*: Political History," *The Review of Politics* 43 (June 1981), 96-97.

17. See *OR* III.3.

18. *OR* III.3.

19. Rousseau notes, "The same vices that make social institutions necessary make their abuse inevitable; and since, with the sole exception of Sparta where the Law primarily attended to the Children's education, and where Lycrugus established morals [*moeurs*] that almost made the addition of Laws unnecessary, Laws, in general less strong than the passions, contain men without changing them." See *The Discourses and other Early Po-*

litical Writings, ed. and trans. Victor Gourevitch (Cambridge: Cambridge University Press, 1997), 182.

20. There is further evidence that points to English novelty. His discussions of England emerge in books where a new category of analysis is introduced: the "purpose" of various states in book eleven and the general spirit in book nineteen.

21. Pierre Manent, *The City of Man*, trans. Marc LePain (Princeton: Princeton University Press, 1998), 47.

22. Quoted in Schleifer, *The Making of Tocqueville's* Democracy in America, 2nd ed. (Indianapolis: Liberty Fund, 2000), 301-302. This passage is also quoted and discussed by Raymond Aron, *Main Currents in Sociological Thought*, Vol. I (New Brunswick: Transaction, 1998), 257-259.

23. This falls in a section of the chapter entitled, "That the laws serve to maintain a democratic republic in the United States more than physical causes, and mores more than laws."

24. Here is the other occurrence, "What one understands by republic in the United States is the slow and tranquil action of society on itself" (I.ii.10, 379).

25. In some of what follows, I have been greatly influenced by Pierre Manent. See *Tocqueville and the Nature of Democracy*, 5-7.

26. Schleifer even suggests that his imprecision with democracy accounts partly "for the brilliance of his observations. If he had fixed definitively on a single meaning, all of the others would have been more or less lost from sight. His vision would have been at once restricted, his message narrowed, and his audience diminished." See *The Making of Tocqueville's* Democracy in America, 339, and this chapter, "Some Meanings of Démocratie" as a whole.

27. Tocqueville to Kergorlay, October 18, 1847, *Alexis de Tocqueville: Selected Letters on Politics and Society*, 191; *Tocqueville: Lettres choicies, Souvenirs*, 586-590.

28. See Lamberti, chs. 5, 8, 9; Schleifer, "How Many Democracies?" in *The Making of Tocqueville's* Democracy in America; and Manent, *Tocqueville and the Nature of Democracy*, ch. 9.

29. Lamberti quotes Tocqueville from his notes for an introduction to volume two: "The first book is more American than democratic. This one is more democratic than American" (140). On the question of the relationship between the two volumes, see Lamberti, 139-143; Schleifer, "How Many Democracies?"; and Seymour Drescher, "Tocqueville's Two Démocraties," *Journal of the History of Ideas* 25 (April-June 1964): 201-116.

30. *EL* XIX.16. "The difference between mores and manners is that the first are more concerned with internal, and the latter external, conduct."

31. On this chapter see the valuable discussion in John Koritansky, *Alexis de Tocqueville and the New Science of Politics* (Durham: Carolina Academic Press, 1986), 136-140.

Chapter 6

Intellectuals and Statesmanship? Tocqueville, Oakeshott, and the Distinction between Theoretical and Practical Knowledge

Richard Boyd and Conor Williams

Introduction: Public Intellectuals as Philosopher-Kings?

One of the most memorable episodes of Plato's *Republic* is Socrates' praise of the rule of "philosopher-kings" in Books V and VI. Whether or not the Platonic "city in speech" was intended as a serious proposal, these passages have been cited frequently as justification for various forms of intellectual meritocracy.[1] They represent an abiding confidence that intellectual eminence and philosophical knowledge are supremely important in political life. In support of this conviction, history provides abundant examples of statesmen who managed to combine philosophical wisdom with inspired political leadership. The lives of Cicero, Marcus Aurelius, Frederick the Great, Edmund Burke, Thomas Jefferson, Abraham Lincoln, and Winston Churchill all seem to demonstrate that intellectual eminence and a philosophical temperament may be attributes of great statesmen.

And yet for every would-be philosopher-statesman, there are countless others whose intellectualism seemingly hampered their political aspirations. That other Socrates—the one who inhabited the "think tank" in Aristophanes' *Clouds*—better confirms the stereotype of intellectuals as inept, abstracted, and even a tiny bit malevolent. At best, philosophers are feckless; at worst, they are dangerous. As Paul Johnson argued in his famous work on intellectuals, utopian philosophers such as Rousseau, Marx, Tolstoy, and Russell offered little to the real world of politics.[2] More often philosophers aspire to be tyrannical than statesmanlike. Under the guise of disinterested humanitarianism, an apocalyptic faith in the perfectibility of human nature, and a hubristic sense of the power of reason, intellectuals have proven to be agents of terror and tragic destruction. Utopian dreams of ridding the world of suffering, inequality, and conflict too often turn out to be nothing more than hypocritical alibis for their own vanity, insecurity, or ambition.

Mark Lilla has recently suggested that something in the philosophical soul makes intellectuals dangerous. Philosophers are passionate creatures with a boundless desire for knowledge. Their reckless temperament and contempt for conventional morality blur easily into an erotic passion for dominance or wholesale social transfiguration.[3] As Karl Mannheim noted in *Ideology and Utopia*, the utopian mind grows impatient with the ambiguities, tensions, contingencies, and contradictions of everyday political life.[4] Intellectuals have a natural affinity for what Raymond Aron, Edward Shils, Elie Kedourie, and others have dubbed "ideological politics," whether of the Left or the Right.[5] Unlike the real world of "civil" politics, which necessarily entails compromise, moderation, discussion, and a healthy dose of moral pluralism, the mind of the intellectual is Manichean.

Much has been written about the moral lapses and sociological proclivities of particular intellectuals. This chapter seeks a more fundamental explanation for the perennial tension between intellectuals and statesmanship. Why, even with the best of intentions, do philosophers so often founder when they get involved in politics? What ultimately keeps the philosophical sage from behaving like a prudent statesman? We argue that the problem arises from the confusion of two different forms of human knowledge. As we will see, the kind of abstract, philosophical knowledge that is the stock in trade of the intellectual differs categorically from the practical, experiential knowledge of the time-tested statesman. While theoretical knowledge—and the public intellectuals who deal in it—might sometimes guide or critique the practical world of politics, it is a dangerous fallacy to think that theory can ever take the place of practice.

In the following sections, we survey the work of Alexis de Tocqueville and Michael Oakeshott and highlight their common appreciation of the tensions between intellectualism and statesmanship. We link their skepticism about the possibilities of combining philosophy and politics to an elemental distinction both make between theoretical and practical knowledge. Finally, we suggest that even though there is an affinity between Tocqueville, Oakeshott, and many other "conservative" political thinkers, the political differences between Tocqueville and Oakeshott clearly show that an epistemological skepticism about the limits of theoretical knowledge need not culminate in an anti-democratic political disposition.

Michael Oakeshott on Theoretical and Practical Knowledge

If there is really a contradiction between the life of the intellectual and that of the statesman, as we have asserted, then what specifically do statesmen have that intellectuals lack? What is this special kind of knowledge that comes from doing and acting, rather than from reading, writing, theorizing, discussing, or contemplating?

Many thinkers in the history of political thought have ventured a distinction between theoretical and practical knowledge. Not long after Plato extolled the virtues of philosopher-kings, Aristotle warned about philosophical reformers such as Hippodamus of Miletus, who thought that complex social and political orders could be divided with geometrical precision.[6] Aristotle's distinction between *phronesis,* or practical reason, on the one hand, and *sophia*, or theoretical knowledge, on the other, stipulates that political prudence comes only with experience. Unlike *sophia* or theoretical knowledge, which can be taught to children, prudence is borne from long engagement in the activity in question.[7]

Analogously, technical arts such as cooking, weaving, riding a horse, piloting a ship, or building a house require skills that can only be acquired through years of practice. Practitioners always "know more than one can tell," in the formulation of Michael Polanyi, and skills like these are inherently unspecifiable in the sense that they cannot be satisfactorily intellectualized.[8] Written instructions, maps, blueprints, theories, maxims, recipes, or how-to manuals are at best cribs, grossly oversimplified abstractions from infinitely more complex realities. They may be of some limited use in guiding conduct, but they are always flawed, incomplete attempts at capturing the totality of the activity in question. Anyone who has ever struggled with assembling furniture, preparing their own taxes, or cooking a gourmet meal can testify that written instructions are poor surrogates for experience. Relying exclusively on theories in the absence of practical experience can lead to catastrophic failures—whether a burnt meal, botched job, wrecked ship, or the destruction of a political system.

Aristotle, Edmund Burke, François Guizot, Max Weber, Michael Polanyi, and many others have warned against entrusting political reform to novices or philosophers. But arguably no thinker has gone so far in depreciating abstract theory as the twentieth-century British philosopher Michael Oakeshott. In *Experience and Its Modes*, Oakeshott argues that human conduct can be understood and interpreted through a plurality of different "modes" such as science, history, practice, and in later writings, poetry. Each of these qualitatively different "modes," "idioms," or "voices" represents an internally coherent and self-contained framework for making sense of human experience. For example, science seeks to apprehend and explain the world in terms that can be expressed impersonally, objectively, and if possible, quantitatively.[9] But the fundamental argument of *Experience and Its Modes* is that science—or any other single mode, for that matter—cannot account for the entirety of human experience. Something about human conduct resists purely objective, rational, or instrumental explanation. This is not to say that there is no legitimate use for science, history, or practice. It is only to say that each is a necessarily partial, abstracted way of making sense of social and political affairs.

Philosophy stands in a unique relationship to these other modes, as well as to the practical activity of politics. Rather than affording specialized knowledge or dictating some particular course of action, "Philosophy [is] the impulse to study the quality and style of each voice [of human experience], and to reflect upon the relationship of one voice to another." Properly understood, philosophy is "a parasitic activity," one that stands above and mediates a plurality of different ways of apprehending the world.[10] While seeking coherence in human arguments and accounts of behavior, the philosopher must inevitably concede the limits of his project. Whereas "the notion of an unconditional or definitive understanding may hover in the background," the activity of philosophy is more like an "adventure" or voyage—intrinsically valuable for its own sake, rather than as a means to get to any particular destination.[11]

What, then, can philosophy offer to politics? Or, put differently, is anything like a *political* philosophy even possible? Strictly speaking, Oakeshott's answer is negative.[12] At most philosophy may help clarify points of incongruity within a regime's ethical, institutional, or historical framework, but the results of this inquiry have the same tenuous relationship to political practice as the rules of baseball have to the activity of a centerfielder judging the arc of a fly ball on a windy afternoon.[13] According to Oakeshott, it is a mistake to confuse philosophical understanding with ethical convictions or metaphysical standards that can be applied to the world of practice. This is the folly of the "theoretician," a pseudo-philosopher who "purports to be concerned with the postulates of conduct, but…mistakes these postulates for principles from which 'correct' performances may be deduced or somehow elicited."[14] Unlike the true philosopher, the theoretician aspires to derive fixed standards from his theorizing instead of mere "platforms of conditional understanding."[15]

These complaints about the "theoretician" are reminiscent of Oakeshott's better-known criticism of the fallacy of "rationalism." In his most famous work, *Rationalism in Politics,* Oakeshott condemns "the rationalist," one who tries to substitute abstract products of the human mind and "pure reason" for the messy contingencies and ambiguities of practical experience. The rationalist thinks that political problems have timeless solutions; indeed, this character expects that politics can be resolved according to readily ascertainable rules and formulas. He practices the "politics of faith," where "governing is understood to be in the service of human perfection."[16] This is in contrast with the "politics of scepticism," which are "the style and habit of governing appropriate to circumstances in which government enjoys only a small opportunity of directing the activities of its subjects."[17] The rationalist pursues the politics of faith because he is convinced that rational analysis and the appropriate methods will lead to certainty, and that political disagreements are always susceptible to a single, "rational" solution. Unfortunately, this rational pursuit of political solutions ignores the inexorable role of habit or custom, to say nothing of the ways in which these are related to political divisions and resulting violence. The answer to the question "rational with respect to what?" cannot be answered without reference to a preexisting set of assumptions—both empirical and normative—which are context-dependent.[18]

The philosopher's fantasy of some Archimedean vantage point from which the theoretician can stand outside of and judge his own society is akin to the spectacle of a fish cleaning its aquarium. The reality is that we always approach ethical or practical problems from within the context of a given tradition. Properly understood by the statesman, the parameters of a given tradition may offer guidance and resources, but more often they serve as boundaries or restraints. Oakeshott's distinction between theoretical and practical knowledge stems from his appreciation of the inescapable role of history, contingency, and context. Whereas Oakeshott's rationalist "strives to live each day as if it were his first," the statesman accepts that political problems are never detachable from long-time horizons.[19] The rationalist thinks that politics corresponds to knowable principles, that its problems may be theorized and conclusively solved. He assumes that humans act in ways which can be calculated, that their behavior aggregates to causal rules, and that these rules can be used to avoid political strife. Theoretical knowledge claims to pursue determinative rules of conduct that gesture to "some over-all scheme of mechanized control" of the political sphere.[20]

Ironically, rather than the dispassionate lens of pure reason, rationalism ultimately collapses into "the politics of the felt need...charged with the feeling of the moment." Rationalist politics lead to comprehensive social planning in pursuit of "perfection" and "uniformity." Political rulers armed with such "certainty" have often found the political world, with its competing interests and ethical ambiguity, to be dissatisfying. Confronted by these frustrations and limitations, they have tragically set out to transform or destroy it. But whereas the theoretician or rationalist seeks finality, certainty and social transformation, Oakeshott's true philosopher resists the urge to offer ethical and political prescriptions. Philosophy can clarify the premises and postulates necessary for a given conclusion, but can never provide a determinative account of how matters *ought* to be conducted.[21]

By contrast, the statesman knows that political solutions require agonistic tradeoffs between mutually incommensurable goods. Politics is "the activity of attending to the general arrangements of a set of people whom chance or choice have brought together . . . all of them aware of a past, a present, and a future."[22] Consequently the statesman's approach to meditating political conflicts must be grounded in the political and cultural resources of his society. He seeks worka- ble, not optimal solutions, and has studied his own tradition to discern both its possibilities and limitations. The mere existence of political power is not a justi- fication for its use. Above all, the statesman recognizes that theoretical know- ledge is dangerous in its aspiration to overcome all limits; he recognizes that "the greater part of what we have is not a burden to be carried or an incubus to be thrown off, but an inheritance to be enjoyed. And a certain degree of shabbi- ness is joined with every real convenience."[23] Experienced politicians accept that some problems may be irresolvable within the constraints of a political tra- dition. Armed with this knowledge, the statesman succumbs neither to the poli- tics of faith nor the politics of skepticism.[24] Instead, his are the politics of pru- dence and tradeoffs.

In *On Human Conduct*, Oakeshott argues that politics never yields deter- minative solutions, only further consideration, debate, and interpretation, unless it abandons the centrality of the rule of law. Decision-making in politics is a matter of making workable choices in the face of competing interests and ethical claims. Each political move stems from a past and alters a future, and as such, is simultaneously limited and expansive. Politics is "to perceive the next step dic- tated or suggested by the character of the society in contact with changing con- ditions and to take it in such a manner that the society is not disrupted and that the prerogatives of future generations are not grossly impaired."[25] In other words, modern politics pursues stability through countless contingent decisions, whereas philosophy aims at the pursuit of truth (measured by the coherence of one's account of the conditions of experience). These are distinct projects, with distinct goals.[26]

Politics is properly confined to debating general conditions for life in civil association and adjusting the "adverbial" terms according to which citizens re- late to one another—what Oakeshott calls "civility." It is not the job of states- men to dictate behavior, impose purposive ends, or inculcate virtue in citizens. The modest task of political leaders is to craft a system of laws that will insure the behavior of citizens is conducted "punctually, considerately, civilly, scientif- ically, legally, candidly, judicially, poetically, morally, etc."[27] This understand- ing of politics is incompatible with any attempt at fixing substantive "postulates for conduct" or directing specific actions.

What, finally, does Oakeshott's distinction between philosophy and politics suggest about the possibilities of statesmanship? Obviously, insofar as politics is an art or skill akin to cooking, weaving, or piloting a ship, Oakeshott has great respect for practical experience. Presumably the statesman is someone with a seasoned, battle-tested appreciation of the contingencies of political life and the requisite judgment to navigate in such a world. Whereas rationalism boils down to the "politics of the politically inexperienced," those who have grown up with the proper political education are intimately acquainted with their own traditions. They know how to "sail a boundless and bottomless sea...[with] neither harbor for shelter nor floor for anchorage, neither starting-place nor appointed destination." The statesman's expertise consists in an invaluable knowledge of how to "keep afloat on an even keel."[28]

Notwithstanding this appreciation of the statesman's art, there is also a deep and abiding skepticism about the value of statesmanship—and of politics more generally. Far from the highest end or *telos*, politics is just one among many activities that make up an interesting human life—an intermittent diversion rather than the *summum bonum*.[29] Oakeshott's "depressing doctrine" is that politics is ultimately an unsatisfying exercise in humility and resignation, demanding "spiritual callousness" and much "false simplification" on the part of its practitioners, and maybe even a "perversion of their genius."[30] Much as it appeared to Max Weber, politics resembles a "slow, strong boring through hard boards."[31] Tradition and circumstances place limits on human agency, creativity, and inventiveness. Mainly we "pursue intimations" within a fixed "groove" or horizon inherited from the past and which we are largely powerless to change or exchange for another.[32] The embeddedness of human conduct within a given tradition or practice sets limits on the most inspired leadership. Rather than playing the part of saviors, redeemers, or Solon-like lawgivers, even accomplished statesmen are powerless to arrest the decline of a given moral tradition.[33]

Democracy and the Intellectual Life?

At first glance, Alexis de Tocqueville seems to be engaged in a very different enterprise than Oakeshott. Where Oakeshott intends a broad philosophical consideration of the nature of human experience and life in civil association, Tocqueville focuses on particular regimes—mainly America and France—and the unique "social state" of modern democracy. Even so, there are actually many affinities between Oakeshott and Tocqueville. Both evince some ambivalence, if not aversion, to mass democracy. Both emphasize the integral role of tradition in political life. And both appreciate the vital function of civic or "enterprise" associations in a free society.[34] In addition to these more obvious similarities, Tocqueville also shares Oakeshott's sense of the tension between theoretical and practical knowledge. As for Oakeshott, Tocqueville is acutely aware of the difficulty of combining philosophical knowledge with prudent statesmanship.

For Tocqueville, this difficulty is at least partially due to the nature of modern democracy. Like J. S. Mill, Nietzsche, Santayana and other "aristocratic" critics, Tocqueville laments democracy's inability to muster a class of intellectual elites capable of elevating public opinion and cultivating the refined tastes and specialized knowledge necessary for civilization.[35] *Democracy in America* famously condemns the leveling effects of democracy: all minds approach a middling standard of mediocrity.[36] Proponents of democracy foolishly maintain "that there is more enlightenment and wisdom in a numerous assembly than in a single man, and the number of the legislators is more important than how they are chosen. It is the theory of equality applied to brains."[37] Widespread social and economic mobility leaves citizens susceptible to envy and *amour-propre*. Democratic regimes instill a debased "taste for equality" in their citizens which makes them wary of intellectual claims to political expertise.[38] The problem goes beyond democratic politics, raising broader questions about the ability of a democratic society to produce an intellectual class and support the life of the mind. Insofar as philosophy, literature, or the fine arts exist at all in America, which Tocqueville doubts, they take on a distinctively pragmatic, Cartesian, or egalitarian cast.[39]

Tocqueville is not the only one who finds the instincts of democratic culture inimical to the specialized knowledge, hierarchy, and elitism represented by intellectuals. From Richard Hofstadter's seminal work on anti-intellectualism in American culture to Edward Shils' treatment of a native current of suspicion toward the intellectual that found fruition in McCarthyism to latter-day conservative polemics on behalf of an unfashionable elitism, Tocqueville's observations about the anti-intellectual character of modern democracy ring uncomfortably true.[40] Democratic citizens are wary of the pronouncements of experts, specialists, or intellectuals. Indeed, being labeled an "intellectual" can be a major liability. Unlike military heroes, lawyers, businessmen, movie stars, or former professional wrestlers—all of whom claim some qualification to rule—intellectuals are generally the last people democratic citizens are willing to entrust with political power. Witness the failures of the "intellectual" presidencies of Woodrow Wilson or Jimmy Carter, not to mention the electoral miscarriages of Adlai Stevenson, Eugene McCarthy, and Michael Dukakis.

If Tocqueville and others are correct about this tension between democracy and intellectualism, should we consider this to be a virtue or a vice of modern democracy? And are these misgivings about intellectuals really unique to democracy, as Tocqueville contends? Strictly on the basis of *Democracy in America*, where Tocqueville seems to take the side of intellectuals and philosophers over and against the leveling tide of mass democracy, one might assume that he would favor greater political engagement by philosophers or intellectuals. But this would be an oversimplified if not inaccurate view. For if we turn to Tocqueville's *Old Regime and the Revolution*, we find a damning indictment of the role of intellectuals and philosophers in political life, a view that is very much in keeping with Oakeshott's skepticism. In contrast to the salutary influence of statesmen well-acquainted with the practice of politics, philosophers and their spurious theoretical knowledge represent a far greater threat to political liberty than the leveling tide of democracy. The *Old Regime* proves that these tensions between the dispositions of intellectuals and the requirements of statesmanship are hardly unique to modern democracy. They reflect a timeless distinction between theoretical and practical knowledge directly analogous to that we have seen in Oakeshott's writings.

The *Old Regime* and the Dangers of Philosophical Rationalism

Notwithstanding Tocqueville's "religious terror" about the providential march of democracy in the modern world, his analysis of the French Revolution differs, at least in emphasis, from that of Edmund Burke, Joseph de Maistre, and other "conservatives," who lamented the caustic nature of democratic equality and blamed the lower classes for disrupting traditional hierarchies and natural inequalities.[41] Rather than being doomed by the ignorance of peasants, small-town lawyers, and obscure country curates, the Revolution of 1789 miscarried because of the ascendancy of intellectuals and the absence of genuine statesman with some modicum of practical experience with politics.

Tocqueville anchors his discussion of the Revolution in a criticism of France's philosophical classes. Despite holding no offices and taking no part in public business, this class "paid sedulous, and, indeed, special attention to the subject of government." Intellectuals were endlessly "discoursing of the origin and primitive form of society, of the primordial rights of the governed and governing power, of the natural and artificial relations of men one to the other, of the soundness or the errors of the prevailing customs, of the principles of the laws." The various schemes they bandied about were united by a single motivating principle, which comprised the "whole of the political philosophy of the eighteenth century." This amounted to the rationalistic fallacy that "it was necessary to substitute simple and elementary rules, based on reason and natural law, for the complicated and traditional customs which regulated society in their time."[42]

Tocqueville's analysis mirrors Oakeshott's critique of rationalism: society is composed of a complex web of inherited institutions. These are inevitably marred by inconsistency, imprecision, and moral ambiguity. Confronted by the illogic, obscurity, and anachronism of so many traditions, the philosopher's first impulse is to dissect them with critical reason. Order can be imposed upon disorder; ambiguities and inconsistencies must be resolved. Institutions and customs that have evolved slowly and episodically over centuries can be dismantled and subsequently rebuilt according to logical rules or abstract systems. The problem, however, as both Tocqueville and Oakeshott appreciate, is that these "complicated and traditional customs" cannot be reduced to simple rules or abstract reason, whether these are inspired by putative "natural laws" or overblown inventions of reason.

Like Oakeshott, Tocqueville appreciates that the rationalistic fallacy is hardly original to the Enlightenment period. Indeed "for three thousand years [this rationalism] had been floating backward and forward through the minds of men without finding a resting place."[43] But if the impulse to substitute the contrivances of human reason for the concrete building blocks of custom and tradition is as old as philosophy itself, why did these theories, formerly "buried in the brain of philosophers," suddenly become a dominating "passion among the masses," even to the point that "the imaginations of women and peasants were inflamed by notions of new systems"?[44] The answer, for Tocqueville, stems from an elective affinity between these ideas and the social conditions of Revolutionary France.

The first factor that accounts for the widespread reception of rationalism in the eighteenth century is the dawning equality of conditions: "There are times in a nation's life when men differ from each other so widely that the very idea of a common law for all seems unintelligible. But there are other times when it is enough to dangle before their eyes a picture, however indistinct and remote, of such a law and they will immediately recognize and grasp it eagerly."[45] Universal rules and principles only make sense in a world where people regard themselves as rough moral equals. In this respect, the democratic age rests upon a paradox: the very same democratic social conditions that make the masses generally suspicious of intellectuals also render them susceptible to the egalitarian dogmas they disseminate.

The second factor is that these ideas were propounded at a time when the nascent equality of social conditions collided with deeply entrenched inequalities. Multitudes of anachronistic taxes, absurd and outmoded privileges, and invidious social distinctions were woven into the fabric of late eighteenth-century French society. The dissonance between newfound social equality and an archaic system of orders and deferences gave rise to popular resentments. Political, social, and economic inequities made the musings of philosophers and public intellectuals attractive to farmers, ordinary tax payers, and other common people and lent a destructive spirit to their reception: "A rage for this political literature seized all who were inconvenienced by the legislation of the day, including many who were naturally but little prone to indulge in abstract speculations."[46] As Tocqueville observes, the literary fascination with speculative philosophy became a vehicle for Revolutionary sentiments: "Popular passions thus disguised themselves in a philosophic garb; political aspirations were forcibly driven into a literary channel, and men of letters, taking the direction of public opinion, temporarily occupied the position which in free countries belongs to party leaders."[47]

As the previous quote suggests, the third and main reason for the appeal of these ideas was the absence of "party leaders" and the atrophy of political knowledge across virtually every strata of French society. Rather than blaming democratic interlopers for the excesses of the Revolution, Tocqueville consistently faults the aristocracy for abdicating their rightful positions of responsibility and governance—a vacancy seized by the *philosophes*. Unlike the English aristocracy who clung to their ancestral rights of governing, sometimes at great personal expense, the French had long since ceased to take part in political life. In the absence of "free institutions and, consequently, of political classes, vibrant political bodies, or organized political parties," Tocqueville complains, "the control of public opinion, when it revived, fell entirely into the hands of the philosophers, that is to say the intellectuals." Under the circumstances it was inevitable that the Revolution "should be conducted less with a view to political realities than abstract principles and highly generalized theories."[48]

The problem is less with these "benign theories" themselves than the inexperience, naivete, and crudeness of the political actors who took them up.[49] Absent any practical experience of governing, the ideas of the intellectuals were destined to go astray. The new political classes of 1789 "had no practical acquaintance with the subject [of political reform]; their ardours were undamped by actual experience; they knew of no existing facts which stood in the way of desirable reforms; they were ignorant of the dangers inseparable from the most necessary revolutions, and dreamed of none."[50] Practical political experience is the only thing that could have impressed upon the Revolutionaries the difference between utopian dreams and sober political realities.

More than anything else, a lack of practical political knowledge explains both the allure of philosophical knowledge and the abuses to which it was put by the Revolutionaries. Just as someone with no actual knowledge of cooking has to resort to cook-book recipes, once the practice of politics has been extinguished, would-be statesmen have nothing left but empty theories. By way of contrast, people who are practiced in the art of government have no need of simplistic formula or recipes. Not only do abstract theories have little appeal, but experienced statesmen apprehend the dangers they present. Having long since lost the habit of self-government, the French had no such political experience to draw upon, which explains their gullibility. Tocqueville notes with irony the aristocracy's zeal for the very philosophical systems that spelled their downfall: "Forgetting that established theories, sooner or later, inevitably become political passions, and find expression in acts, they made no objection to the discussion of doctrines that were wholly subversive of their private rights, and even of their very existence."[51] Treating philosophical systems as "ingenious exercises for the mind," the aristocracy diverted themselves while ignoring their explosive potential.[52]

The problem is not just with aristocrats squandering their political capacity and abdicating responsibility. Philosophical systems appeal to those who have never enjoyed political liberty in the first place. They know no better than to be taken in by imagined schemes for reforming government. They have no direct experience or habit of the art of government: "If the French people had still participated in the government by means of States-General, if they had still taken part in the administration of the public business in Provincial Assemblies, it is certain that they would have received the lucubrations of these authors with more coolness; their business habits would have set them on their guard against pure theory."[53] The fanciful flights of the philosophical mind and the sober-minded judgment of the statesman are inimical to one another. Referencing Hume's disagreement with Diderot on the question of religious toleration, Tocqueville asserts that "it was the Scotsman who was right. Living in a free country, he had practical experience of freedom; Diderot's was the viewpoint of a man of letters; Hume's that of a statesman."[54]

But what were these problems with which practical political men should have been acquainted? What accounts for the alleged dangers of this spirit of philosophical rationalism, making it equally undesirable for democrats and aristocrats alike? Above and beyond their blatant disregard for tradition and their inflated sense of human reason, intellectuals exacerbate the tendency toward state centralization. The atrophy of practical political experience is both the cause and consequence of that centralization of political power that Tocqueville sees as the most formidable danger to political liberty. The atomization of society, the abdication of political responsibility by traditional ruling classes, the growth of a centralized bureaucracy—all these developments have served not only to extinguish the practical experience in politics that might resist the intellectuals' siren song, but they further empower the centralized state: "Though the central power had not acquired in the eighteenth century the strong and healthy constitution it has since possessed, it had, notwithstanding, so thoroughly destroyed all intermediate authorities, and left so wide a vacant space between itself and the public, that it already appeared to be the mainspring of the social machine, the sole source of national life."[55]

Already in the eighteenth century the French confronted a state that was "highly centralized, supremely powerful, [and] prodigiously active."[56] All power and political knowledge were concentrated in Paris. The centralization of state power under the Bourbon monarchs had absorbed all intermediary organizations and sapped society of its vitality. The state had already begun playing the role of paternalistic tutor over its dependent children, rather than governor of its subject-citizens.[57] The last vestiges of local liberties, entrepreneurial initiative, personal responsibility, and dignified freedom had long since passed away. With this enervation of practical political experience, it never would have occurred to citizens that any large-scale undertaking could succeed without the assistance of the state.[58]

It makes perfect sense that intellectuals would recur to the centralized state with their philosophical schemes for remaking society. After all, only a powerful state has sufficient resources to undertake the wholesale transformation of society. There is a symbiotic relationship between intellectuals and the omnipotent state: while "the philosophers confined themselves, for the most part, to abstract and general theories on the subject of government; the Economists dealt in theory, but also deigned to notice facts."[59] In their eyes, the function of the state was not just governing the nation, but also recasting it in a given mold and forming the minds of the population to fit their utopian visions of a new society. They set "no limit either to its rights or its powers." The state's duty was to transform its subjects, making them over from scratch if necessary. Only the centralized state was up to such a Promethean task.[60]

Even with all the state's power at their disposal, however, the enduring lesson of the French Revolution is the insurmountable force of tradition. Notwithstanding the "greatest effort that has ever been made by any people to sever their history into two parts, so to speak, and to tear open a gulf between their past and their future," one which attempted to remake all of French society and to obliterate everything that came before it, the Revolutionaries ironically succeeded only in perpetuating the original tradition of centralization. As Tocqueville wanly observes, "I have always fancied that they were less successful in this enterprise [of wholesale social revolution] than has been generally believed...they unconsciously retained most of the sentiments, habits, and ideas which the old regime had taught them."[61] Sadly, if public intellectuals manage to have any effect on society at all, it is likely to be strictly negative: the power to destroy but not to rebuild.

If Tocqueville is right that intellectuals are powerless to effect more than negligible and (largely destructive) reforms, doesn't this have dispiriting implications for statesmanship? He remarks that both "philosophers *and* statesmen may learn a valuable lesson of modesty from the history of our Revolution."[62] With all of his emphasis on the unshakeable weight of tradition, political culture, and a nation's determinative "point of departure," Tocqueville is sometimes criticized for giving in to a paralyzing kind of sociological determinism. There is surely something to his observations about the "stickiness" of institutions, the inexorable constants of circumstances and mores, and the futility of wholesale social revolution.[63] Even so, Tocqueville denies that the limits posed by custom are absolute. While stressing humility and moderation, Tocqueville consistently opposes political fatalism: "I am tempted to the belief that what are called necessary institutions are only institutions to which one is accustomed, and that in matters of social constitution the field of possibilities is much wider than people living within each society imagine."[64] Providence may have drawn a "predestined circle" around the fate of each nation or individual "beyond which he cannot pass," but Tocqueville is adamant that "within those vast limits man is strong and free, and so are peoples."[65] The boundaries of politics may be circumscribed, but experienced statesmen, rather than literary philosophers, are capable of bringing about modest reforms.

All hope should not to be abandoned. Unlike Oakeshott, who insists that philosophy cannot be political, and that politics must never be philosophical, Tocqueville has modest hopes for a rapprochement between intellectuals and statesmen. In his writings and by personal example, Tocqueville suggests a possible accommodation between the specialized knowledge of intellectuals and the expertise of the political art. In England, for example, "political writers and political actors were mixed, one set working to adapt new ideas to practice, the other circumscribing theory by existing facts; whereas in France, the political world was divided into two separate provinces without intercourse with each other. One administered the government, the other enunciated its principles among themselves."[66] At best, it seems, public intellectuals can indirectly inform and support political life so long as the distinction between the two activities is acknowledged and appropriately maintained.

Tocqueville's thoughts on the political function of the intellectual leave us with a conundrum. On the one hand, modern democracy's reluctance to accord political respect to the intellectual represents an undeniable threat to political liberty. Abandoned to its instincts, democracy may drift toward intolerance, know-nothingism, *ressentiment*, and leveling. The passionate love of equality, even to the point of denying specialized knowledge or intellectual eminence, is an ominous trend for liberty. On the other hand, we have seen that Tocqueville is no less troubled by the opposite tendency. The dominance of political life by intellectuals lacking practical political experience poses an even greater threat. Thus, and paradoxically, Tocqueville can lament the debasement of popular culture in modern democratic society while at the same time recognizing that the dominance of political life by intellectuals, with all their peculiar foibles, would probably be even worse.

The Politics of Epistemological Skepticism?

We have suggested that Tocqueville's criticism of abstract, philosophical knowledge shares much with that of Michael Oakeshott, Edmund Burke, and other "conservatives." At first glance, Tocqueville's political sociology looks to be supportive of the elitist notion that political activity should be reserved for a cadre of time-tested political leaders versed in the practical arts of governance. Politics—like cooking or riding a bicycle—is an art that comes from experience, and just as not everyone can be a gourmet chef, or even a competent cook, practical political experience draws clear lines between statesmen, ordinary citizens, and the naive and untrustworthy masses. The epistemological distinction between theoretical and practical knowledge has a long and distinguished anti-democratic lineage, after all, and Tocqueville appears to share the anti-democratic bias of Burke, Oakeshott, and other conservatives wary of the role of the "masses" in modern democracy.[67]

And yet for all of these similarities between Tocqueville and Oakeshott, what explains their apparent divergence on the question of moral equality, civic engagement, and democratic participation? What gives Tocqueville his Rousseauean soft spot for democracy? Unlike Burke, Maistre, and other counterrevolutionaries who resist the democratic tide, Tocqueville thinks that the solution to the problem of democracy is, somewhat paradoxically, more democracy.[68] Given the inevitability of democracy thrusting into power a new political class, the main problem of the democratic age is to educate this class. According to one of the most celebrated passages in *Democracy in America,* the work is written in the hope of "educating" democracy in order to render it safe for liberty: "to put, if possible, new life into its beliefs; to purify its mores; to control its actions; gradually to substitute understanding of statecraft for present inexperience and knowledge of its true interest for blind instincts."[69] Presumably democracy can develop a sense of statecraft from the right kind of education, which consists first and foremost of practical experience in the arts of self-government.

For the Anglo-Americans, favored by history and long accustomed to the practice of self-rule, democracy is problematic at the margins. But for a people like the French, whose citizens have either relinquished the practice of freedom, or never enjoyed it in the first place, the dilemma of democracy is more acute. Even here, however, Tocqueville's take on the distinction between philosophical and practical knowledge leads in more hopeful, democratic directions. If one takes if for granted that the masses are destined to assume a greater role in their own self-government than has heretofore been the case, as did Tocqueville, then it behooves political leaders to give them the opportunity to learn the practical knowledge that can only be mastered by actually participating in political life. This was a position that Tocqueville consistently espoused throughout his life, championing suffrage reform, public education, and other social legislation that would gradually integrate new political classes into the habits of self-rule.[70]

Tocqueville's argument opens up democratic vistas in several directions. First, Tocqueville is quite explicit in shattering the link between practical political experience and social class that has been a mainstay of the conservative political tradition. As his withering criticism of the behavior of the French aristocracy demonstrates, being an aristocrat is hardly a sufficient condition for political knowledge. Indeed the French aristocracy is arguably more to blame for the miscarriages of the French Revolution than the masses. Whereas the latter needed only to be guided and educated, the former squandered what political experience they once possessed and shirked their responsibility to lead, fleeing the country or withdrawing from public life.[71] Whether wielded by the nobles, middle classes, or the masses, the "great science of government" can only be learned by the "practical working of free institutions."[72] Clearly, then, aristocracy is hardly a qualification, in and of itself, for political rule.

More radically, Tocqueville implies that neither aristocratic breeding nor privileged social position is a necessary condition for responsible statesmanship. Although democracies are unlikely to be truly wise or capable of adopting a long-term perspective on the public good, the general tendency of their laws does tend toward the overall well-being of society. Aristocratic regimes may occasionally summon up great and magnanimous acts of patriotism, and they are capable of finer administration, but they are also prone to partiality, callousness if not outright cruelty, and self-indulgence. In contrast, democratic nations are distinguished by a conspicuous sympathy for all of their fellow creatures. They rarely inflict unnecessary cruelty and are inclined to come to the aid of others when they can do so with little trouble to themselves.[73]

Finally, Tocqueville understands that the genius of democratic citizenship subsists less in the disinterested patriotism of a few august statesmen than in the mores, habits, and practices of everyday life. Rather than extolling an aristocratic ideal of statesmanship from an age that is irretrievably past, the emphasis throughout *Democracy in America* is on the practical, experiential nature of democratic citizenship open to all who participate. While the French were promised universal rights in the Revolution of 1789 (even as they trampled those of others underfoot), "the American man of the people has conceived a high idea of political rights because he has some; he does not attack those of others, in order that his own may not be violated."[74] Experience and practice play a major role in explaining this difference.

Democratic citizens take advantage of "an infinite number of occasions" for meeting and collaborating. Instead of the rare, heroic deeds of the aristocratic statesman, democratic citizens are drawn into the civic life of their community by the administration of trivial affairs—a "long succession of little services rendered and obscure good deeds," rather than "great matters" or "brilliant achievements."[75] The objects of these common enterprises are largely irrelevant. Nor does it really matter whether citizens are more efficient than government. Rather, the practice of democratic life is important for the education it brings in the practice of political liberty. Describing civic engagement and political liberty as an "art," "taste," "habit," "experience," "skill," "technique," or "apprenticeship," Tocqueville's language is evocative of the experiential nature of politics.[76] "[K]nowledge of how to combine," Tocqueville concludes, "is the mother of all other forms of knowledge."[77] Once democratic citizens have met and worked together, "they always know how to meet again."[78]

Ironically, then, it may be Tocqueville's depreciation of the importance of philosophy in political life that allows him to be relatively sanguine about the fate of democracy. Most ordinary citizens are never going to be philosophers. But given the primacy of practical, experiential knowledge, democratic citizens hardly suffer for their anti-philosophical dispositions. As long as they maintain the everyday habits of civic engagement, self-government, and local liberties, statesmanship is never far from their grasp.

Notes

1. For the most influential reading of Plato's *Republic* as a blueprint for totalitarianism, see Karl Popper, *The Open Society and Its Enemies* (Princeton, NJ: Princeton University Press, 1971), esp. 86-168.

2. Paul Johnson, *Intellectuals* (New York: Harper & Row, 1990).

3. Mark Lilla, *The Reckless Mind: Intellectuals in Politics* (New York: New York Review of Books, 2006), xii, 3-4, 193-216.

4. Karl Mannheim, *Ideology and Utopia* (New York: Harcourt, 1985), 9-10, 84-85.

5. Raymond Aron, *Opium of the Intellectuals* (New Brunswick, NJ: Transaction Publishers, 2001), 43, 289-90; Edward Shils, *Intellectuals and the Powers* (Chicago: University of Chicago Press, 1983); Elie Kedourie, *Nationalism* (Malden, MA: Blackwell Publishers, 1993), xiii-xiv, 38. Others have characterized political ideologies as "fantasies," "religions," or "myths." See especially Jacob Talmon, *Political Messianism: The Romantic Phase* (London: Secker and Warburg, 1960); Vladimir Tismaneanu, *Fantasies of Salvation: Democracy, Nationalism and Myth in Post-Communist Europe* (Princeton: Princeton University Press, 1998); Emilio Gentile, *Politics as Religion* (Princeton: Princeton University Press, 2001).

6. Aristotle, *Politics*, trans. Ernest Barker (Oxford: Oxford University Press, 1995), II.8.1267b-1269a, 61-66.

7. Aristotle, *Nichomachean Ethics*, trans. Martin Ostwald (Upper Saddle River, NJ: Prentice Hall, 1999), VI.5-13, 152-73.

8. Michael Polanyi, *The Tacit Dimension* (Gloucester, MA: Peter Smith, 1983), 8; Polanyi, *Personal Knowledge* (Chicago: University of Chicago Press, 1962), 49-62.

9. Michael Oakeshott, *Experience and Its Modes* (Cambridge: Cambridge University Press, 1985), 170-1.

10. Michael Oakeshott, "The Voice of Poetry in the Conversation of Mankind," in *Rationalism in Politics and Other Essays*, ed. Timothy Fuller (Indianapolis: Liberty Fund, 1991), 491. Though Oakeshott's terminology evolves, the concepts of "modes," "idioms," and "voices" of human experience are largely analogous. On the evolution of this terminology and an account of the importance of modality for Oakeshott's thought, see Richard Flathman, *Pluralism and Liberal Democracy* (Baltimore: Johns Hopkins University Press, 2005), chapter 5.

11. Michael Oakeshott, *On Human Conduct* (Oxford: Oxford University Press, 2003), 3.

12. See especially, Michael Oakeshott, "The Claims of Politics" and "Political Philosophy" in *Religion, Politics, and the Moral Life*, ed. Timothy Fuller (New Haven: Yale University Press, 1991), 91-6, 138-55. Oakeshott has frequently been criticized for his retreat from politics and denial of the political. See especially, Benjamin Barber, *The Conquest of Politics: Liberal Philosophy in Democratic Times* (Princeton: Princeton University Press, 1988), esp. chs. 1, 6; Bhikhu Parekh, "Oakeshott's Theory of Civil Association" *Ethics* 106 (October, 1995): 158-186; Hannah Pitkin, "Inhuman Conduct and Unpolitical Theory" *Political Theory* 4 (August, 1976): 301-320. Terry Nardin's work is particularly instructive on the relationship between philosophy and politics. See Nardin, *The Philosophy of Michael Oakeshott* (University Park: Penn State University Press, 2001).

13. Cf. Oakeshott, "Rationalism in Politics," in *Rationalism in Politics*, 12.

14. Oakeshott, *On Human Conduct*, 26. Cf. 27-31. Cf. Andrew Sullivan, *Intimations Pursued: The Voice of Practice in the Conversation of Michael Oakeshott* (Charlottesville, VA: Imprint Academic, 2007), 3-4.

15. Oakeshott, *On Human Conduct*, 2-3.

16. Michael Oakeshott, *The Politics of Faith and the Politics of Scepticism* (New Haven: Yale University Press, 1996), 45.

17. Oakeshott, *Politics of Faith*, 69.

18. Oakeshott, "Rational Conduct," in *Rationalism in Politics*, esp. 100-17.

19. Oakeshott, "Rationalism in Politics," 7.

20. Oakeshott, "Rationalism in Politics," 28.

21. Oakeshott, "Rationalism in Politics," 9-10, 25-29; Oakeshott, *Experience and Its Modes*, 83. See also Oakeshott, "Political Philosophy," 151-52.

22. Oakeshott, "Political Education," in *Rationalism in Politics*, 44.

23. Oakeshott, "Political Education," 45.

24. Oakeshott, *Politics of Faith*, 17. For a more detailed discussion of the politics of faith and the politics of skepticism, see Paul Franco, *Michael Oakeshott: An Introduction* (New Haven, CT: Yale University Press, 2004), 74-75, 102-7.

25. Oakeshott, "The Political Economy of Freedom," in *Rationalism in Politics*, 396.

26. Oakeshott, "Political Education," 57.

27. Oakeshott, *On Human Conduct*, 56.

28. Oakeshott, "Rationalism in Politics," 28-30; Oakeshott, "Political Education," 60-2.

29. Oakeshott, "The Claims of Politics," 94.

30. Oakeshott, "Political Education," 60; Oakeshott, "The Claims of Politics," 93-94.

31. Max Weber, "The Profession and Vocation of Politics," in *Political Writings,* ed. Peter Lassman and Ronald Speirs (Cambridge: Cambridge University Press, 1994), 369.

32. Oakeshott, "Political Education," 57-62.

33. Oakeshott, "On Being Conservative," in *Rationalism in Politics*, 432-35; Oakeshott, "Rational Conduct," 128-9; Oakeshott, "Rationalism in Politics," 40-42; Oakeshott, "The Claims of Politics," 94-6.

34. Oakeshott, *On Human Conduct*, 114-15. On the Tocquevillean role of enterprise associations in Oakeshott, see especially Richard Boyd, "Michael Oakeshott on Civility, Civil Society, and Civil Association," *Political Studies* 52 (October 2004): 603-22. For a balanced consideration of the role of civic associations in Tocqueville, see especially Aurelian Craiutu, "From the Social Contract to the Art of Association: A Tocquevillian Perspective," in *Freedom of Association*, eds. Ellen Frankel Paul, Fred D. Miller, Jr., and Jeffrey Paul (Cambridge: Cambridge University Press, 2008) and Richard Boyd, *Uncivil Society: The Perils of Pluralism and the Making of Modern Liberalism* (Lanham, MD: Lexington Books, 2004), chapter 6.

35. For a sense of Tocqueville's affinity for nineteenth-century criticisms of democracy, see especially Alan Kahan, *Aristocratic Liberalism: The Social and Political Thought of Jacob Burckhart, J. S. Mill, and Alexis de Tocqueville* (New York: Oxford University Press, 1992). Aurelian Craiutu has characterized this sensibility as an "elitist liberalism." See *Liberalism Under Siege: The Political Thought of the French Doctrinaires* (Lanham, MD: Lexington Books, 2003).

36. Alexis de Tocqueville, *Democracy in America*, ed. J. P. Mayer and trans. George Lawrence (New York: Harper & Row, 1988), volume 1, "Introduction," 12; volume 1, part 2, chapter 7, 247-50; volume 1, part 2, chapter 9, 311.

37. Tocqueville, *Democracy in America*, volume 1, part 2, chapter 7, 247.

38. Tocqueville, *Democracy in America*, volume 1, part 1, chapter 3, 57; volume 2, part 2, chapter 1, 503-6.

39. Tocqueville, *Democracy in America*, volume 2, part 1, chapter 1-2, 429-36; volume 2, part 1, chapter 9, 454-58; volume 1, "Introduction," 10-11.

40. Richard Hofstadter, *Anti-Intellectualism in American Life* (New York: Vintage Books, 1963); Edward Shils, *The Torment of Secrecy* (Glencoe, IL: Free Press, 1956); William A. Henry, III, *In Defense of Elitism* (New York: Doubleday, 1994).

41. For a brilliant and systematic analysis of the ways in which Tocqueville's account of the French Revolution differs from Edmund Burke's, see Robert T. Gannett, *Tocqueville Unveiled: The Historian and His Sources for the Old Regime and the Revolution* (Chicago: University of Chicago Press, 2003), esp. chapter 4.

42. Alexis de Tocqueville, *Old Regime and the Revolution*, ed. John Bonner (New York: Harper & Brothers, 1856), 170-71. All references are to this edition of the *Old Regime*, though we have modified some translations slightly.

43. Tocqueville, *Old Regime*, 171; Cf. Oakeshott, "Rationalism in Politics," 17-25; Oakeshott, *On Human Conduct*, 198, 313, 320.

44. Tocqueville, *Old Regime*, 171.

45. Tocqueville, *Old Regime*, 27-28.

46. Tocqueville, *Old Regime*, 174.

47. Tocqueville, *Old Regime*, 174.

48. Tocqueville, *Old Regime*, 247-48.

49. Tocqueville, *Old Regime*, 249.

50. Tocqueville, *Old Regime*, 172-73.

51. Tocqueville, *Old Regime*, 174.

52. Tocqueville, *Old Regime*, 175.

53. Tocqueville, *Old Regime*, 173.

54. Tocqueville, *Old Regime*, 153.

55. Tocqueville, *Old Regime*, 90.

56. Tocqueville, *Old Regime*, "Preface," iii.

57. Tocqueville, *Old Regime*, 71-72.

58. Tocqueville, *Old Regime*, 91-94.

59. Tocqueville, *Old Regime*, 193.

60. Tocqueville, *Old Regime*, 197.

61. Tocqueville, *Old Regime*, "Preface," i.

62. Tocqueville, *Old Regime*, 13. My emphasis.

63. See especially Tocqueville, *Democracy in America*, volume 1, part 1, chapter 2, 31-49; volume 1, part 1, chapter 8, 163-70; volume 1, part 2, chapter 9, 277-315.

64. Alexis de Tocqueville, *Recollections: The French Revolution of 1848*, ed. J. Mayer and A. Kerr (New Brunswick, NJ: Transaction Publishers, 1997), 76.

65. Tocqueville, *Democracy in America*, volume 2, part 4, chapter 8, 705.

66. Tocqueville, *Old Regime*, 178.

67. For Oakeshott's apparently "conservative" statement on this dilemma, see especially "The Masses in Representative Democracy," in *Rationalism in Politics*, 370-83. While many have (correctly) linked Oakeshott with a tradition of modern conservatism, the consensus seems to be that his thought is better described as a peculiar blend of skeptical liberal pluralism. For the more extreme view of Oakeshott as a theorist sympathetic to participatory democracy, see especially Richard Flathman, *Reflections of a Would-Be Anarchist: Ideals and Institutions of Liberalism* (Minneapolis: University of Minnesota Press, 1998); Steven Gerencser, *The Skeptic's Oakeshott* (New York: Palgrave Macmillan, 2000).

68. Tocqueville, *Democracy in America*, volume 1, part 2, chapter 4, 195.

69. Tocqueville, *Democracy in America*, volume 1, "Introduction," 12.

70. See especially, Edward T. Gargan, *Alexis de Tocqueville: The Critical Years, 1848-1851* (Washington, DC: Catholic University Press, 1955), 79, 100-3, 106-7, 114-15.

71. Tocqueville, *Old Regime*, esp. 44-49, 176-77.

72. Tocqueville, *Old Regime*, 177.

73. Tocqueville, *Democracy in America*, volume 1, part 2, chapter 6, 231-37, 244-45; volume 2, part 3, chapter 1, 561-65.

74. Tocqueville, *Democracy in America*, volume 1, part 2, chapter 6, 238.

75. Tocqueville, *Democracy in America*, volume 2, part 2, chapter 4, 511.

76. Tocqueville, *Democracy in America*, volume 1, part 2, chapter 4, 194; volume 1, part 2, chapter 6, 240; volume 2, part 2, chapter 1, 506; volume 2, part 2, chapter 4, 512-13; volume 2, part 2, chapter 5, 517; volume 2, part 2, chapter 7, 521-24.

77. Tocqueville, *Democracy in America*, volume 2, part 2, chapter 5, 517.

78. Tocqueville, *Democracy in America*, volume 2, part 2, chapter 7, 521.

Part II
Statesmanship and Government

Chapter 7

Tocqueville's View of the American Presidency and the Limits of Democratic Statesmanship[1]

William B. Parsons, Jr.

This chapter will evaluate the role of the American president as democratic statesman by examining Tocqueville's treatment of that executive in *Democracy in America* and comparing it to the debate concerning the executive that occurred at the founding. Tocqueville's treatment of the presidency is especially helpful to those who wish to escape the partisan limitations of the ratification debates. In their efforts to persuade a wary public to ratify the U.S. Constitution, the founders make several problematic arguments that unjustifiably diminish the dangerous potential of the American executive: among these are Publius' claims that the powers of the office are limited and that the president represents a crucial check on popular passions. Tocqueville's subtle appraisal of the office's character informs our understanding of the presidency in important ways: his understanding of the inherently popular character of the executive and his shrewd evaluation of the potentially broad powers of the office are particularly prescient and, moreover, are consistent with his most pressing fear for democracy's future: the rise of administrative despotism. Tocqueville—unlike many of the antifederalists—acknowledges the important strengths of the office, but his philosophic perspective allows him to perceive the potential dangers posed by the American executive. While he views the presidency as relatively weak in 1830, he asserts that it cannot remain so. Tocqueville's oracular predictions concerning dangerous growth of executive power distinguish him from the founders, who argue that their executive improves the science of government. Ultimately, this chapter concludes that Tocqueville's analysis of the American presidency reveals the limits of democratic statesmanship and the perils of seeking political wisdom from executive power in a democratic age.

Surprisingly, Tocqueville's treatment of the presidency in *Democracy in America* has earned limited attention. Robert Kraynak describes Tocqueville as a "student and admirer of *The Federalist*," who nonetheless identified the chief weakness of the Constitution of 1789: the inability of its institutions to prevent the rise of majority tyranny.[2] In particular, Kraynak rightly maintains that according to Tocqueville, the presidency appears susceptible to popular passions and impotent in comparison to an overbearing legislative.[3] Consequently, Kraynak concludes that among Tocqueville's chief goals are "strengthening the federal judiciary and concentrating more power in the executive branch."[4] Kraynak's claim that Tocqueville is seeking judicial statesmen who might serve as "the ultimate 'executive' of the laws" is certainly correct; indeed, in Part One, at least, the future of America seems to depend largely on the virtue and judgment of the federal judiciary.[5] It is striking, however, that Tocqueville never places such high hopes in the presidency: although he concedes "executive power plays . . . a great role in the destiny of nations," he remains deeply ambivalent about the institution.[6] While he criticizes the weaknesses of the American executive, Tocqueville refrains from recommending an increase in the power of an office that he describes elsewhere as possessing "almost royal prerogatives."[7] Thus, Kraynak's contention that Tocqueville argues for a stronger president is not persuasive.[8] Also unsatisfactory is Hugh Brogan's assertion that "Tocqueville blundered" by describing the presidency as weak: Brogan maintains that Tocqueville misunderstood President Jackson's important role as the leader of a national majority party and a proponent of stronger executive power.[9] As this chapter will demonstrate, Tocqueville does not view the presidency as weak, simply, and he certainly is not unaware of the popular support that a president may garner—instead, he appears wary of this ability. Indeed, Tocqueville's ambivalent view of the executive is due partly to his negative appraisal of Jackson; in his judgment, a Jacksonian president who was responsible for managing great international affairs would constitute a grave danger to the institutional balance that the Constitution seeks to achieve. Thus, Jackson's strength, and not his weakness, reveals the potential dangers of executive power in America. Much of the Tocqueville scholarship resembles Kraynak's and Brogan's, insofar as it does not capture adequately Tocqueville's profound ambivalence concerning the American executive. This chapter intends to make sense of Tocqueville's presentation by comparing his views to federalist and anti-federalist opinions of the presidency.

The Presidency at the Founding: Federalist and Anti-federalist Opinion

The *Federalist* papers suggest that if the legislative supremacy enshrined in the Constitution is born of republican political principles, then the executive is crucial to political practice; in Publius' view, the executive was necessary to supply the defects of power and judgment observed even in a properly constituted legislature.[10] The failure of the Articles of Confederation, which provided for no strong executive power, also informed this judgment. Although anti-federalist opinion varies significantly, anti-federalists were generally suspicious of this proposed institution. While some of the more radical anti-federalists maintained that legislatures could and should properly exercise executive power, most objected only to certain features of the American presidency: the length of term, the eligibility for reelection, the power of appointment, and the establishment of the electoral college, were among the most common complaints about the executive created by Article II of the Constitution. What follows is a brief survey of federalist and anti-federalist arguments concerning the proposed American executive.

In part because the founders maintain that "the accumulation of all powers, legislative, executive, and judiciary, in the same hands . . . may justly be pronounced the very definition of tyranny," they contrive to establish an independent executive.[11] Sensitive to republican fears of executive power, Publius insists that the president's powers are consistent with most of the powers accorded to many of the state governors.[12] Nonetheless, in comparison to state governors at the time, the powers granted to the national executive are expansive: he possesses a qualified veto, may appoint his subordinate officials, is commander-in-chief of the armed forces, is supreme executor of the law, and is charged with the powers to conclude treaties and manage diplomatic relations, which are to be exercised with the "advice and consent of the Senate."[13] The president is granted such extensive powers because the founders regard the creation of a "vigorous Executive" as crucial to a free republic.[14]

> It is essential to the protection of the community against foreign attacks; it is not less essential to the steady administration of the laws; to the protection of property against those irregular and high-handed combinations which sometimes interrupt the ordinary course of justice; to the security of liberty against the enterprises and assaults of ambition, of faction, and of anarchy.[15]

To ease the fears that this powerful institution would incite in republican America, Publius reminds his audience repeatedly that the executive is ultimately controlled by Congress. He rejects the suggestion that the executive be "sacred."[16] In addition to the Senate's duty to offer advice and consent to the president in foreign policy and approve most executive appointments, Congress has the power to impeach and convict the president for high crimes and misdemeanors.

Congress also retains control over the formation, dissolution, and funding of the national army. The president's veto offers the executive some legislative power, but even that power is qualified. In short, Publius argues that the Constitution aims to give presidents with tyrannical aspirations little means to accomplish their schemes. In comparison to the Congress's powers, the president's constitutional defenses are meager.[17]

To strengthen the presidency against a powerful Congress, Publius recommends a four-year term of office. This term, longer than the terms of governors under the original state constitutions, would help the president's efforts to oppose injudicious congressional measures, and would promote good governance.[18] Publius also considers the re-eligibility of the president to be essential to stability. He views this stability in three ways: first, the reelection of a competent president would help ensure stability in the nation's most vital policies; second, re-eligibility would encourage the ambitious to pursue grand projects; and third, re-eligibility would deter the ambitious from usurpation by slaking their thirst for fame, which Publius deems "the ruling passion of the noblest minds."[19] Finally, the contrivance of an electoral college would accomplish the desire of all modern republics: orderly elections that express the national will, but are insulated from the violence and passion of direct elections.

Despite Publius' arguments, most anti-federalists deemed this executive power unsafe. Some argued for the creation of an executive council that would decentralize executive power and prevent the growth of a monarchical prerogative, but they were a minority: most conceded the necessity of a single executive; they agreed with Publius' argument that a plural executive would increase intrigue and decrease effectiveness. Nonetheless, anti-federalists believed that the presidency was too powerful. First, almost all anti-federalists objected to the president's power of appointment. They thought Congress should appoint certain important positions (for example, Treasurer) and predicted that this executive power would lead to the establishment of a quasi-royal court, replete with flatterers and intriguers.[20] They also feared the power of appointment would be used "to multiply officers in every department: judges, collectors, taxgatherers, excisemen and the whole host of revenue officers will swarm over the land, devouring the hard earnings of the industrious. Like the locusts of old, impoverishing and desolating all before them."[21]

Second, anti-federalists objected to the term of the executive. Most of them deemed it too long, and viewed the president's eligibility for reelection as profoundly dangerous. Cato comments that "great power in the hands of a magistrate . . . with considerable duration, may be dangerous to the liberties of a republic," and opines that if the country is to have a single executive, he ought to be elected directly for a term of one year.[22] The Federal Farmer, by contrast, argues that the term be extended to seven years: this would "avoid instability in the execution of the laws . . . [but not be] so long as to enable him to take any measures to establish himself."[23] He nonetheless insists that reelection ought to be abandoned. Like most anti-federalists, he predicted that this provision would distract presidents from their constitutional duties, breed an un-republican attachment to the office of chief magistrate, and invite corruption—or even usurpation. Anti-federalists disagreed among themselves about the advisability of the Electoral College: while some considered it a necessary bulwark against tyranny and confusion, others decried it as a secret aristocratic cabal that would eventually subvert the republic.[24]

Finally, anti-federalists feared that the establishment of a standing army, combined with the president's power as commander-in chief, would lead America into wars abroad that would eventually destroy liberty at home. Many judged that Congress' power to fund armies and declare war was in unsustainable tension with the executive's unchallenged power to command the army. Patrick Henry predicts that an ambitious and corrupt president will employ his powers to place America under "absolute despotism."[25] How, then, do anti-federalists respond to Publius' assurance that only Congress may declare war? Cato notes that the King of Great Britain customarily consults parliament before declaring war, and yet this does not reduce the number of wars in which Great Britain is involved; as "generalissimo of the nation," he predicts that the American president would develop a similar relationship with Congress, regardless of the constitutional provisions that dictate otherwise.[26] The president will lead the nation into war, and Congress will follow dutifully.

Tocqueville's Treatment of the Executive in Part One of *Democracy in America*

Tocqueville discusses the presidency in his chapter on the Federal Constitution.[27] He evidently considers the subject important: he devotes more space to a discussion of it than any other federal institution. Even the crucially important federal judiciary, to which he devotes one-fifth of the chapter, receives less attention than the presidency. The following treatment will seek to clarify Tocqueville's answers to the following three questions: What is the institutional power of the presidency? How might the presidency's power increase over time? How do elections affect the presidency? This chapter will end with a consideration of the promise and perils of seeking democratic statesmanship in the president of the United States.

Institutional Powers of the President

Much of Tocqueville's presentation in this chapter relies on *The Federalist*, a book he judges "ought to be familiar to statesmen of every country."[28] Following Publius, Tocqueville describes the difficulty of creating a powerful and independent presidency that can correct the error and caprice of the majority but is not fatal to majority rule. He considers the institutional independence of the federal executive an improvement upon the relatively weak gubernatorial powers found in state constitutions: a four-year term, the qualified veto, and the lack of a presidential council all conduce to relative executive independence.[29] Nonetheless, Tocqueville concedes that Congress would be able to overcome the president in an ultimate contest of constitutional powers. He implies, however, that only a corrupted people would permit this to happen.[30] The demise of the independent presidency would thus be synonymous with the moral decline of America, and the triumph of the cruder democratic mores of majority tyranny.

Tocqueville finds the presidency of 1830 to be much as Publius described it: a relatively circumscribed power in American national politics. In *Federalist* 68 and 69, especially, Publius argues that the president rarely will act alone: instead, he must gain the support of Congress (especially the Senate) to execute any major change in American policy.[31] Tocqueville agrees with this assessment. Unlike Publius, however—who offers this argument to assuage fears of an overbearing executive power—Tocqueville considers the presidency's weakness a significant defect. The president, writes Tocqueville, cannot make laws, and he must execute them; he may be removed from office by Congress and remains ultimately accountable to the people; if he does not command a majority in Congress, he may nonetheless remain in office—a sure sign, in Tocqueville's estimation, of the relative insignificance of the office.[32] Even in the sphere in which a president may act—for example, to name his cabinet or conclude treaties—he must seek the advice and consent of the Senate. Tocqueville adds that the small number of civil servants who currently serve at the pleasure of the president is another indication of his weakness, especially in comparison to European monarchs, who command vast administrative systems populated by political supporters. The president, concludes Tocqueville, is "an inferior and dependent power" in relation to Congress.[33] The main consequence of this weakness is that the presidency is not an adequate check on the passions of the majority. In *Federalist* 70, Publius assures his readers that the unitary executive is most necessary as a bulwark against the bias, passion, and schemes of oppression that arise in republican governments.[34] Tocqueville doubts the ability of the presidency to perform these laudable functions. Tocqueville's presentation thus highlights a tension in Publius' (admittedly political) presentation: is the executive to be restrained and superintended by Congress (as *Federalist* 68 and 69 indicate), or will it possess the prerogative to act forcefully and independently of Congress (as *Federalist* 70 through 74 imply)?[35]

Nonetheless, while Tocqueville may identify the institutional weakness of the presidency, he never suggests that the Constitution be revised to grant it greater independence. Instead, Tocqueville implies that republican governments will always struggle to create effective and independent executives. While all republics require the prudence and decision of a single man, "[m]aintenance of the republican form require[s] that the representative of the executive power be subject to the national will."[36] Earlier, Tocqueville argued that due the fear of tyrants, American political judgment had one "principal goal": to maintain the ability to remove from office those who abuse power.[37] Any proposal that would make the executive truly independent would be fatal to this principle; hence, the constitutional provisions that allow Congress to impeach and convict a president are quintessentially American. While hereditary constitutional monarchs enjoy greater independence, democratic America—as described in detail earlier in the book—could not tolerate such an office. Tocqueville thus concludes, "dependence of the executive power is one of the vices inherent in republican constitutions. The Americans were not able to destroy the inclination that brings legislative assemblies to take hold of the government, but they rendered this inclination less irresistible."[38] The role of executive power in a republic is always problematic. When one considers the intractability of this problem, the American executive appears an impressive contrivance. The American founders may not have created an executive of sufficient independence to ensure good governance, but they were as successful as democratic conditions allowed.

Tocqueville's arguments in favor of an independent executive (as far as one is possible, in a democratic government) contradict many of the arguments advanced by the anti-federalists. In particular, Tocqueville's insistence that the presidency is too weak to oppose the majority contradicts the predictions of Cato and Patrick Henry, who imagine an absolutist European court rising from the swamps of Washington, D.C. Indeed, Tocqueville also seems to reject their understanding of monarchs: he insists that public opinion serves as a "directing power" over even monarchs.[39] The most prominent difference between France and America, then, is that American public opinion directs the government by elections, rather than revolution.[40] This claim is perfectly consistent with Tocqueville's central claim that "a great democratic revolution is taking place among us," evident even within the monarchies of Europe.[41] Legislators who arrange governments to thwart absolutist tyrants are wrestling with ghosts.

The Potential Increase of Presidential Power

While the thrust of Tocqueville's argument is that the executive is too weak to resist the determined will of the majority, he does offer a scenario in which the executive becomes the preponderant power of American politics in a section entitled "Accidental Causes That Can Increase the Influence of the Executive Power."[42] Though brief, the observations in this section alter significantly Tocqueville's presentation. While generally he claims that the laws of America circumscribe presidential authority, here he reasons that "[i]f the executive power is less strong in America than in France, one must attribute the cause of it perhaps more to circumstances than laws."[43] What are these circumstances, and how might they change? Tocqueville begins by observing that the executive power of any country, including America, is most free when conducting foreign relations. He then comments on the current isolation of the United States: it has a small army and an even smaller navy; it has no powerful neighbors; it exhibits little desire to engage in foreign relations, and is not possessed by a lust for conquest. According to Tocqueville, these idyllic conditions cannot last. War must eventually visit America's shores and alter its government: "[t]his makes one see well that the practice of government must not be judged by the theory."[44] This general teaching seems to qualify Tocqueville's earlier consideration of the presidency, which appears now to have been insufficiently practical, insofar as it did not consider the effect of war on the constitutional arrangement. Does this imply that Publius' arguments are also defective? When Tocqueville introduces the necessity of war, his description of the presidency certainly departs sharply from Publius' own: "[t]he president of the United States possesses almost royal prerogatives, which he has no occasion to make use of, and the rights which, up to now, he can use are very circumscribed: the laws permit him to be strong, circumstances keep him weak."[45] Tocqueville thus foresees that presidential power will increase as America begins to engage other nations; amazingly, he even predicts the location of the first American war of expansion: Mexico.[46] As further confirmation of Tocqueville's oracular ability, history confirms that war was instigated by the actions of an imperious president, acting with a dubious congressional mandate.[47]

What can we learn from this aspect of Tocqueville's consideration of the presidency? First, he rejects flatly the radical anti-federalist claim that America does not require a single, vigorous executive: in Tocqueville's opinion, anti-federalists could only argue this because America was isolated from the wider world. This condition could not last. If Cato's proposals had carried the day, America would have been conquered eventually—if it had been able to avoid majority tyranny. Second, Tocqueville's analysis suggests that the American legislators, like all legislators, have limited powers; although they attempted to combine a strong executive with republican governance, the preservation of that institutional arrangement—the Constitution—depended ultimately on events beyond their control: the vagaries of international relations. Tocqueville predicts, "If the life of the Union were constantly threatened, if its great interests were mixed every day with those of other powerful peoples, one would see the executive power grow larger in opinion, through what one would expect from it and what it would execute."[48] This observation vindicates anti-federalists like Cato, who viewed the president's role as commander-in-chief as a threat to the constitutional balance promised by Publius. Furthermore, U.S. history has vindicated both Cato and Tocqueville. Since World War II and the rise of permanent international security threats such as nuclear war and terrorism, the executive branch (and its enforcement arm, the bureaucracy) has steadily accumulated powers at the expense of Congress. This trend signals an erosion of legislative supremacy and popular sovereignty inconsistent with Publius' hopes for government and perfectly consistent with Cato's and Tocqueville's predictions. Of course, Tocqueville and Cato do not agree entirely. Based on these concerns, Cato, like many of the radical anti-federalists, argues for an executive that is administrative and subordinate to Congress, while Tocqueville reflects philosophically on the insolubility of the problem of executive power.

Hence it is that all peoples who have had to make great wars have been led almost despite themselves to increase the strength of the government. Those who have not been able to succeed at this have been conquered. A long war almost always places nations in this sad alternative: that their defeat delivers them to destruction and their triumph to despotism.[49]

It is likely that Tocqueville would accuse followers of Cato of thinking America safer in the hands of Charybdis rather than Scylla.

The Election of the President

Early in *Democracy in America,* Tocqueville explains that

[t]he presidency is a high magistracy that one can scarcely reach except at an advanced age; and when one arrives at other federal offices of an elevated rank, it is in a way haphazardly and after one has already become celebrated by following another career. Ambition cannot make them the permanent goal of its efforts.[50]

Nonetheless, Tocqueville concludes that the election and re-eligibility of the president strain the constitutional mechanisms of America and constitute a threat to the republican institutions of government.

The subject of elections is relevant to Tocqueville's earlier discussion of the increase in presidential power that will accompany war. As the executive grows more powerful, it will attract the ambitions of the unscrupulous and their supporters. Because the presidency is still relatively weak, "no one has yet been encountered who cares to risk his honor and his life to become . . . [president.] . . . Fortune has to put an immense prize in play for desperate players to present themselves in the lists."[51] Nonetheless, Tocqueville observes that even while the presidency is weak, its election disturbs significantly the execution of the office: the "lame duck" president is paralyzed by the knowledge that any project he begins is the political equivalent of a sandcastle and the president who is eligible for re-election becomes "absorbed by the care of defending himself. He no longer governs in the interest of the state, but in that of his reelection; he prostrates himself before the majority and often, instead of resisting its passions, as his duty obliges him to do, he runs to meet its caprices."[52]

The vitriolic campaigning undertaken by presidential candidates' supporters only increases the "feverish state" of election season.[53] Tocqueville explains that these partisans support their candidate for two principal reasons: many are desirous of a political appointment, but the party as a whole uses the president as a symbol of its political principles. They hope "to show by his election that [their] doctrines have acquired a majority."[54] In both cases, the partisans view the presidential candidate instrumentally. In democratic America, it is unlikely that any president will disappoint—or lead—the majority, especially if he entertains hopes of reelection. Tocqueville thus treats the presidency as inherently popular.

It is primarily a tool of the majority, and generally incapable of opposing its will. This interpretation departs significantly from that of both federalists and anti-federalists. The former hoped that the president would be able to oppose the unwise majority at crucial moments; the latter feared that the president would exercise arbitrary, kingly power. Tocqueville argues that they were both wrong: even if he steadily accumulates powers and prerogatives at the expense of Congress, the president will remain chained firmly to majority opinion.

Tocqueville concludes that because of the circumscribed powers of the president, America is spared—for now—from the worst effects of the elective presidency. When, however, the president's powers expand, presidential elections will create a "profound disturbance" that will endanger American security and domestic peace.[55] Even the Electoral College, which Tocqueville praises as prudent innovation, cannot ensure orderly elections. Given the dangers of this system, Tocqueville, like the Federal Farmer, expresses a reluctant preference for constitutional hereditary monarchies, which escape the dangers of election: still, Tocqueville does not recommend that future republics adopt such an institution, probably because unelected monarchs are incompatible with the dominant spirit of equality.[56] It seems that the perils attendant on the elective executive are permanent features of the democratic age.

If the American executive must be elective, and, therefore, must be beholden to the majority, how might America remedy the ill effects these conditions produce? Tocqueville's analysis suggests two possible innovations to the American system: the abandonment of the president's re-eligibility for election and civil service reform. Publius hoped the president would be able to prevent the worst tendencies of the majority, but Tocqueville observes that the possibility of reelection ensures that the presidency will be a "docile instrument in the hands of the majority. He loves what it loves, hates what it hates; he flies to meet its will, anticipate its complaints, bends to its least desires: the legislators want him to guide it, and he follows it."[57] He also rejects Publius' argument that reelection promotes stability and prosperity. Like the Federal Farmer, Tocqueville views an incumbent's role in elections as dangerous.[58] If a private citizen corrupts an election, it damages only his reputation. If, however, the executive does the same, he damages the entire government.

Tocqueville's rejection of reelection seems informed by an opinion expressed by the Federal Farmer, who opined "we may have, for the first president, and, perhaps, one in a century or two afterwards . . . a great and good man, governed by superior motives; but these are not events to be calculated upon in the present state of human nature."[59] By defending presidential reelection, did Publius exhibit too much faith in human nature? Given Publius' general argument, this is unlikely. Instead, he supports the reelection of the president because he, like Tocqueville, knows the office is crucial to sound political practice; therefore, he does not think it is advisable to prevent good men from serving indefinitely. Tocqueville judges that this decision was too risky. Even the twenty-second amendment, which established a two-term limit for a president, does not satisfy Tocqueville's complaints; indeed, it might breed greater corruption in an incumbent. More than ever before, reelection, rather than good works and steady administration, indicates a president's success; no one-term president of the modern era has been considered successful. Who knows what an ambitious incumbent might do to secure the reputation of a successful president? Tocqueville clearly foresees that such a man might descend to the pettiest criminal acts. By allowing the reelection of the president, Tocqueville concludes that the founders planted the "seed of death" in the American system.[60]

Tocqueville is also sharply critical of a new president's prerogative to replace federal officials with his political supporters. He contends that it conduces to governmental instability and produces thousands of hardened partisans who corrupt the public deliberation that occurs during presidential elections. While he is sympathetic to the notion that the president ought to be able to choose his most powerful agents, he expresses a qualified preference for the permanent civil services found in the monarchies of Europe. Although European bureaucracies can be aloof and obscure, they contribute mightily to the steady administration of government.[61] One might suggest here that America has answered these Tocquevillian objections by accomplishing civil service reform. Tocqueville would probably disagree. While the election of a new president no longer results in the replacement of the entire bureaucracy, the vast size of the modern bureaucracy means that the new president still appoints about 3,500 officials, many of whom work immediately to politicize the permanent bureaucracy.[62]

Moreover, the size of the modern bureaucracy would concern Tocqueville for another, more important, reason. Earlier, he commented that an indication of the American president's weakness was the relatively small size of the executive bureaucracy.[63] This condition also signaled the relative strength of republican mores: Congress generally dominated the national government and the people largely determined for themselves the course of everyday life.[64] Yet these conditions, as with so many found at the beginning of the American republic, were unlikely to last. Tocqueville judges that "no nations are more at risk of falling under the yoke of administrative centralization than those whose social state is democratic."[65] He explains that administrative centralization at first appears as a great boon to republican government, because it renders administration more orderly and effective; yet he warns that it will eventually "enervate the peoples who submit to it."[66] This observation prefigures Tocqueville's most dire warnings for the future of the democratic age: the rise of administrative despotism. In this scenario, the administrative and bureaucratic elements of the democracy grow gradually, eventually resulting in the development of

> an immense tutelary power . . . which alone takes charge of assuring their enjoyments and watching over their fate. It is absolute, detailed, regular, far-seeing, and mild. It would resemble paternal power if, like that, it had for its object to prepare men for manhood; but on the contrary, it seeks only to keep them fixed irrevocably in childhood; it likes citizens to enjoy themselves provided that they think only of enjoying themselves. It willingly works for their happiness; but it wants to be the unique agent and sole arbiter of that; it pro-

vides for their security, foresees and secures their needs, facilitates their pleasures, conducts their principal affairs, directs their industry, regulates their estates, divides their inheritances; can it not take away from them entirely the
trouble of thinking and the pain of living?[67]

Tocqueville thus summons an anti-federalist bogeyman. In their broadside
against the proposed constitution, the minority of the Pennsylvania Convention
predicts that the administrative institutions of the government will grow to a size
sufficient to smother liberty.[68] Although Tocqueville imagines that this power
will grow more slowly and be less harsh—and and yet, more insinuating—than
the anti-federalists imagine, they agree as to the principal effect of this power.
The rise of administrative despotism is identical with the extinction of liberty,
that quality that Tocqueville—and the anti-federalists—repeatedly identify as
crucial to the development of healthy and virtuous democracies. The growth of
an administrative system capable of this despotism is evident: in the twentieth
century, its growth has been due largely to the actions of presidents who have
been unconstrained during times of crisis.[69] It is apparent that the American
experience confirms Tocqueville's ambivalence concerning the American executive.

Conclusion: The American President and Democratic Statesmanship

In some ways, the Presidency would seem to offer democracy something crucial
to its flourishing: Tocqueville judges that the central task of democratic leaders
is

> to instruct democracy, if possible to reanimate its beliefs, to purify its mores, to
> regulate its movements, to substitute little by little the science of affairs for its
> inexperience, and knowledge of its true instincts for its blind instincts; to adapt
> its government to time and place; to modify it according to circumstances and
> men.[70]

Tocqueville is describing the task of a democratic statesman: one who is wiser
and more prudent than the majority, and can compensate for the democracy's
inclination to follow passion and ignorance. Because of his unique position in
the constitutional order and his potential independence in international affairs,
Tocqueville thinks the presidency is the only elective American institution that
could possess the flexibility and judgment necessary to this democratic statesmanship. As a laudable example, he cites George Washington's refusal to ally
with the French during his second term, despite overwhelming public support
for the alliance.[71] Yet, would the America that Tocqueville describes elect
Washington to the presidency? Would it tolerate a man who disdained party
politics and opposed the majority opinion? Would Washington willingly con-

descend to the office, as it existed in 1830? It seems likely that America is destined to elect to the presidency many Jacksonians and few—if any—Washingtonians.

While Tocqueville praises the presidency as a potentially helpful corrective to legislative error and excess, he also emphasizes—more explicitly than Publius ever does—that the presidency is likely to follow public opinion. In an educated and virtuous democracy, this tendency might contribute to an executive's resolution in confrontations with an overreaching Congress; in a corrupted democracy that bows reflexively to majority opinion, however, Tocqueville bluntly states the president will not oppose the majority. Virtue, and not constitutional innovation, is the only sure solution to the problem of executive power; a civic education that inculcates a healthy distrust of majority rule is thus most necessary to maintain an effective and independent executive. The difficulty of designing and implementing such an education only further complicates Tocqueville's estimation of the American executive.

Like Publius, Tocqueville repeatedly stresses that the executive remains compatible with republican mores because of its limited nature. However, unlike Publius, and like the anti-federalists, he also argues that the limited powers of the president in 1830 are largely a result of historical circumstance, and he predicts that the emergence of a more dangerous world will lead to the expansion of presidential power, which he characterizes as "almost royal prerogative" in theory.[72] Tocqueville views the expansion of executive powers in two ways. First, he concedes that a strong executive is necessary if a country wishes to conduct a successful foreign policy. Second, Tocqueville envisions how this growing executive power could easily endanger the republican spirit of liberty for which he praises early nineteenth century America. Thus, the flexibility of the American Presidency is simultaneously a great boon to good government and a great danger to the goods that government is to protect.

Perhaps most dangerous is the tendency of executive power to multiply bureaucracies. While Congress is capable of doing the same, executive bureaucracies are particularly pernicious to republican mores. The stultifying effects of administrative despotism, which Tocqueville views as the worst possible outcome for modern democracy, should lead us to consider the limits of presidential power. To what degree can any republic trust in a power that naturally creates institutions fatal to republican virtue? Finding a democratic statesman in the person of a single executive at the head of a massive bureaucracy appears very uncertain.

Tocqueville's opinion of the growth of executive power in democracies would seem to mirror Matthew's view of sin: "Woe unto the world because of strong executives! for it must needs be that such executives come; but woe to that republic by which the strong executive cometh!"[73] Executive power is a crucial feature of all political ages. The democratic age is unique because it inexorably works to undermine the traditional bases of executive power: hereditary right, divine sanction, and overwhelming force are illegitimate claims to power in the age of democracy. The modern democratic executive must instead rely on the will of the majority for his support. This fact makes it difficult for him to accomplish the customary work of executives: chief among these is opposing the baser instincts of the majority. Thus, the modern democratic executive is unlikely to subvert democracy; instead, he is much more likely to hasten its descent into corruption.

Tocqueville teaches us that the American president is unlikely to be a democratic statesman. His consideration of the presidency suggests that while democratization has resulted in an increase in human freedom, material progress, and domestic peace, the revolution in government has created new and difficult problems for the modern legislator. The problematic status of executive power is perhaps the most salient—and the most troubling.

Notes

1. I am grateful for the helpful comments offered by Brian Danoff and Joe Hebert.

2. Robert Kraynak, "Tocqueville's Constitutionalism," *The American Political Science Review* 81, no. 4 (1987), 1187.

3. Ibid., 1187.

4. Ibid., 1190.

5. Ibid., 1192.

6. Alexis de Tocqueville, *Democracy in America*, ed. and trans. Harvey C. Mansfield and Delba Winthrop (Chicago: University of Chicago Press, 2000), I.I.8, 115.

7. *Democracy*, I.I.8, 119.

8. Kraynak seems aware of the problematic character of this argument, writing guardedly: "Tocqueville makes a similar though less conclusive argument in recommending a stronger executive." See "Constitutionalism," 1192.

9. Hugh Brogan, "Tocqueville and the American Presidency," *Journal of American Studies* 15, no. 3 (1981), 365.

10. Portions of this part of the chapter appeared originally in William B. Parsons, Jr., "Thomas Paine's Problematic (and Prescient) Critique of the American Constitutional Arrangement" (Paper presented at the annual meeting of the Midwestern Political Science Association Conference, Chicago, IL, April 2009).

11. Alexander Hamilton. "*Federalist* 47," in *The Federalist,* ed. John C. Hamilton (Washington: Regenry Press, 1998), 373-374.

12. According to Publius, the power that most clearly distinguishes the president from the governor of New York is the "concurrent authority of the president in the article of treaties." *Federalist* 69, 520.

13. *Federalist* 69, 519.

14. *Federalist* 70, 522.

15. *Federalist* 70, 522.

16. *Federalist* 69, 514.

17. *Federalist* 69, 513-521.

18. *Federalist* 71, 536. The original state constitutions may be viewed at The Avalon Project: Documents in Law, History, and Diplomacy, "18th Century Documents: 1700–1799," Avalon Project, http://avalon.law.yale.edu/subject_menus/18th.asp.

19. *Federalist* 72, 540.

20. Cato, "Cato No. 4," in *The Essential Federalist and Anti-Federalist Papers,* ed. David Wootton (Indianapolis: Hackett, 2003), 59.

21. "The Address of the Minority of the Pennsylvania Convention," in *The Essential Federalist and Anti-Federalist Papers*, ed. David Wootton (Indianapolis: Hackett, 2003), 24.

22. *Cato* No. 4, 59.

23. Federal Farmer. "Federal Farmer XIV," in *Classics of American Political and Constitutional Thought*, eds. Scott J. Hammond et al. (Indianapolis: Hackett, 2007), 563.

24. See *Federal Farmer* XIV and *Cato* no. 4, respectively, for these opinions.

25. Patrick Henry, "Speech of Patrick Henry before the Virginia Ratifying Convention," in *The Essential Federalist and Anti-Federalist Papers*, ed. David Wootton (Indianapolis: Hackett, 2003), 38.

26. *Cato* No. 4, 61.

27. *Democracy*, I.I.8, 105-161.

28. Ibid.,, 108, fn. 8.

29. Ibid., 114. Tocqueville apparently disagrees with Publius, who claims hyperbolically in *Federalist* 69 that the governor of New York is almost equal in power to the American president.

30. Ibid., 115.

31. *Federalist* 68 and 69, 508-521.

32. *Democracy*, I.I.8, 119-120.

33. Ibid., 117.

34. *Federalist* 70, 522.

35. One could argue, of course, that the actions of the president described in *Federalist* 70 are to be pursuant to the laws of the United States, and therefore do not amount to the exercise of genuine prerogative. Given the broad language of Article II of the U.S. Constitution, however, I am not persuaded by this interpretation.

36. *Democracy*, I.I.8, 114.

37. *Democracy* I.I.7, 102.

38. Ibid., 114.

39. Ibid., 116.

40. Ibid., 116.

41. Ibid., 3.

42. Ibid., 118-119.

43. Ibid., 118.

44. Ibid., 118.

45. Ibid., 119.

46. Ibid., 160.

47. Daniel Walker Howe, *What Hath God Wrought: The Transformation of America, 1815-1848* (Oxford: Oxford University Press, 2007), 740-743. The president in question is James K. Polk.

48. *Democracy* I.I.8, 118.

49. Ibid., 159.

50. *Democracy* I.I.5, 64.

51. *Democracy* I.I.8., 121.

52. Ibid., 127.

53. Ibid., 127.

54. Ibid., 127.

55. Ibid., 122.

56. *Democracy* "Introduction," 3. That the staunchly republican Federal Farmer entertains the creation of a hereditary monarchy is indicative of how dimly he viewed the proposed presidency. He writes: "On the whole, it would be, in my opinion, almost as well to create a limited monarchy at once, and give some family permanent power and interest in the community, and let it have something valuable to itself to lose in convulsions in the state, and in attempts of usurpation, as to make a first magistrate eligible for life, and to create hopes and expectations in him and his family, of obtaining what they have not. In the latter case, we actually tempt them to disturb the state, to foment struggles and contests, by laying before them the flattering prospect of gaining much in them without risking any thing." *Federal Farmer* XIV, 564.

57. *Democracy* I.I.8, 130.

58. *Federal Farmer* XIV, 563-564.

59. *Federal Farmer* XIV, 564.

60. *Democracy* I.I.8, 129.

61. Ibid., 123.

62. David E. Lewis, *The Politics of Presidential Appointments: Political Control and Bureaucratic Performance* (Princeton: Princeton University Press, 2008), 100, figure 4.3.

63. *Democracy* I.I.5, 118.

64. Ibid., 91.

65. Ibid., 91.

66. Ibid., 83.

67. *Democracy* II.4.6, 663.

68. "The Address of the Minority of the Pennsylvania Convention," 24. See the minority quoted above, on page 6.

69. Richard E. Neustadt, *Presidential Power and the Modern Presidents: The Politics of Leadership from Roosevelt to Reagan* (New York: Simon and Schuster, 1991).

70. *Democracy,* "Introduction," 7.

71. *Democracy* II.V.15, 218-219. I am indebted to Brian Danoff, whose invaluable commentary on this section of the chapter benefitted me greatly.

72. *Democracy* I.I.8, 119.

73. The original passage is Matthew 18:7.

Chapter 8

Changing the People, Not Simply the President: The Limitations and Possibilities of the Obama Presidency, in Tocquevillian Perspective

Thad Williamson

Attempting to elucidate what precisely Alexis de Tocqueville would have made of either Barack Obama the politician or the astonishing political phenomenon that swept the nation's first African-American president into office in 2008 is a fruitless endeavor. In *Democracy in America*, Tocqueville devotes relatively little attention to the presidency as an institution, and still less to the merits and accomplishments of particular presidents. In his account, what made American democracy unique and functional was neither its federalist institutional arrangements nor the virtues of its national leaders, but its culture of political participation in local democratic institutions. Tocqueville recognized the power of private pursuits, especially the pursuit of material gain, in American culture, and viewed political participation as a central mechanism for broadening the self-interest of Americans, to force them to temper individualistic tendencies with consideration of the good of the whole. The idea that the fate of the American republic could rest in the hands of an individual leader is not prominent in *Democracy*. Indeed, many of Tocqueville's observations about the presidency stress its weakness, especially vis-à-vis the force of public opinion.[1]

Yet if Tocqueville's likely assessment of Obama is necessarily shrouded, the view of many neo-Tocquevillian scholars and public intellectuals with a centrist or progressive bent is clear. Political scientists such as Robert Putnam excitedly praised Obama's candidacy and speculated that his election and the grassroots campaign he mobilized might represent a civic turning point, as well as an extraordinary breakthrough in America's racial history.[2] Political theorist Michael Sandel suggests in the final chapter of his recent treatise *Justice: What's the Right Thing to Do?* that Obama represents exactly the sort of "politics of moral engagement" that has been missing in recent decades.[3] By marrying social concern and a commitment to using public power on behalf of public purposes with talk about civic and personal obligation, Obama is a potent example of what contemporary civic republicanism (in Sandel's view) should look like.

As I show later in this essay, the description of Obama as a latter-day civic republican, not a conventional liberal, is well grounded. The tougher question, however, is whether Obama's civic republicanism has teeth. In contrast to the optimistic interpretation of Obama's election offered by many progressive academics, consider the alternative view of Sheldon Wolin—a perspective that is itself strongly shaped by detailed engagement with Tocqueville's work. In Wolin's view, American democracy has deteriorated beyond recognition from the culture of participatory local engagement Tocqueville describes. Instead, the American political system can be best described as a corporate-dominated state with policies more befitting an oligarchy than a democracy, combined with a worldwide military empire. The role of citizens in this system is fundamentally passive, and "politics" has become circumscribed to increasingly narrow choices between different factions of the political elite. According to Wolin's diagnosis, it will be no surprise if Obama, despite the fanfare attached to his election, is not able to move the status quo very far—or if he himself transforms from a quasi-oppositional figure into essentially a representative of the institutional status quo.[4]

This essay argues that while Wolin's diagnosis of American democracy is largely accurate, his unrelentingly pessimistic assessment of what Obama might accomplish is overstated (or at least premature). Here I argue that Stephen Elkin's proposals for reconstructing a "post-Madisonian" commercial republic offer a fruitful way for thinking about how a president like Obama might take meaningful steps to re-shape the long-term political culture of the United States—particularly by (following Tocqueville) restoring attention to the importance of local politics and local political participation.[5] In short, insofar as Obama aspires to be a statesman who does not simply deal with immediate crises but who helps redefine the meaning and practice of American democracy, he needs to have an accurate assessment of the institutional and political obstacles to change, and an imaginative response aimed at re-establishing a political culture based on informed, active citizens taking political responsibility for the society in which they live.

We begin by spelling out what neo-Tocquevillians found attractive about Obama's candidacy in 2008. Obama, from the outset, framed his campaign as a social movement, and continuously claimed that his candidacy was not about him personally but about "ordinary Americans" (i.e., his supporters) becoming mobilized on behalf of "change." Empowerment of those who participated in the campaign was stated as an explicit goal. As noted above, Obama's candidacy can be accurately described as an experiment in what I (following Michael Sandel) term "civic republicanism"—a public philosophy that puts primary emphasis on our shared identity, shared responsibilities and shared obligations as citizens involved in a common project of building a just, democratic society.[6]

Civic republicanism, so understood, can be distinguished from approaches to politics that either a) view politics as primarily a vehicle by which one advances or defends one's self-interest, narrowly construed or b) view politics simply as a mechanism for determining how different goods such as income and jobs are to be allocated. Rather, civic republicanism involves a) a deliberate effort to appeal to citizens' wider interests—such as the interest we have in living in a community with certain moral qualities; b) calls for citizens to themselves become directly engaged in addressing matters of shared, public concern; and c) rehabilitating the idea of using public power to undertake bold public action to redress public problems and advance a wider public interest.

Obama's distinctive civic republican themes can be brought out by comparing his campaign themes to those of first Hillary Clinton, and then John McCain. Hillary Clinton ran a primary campaign oriented around her promise to "fight for you"—that is, to be an effective advocate of working class Americans on fundamental economic issues. The basis for this claim was both Hillary's own policy positions and the record of Bill Clinton's administration on economic growth and job creation. The claim that American politics is fundamentally broken was not a central theme of Hillary's campaign; nor did she attempt to offer big-picture thinking or engage in public philosophizing about controversial issues. Rather, she staked her candidacy on the claims that she could best serve as a "champion" of middle and working class voters' interests, and that she had the experience and tenacity to fight and win against those who would thwart those interests. "I'm in this race to fight for you, to fight for everyone who has ever been counted out, for everyone fighting to pay the grocery bills or the medical bills, the credit card and mortgage payments, and the outrageous price of gas at the pump today," Clinton told a Pennsylvania audience in April 2008. "You know you can count on me to stand up strong for you every single day in the White House."[7]

John McCain's campaign primarily focused on his own narrative as a former prisoner-of-war, as a conservative capable of taking independent stands, and as an expert on national security matters. But his domestic policy, such as it was, consisted of, first, claims that his policies would not raise taxes, and second, critiques of Obama's policy ideas as redistributive and "socialist." McCain in effect appealed to self-interest of middle class voters in keeping what they have.

In contrast, Obama repeatedly portrayed his candidacy as a collective effort to work *with* supporters, first to win the nomination and subsequent general election, and then to convert that grassroots mobilization into an effort to change the status quo in Washington. Obama talked about foreign policy failures and about serious economic problems, but linked these not just to the policies of George W. Bush but to broader problems in the American polity: excessive influence of powerful corporate interests, citizen disengagement, disregard for the public sphere, timid leadership. Frequently he intimated that these problems ran deeper than the rule of any one party. Further, he demonstrated a willingness (and capacity) to model more ambitious, public-minded leadership by directly addressing the role of race and religion in American politics and American life more generally, at considerable risk to his own candidacy.

Crucially, these high-minded words were matched by a potent grassroots mobilization effort that lent substance to the claim that the candidacy represented a movement of citizens acting on their own behalf, using the vehicle of a campaign to advance shared interests. The campaign did not just send professional staffers and recently hired college kids out into communities. Rather, they used the staffers as leverage to bring hundreds of thousands of campaign volunteers aboard, many of whom obtained locally significant roles, such as "precinct block captain" or head of phone banking and data entry. On Election Day, the Obama campaign in swing states implemented an elaborate Get Out the Vote operation—"Project Houdini"—which involved two to three poll watchers in each precinct documenting from six a.m. who had voted, then passing that information to campaign workers at mid-morning and then early afternoon. That information was quickly entered into computer databases to generate a new, targeted phone list for volunteer phone-callers and door-knockers to contact in the waning hours of Election Day. The object was to contact all expected supporters who had yet to vote as efficiently as possible.

Needless to say, such a labor-intensive operation would have been impossible without the presence of thousands of highly-motivated volunteers. That operation was unquestionably the margin of victory in formerly solid Republican states that Obama won, especially Virginia and North Carolina. In the heavily Democratic city of Richmond, Virginia, turnout spiked to roughly ninety-three thousand voters, nearly a 25 percent increase over 2004. Equally important, the campaign was an unusual example of a multi-racial, multi-generational political effort; in the Richmond area alone, hundreds of volunteers devoted time around the clock to the campaign, particularly in the final three months. For many volunteers, the election felt like a triumph that they had made happen, in a tangible way.[8]

Indeed, the Obama campaign did delegate remarkable responsibility and autonomy to grassroots-level volunteers. The campaign deliberately adopted a community organizing model emphasizing the training of local-level leaders who acquire both responsibility and practical capabilities over the course of the campaign.[9] During the primaries, the Obama campaign was often understood by its supporters to be a challenge to the dominant apparatus of the Democratic Party, an effort to take down the presumed all-powerful Clinton political machine. In the general election, the same rhetorical stance held as the target shifted; the general election campaign was understood by its most active supporters as both an effort to unseat the (much-feared) Republican Party and as a historic effort by the citizenry to re-shape the direction of the nation. Equally significant from a Tocquevillian perspective, grassroots participation in the campaign—nationwide—was dramatically larger and in many ways more so-phisticated than previous efforts by either party in the modern era.

Many supporters expected that the energy and high level of engagement characteristic of the campaign would carry over into Obama's presidency. At times during the campaign Obama seemed to promise a new mode of gover-nance, in which the president would directly ally with mobilized citizens to chal-lenge vested special interests and achieve meaningful shifts in policy. In some respects, this was a typical "outsider," anti-Washington message, but the notion that the outburst of civic energy seen during the 2008 campaign could be sus-tained, even institutionalized, as a potent force in the legislative process was a bold, albeit implicit claim. The route to change, Obama stated in one campaign stop just before the breakthrough Iowa caucuses, would involve "imagining, and then fighting for, and then working for, what did not seem possible before."[10] Obama's frequent statements that the campaign "is not about me, it's about you" fit squarely with James McGregor Burns's conception of "transformational lea-dership" as involving an ongoing relationship between leaders and followers of mutual responsibility in pursuit of shared, morally relevant goals.[11]

Obama's Inaugural Address carried forward many of these themes. The address consisted not just of a promise to deliver specific material goods and reforms (jobs, health care reform, energy independence) but a call to change what kind of country the United States is. On several occasions the speech chal-lenged Americans to be more engaged in their communities and less preoccu-pied with material pursuits and entertainment. "[G]reatness is never a given. It must be earned. Our journey has never been one of short-cuts or settling for less. It has not been the path for the faint-hearted, for those that prefer leisure over work, or seek only the pleasures of riches and fame." Equally important, Obama critiqued America's civic condition, including "our collective failure to make hard choices and prepare the nation for a new age"; Obama later added "our time of standing pat, of protecting narrow interests and putting off unpleasant decisions—that time has surely passed." Obama made a call for reinvigorated citizenship the punch line of the address: "What is required of us now is a new era of responsibility—a recognition on the part of every American that we have duties to ourselves, our nation and the world; duties that we do not grudgingly accept, but rather seize gladly, firm in the knowledge that there is nothing so satisfying to the spirit, so defining of our character than giving our all to a diffi-cult task. This is the price and the promise of citizenship."[12]

The tough question, of course, is what exactly this means in practice. Win-ning elections with attractive promises to reinvigorate the practice of democra-cy, and actually translating that promise into a mode of governance that tangibly shifts not just what gets done but how it gets done, are two different things. The latter aim, changing governance, in Obama's first year proved much more diffi-cult—sufficiently difficult to invite cynicism, both on the left and the right, about Obama's campaign promises to deliver "change we can believe in."

At the heart of this difficulty is the ambiguity inherent in the phrase "change we can believe in." What does this actually mean? One conception focuses primarily on policy changes and delivering promised shifts of direction on a wide array of issues, from jobs to energy policy to climate change. Success on major policy initiatives generally requires winning favorable legislation, and that in turn means making the system work: shepherding through Congress acceptable bills that meaningfully shift policy. The track record of Democratic presidents passing large-scale social and economic legislation in the decades since the New Deal generally is not impressive, but (like Hillary Clinton) Obama made it abundantly clear that he intended to deliver a new era of public policy activism, led by government, aimed at addressing concrete, tangible problems. Indeed, some serious analysts believed that with the severity of the financial crisis, a New Deal-type programmatic initiative might have been a viable political possibility at the beginning of 2009. Obama did not declare a new New Deal, but he did seek dramatic action on several policy fronts simultaneously.[13]

Note however that the commitment to an ambitious legislative agenda subtly, and perhaps necessarily, stands in tension with Obama's campaign criticisms of Washington politics-as-usual. By defining "change" as legislative success, the Obama administration essentially committed to a form of this statement: "The American political system is broken, but it is not so broken that my Administration, along with my good friends in Congress, cannot fix it. The system can be made to work, and we are the ones to do just that." Why should anyone have believed that the administration was capable of delivering on such a bold claim? The popularity of the president during his honeymoon phase, his communication skills in speaking directly to the public, the solid majorities in each hall of Congress (including for seven months, a sixty-vote majority in the Senate), the seeming disarray of the Republican opposition, and the severity of the problems themselves all made large-scale domestic legislation seem quite possible to many observers at the start of 2009. Further, Obama would bring to the table something no other president had ever had: an infrastructure to convert his campaign operations into a mobilizing tool for generating grassroots engagement on behalf of his legislative agenda, including a vaunted thirteen million name email list and a new organization, Organizing for America, headed by campaign strategist David Plouffe. Obama thus would not be left to make generalized bully pulpit appeals calling for citizen pressure on Congress to pass his agenda; instead, he would have a direct mechanism to communicate with those most likely to take such action. In this manner, Obama might be able to introduce a new form of governance marrying presidential charisma and top-down strategic direction with the ability to mobilize—over and over—millions of committed citizens to impact legislative debates. This would provide a solution to both legislative gridlock and the persistent, disproportionate influence of special interests: large-scale citizen pressure demanding change.

This narrative—at least for a moment—persuaded many sober people that Obama's election did not just represent a transformative *event*—an episode of what Wolin would term "fugitive democracy"—but potentially heralded a transformation in American politics itself. Yet while Obama has certainly shifted policy in numerous areas, and tackled a mind-bogglingly large number of complex issues, all at the same time, it would be highly implausible to claim that the Obama era has substantially altered the relationship of ordinary Americans to the legislative process or the federal government more generally. In particular, the attractive notion of highly mobilized citizens placing sufficient pressure on Congress to neutralize the influence of the health care industry and pass a health reform bill that significantly challenged the interests of the insurance industry never came to fruition in 2009.

Instead, Obama was faulted by many allies and supporters for not taking an aggressive enough role in the health care debate, allowing Congress to write the bill(s), waiting months before addressing the public with his views on the topic, and refusing to commit to clear guidelines as to the minimum content of an acceptable bill. The result was a bill widely regarded as an agreement to subsidize private health insurers to allow them to cover more people, with insufficient mechanisms in place to contain costs or provide consumers an alternative to the large insurance companies. At the same time, the bill inspired much more visible grassroots opposition than support; public opinion regarding the plan sank as the debate carried on, less because of the details of the plan (which few citizens seemed to understand) than because of the sheer fact that the horse trading and prolonged debate gave the opposition time to mount a variety of attacks, ranging from legitimate questions to blatant fear-mongering. The upset election of Scott Brown of Massachusetts to the Senate as the chamber's forty-first Republican in a January 2010 special election forced Obama to change tactics to get the bill passed. Eschewing any pretense of bipartisanship, Obama focused energy on getting House Democrats to approve the Senate's version of health reform in March 2010, with further amendments added through the budget reconciliation process. On its own terms, the leadership the president displayed in getting his own party on board and rescuing the health care bill was impressive, but the entire episode raises the question of whether Obama might have been able to deliver a better bill (including a "public option") had he pursued a less compromise-minded strategy from the start. Further, while the passage of the health bill indeed represented (to paraphrase Joe Biden) a big deal, the impact of the bill on Obama's political prospects remain at this writing highly uncertain.[14]

Meanwhile, unemployment continued to remain very high by historic standards with no obvious prospects for improvement in the near term, and no serious, large-scale plan forthcoming from the White House or the Democratic leadership as to how to attack that problem prior to the midterm elections. The February 2009 stimulus bill, Obama's first legislative triumph, proved to be large enough to invite criticism from the right but not large enough to make a visible dent in the fundamental economic trends; Obama advisers were reduced to the claim that the economy would have been much worse without the bill, a claim accurate enough on its own terms but not likely convincing to voters inclined to hold the president directly responsible for the state of the economy.

Perhaps most disturbing of all, Obama's economic team showed little inclination in its first year to challenge the prerogatives of powerful Wall Street firms, instead continuing the outgoing Bush administration's problematic strategy of bailing out favored financial firms on sweetheart terms.[15]

In short, feeling was widespread at the end of Obama's first year that his "moment" had passed and with it the opportunity to transform the tone and substance of American politics—if there ever was such an opportunity. In particular, the efforts of David Plouffe's Organizing for America (OFA) to influence legislative debate, by almost all accounts, had a marginal impact on Congressional behavior. Initial analyses of OFA by both political scientists and journalists point to several reasons why. First, the number of OFA email members who remained highly engaged was small; even if 130,000 members sent emails to their representative of Congress, this would represent just 1 percent of members (allowing Republicans to say—as they did—that even 99 percent of the president's base supporters were not all that fired up). Second, attempts to target House Republicans from districts carried by Obama in 2008 were ineffective both because of Republican party discipline and because such efforts invited a counter-response from conservative activists. Third, increased contacts with members of Congress via emails and phone calls generally has, whatever the quantity, only limited impact on positions taken by members. Fourth, OFA did not develop effective mechanisms by which members could not just contact Congress but attempt to shape local public opinion. Fifth, as the president made high-profile compromises on health care, the enthusiasm of some supporters waned, especially in the long summer months when visible presidential leadership seemed to be absent. Sixth, the OFA did not encourage members to target Democratic members of Congress (even those who put roadblocks in the way of health care reform) or to lobby for any particular version of health care reform; members were asked to simply lobby for passing a "health reform" bill they had no real role in shaping, and to target only Republicans.

In short, having direct email contact with supporters has to date proven far less valuable an asset in the work of governance than it was during the campaign. From a civic republican point of view, the OFA effort as presently constituted is inherently flawed as a mechanism for facilitating robust political engagement. First, the organization itself is not controlled by its members, but rather via top-down directives, with strategy controlled by close allies of the White House. Many OFA members likely would have favored campaigns targeting Blue Dog Democrats wavering in their support for Obama's legislative agenda, but (for understandable political reasons) Obama could not be seen as endorsing attacks on fellow Democrats. There is a place for being a loyal foot-soldier in an army controlled by someone else, faithfully donating money and signing petitions and calling Congress when an email arrives from David Plouffe, but such activity does not develop the independence of judgment a healthy civic republican political culture requires. Second, as argued by Peter Dreier and Marshall Ganz (Ganz was a key figure in shaping Obama's community organizing approach to the campaign), the OFA approach simply sets aside key elements of the social movement advocacy model that worked so well in the campaign: state a clear goal (i.e., what we want in a health care bill), name a clear opponent (the health care industry), and call not just for "polite" emails to legislators but for direct action and the full array of activist tactics to push Congress in the intended direction. OFA allowed itself to be tangled in the contradiction of *being* the power and at the same time trying to fight it; this contradiction in turn mirrored the tension between on one hand Obama's pledges to fight for needed changes (implicitly using an organizing model) and on the other hand his calls for bipartisan cooperation and more deliberative public debate as well as his (sincere) desire to be a unifying, not polarizing figure.[16] This critique of Obama's 2009 strategy argues that the community organizing model failed because it was not sufficiently tried, or tried only in a half-hearted way that failed to energize citizens and squandered the momentum generated during the election.[17]

But even if the effort had been more successful there is good reason to suspect that national politics is simply the wrong scale to expect sustained political activism to make a major difference on a regular basis, or to develop the distinctive civic virtues that come with experience in both dealing with those with whom one disagrees and in learning to make complex judgments about the public interest. It is a truncated civic republicanism indeed that reduces desirable political engagement to electronic communication and periodic face-to-face pressure on members of Congress. Put another way, at no point to date has the Obama administration attempted to connect the dots between what it means to support the president's broad goals and concrete steps that can be taken in support of those goals at the local level. Being a good citizen cannot simply mean communicating frequently with members of Congress and then hoping bills pass. Such a conception of citizenship leaves citizens without any *power* to directly affect or achieve social change. Rather than affect change directly, citizens are to *hope* (based on very uncertain evidence) that Washington will somehow respond to all the pressure, and if it does not, then try harder or hope the next charismatic president who comes along will do better. Obama has not been shy about telling students they must study, parents that they must put away the video games and read to kids, and young people in general that they should exercise personal responsibility. But how can or should residents act *within* their local communities—as *political* actors, not just as do-gooders—to support the broad vision of America Obama endorses? The answer to that question has remained very unclear, in large measure because there is no evidence it has been asked by either the White House or the Democratic Party leadership, including Organizing for America.[18]

There is some irony in the fact that Barack Obama, the former community organizer, has not called on the young or citizens more broadly to follow his example and make a serious commitment to bringing about social change at the local level, or make a serious effort to engage in local issues more generally. Perhaps this omission is because his own difficult Chicago experience persuaded

Obama that there really is not all the much that can be done at the local level in the absence of larger-order changes. Perhaps it is because inviting large-scale civic activism at the local level might unleash movements that the White House could not control or shape, with unpredictable consequences.[19] Or perhaps it is because Obama has not yet considered revising the implicit claim that *his* presidency and *his* administration can make Washington work, even though others could not.

Consider, now, an alternative formulation of what the slogan "change we can believe in" means. This formulation is delivered in the form of a short presidential speech, delivered some time in 2011.

Speaking from the Oval Office, President Barack Obama: Good evening. Washington, DC, is broken, and it is so broken that is beyond the capacity of my President or my Administration to fix all that is wrong with it. I knew this job was tough when I took it, but I didn't realize how tough. I may have overestimated my ability to get the things done that need to get done. I had and continue to have a responsibility to do the best I can given the powers invested in the President to address our urgent problems. I do not plan to waver in those efforts in the future. But I now recognize that those efforts alone are not enough to bring about the changes we need.

I can already hear what some of the pundits will say. They will compare tonight's speech to Jimmy Carter's "national malaise" speech of 1979. They will say that I am trying to mask my failure to deliver what I promised to deliver in my election campaign and in my Inaugural Address. I will admit that there have been leadership failures and things I could have done differently. But we will never have a president who does not make mistakes. More importantly, many of the failures have as their root cause not the actions or inactions of any particular person or leader, but institutions that no longer function in a way that allows us to act on the majority's shared interests—the promise of democracy—or to solve our urgent common problems—our imperative as a society.

Consider some of the institutional and political obstacles the pursuit of "change we can believe in" has encountered during my term of office to date.

First, the American political system is deliberately structured so as to frustrate significant legislative change. Unlike in a parliamentary system, it's no simple matter for the majority party, even if it controls the executive branch and Congress at the same time, to pass major legislation. Further, by Senate rules, a super-majority is needed to pass legislation, and because Senate elections are spaced out, it's unlikely that either party will ever have a sufficient majority to ram its own favored legislation through without being held hostage to the demands of individual senators. Even for that brief period in which my party's caucus had a super-majority in the Senate, the result was to allow individual Senators to hold up reform with their own demands, demands we could not easily ignore since we needed each and every vote.

Second, the Democratic Party, even when we enjoyed a comfortable majority in the House and Senate, is internally diverse, and far more ideologically diverse than the Republican Party. It includes many liberals, but also moderates and substantial number of moderate conservatives. My sometime friends the "Blue Dogs" have the capacity to torpedo social legislation, or to get it watered down in order to win approval for it. We Democrats have never been very big about practicing strong party discipline, or gung-ho about congressional leaders forcing recalcitrant members to vote for legislation.

Party discipline—that's what Republicans do, and that's why the Republicans are the third severe obstacle I have faced. The GOP is ideologically relatively homogenous with only a handful of members willing to support any legislation I sponsor or that might benefit me politically. I've got to hand it to them—no one does obstruction any better. I have had to learn the hard way that "bipartisanship" is not a realistic aim in this environment.

Fourth, political influence in the United States remains highly skewed towards powerful interest groups. Large-scale civic mobilization of voters on domestic legislation is not a regular feature of American politics, but corporate influence over both Republican and Democratic Administrations is assumed as a fact of life. When possible, I've tried to make an end run around that fact by making tactical alliances with particular corporate interests to help get bills passed, as when I met with Big Pharma to get their industry support for our health proposals. Those alliances, I understand, may have made some of my supporters less enthusiastic about fighting for my agenda. One thing I've learned though, is that while the passion and enthusiasm of voters for engagement waxes and wanes, the largest corporations and industries never take a day off from trying to advance their interests. I have to admit, I haven't quite figured out how to cope with this, but I'm just letting you know that this is a fact of life I have to deal with.

Of course, and this is my fifth point, it would be a whole lot easier to deal with if we have what my friends in Europe have, namely a strong and active labor movement. The labor movement has shown some resurgence in its ability to influence elections—they helped get me elected—but does not have a major influence on domestic legislation, even on its top priorities. So to all you union members out there, thanks for voting for me and for working for me, and for using your dues to try to get health care reform passed. I'm sure I will hit you up again next year. I'm sorry I couldn't help get labor law reform passed either—it would be great for me if I could help create more union members—but the votes just aren't there to do something real.

Sixth, I inherited a triple economic crisis. The first economic crisis is the current economic downturn of 2008 and the very high unemployment rate that has persisted throughout my term. The second is the decades-long trend in the United States towards growing inequality that has undermined long-term purchasing power of working Americans and made growth contingent on various financial bubbles. The third is the almost-as-long trend towards deregulation of financial markets in the United States, creating the possibility and then the reality of a major financial crisis. Since we finished with all the bailouts, there hasn't been a lot of money slushing around for new initiatives, even for job creation. And while I wish we could do more for the unemployed, the votes in Congress for a really big jobs program just aren't there, because so many of our fellow Americans are convinced that a bigger short-term deficit is worse than keeping unemployment around 10 percent for another year. My advisors and I decided it would be better to be hammered over high unemployment than to be hammered over not caring about "fiscal discipline."

Seventh, believe it or not, all my domestic initiatives are just a part-time job. I've got a worldwide military empire to run too, you know. I have gotten us almost all the way out of Iraq, and want to do the same with Afghanistan before long. But I can't just pack up all the army's equipment and tell them to go home. Well, technically I could but it would be political suicide—I cannot have the generals on my case or the elite newspaper columnists saying I "lack seriousness" or having Joe the Plumber saying I'm soft on terrorism. You voters don't have any real say over my war policy, and there's not much point in challenging the huge military budget—it is what it is. I ran for President claiming I had better judgment than McCain or Bush about the wisdom of Iraq, not that I shared the views of American peace activists. As I told my Scandinavian friends in Oslo back in 2009, while I want to be an enlightened realist in foreign affairs, I am a realist, and I'm not going to be dismantling our military-industrial complex.

Now I can hear what some of you may be saying. Some of you might be thinking that it's a good thing that our system is designed to frustrate change and that major reforms have to pass a high bar. Fair enough, but the specific nature of our system adds an additional bias against progressive reforms: residents of rural states are dramatically over-represented in the Senate, while residents of our biggest cities are under-represented. Others of you, especially my friends on the left, might think that however tough a hand I have had to play, I haven't played it as well as I might have. That's fair enough, too. But I'm here to tell you that those of you who expected me to be a miracle worker and succeed in delivering an adequate economic recovery plan, serious financial reform, a health care plan that provided a real alternative to the private insurers, and a serious energy and carbon reduction plan in this political climate just aren't being realistic. I'm doing the best I can to achieve these goals given some pretty significant constraints. I'm proud of what we've tried to do, but fully aware how far short we've fallen compared to what we set out to do and what needs to be done.

As we all know, the time cycle of American politics is quite short, with significant elections every two years. Sometimes it is possible to win political points for long-term diagnoses of the nation's civic condition, and I have done so in the past. But I have also learned that attempting to do anything substantial about it rarely does. What will drive my fate the most is the condition of the American economy, not the quality of our civic life. You know that, I know that and I will act accordingly between now and the election next year. As Tocqueville put it long ago, "It is impossible to observe the normal course of affairs in the United States without realizing that the wish to be re-elected dominates the President's thoughts and that all the policies of his administration are geared to this objective."[20] Tocqueville was right about that.

But let me make one more promise that hopefully you can believe in. Like the prison convict who wins his release from the parole board the day he stops claiming he's reformed, I have come to believe that leaders like myself can make the most valuable contribution to improving our political system when we stop pretending that we can fix it or that if you put me in office—even the highest one—I will become immune to its logic and limitations. If you re-elect me, the system will still be broken. I'll do what I can to get the urgent things that need to be done through the system, but I can't fix it. Let me turn to my old friend Tocqueville again to explain why. He wrote that "In America, the President"—that would be me—"exercises quite an influence upon state affairs but he does not direct them; the preponderant power resides in the representatives of the nation as a whole. You have, therefore, to change the people en masse, not simply the President, if you wish to alter the guiding political principles."[21] To me, what that is saying is that we have to pay attention to all the capillaries of power, not just the big heart muscles. Changing Presidents doesn't make that much difference if we don't also change the nature of our political culture, from bottom to top. I've been reading up on Tocqueville, and that's my conclusion. It really isn't all about me—it's about you and our shared civic culture.

What does it mean to say there's something wrong with our political culture? Let's go back to 2009 and let me try to explain once again why our health care efforts ran into such difficulty. It wasn't only because Martha Coakley blew the Massachusetts election, or because of Joe Lieberman, Rahm Emanuel, or anyone else you care to blame. Here's the deeper reason: the generally weak state of political mobilization in the United States, combined with the generally low level of political awareness and sophistication of the American public. All throughout 2007 and 2008 as I traveled the country campaigning for this job, voters told me how much they needed health care reform, how terrible the status quo is, how many people they knew whose lives had been disrupted by illnesses and injuries they weren't covered for. At the start of 2009, Americans in the abstract strongly supported fundamental changes in the health care system, including measures to expand coverage to the uninsured and to rein in rapidly spiraling costs.[22] All of us running for President in 2008 as Democrats supported one version or another of comprehensive reform, as did the general public. But we knew all along that health care reform would attract major ideological opposition from conservatives as well as many business interests.

As the legislative process dragged on throughout 2009, public support for my party's plan fell, in part due to sustained attacks on the plan launched by the Republicans and the substantial right-wing media machine that attracts many millions of listeners and viewers, day in and day out. (I wish I had a nickel for every time those radio guys had called me a Kenya-born socialist over the last three years.) Patently false claims about "death panels" and "subsidizing illegal aliens" came to be accepted by many people as factual accounts of what my "Obamacare" intended to do. They made it seem like my goal was to bankrupt as many small businesses as possible, force everyone to change their doctors, and have a government panel decide whether grandma really needs treatment anymore. The Tea Party movement launched a grassroots campaign intended to target Congressional representatives who favored the bill. Protests of town hall events sponsored by Congressmen in their constituencies had the precise aim of disrupting the ability of legislators to communicate the goals and fundamental mechanisms of the health care plan to voters.

To be sure, there was and is plenty of room for both principled and pragmatic disagreement with our health care reform plans. I went back and forth on some of the details myself a few times. The key point is not that the plan attracted some opposition—I don't expect everyone to agree with me—but the nature of the debate itself. Only rarely did it resemble well-structured deliberation between parties committed both to respecting one another as fellow citizens and seeking to judge the plan not in terms of its political ramifications but in terms of its capacity to further the public interest. Few Americans possessed sufficient knowledge of the plan and its details to have informed debate about its pros and cons. That's partly my fault—I should have explained it better—but it's partly your fault. You should be sophisticated enough to understand why every story about an affluent Canadian getting elective surgery in the United States does not mean their system is a disaster and ours is great. You should know the difference between arguing from systematic evidence and arguing by anecdote. You should also be capable of thinking about other citizens, not just your own narrow interests, when we have a debate like this. Because not enough of you have those basic civic habits, the conservative activists made hay by framing the bill as a fundamental threat to the American way of life and an attempt by socialist bureaucrats to micro-manage the details of individuals' lives and decide who lives and dies. Now I don't expect the entire country to become big government liberals, and I never expected the health plan to garner 100 percent or even 80 percent approval from the public. But is it too much to ask that citizens not be taken in by obvious distortions, and that citizens punish rather than reward leaders who engage in over-the-top exaggeration designed to inflame rather than educate? Those criticisms and distortions did not kill the bill, but they helped make it weaker—and less popular—than it should have been. Again, this is partly my fault, but it's partly yours. We've got to be better informed and less easily manipulated, or nothing will ever get done, be it further improvements to health care down the line or addressing other critical issues.

Now it turns out that Tocqueville also had some pretty interesting observations about how a truly democratic political culture emerges and what sustains it. Some of those ideas, we can update, draw on, even try to implement. I've got some ideas on how to help do just that, or at least start the ball rolling. For instance, Tocqueville said that "Town institutions are to freedom what primary schools are to knowledge: they bring it within people's reach and give men the enjoyment and habit of using it for peaceful ends." Put another way, real freedom isn't just about consumer choice and people not telling you what to do—it also must involve skill in self-governance. That skill requires practice, and I fear that too many of us have not graduated from the primary schools of freedom Tocqueville is talking about. So we need to find some ways to again make local politics relevant, and breathe back into our everyday experiences what Tocqueville called the "spirit of freedom."[23] Tocqueville worried that one day we might lose that spirit of freedom, by trading it for a cheap consumerism. I'm optimistic enough to believe that we are not too far gone yet—in 2008 we saw that Americans' "concern for their future and that of their descendants" has not vanished, and that Americans are still capable of making a "sudden and capable effort to set things right when the need arises."[24] But I've come to understand that just mobilizing people to win an election isn't enough to heal our civic culture and begin solving our urgent problems.

Now I realize that most of you don't care about that right now and just want me to fix the economy. I'm trying, and I hope my efforts pay off in time so that I can get that second term. In the meantime, if you want to see the country change, don't depend on me to do it. Go out and organize the communities you live in, remembering that organizing isn't just about talking to people who are like you or who think like you, but about pulling people together across differences and learning to deal with people who disagree with you. I can't teach you how to do those things. You have to go learn it for yourself. When more of you start doing that, we'll have a better country and I—or whoever you elect to replace me—will have a little easier job.

Good night, thank you, and God bless the United States of America.

The speech cited above is fictional, but the political and institutional constraints it describes are not. Those constraints must be kept foremost in mind in trying to evaluate Obama's presidency. His presidency may in time come to be seen as a case study of the difficulty of achieving substantial social changes within the American political system, even in relatively favorable political circumstances and with a competent, far-sighted president who enjoys widespread popularity, and even when there is fairly widespread majority support for significant change.

For some observers, this outcome would be no surprise. Sheldon Wolin argues in *Tocqueville Between Two Worlds* as well as *Democracy, Inc.* that contemporary American politics is best characterized not as democracy but as a form of permanent corporate rule, with citizens limited to a plebiscitary role in which they are asked to choose between (generally) two candidates who may have significant differences on certain philosophical and social issues but are each fundamentally committed to perpetuating a regime in which a) corporations are the predominant economic institution and have disproportionate political power and b) the United States maintains a permanent, quasi-imperial military presence around the world. Republicans and Democrats may have substantial differences in identifying, prioritizing, and crafting responses to particular problems, but they are each committed to the presumption that these problems are to be addressed within the framework of regime features a) and b). Exhibit A in contemporary politics for these propositions is the gargantuan federal bailout of the financial industry, in which there was bipartisan support for committing huge amounts of public resources to benefit private actors, without at the same time establishing meaningful control over the bailed-out firms or challenging investor prerogatives. Many of the specific institutional features of American politics noted above reinforce this corporate-dominated regime and contribute to rendering political majorities in America almost toothless.

Consider again the health care debate of 2009-2010, in which Obama sought to pass reform that would be comprehensive, yet not directly attack the core idea of profit-driven provision of medical care and health insurance. One might reasonably criticize Obama's performance in swaying and attempting to educate public opinion on health care during 2009—he took a back seat in drawing up legislation, and arguably waited much too long to frame the debate. But the underlying issue is not whether Obama got the tactics right, but the difficulty of passing complicated, comprehensive reform given a climate characterized by a) determined opposition from some corporate interests, b) determined ideological opposition from a substantial minority, and c) inability to appeal to a middle, "even-handed" center of American politics consisting of independent-minded, highly informed voters who make calls based on a reasonably informed judgment of the merits of particular cases. Political communication in this climate

resembles not even a crude form of public deliberation, but sheer political war-
fare, couched in highly ideological terms and driven by the quest for tactical
political advantage.

Could American democracy become anything more promising than this?
Wolin's conclusion is largely negative: he contrasts Tocqueville's effusive
praise of the New England township in volume 1 of *Democracy in America* with
the stark warnings in volume 2 of popular rule decaying into a form of soft tyranny—"democratic despotism"—as citizens become consumed with private
affairs and lose their civic habits. At one point, the American political system
had institutional elements that both permitted and moderated a form of rule by
an informed majority capable of recognizing and acting on the public interest;
now it consists of elite manipulation of (and contempt for) a largely uninformed
majority, a "society of stunted individuals who have embraced lives empty of
political responsibility."[25]

Yet if Tocqueville's description of the New England township seems
quaint, it remains the most plausible account of the *kind* of political experience
and education citizens must acquire if they are to become skilled in making
judgments about the common good, either on a small-scale basis or writ large.
Consider the nature of local political participation, as described by Tocqueville
and re-described as a normative aspiration by Stephen Elkin. First, involvement
in local politics is most often motivated by a practical concern touching one's
self-interest: the condition of the schools, the quality of the local infrastructure,
proposed changes in land use, the provision of public space and recreational
facilities, local tax rates, local economic development plans—down to such
mundane questions as how to fund the removal of chewing gum from city side-
walks. The content of local politics is thus more pragmatic than ideological
(though ideologies may be invoked). Second, the effects of local politics are
generally immediately visible and concrete. Third, the scale of local politics
means that active citizens are likely to be placed into fairly direct contact with
parties or interests they oppose, and will be compelled to hear what the other
side has to say. Fourth, the scale of local politics ought to make it easier to directly judge the competence and skill of leaders.

When local politics have these qualities, we might expect the following
civic virtues to emerge: citizens learn to move from narrow consideration of
their own interest to consideration of the public interest, and learn to frame their
arguments in terms of the public interest; citizens become aware of the tradeoffs of alternative courses of action, and come to recognize the legitimacy of
perspectives other than their own; and citizens learn to distinguish better from
worse arguments and proposals. In Elkin's view, local politics of this kind can
produce better citizens as well as better leaders (persons skilled in taking account of multiple perspectives to shape a public interest). Leaders who are
judged to be successful stewards of the public interest in the immediate setting
of local politics in turn become strong candidates to practice statesmanship at a
higher level of government—i.e., to become a candidate for governor or for
Congress. Similarly, virtuous civic habits learned through the experience of ac-

tive engagement in local politics might carry over to engagement in national-level politics.

This last point is crucial for Elkin: Elkin is concerned not just with local politics, but with the institutional design of a "reconstructed commercial republic"—that is a Madisonian constitutional theory updated for modern conditions. A continental-scale republic simply cannot work if citizens do not have some skill and experience in judging public matters, and if leaders do not have the proper kind of education in judging and acting on the public interest. While in Elkin's view reviving local politics is not a sufficient condition for achieving a significantly improved commercial republic—he also cites strengthening the middle class and broadening the ownership of property as key goals for a healthy republic—it is certainly a necessary condition.

But local politics in the United States do not always—or even usually—have all the desirable qualities stipulated by Tocqueville and Elkin. The fragmentation of the American metropolis into relatively homogenous, independent municipalities has damaged interest in and participation in local politics.[26] Evidence also suggests that the automobile-oriented design of most contemporary suburban communities, and the associated loss of public space, inhibits several types of nonelectoral political participation.[27] Thus many residents of suburbia (the spatial setting of the majority of Americans) inhabit neighborhoods and municipalities where interest in local political participation is weak, precisely because of both the homogeneity and the spatial design of the communities. Where there are no fundamental conflicts between residents that must be adjudicated by politics, participation is likely to recede, and such participation as remains is less likely to teach citizens how to interact with and learn from people different from and with different interests than themselves.

Turning from suburbs to central cities, in cities we are likely to find higher levels of nonelectoral political engagement, and higher levels of local political conflict among competing groups and interests.[28] Yet urban "regime theorists" have long stressed that central city politics tend to be dominated by coalitions between elected officials and local business interests, and oriented primarily around the pursuit of new economic development. The economic dependence of cities on mobile corporate investment means that attracting new development, or retaining existing jobs, becomes the top priority of urban political leaders. In this context, citizens' political activism often becomes reactive and defensive, and city officials are likely to view civic groups that question elite priorities as impediments to progress and action rather than partners and collaborators. Further, cities are typically under tight fiscal constraints, with few additional resources available to advance the public interest. When such resources do become available, privileged political actors (particularly business interests) have the largest role in shaping how they are used. Urban politics in this mode rarely resembles a deliberative conversation between a variety of actors about how best to advance the public interest. Instead, it more likely takes the form of public officials allying with private business interests to advance initiatives intended to stimulate economic development; civic mobilization becomes oriented around attempting to block or modify elite-sponsored initiatives, or becomes reduced to symbolic or identity politics. Meaningful public action in the direct interests of the majority becomes unlikely, in the dominant sort of urban regime; instead, public action and resources are steered towards and guided by the most powerful economic actors, with any benefits to the broader public coming in trickle-down form.[29]

Elkin's vision of a commercial republic accepts this critical description of contemporary urban politics (indeed Elkin himself has played a prominent role in development of urban regime theory), but unlike many other regime theorists he suggests it is possible to imagine a reformed form of city politics not dominated by the economic imperative to attract and keep jobs. The basic idea is simple: for local politics not to be dominated by economic concerns and the need to retain investment, localities must in fact have a stable economic base that is not likely to move or evaporate. Obvious examples in the United States include moderate-sized college towns (Chapel Hill, Ann Arbor; Madison) where state universities provide a permanent source of employment and income. Such communities are not devoid of conflict, but they need not be nearly as preoccupied with maintaining and retaining investment as other urban areas. In the absence of a major state university or other form of public investment, alternative urban regimes could instead be anchored around locally owned firms, including small businesses, worker-owned firms, cooperatives, city-owned firms, and public-private partnerships. If such locally controlled capital achieves sufficient mass, it might serve as the basis for a politics oriented around the interests of the majority and responsive to meaningful public deliberation about the public interest.[30] Such a politics in turn might reasonably aspire to produce at least some of the positive civic effects Tocqueville attributed to local political engagement.

At first glance, this line of reasoning might seem utterly irrelevant to an assessment of the Obama presidency. We expect presidents to tackle national and global problems, not worry about the nature of local politics. But federal policies set in Washington have important effects on metropolitan areas, and an administration seriously committed to the project of revitalizing local democracy could take at least three kinds of policy initiatives (two of which could be launched at minimal or modest cost). First, the federal government could take aggressive steps to promote regional cooperation at the metropolitan level, and to compel municipalities within the same region to cooperate with one another, by making award of federal funds contingent on the presence of regional cooperation. Existing metropolitan planning organizations (MPOs) could be reorganized as democratically elected bodies and given real power in shaping local priorities. Other scholars have gone further, and envisioned the establishment of regional legislatures consisting of elected representatives from a region's cities.[31] Second, the government could direct community development funds toward a deliberate strategy to build up place-based, community-anchoring economic enterprises, building on past community development precedents as well as exciting new initiatives such as the "Cleveland Model" of cooperative development.[32] Third, the federal government could undertake major public infrastructure investments designed to upgrade transportation networks, particularly public transit, in and around central cities, with the aim of strengthening urban economies. The guiding principle behind these reforms is the observation that meaningful democratic governance at the city, metropolitan and state (or regional) level will always be hamstrung so long as localities remain economically insecure and in competition with one another for capital. The goal of larger-order policy units at the state and federal level should be to relieve that insecurity through place-based investments and the nurturance of forms of capital that stabilize local community economies over the long term.

We thus confront a paradox: the climate of national politics is distorted in part because an insufficient number of citizens possess the substantive knowledge, skill in judging the public interest, and disposition to listen to and take seriously the viewpoints of others that a healthy deliberative political culture requires. This is in part because one key mechanism generating such a political culture—training and experience in judging the public interest at the local level—has been allowed to atrophy in most places in the United States, for a variety of reasons. Yet it is difficult to see how meaningful local-level democracy could be revitalized in this country without substantial alterations in the way local politics are organized. The most plausible way by which such an alteration could be achieved involves substantial interventions by the federal government to promote the formation of more effective local and metropolitan-scaled democratic institutions, in the ways described above.

Any move in this direction by the Obama administration—or any other president in the near to mid-term—would represent, of course, an admission that the current mode of governance is unworkable, for reasons that are deeper than can be solved by any president. Many Americans, across the ideological spectrum, in fact already share that judgment. Nonetheless, it would take some courage (in terms of the conventional political wisdom) for Obama to openly state that he cannot cure what ails American democracy, and that he has very little hope of realizing his largest policy ambitions because of the obstacles, both institutional and cultural. Indeed, the political risks of doing so—"Obama admits failure"—are probably too steep for a first-term president to take on. (Here Tocqueville's critique of the way political concerns and bending to the views of the majority militate against presidents seeking re-election *leading* the citizenry is right on point.) Such a message would both invite stinging attacks from the opposition and undercut the enthusiasm of the president's progressive and liberal supporters, most of whom respond more instinctively to positive themes about "hope" than sober assessments of the severe difficulties of achieving meaningful change.

So the course recommended here could probably only be taken by a president who had already achieved re-election. Ironically, however, the honest admission that the American political system is in need of fundamental reconfiguration, and that no elected official can magically "fix Washington," would likely achieve wide resonance among the citizenry. It also would open the door to a serious conversation not just about policies and problem-solving, but about the advantages and disadvantages of our current political institutions, and about plausible ways they might be improved—a conversation that is now confined largely to academic political scientists (and is relatively rare even there). Elkin's critique of the American constitutional system, as it is practiced, both illustrates the kind of discussion that needs to take place and offers a fairly well-developed argument for the proposition that there is no way to heal or improve the larger-order constitutional regime without providing a regular outlet in which citizens can learn to exercise judgment and to wield the responsibility of authority—an outlet which, now as in Tocqueville's era, must generally be in local politics. But not all local politics are equally efficacious in producing the sorts of civic habits valued by Tocqueville and Elkin, and alterations in federal policy vis-à-vis urban areas with the aim of producing urban regimes that are more responsive to the public interest are imperative if local politics are to once again become formative schools of democratic virtues.

Without a programmatic agenda of this kind, Obama's civic republicanism runs the risk of being reduced to occasional bully pulpit advocacy of greater "civic engagement," with no real effort to encourage and nourish a healthier, more knowledgeable and more vigilant political culture. Obama secured tactical advantage in the 2008 campaign from mobilizing partisans, encouraging them to network with one another, providing opportunities for meaningful participation, and encouraging them to give money (early and often). No one would deny that there is an important place for partisan political participation of this kind, but the Obama campaign model does *not* in itself cultivate the full range of political virtues associated with Tocquevillian local political participation—in particular, the imperative to deal with and listen to those with whom one disagrees (rather than just check them off one's prospective voter list). More generally, Obama, as president, needs to be concerned not just with maximizing the participation and engagement of liberal activists, but with promoting stronger civic virtues among the citizenry as a whole. Reasoned pitches to the putative political center cannot work if there is not an informed, highly engaged political center to appeal to. The less partisan, more pragmatic terrain of local politics, despite its imperfections, remains the most promising terrain for developing those virtues across a broad cross-section of the population.

To be sure, national politics will always be contentious and potentially ugly, and the job Obama signed up for demands trying the best he can to advance his agenda within the cross-currents of the existing political culture. The argument of this essay is that Obama could make a lasting impact on American civic culture beyond the parameters of what he is or is not able to accomplish legislatively by seeking ways to address the root causes of America's highly polarized and near-dysfunctional political culture. This is not an easy task: to make the argument for the value of political engagement in an era when politics strikes many people as ugly, and perhaps fruitless. But as president, Obama should not settle for bemoaning the civic status quo or for bully pulpit exhortations to be better citizens. Rather, he should take concrete steps to support institutional arrangements at the local level designed to maximize opportunities for genuine civic participation, with the aim of turning America's localities back into genuine schools for democracy, not simply comfortable places where Americans can escape politics. Meaningful steps in that direction are well within the scope of presidential power, and need not require extremely expensive fiscal commitments. Obama himself would be long out of office before the benefits of a re-engaged citizenry with stronger civic habits made any tangible effect on the tone and parameters of national political culture. The agenda suggested here thus should be understood as a long-term—but indispensable—investment in improving America's civic condition. A society based on the force of majority opinion cannot work if the majority are not engaged, informed, and experienced in exercising political responsibility. Likewise, as Tocqueville observed and the Obama presidency is helping to prove, electing a talented, occasionally brilliant leader with legitimate statesmanlike qualities as president cannot in itself cure the dysfunctions of a political system unable to address society's most urgent problems, so long as the bulk of citizens remain both unskilled in exercising independent judgment about what the public interest requires and inclined to believe that taking responsibility for the nation's pressing problems is someone else's job.

Notes

1. Alexis de Tocqueville, *Democracy in America*, trans. Gerald E. Bevan (London: Penguin Books, 2003), volume 1, chapter 8. Quotations and specific page references from *Democracy* in this chapter refer to this edition.

2. See, i.e., Tom Clark, Robert Putnam, and Ed Fieldhouse, *The Age of Obama* (Manchester, UK: University of Manchester Press, 2010), and Robert Putnam, "The Rebirth of American Civic Life," *Boston Globe*, March 2, 2008.

3. Michael J. Sandel, *Justice: What's the Right Thing To Do?* (New York: Farrar Strauss, 2009).

4. See Sheldon Wolin, *Tocqueville Between Two Worlds* (Princeton: Princeton University Press, 2001); and Wolin, *Democracy, Inc.* (Princeton: Princeton University Press, 2008). In February 2009, Wolin was quoted as follows by journalist Chris Hedges, when asked to describe the likely direction of the Obama administration:

> The basic systems are going to stay in place; they are too powerful to be challenged. . . . This is shown by the financial bailout. It does not bother with the structure at all. I don't think Obama can take on the kind of military establishment we have developed. This is not to say that I do not admire him. He is probably the most intelligent president we have had in decades. I think he is well meaning, but he inherits a system of constraints that make it very difficult to take on these major power configurations. I do not think he has the appetite for it in any ideological sense. The corporate structure is not going to be challenged. There has not been a word from him that would suggest an attempt to rethink the American imperium.

Chris Hedges, "It's Not Going to be Okay." Interview with Sheldon Wolin. *TruthDig*, February 2, 2009. Available at www.truthdig.com/report/item/20090202_its_not_going_

to_be_ok/

5. Stephen L. Elkin, *Reconstructing the Commercial Republic: Constitutional Design after Madison* (Chicago: University of Chicago Press, 2006).

6. For accounts of contemporary civic republicanism, see among others, Michael J. Sandel, *Democracy's Discontent: America's Search for a Public Philosophy* (Cambridge: Harvard University Press, 1996); Iseult Honohan, *Civic Republicanism* (New York: Routledge, 2002); and Cecile Laborde and John Maynor, eds. *Republicanism and Political Theory* (Oxford: Blackwell, 2008).

7. Hillary Clinton. Speech to supporters, Philadelphia, Pennsylvania, April 23, 2008. Available at http://blogs.suntimes.com/sweet/2008/04/clinton_pennsylvania_victory_s.html

8. Thad Williamson, "Obama's Vote Machine." *Style Weekly* (Richmond, VA) online, November 6, 2008. The dramatic increase in voter turnout seen in Richmond was not typical of the national pattern: the presence of a large African-American community, many Democratic voters, college age voters (and volunteers), and heightened interest in the election in Virginia due to the close race in the state made Richmond ripe—and strategically important—terrain for Obama's ground operation. In some parts of the country, voter turnout in 2008 actually declined compared to 2004. For analysis, see Thom File and Sarah Crissey, "Voting and Registration in the Election of November 2008," United States Census Bureau, May 2010, available at www.census.gov/prod/2010pubs/p20562.pdf, as well as Curtis Gans, "African-Americans, Anger, Fear and Youth Propel Turnout to Highest Level since 1960," Center for the Study of the American Electorate (American University), December 17, 2008, available at www1.american.edu/ia/cdem/csae/pdfs/2008pdfoffinaledited.pdf.

9. For detailed description, see, David Plouffe, *The Audacity to Win: The Inside Story and Lessons of Barack Obama's Historic Victory* (New York: Viking, 2009).

10. Quoted in Peter Dreier and Marshall Ganz, "We Have Hope. Now Where's the Audacity?" *Washington Post*, August 30, 2009.

11. James McGregor Burns, *Leadership* (New York: Harper & Row, 1978).

12. Barack Obama, "Inaugural Address." January 20, 2009.

13. For a helpful overview of the policy agenda Obama took up in 2009, See Thomas Dye, George Edwards, Morris Fiorina, Edward Greenberg, Paul Light, David Magleby, and Martin Wattenberg, *Obama: Year One* (New York: Longman, 2009). For a detailed, informative critique of Obama's first year in office from a progressive perspective with special attention to the handling of the financial crisis by Obama's economic team, see Robert Kuttner, *A Presidency in Peril* (White River Junction, VT: Chelsea Green, 2010).

14. First, it is possible that if Republicans return to power across the board in 2012, the reform bill will be scrapped before most of it is implemented. Second, the bill's mandate that the uninsured buy private health insurance may prove sufficiently unpopular to drive a powerful backlash against the reform.

15. For detailed assessment of Obama's handling of the financial crisis in 2009, see Kuttner, *A Presidency in Peril*. Partly in response to the election of Scott Brown, Obama in 2010 began taking a tougher line on financial reform; at this writing Congress is considering a reform bill intended to at least reduce the risk of future financial meltdowns and bailouts.

16. For discussions of Organizing for America's efforts in 2009, see Ari Melber, "Year One of Organizing for America: The Permanent Field Campaign in a Digital Age," *techPresident Special Report* (Jan. 2010). Available at www.techpresident.com/ofayear1;

Dreier and Ganz, "We Have the Hope"; and George Edwards, "*Creating* Opportunities for Policy Change?" in Dye et al., *Obama: Year One.*

17. Some observers did credit OFA with having a notable role in the final days of the health care reform debate in March 2010; volunteers affiliated with the organization were responsible for over 500,000 phone calls and 324,000 letters to Congress in a ten-day period in mid-March. See Micah Sifry, "Organizing for America's Role in Health Care Battle," March 21, 2010, at http://techpresident.com/blog-entry/organizing-americas-role-health-care-battle.

18. OFA frequently sponsors neighborhood events aimed at local social capital-building, and in 2009 encouraged volunteers to do community service work in their local communities. Both these activities are different from mobilizing people to engage in local issues.

19. For instance, mobilized citizens might begin directly challenging the policies of Democratic officeholders at the local level—creating a political headache for the president who endorsed such mobilization. For discussion of the tension between local public officials and the federal government generated by federal Community Action Programs in the 1960s, see Noel Cazenave, *Impossible Democracy: The Unlikely Success of the War on Poverty Community Action Programs* (Albany: SUNY Press, 2007).

20. Tocqueville, *Democracy in America*, 160.

21. Tocqueville, *Democracy in America*, 151-52.

22. In April 2009, polls showed that 53 percent of Americans approved of Obama's handling of health reform, compared to 28 percent opposed. By April 2010—after the bill had passed—only 44 percent approved, while 52 percent opposed. A July 2009 Gallup Poll found that 56 percent of Americans at that time supported passage of a reform bill, with an identical number agreeing that all Americans should be required to have insurance. Polls taken in April 2010 generally show that roughly 40 percent of the public approve the bill as passed, although solid majorities believed it would have beneficial effects for the uninsured and the poor. Notably, over half of respondents in one poll reported that they needed more information to be able to adequately gauge how the reform would impact their personal situation. See Jeffrey M. Jones, "Majority in U.S. Favors Health Care Reform This Year," Gallup Report, July 14, 2009, available at www.gallup.com/poll/121664/majority-favors-healthcare-reform-this-year.aspx. See also Kaiser Family Foundation and AP-Gfk polls on health care from 2010, as well as other polling data on health care assembled at www.pollingreport.com/health.htm.

23. Tocqueville, *Democracy in America,* 73.

24. Tocqueville, *Democracy in America,* 750.

25. Wolin, *Tocqueville Between Two Worlds*, 570.

26. J. Eric Oliver, *Democracy in Suburbia* (Princeton: Princeton University Press, 2001).

27. Thad Williamson, *Sprawl, Justice and Citizenship: The Civic Costs of the American Way of Life* (New York: Oxford University Press, 2010).

28. Williamson, *Sprawl, Justice and Citizenship.*

29. On these points, see among many others, Stephen Elkin, *City and Regime in the American Republic* (Chicago: University of Chicago Press, 1987); Clarence Stone, *Regime Politics: Governing Atlanta, 1946-1988* (Lawrence: University Press of Kansas, 1989); and David Imbroscio, *Reconstructing City Politics: Alternative Economic Development and Urban Regimes* (Thousand Oaks, CA: SAGE, 1997).

30. See Thad Williamson, David Imbroscio, and Gar Alperovitz, *Making a Place for Community: Local Democracy in a Global Era* (New York: Routledge, 2002). See also

Imbroscio, *Reconstructing City Politics*, and Imbroscio, *Urban America Reconsidered: Alternatives for Governance and Policy* (Ithaca: Cornell University Press, 2010).

31. Gerald Frug, "Beyond Regional Government," *Harvard Law Review* 115 (2002): 1763-1836.

32. See Gar Alperovitz, Ted Howard, and Thad Williamson, "The Cleveland Model." *The Nation*, March 1, 2010; and Williamson et al., *Making a Place for Community.*

Chapter 9

Moderating the Penal State through Citizen Participation: A Neo-Tocquevillian Perspective on Court Professionals and Juries in a Democracy[1]

Albert W. Dzur

And so the virtues arise in us neither by nature nor against nature. Rather, we are by nature able to acquire them, and we are completed through habit. . . . Correct habituation distinguishes a good political system from a bad one.
—Aristotle

Democracy and the Penal State

Ours is a time when so much of what might concern citizens, should they be attuned to the suffering of others, is as if invisible while what is trivial remains all too visible. At this writing one in a hundred American adults are in prison and many more are economically dependent on the penal state. Alexis de Tocqueville, one of the earliest and brightest students of American penal policy, was well aware of the dangers and cruelties of democracy, its arbitrariness, incompetence, and vulnerability to majority pressure, its potential for apathy and self-involvement.[2] But even such an apt predictor as he did not imagine that a democratic republic would both lead the world in imprisonment and lack any discernable public embarrassment for that fact. In his darkest worries he saw a nation of sheep not convicts.

179

Within criminal justice circles the main culprit of this bloated penal state is what has been called, somewhat presumptuously, "populist punitiveness." This is a socio-political complex afflicting most modern Western states, but with particular virulence in the Anglo-American world of the United Kingdom, New Zealand, Australia, and the United States. It includes the decline of trust in officials in all branches of government as well as in the policy experts and professionals who advise them, the erosion of traditional barriers between electoral politics and criminal justice policy, and the lessening of checks on severe penalties. It is exacerbated by commercial and infotainment tendencies in the mass media that discount independent analysis and rational debate while privileging rapid, shocking, and raw stories and images.[3]

In response, prominent scholars have advocated a program of de-politicized democracy that would remove certain issues—such as how to calibrate sentencing for violent or sex offenders and how to determine which offenses should be punished with prison—from public influence. Some have endorsed expert panels modeled after the Federal Reserve Board to insulate such "hot" issues from an irascible public.[4] There are, however, diagnostic, practical, and normative problems with this approach. First, it misdiagnoses the public as punitive when in fact attitudes toward offenders are more complicated. Studies reveal that punitiveness is not a natural default public attitude; when confronted with the context of offenses and thick descriptions of offenders, public attitudes tend to be more moderate than when there is no context provided.[5] Practically, it is inconceivable that criminal justice policy could be transferred to experts under contemporary political conditions marked by distrust of experts. Bridges rather than further barriers between the current, highly mediated and technocratic world of official policymaking and the general public are what are needed. Finally, the normative implication of the argument that without strict elite guidance the American public is unable to self-regulate, unable to develop a more measured approach to criminal justice, to punish but in a more thoughtful, consistent, and humane fashion is that a guardian state not a democracy is what the United States requires.

In the context of these concerns over the penal state and the role of public attitudes and citizen participation in contributing to it, this chapter considers, critically, a different approach suggested by Tocqueville and then further elaborated by John Stuart Mill, a kind of statesmanship in the juridical realm that leads by example but does not assert direct control over a discrete set of criminal justice issues the demos is allegedly incapable of handling with care. While both thinkers were sensitive to the limitations of the public, so much so that they are sometimes called "strange" and "aristocratic" liberals, they nonetheless believed that citizen participation within the criminal justice domain was needed for more moderate policy.[6]

The centerpiece of Tocqueville's argument is what I will call the "civic schoolhouse" account of jury trials that stresses the value of a certain kind of popular participation, one that empowers citizens, provides an institutional place for their action, and grants importance to their decisions yet at the same time renders public faith in majority will and unvarnished opinion less certain and more malleable.[7] I will start by distinguishing two dimensions of Tocqueville's civic schoolhouse account, a micro-level attention to the beneficial influence of jury service on citizens (its socializing effects) and a macro-level attention to the positive impact of the jury on the legal and political system (its legitimacy effects). Then, I will draw attention to the merits and the flaws of the way Tocqueville and Mill articulated the argument's two dimensions and how they linked them together. Finally, I will suggest that a reconstructed form of the civic schoolhouse argument shows how more not less popular participation in the criminal justice process might help combat the penal state. These conclusions pose a clear but difficult set of leadership tasks for reform-minded court professionals.

Tocqueville's Jury[8]

A Trojan Horse in Reverse: Tempering Majority Power One Juror at a Time

Tocqueville interpreted the American jury as a critically important stabilizing and moderating institution, one whose efficacy stems from being both an expression of majority power and a mechanism for limiting it through the socialization of jurors. In theory the embodiment of popular sovereignty, the jury in practice is a Trojan horse in reverse that carries ordinary citizens into the quasi-aristocratic corridors of professional legal power only to find them acclimate and return to the democratic public sphere with increased respect for the rule of law. In the American courtroom, even as the people formally hold sway through the jury, they themselves are informally influenced by forces that shape their "habits of mind and even the souls."[9] By sharing and exercising judicial power, jurors are required to become for the duration of a trial not just a little like a judge and this has major transformative cognitive, moral, and political effects.

Cognitively, jurors learn, by doing, "some of the habits of mind of the judge," which are the "habits of order, a taste for forms, and a sort of instinctive love of regular sequence of ideas," a preference for tradition and precedent over innovation, and an appreciation for the boundaries set on judgment by particular facts and rules.[10] No temporary shift in consciousness, jurors carry this way of thinking with them out of the courthouse. "The human mind becomes habituated to the jury's forms, and the jury itself comes to be identified, as it were, with the very idea of justice."[11] Tocqueville notices a pervasive culture of legalism—in the ways American children resolved conflicts, for example, or the mock jury trials held by inmates in a juvenile detention center.[12] He praises the use of the jury in both civil and criminal trials because it maximizes the opportunities for lay citizens to serve in the administration of justice and extends the range of issues and interests they must consider.

Morally, jury service helps scour the "rust" of individualism by compelling people to take up matters that affect others and to treat them seriously and fairly.[13] As in Aristotle's sense of the true citizen being ruler and ruled in turn, jurors taking up the power of judgment recognize that they are part of their government not merely as subjects with wants, sovereigns with wills, but as governors with reason and charged with making difficult decisions deliberatively not putting them off or rendering them hastily or by default. Vested with magistracy and seated in somber judgment over others, citizens are pressed into a more universal standpoint. They realize that the justice of this very courtroom, which they are meting out and which might be meted out to them in the future, is something for which they are responsible not theoretically but actually. Habits of the heart like commitment to equity, impartiality, and a robust sense of social responsibility are nurtured through these intensely public and personal experiences on the jury.[14]

Politically, and above all else, jury service is a civic education. The jury is a "free school, and one that is always open, to which each juror comes to learn about his rights, and where he enters into daily contact with the best educated, most enlightened members of the upper classes and receives practical instruction in the law in a form accessible to his intelligence."[15] "I think that the primary reason for the practical intelligence and political good sense of Americans is their long experience with juries in civil matters."[16] Throughout *Democracy in America* Tocqueville compares Americans' awareness of institutions and rules, their realism about government with the passion for general ideas he finds among the French citizenry.[17] This practical intelligence is formed by taking part in "free institutions" like town meetings and the jury and muddling through to difficult and often imperfect decisions.

Being a juror is a political education in another sense as well; it is a lesson in taking guidance from one who knows more about the law, a lesson in the legitimate power of the judge: "The jury instills in all classes a respect for judicial decisions and the idea of law."[18] It is one thing to have judges; it is another to work with them on issues one knows something about, as in criminal law; it is another indeed to work with them on issues one knows little about, as in civil law. What jurors learn by doing and by needing to rely on and to defer to judges in order to reach a decision on serious civil matters is that though they are vested with magistracy, they cannot perform their role well without the guidance of real magistrates.[19]

The schoolhouse that is the courtroom is staffed by lawyers, who "take from their work certain habits of order, a taste for forms, and a sort of instinctive love of regular sequence in ideas that naturally foster in them a strong opposition to the revolutionary spirit and the unthinking passions of democracy."[20] Though

Americans in the age of Jackson try to keep the wealthy and the natural aristocrats out of political office, they do elect lawyers, who belong "to the people by
interest and birth and to the aristocracy by habit and taste." Lawyers are, for
Tocqueville, functionally quasi-aristocratic because they resist the "democratic
instincts," "love of novelty," grand ambitions, "contempt for rules," and "ardor"
of lay people and hold countervailing tendencies: "aristocratic inclinations,"
"superstitious respect for what is old," narrow perspective, "love of formalities,"
and "habitually dilatory ways."[21] The jury trial provides the opportunity for the
American legal profession, as an "aristocratic element," to "mix readily with the
natural elements of democracy to form useful and durable compounds."[22]

Keeping Judges from Being "Outside the People": The Jury Trial as a Circulatory System to Purge Distrust

Though Tocqueville's driving point is how much the juror can learn from the
judge and, ultimately, how much democracies benefit from a judiciary and rule
of law that are independent of direct popular control, what allows this independence is a deference to professional legal authority that is granted by the people
not seized by the professionals.

In other words, the jury trial is a place where legitimation happens, where
official authority inside must gain critically needed support from the outside.
The jury is a reminder that the power of judgment is to be grounded in widespread citizen participation not only in extraordinary circumstances, as in a
process that produces a constitution, but constantly and concretely day after day
in ordinary courtrooms. Judicial authority, with all the resources of respect already at its disposal—professional training, legal experience, the age-old symbolism and hierarchy of the courtroom—must be shared and still has to prove
itself to the jury all the time.

Without the jury, the demos would be suspicious of judges and seek to rein
in their powers. After a conversation with Charles Pelham Curtis, legal solicitor
of Boston, Tocqueville wrote in his travel notebook that the jury "gives a great
outward strength to justice, it prevents the magistracy from becoming a body
outside the people and gives it immense and almost always useful power in political questions."[23] He understands the power of judicial review as dependent
upon lay participation in the courtroom and the gradual relaxing of distrust that
occurs there. Only by working with the judge in civil trials and noticing that he
is a "disinterested arbiter" do citizens begin to "have confidence in him and listen with respect to what he says," a confidence that spreads to criminal trials,
where the lay juror could more readily rely on his own opinion rather than the
judge's.[24] Such trusting and indeed deferential collaboration in civil and then
criminal trials prevents judges from being viewed as official entities with interests that are separate from the public, even as their interests are in fact separate,

and it leads lay citizens to accept transfers of power to the judicial branch inconceivable under other arrangements. "Thus the jury," writes Tocqueville, "though it seems to diminish the rights of the magistracy, actually establishes its empire, and nowhere are judges more powerful than in countries where the people share their privileges."[25]

Without the jury, the demos would lack adequate knowledge of the complexity of legal decisionmaking and, failing to realize their inabilities in making justice, would remain in their default mode of distrust of judges. Tocqueville sketches in rough outline a picture of the jury as a circulatory system enabling courthouse regulars to share language, ideas, and experience with lay citizens and thus purging the distrust that can grow when professional and official domains are "outside" the people. As a place of significant interaction between professionals and laypeople, the jury renders transparent the complicated norms, rules, and procedures best understood in practice. Jurors become confident enough to grant appropriate authority to court professionals, building up their civic competencies enough to trust and honor the ones who know.

These crucial trust-building and moderating effects on the political system, the macro-level of American democracy, are dependent on the socialization effects Tocqueville believed happened at the micro-level of the courtroom. The jury shapes citizens' attitudes and sense of responsibility toward one another, reverses their initial distrust of external authority, and thus channels majority power in a productive and ultimately authority-enhancing fashion. While it can be said to build civic capacity, the jury's equally important function is to instruct the people to use that capacity not to serve as judges themselves but to appreciate the work of the real judges. The civic schoolhouse of the jury thus does not in fact quite resemble normal classrooms, where students' natural capacities for reading and writing, for example, are "completed by habit," in Aristotle's words, but is instead a setting where students become convinced that they could never actually write anything of their own, but only read and appreciate what was written by others. Later in this chapter, I will argue that this hierarchical professionalism, though a core feature of the civic schoolhouse model for Tocqueville as well as Mill, is more problematic and less necessary than they believed.

Mill's Jury

Apprentices to Government Work: Active Learning on Mill's Jury

The jury helps accomplish what Mill understood as the two core goals of well-functioning governments: "to increase the sum of good qualities in the governed" and "to take advantage of the amount of good qualities which may at any time exist, and make them instrumental to the right purposes."[26] The government's use of jury trials fosters an indirect civic education among the governed that in turn ultimately improves the "quality of the machinery" of government itself. [27] While staying close to Tocqueville's framework, which influenced him, Mill develops his own version of the micro-level civic socialization and macro-level circulatory legitimacy arguments and casts additional light on both.

Both perfectionist and liberal in his thinking, Mill held government responsible for actively promoting a universal civic education that can foster good qualities such as "industry, integrity, justice, prudence," as well as "mental activity, enterprise, and courage," but he stressed that it is to prosecute these objectives indirectly.[28] Sensitive to the many hazards of government action on citizens, such as the accumulation and abuse of power by service providers and the threats to the self-development of service recipients, Mill sought educational opportunities government could offer that citizens would seize hold of and pursue themselves. These were meant to activate and affirm citizens' capacity to stand up for their own interests as much as they were to cultivate new cognitive skills and moral perspectives.[29]

Jury service was, for Mill, a powerful example of such an indirect civic education program, one that, as Tocqueville had argued, could inform citizens about government and stretch their intellectual capacities. Just as jury courts served in ancient Athens to dramatically elevate the intellectual abilities of average citizens, Mill writes, so British juries make "Englishmen of the lower middle class . . . very different beings, in range of ideas and development of faculties, from those who have done nothing in their lives but drive a quill, or sell goods over a counter."[30] Without civic education opportunities like jury service, citizens are more ignorant about government functions and less capable of acting politically than they should be in order to protect and further their individual and collective interests.

Echoing Tocqueville, Mill described juries as one of the few ways an individual can learn public morality by practicing it:

> He is called upon, while so engaged, to weigh interests not his own; to be guided, in case of conflicting claims, by another rule than his private partialities; to apply, at every turn, principles and maxims which have for their reason of existence the common good: and he usually finds associated with him in the same work minds more familiarized than his own with these ideas and operations, whose study it will be to supply reasons to his understanding, and stimulation to his feeling for the general interest. He is made to feel himself one of the public, and whatever is for their benefit to be for his benefit. Where this school of public spirit does not exist, scarcely any sense is entertained that private persons, in no eminent social situation, owe any duties to society, except to obey the laws and submit to the government.[31]

Without attending such schools, a person is unable to conceive a public good that is different from his own interest, is unable to recognize different but equally valid claims of others, and perhaps most important, is unable to see others as collaborators and allies in a collective project that depends for its success on his public-minded action, but is stuck with disabling default perceptions of a Hobbesian social world consisting only of competitors and rivals.[32] Jury service is a liberation from the servitude of private habit and routine that forestalls possibilities of a better individual and collective life.

Since many today think of the jury as a symbol rather than a significant concrete expression of our constitutional commitments to popular sovereignty, it is important to notice that both Tocqueville and Mill view the jury as having an effect because it actually is a civic schoolhouse in which a large number of citizens matriculate.[33] It has a cognitive and normative impact not simply because it is read about in the newspaper or witnessed by spectators in the courtroom, but because citizens take up responsibilities in it. As a juror, the citizen is "called upon," "guided," "made to feel" the moral and political standing of others in a way that cannot be replicated outside the forums in which power over others is not exercised concretely.

Mill makes explicit a point Tocqueville made more indirectly, though no less insistently, that civic education in the moral and practical dimensions of government cannot be acquired in any way other than by *action*, by concrete participation in decision making: "books and discourses alone are not education," "life is a problem, not a theorem," and "action can only be learnt in action."[34] This is so first, because only by doing something repeatedly, as a matter of habit, can one gain the facility that leads to a desire for further practice and perhaps attempts at higher levels of complexity. But, second, both thinkers were aware of the more basic and emotionally attractive economic and familial claims on people's time, attention, and desires. Even the best drafted books and essays were uncompetitive modes of education, doing little to disrupt the personal and vocational habits of the heart and pocketbook. Pressing public responsibilities on people so that they would be required to learn on the job, gain competence and confidence, if just for a few days a year, was the only way to lead them to desire further learning and greater responsibilities.

Though sometimes expressed condescendingly, as if civic education were a matter of cleaning up the masses so they do not make a mess of popular government, an equally strong strand in Mill's thought has to do with the requisite characteristics that secure human beings "from evil at the hands of others," namely those that allow them to be "self-protecting," and "self-dependent, relying on what they themselves can do, either separately or in concert, rather than on what others do for them."[35] An individual's "rights and interests" "are only secure from being disregarded, when the person interested is himself able, and habitually disposed, to stand up for them."[36] Thus Mill insists that if the masses are to participate in government, they must do more than simply cast a ballot every one or two years; otherwise, ordinary voters are vulnerable targets for manipulation by political elites.[37]

Justice Coram Populo

The second way the jury is politically valuable is by helping government become more transparent and accountable. For Mill, even the best designed criminal justice system containing the right rules and procedures will nonetheless fail to deliver justice if it is not constantly held open to scrutiny and if it is not embedded in a dynamic, ongoing public culture attentive to the process and the decisions made within it.

The judicial system being given, the goodness of the administration of justice is in the compound ratio of the worth of the men composing the tribunals, and the worth of the public opinion which influences or controls them. But all the "difference between a good and bad system of judicature lies in the contrivances adopted for bringing whatever moral and intellectual worth exists in the community to bear upon the administration of justice, and making it duly operative on the result."[38]

Judicial selection, procedural clarity, open courtrooms, public dissemination of court decisions, press freedom to discuss and criticize, are all crucial to the proper functioning of the machinery of justice, but Mill insists that the indispensible ingredient is an educated, active, and attentive public.

By activating, cultivating, and focusing the civic intelligence of lay citizens, the jury keeps people interested in a complex and otherwise remote domain. Such attentiveness to the justice system is needed, first, to check malfunctioning elites. Mill has no confidence that professional self-monitoring or regular internal review and assessment procedures alone can adequately check poor performance. Second, the jury spreads the awareness of how public duties such as citizens coming forward as witnesses are essential to the rule of law, how the justice system could not function without ordinary citizens doing their part.

It is important to notice that Mill, like Tocqueville, does not endorse the jury trial as a decision-making body, but only as an indirect contributor to help the public sphere operate as a checking mechanism. Devlin uses the revealing phrase *justice coram populo*, or justice before the people, to make a similar claim about the role of the jury:

> They see the way the accused is treated, listen to the police evidence of character, hear the sentences that are passed, and silently approve or disapprove. That Justice should be done *coram populo* is a good thing for the lawyers as well as for the public. It reminds them that they are not engaged upon a piece of professional ritual but in helping to give the ordinary man the sort of justice he can understand. Upon what jurymen think and say when they get home the prestige of the law in great measure depends.[39]

None of these thinkers asserts that justice *by* the people is what makes for a good legal system. The people can check, witness, silently judge the performance of court professionals. No mere spectators, they moderate and indirectly steer the power-holders, yet they do not, ultimately, exercise power independently.

Tightening Loose Connections Between the Jury, the Trial, and the Public Sphere

The civic schoolhouse account of the jury initiated by Tocqueville and further developed by Mill suggests it is a transformative space, one that can help change individuals into more civic beings and modify and moderate public attitudes toward justice. Such a space could have immense value today, I believe, as a corrective to the bloated penal state, but only if we clear away the elements of hierarchy and dependence found in both theorists and join together the micro and macro elements of the civic schoolhouse argument differently. I will focus on "how" and "what" questions at both the micro and macro levels of transformation: *how* are citizens educated in the courtroom, *how* does their education then translate into something meaningful in the wider realm of politics, *what* kind of education is this, and *what* is its range of impact in the wider realm? The answers to these questions offer a new way of conceiving democratic leadership and reform in the criminal justice domain, but before addressing them I want to very briefly consider a "why" question that fuels longstanding theoretical skepticism about the civic schoolhouse argument: why, exactly, do individuals need to engage in robust civic participation such as jury service?

Some critics hold that participatory democratic thought presumes that citizens deep down want to participate even if their current unreflective preferences point toward more superficial apolitical pursuits, and that once they do participate they will then realize the error of their earlier ways. Therefore it counts against this mode of thought that it appears to make essentialist and atavistic assumptions about the deep structure of human well-being and about the priority of political activity to achieving good lives. In response, we must recognize that although both Tocqueville and Mill do appear to believe that participation in public load-bearing activities will spawn further engagement, this is not the primary normative thrust of their arguments. Rather, it is that without load-bearing participation, the entire political system under democratic conditions will worsen: be less stable, more short-term in its choice-making, more wanton in its leadership. Participation on the jury is what Joel Feinberg has called a "mandatory right," something that, like elementary education in non-political matters, presses on individuals both for their own good and to serve fundamental collective purposes, indeed to prevent public ills.[40] Public enlightenment and attentiveness in the judicial domain are not optional if these qualities make the difference between a good and bad system of judicature; this is a system, after all, where decisions carry heavy meaning and potential consequences for plaintiffs and defendants.

A related critique suggests that the jury as civic schoolhouse is not a premodern account but a dystopian nightmare that sets citizens up for real-world experiences that will spoil rather than positively transform individual participants as a result of hierarchical, patriarchal, and inegalitarian tendencies in the political world. Scholars such as Lynn Sanders have pointed out how the contributions of women and members of marginalized social groups are often discounted in jury deliberations and other small group discussions dominated by members of the majority group, who are chosen as forepersons and typically steer discussions and voting.[41] Though marginalization is a valid problem, it leaves the normative argument untouched; jury service at the very least provides an opportunity to make more public these considerable flaws of current institutional practices. Non-jury bench trials and non-trial settlements are no less affected by cultural constraints and social inequalities, but they have the added disadvantage of being less public and less accountable. Moreover, the dystopian argument does not claim that jury service *cannot* play a positive transformative role, only that it currently reproduces existing tendencies of the dominant culture, so the core question is which, if any, court practices help contest rather than acquiesce in these tendencies.

Mark Warren has suggested that while the "romantic dogma" of currently apolitical citizens leaping at the chance to improve themselves through civic involvement should be discarded in light of the often conflictual and degrading reality of contemporary political institutions, nevertheless democratic participation offers valuable transformative opportunities. In particular, it presses participants to "take up a reflexive attitude toward the interests, desires, commitments, and entanglements that constitute one's life."[42] Though Warren emphasizes the contributions of reflexivity to more autonomous selves for individuals, the point can equally extend to the public good of a more reflexive society: one that makes difficult choices, such as when and how much to punish, with sobriety.

Mechanisms for Transformation: How Civic Beings Are Formed

Tocqueville and Mill stress responsibilization and elite guidance as the two critical mechanisms for civic transformation, but these fit oddly together and create an unsteady foundation for their argument.[43] Real power-sharing in court decisions is precisely what jolts citizens out of a default mode of self-interest and solipsism; they recognize that their verdict will have an impact on someone's life and sober up to their public responsibility. Yet the prime catalyst is the judge, who models the kind of rationality jurors are to use in their own decisionmaking. So civic beings are formed by holding power they recognize they need assistance in discharging appropriately; what begins as ownership leads to deference to judges as trustee professionals.[44]

As the incongruity indicates, this top-down understanding of the resources of transformation available in the jury is incomplete and overly hierarchical. It curiously ignores the bottom-up or peer-to-peer aspects of jury activity: pressed by the need to reach consensus because of the goal of a unanimous verdict, jurors work closely with others from different walks of life, reason together using a common language, and cooperate to serve a larger public purpose. This potential for horizontal political socialization is overlooked by Tocqueville and Mill, who stress juror dependence and deference to court professionals. These elements of hierarchy and dependence are inconsistent with the development of the independent self-protecting citizenry both theorists idealize.

Interestingly, the late eighteenth and early nineteenth century American views of the jury Tocqueville was aware of grant more credit to juror capabilities, rely less heavily upon on professional influence, and therefore render a more congruent account of how jury service can lead to an attentive public sphere. One discussion with which both Tocqueville and Mill may have been familiar was Edward Livingston's widely distributed 1822 report on the penal code he had crafted for Louisiana, in which he too celebrated the jury as a civic schoolhouse.[45] Arguing for non-optional jury trials in criminal cases, Livingston notes their significant advantages beyond the due process benefit of ensuring defendants a fair trial:

> [I]t diffuses the most valuable information among every rank of citizens; it is a school, of which every jury that is empanelled, is a separate class; where the dictates of the laws, and the consequences of disobedience to them, are practically taught. The frequent exercise of these important functions, moreover, gives a sense of dignity and self-respect. . . . Every time he is called to act in this capacity, he must feel, that though perhaps placed in the humblest station, he is yet the guardian of the life, the liberty, and the reputation of his fellow citizens, against injustice and oppression; and that, while his plain understanding has been found the best refuge for innocence, his incorruptible integrity is pronounced a sure pledge that guilt will not escape. . . . While the people enjoy the trial by jury, taken by lot from among themselves, they cannot cease to be free. The information it spreads; the sense of dignity and independence it inspires; the courage it creates, will always give them an energy of resistance, that can grapple with encroachment; and a renovating spirit that will make arbitrary power despair.[46]

Livingston's jury enrolls citizen students who, though receiving lessons on the laws, are able by dint of their own natural capacities—their plain understanding and incorruptible integrity—to serve as guardians of each other in the courtroom and in the wider expanse of political life. Power-sharing in the courtroom is connected in an unmediated way with the sober exercise of broader public responsibilities outside. Indeed, the obligatory nature of jury service is meant both as a check on public ignorance and on the judicial power, and judges appear less as domineering teachers than distant principals over whom one must keep a watchful eye.

Impact of Transformation: What Newly Civic Beings Do

As Livingston's rhetoric suggests, American views of the jury as civic school-house at the time of Tocqueville's visit linked its full-blown juridical functions to its political impact. Indeed, without tight connections drawn between the ju-ridical work of the jury trial and its political work, the alleged offense, defen-dant, and complainant would all appear as instrumental to the public good of civic education rather than the reason for the jury trial. Neither Mill nor Tocque-ville believed jurors brought anything juridically valuable into the courtroom, but rather had their natural capacities for justice triggered and directed once there. They argued from baseline assumptions of rational ignorance on the part of the public that place the schoolhouse argument at odds with the historical context out of which it emerged and weaken the normative force of the argu-ment for a revitalized role for the jury in contemporary justice.

The jury emerged historically as a result of precisely the opposite assump-tions, namely that lay citizens had something to contribute to the process of ad-judication that would help improve justice. Early jurors were viewed as wit-nesses of the character and actions of defendants, while judges had knowledge of neither.[47] Eighteenth and nineteenth century jurors were held to be cognizant of basic principles of natural right, aware of community norms, and guardians of citizen interests.[48] Twentieth and twenty-first century jurors have been seen as possessing common sense and a store of community values that counterbalance the sometimes overly procedural legal reasoning of court professionals.[49] Func-tional arguments like these hold lay participation to be critical to due process writ large, as juror participation helps courts become more attentive to particular facts, more capable of reaching a decision that is true to the facts and the law.

Long ago Aristotle considered two epistemic arguments for popular partici-pation in jury trials. First, the people have an advantage of collective wisdom when they gather together. While experts must know everything about a given matter to judge it well, individuals in a group need only bring partial knowledge of all the different aspects of a case. As long as the group can utilize this divi-sion of cognitive labor and join these perspectival attributes together, the group functions at the same high level of decisionmaking as the expert. Second, be-cause of a lived experience with the law that may be different from that of the lawmakers, the people bring relevant practical reason into their public judg-ments: as the sailor's knowledge of his ship or the homeowner's knowledge of his house may differ from the designers and builders of these structures and yet be apt for any judgment of their performance. The wearer of the shoe, after all, knows better than the cobbler where it pinches.[50]

Jury advocates today point precisely to collective wisdom and practical reason capabilities in their arguments for more rather than fewer jury trials. Because of natural limits of the human attention span, a group of twelve individuals can remember more details of evidence presented during trial than one person would.[51] Even in cases involving complex evidence, a group of twelve including one high school science teacher, or an engineer, for example, may very well be better equipped than a judge who avoided such topics in school.[52] "Jurors with expertise on a topic," write Neil Vidmar and Valerie Hans, "often take a lead role when the jury discusses that topic, and errors made by one juror are frequently corrected by another juror."[53] As for practical reasoning, members of the jury may well be more "street smart" than the judge and therefore better able to assess some kinds of evidence and especially well placed to gauge the credibility of witnesses.[54]

Moving beyond Aristotle, who knew only the large juries of ancient Athens that did not deliberate as a group before casting their verdicts, advocates also point to added epistemic benefits resulting from the goal of consensus, which presses jurors to confront each other's biases and to search for reasons and arguments that can transform the views of the evidence and legal narratives one person or group holds into a view all can accept.[55] Consensus forces the majority to work through the specific strengths of their position with those in the minority, sometimes revealing previously unseen weaknesses in the majority position.[56] Nothing like the epistemic power of dialogue and deliberation can occur when one person is in charge of reaching a decision.

Once we take jurors seriously in their juridical capacity we can envision attitudes other than generalized deference to experts and professionals in the larger public sphere. We can see how harnessing and focusing local knowledge, collective wisdom, and practical reason in the courtroom might spark continued attunement to issues of law, order, crime, and punishment outside the court.[57] Additionally, there is an even more direct connection between the juridical and political, sometimes characterized as the policymaking role of the jury or the jury as a "little parliament," in Devlin's words.[58]

When criminal justice policy appears mistaken or overly severe, or when patterns of judicial behavior have become too rigid, jurors have historically used their general verdict powers to both protect a defendant and to signal the need for change.[59] The antebellum juries in the North that acquitted defendants who assisted fugitive slaves, prohibition era juries that acquitted defendants who had violated liquor laws, Vietnam era juries that acquitted draft violators were all acting as policymakers. "At times," James Levine writes, "the jurors in effect become legislators—infusing their responses to trials with their political beliefs about the proper direction of public policy."[60] Even as draft laws grew more severe, signaling how the rule of law should be applied, juries responded with acquittals that reflected a public that had grown dissatisfied with Vietnam War policy.[61] In these instances, "jurors judge laws as well as defendants—convicting more frequently when the public approves of legal norms or the purposes they are serving, and convicting less frequently when the government policy being supported through the criminal law is in disrepute."[62]

While the verdict of a single trial, of course, does not make policy, a pattern of verdicts over time regarding the same offense does. In fact, this pattern in itself is policy even if the relevant legislative or executive bodies themselves do not react and make changes to the law or how it is applied.[63] Jury decisions in the aggregate can be seen as straightforward inputs to a policy process that incrementally adjusts to shifts in public opinion regarding a policy.

One might reject the jury as policymaking body as an unjustified exercise of discretionary power, an unfortunate infusion of populism into the legal arena that undermines the democratic system by second-guessing the proper authorities. Yet experience teaches that sometimes these authorities do not best represent the public will, because they are caught up in their own inside world of political combat, or, as Aristotle's epistemic arguments would hold, because they have not thought of everything. And sometimes, as in the fugitive slave, prohibition, and draft cases, the public sphere has reached a conclusion about policy more quickly than the formal political bodies, so the jury system allows the law to catch up before more lives are damaged.

Though judges are commonly believed to be above politics and public opinion, this is not accurate. Judges, not juries, are required to stand for re-election or for performance evaluation, and are therefore held accountable for conviction rates. Judges, not juries, must have had a strong history of political activism within a party establishment in order to rise to the bench. None of these routine pressures of formal electoral and organizational politics are felt by jurors, who "disappear into anonymity" after rendering their verdict.[64] Though reflective of public sentiments, the jury as an informal juridical body can sometimes be more independent of the pressures of public opinion than the bench because jurors' careers are not at stake in a decision.

As it stands, the traditional civic schoolhouse argument draws only vague and wishfully elitist connections between citizen socialization during trials and the moderating effects that result for the wider political sphere. Tocqueville and Mill did not have enough faith that the public could make a direct positive impact on the justice of the courtroom or the legislative decisions that set the underlying criminal justice framework. A more theoretically complete and normatively appealing version of the argument posits the jury trial as more than a deference machine for shaping respect for the rule of law; rather, to put it crudely, it is a deliberation machine for critically attuning public reflections on law and order and ultimately for helping to create a justice system in which citizens can take pride. Indeed, I think the spirit of Tocqueville's argument points outward to a more dynamic and critical civic consciousness than he thought possible for mass publics, one that would reject the demagogic emotional appeals of politicians who capitalize on fear and insecurity.[65]

Rebuilding the Schoolhouse: A Task for Democratic Court Professionals

We live in an age of profound and profuse distrust of both government and citizen action, even as the access to information about our political institutions has exploded. How, embedded as we are in mass media and instant, constant digital communication, would we need such a quaint and seemingly pointless activity as jury service for the purpose of civic education? The civic schoolhouse argument suggests that face-to-face, active learning about real institutions where concrete decisions are made is precisely what is needed for coping with a media-world that has unmoored us from the political realities of crime and punishment we are all too comfortable drifting around in distrust. Action clarifies, anchors, responsibilizes.

A neo-Tocquevillian normative reconstruction of the civic schoolhouse argument would proceed along two tracks that aim to demonstrate how the jury trial as a public transformative space has positive juridical and political impact: first, the micro-level track that explains how the jury contributes communicative elements that help the trial's normal functions work better, and second, the macro-level track that shows how the jury shapes the contours of the justice system in beneficial ways. The limited space remaining permits only a sketch of these arguments, which support more citizen involvement in criminal justice and point to a more democratic mode of court professionalism.

Co-creating Justice in a Public, Communicative Space

Because juries are small groups of lay people ordinarily untrained in the law, they help shape the communicative dimensions of the courtroom. Following Antony Duff, we can see that trials aim to call defendants to account for their actions, to encourage an exchange of reasons that explain, justify, excuse, or, alternatively, to draw attention to culpability. A criminal trial should seek to fix blame but also to incorporate the offender into this dialogical process to remind as much as penalize, to remind the offender of the values the law embodies that he also shares, to regain his assistance in defending the polity from lawbreaking. As a forum for communication and moral deliberation, the trial must be conducted so that the offender can come to a heightened awareness of the meaning of the offense. It cannot be purely instrumental—a platform of great power to scare an offender into future compliance or a vehicle of mere recompense for the victim. Trials should seek the assent and not merely the obedience of the offender.[66]

Yet there are many ways court formality impedes communication: the imposing architecture of court buildings, black robes of judges, technical language of the lawyers, the complex rules and procedures court professionals need to follow to "manage" a case. All these normal features of court process, Duff et al. write, "contribute to the creation of an environment in which the participation of the defendant as a responsible citizen who can speak in his own voice is substantially hampered."[67] Juries inject an informal element into the courtroom that both corrects for the deficiencies of overly formal procedures while also adding substantive benefits.

A jury of the defendant's peers has value on this account because it forces courtroom dialogue to be in the language of everyday life, rather than the default language of court professionals. Though jurors themselves do not engage in spoken dialogue with the complainant and defendant, their presence ensures that this dialogue is conducted using terms, concepts, and narrative forms that all will understand. The presence of lay citizens also communicates to the defendant that the alleged offense is something for which he is accountable not just to the victim but to the society of which he is a member.

The fact that juries hold responsibility for determining the guilt or innocence of a defendant signifies that "ordinary people" are listening to his reasons and weighing their merits. Unlike court professionals, these ordinary people have not seen hundreds of similar cases and they are not accountable for conviction rates or reelection or performance reviews. In short, they are not officials holding seats in bureaucratic systems; therefore, they help the court produce a decision that is legitimate for both victim and offender. The jury's role, as Robert Burns puts it, is to engage "in highly contextual moral evaluation," "a kind of factfinding enormously more serious than the clichés of mass political discourse and a kind of evaluation continuous with the moral world, not the implicit norms of public and private bureaucracies."[68] A jury trial has juridical merit, therefore, not because it follows judges but precisely because of its independent, democratic elements.

This micro-level argument for the jury as a form of justice-making by lay people that creates a better form of punishment than professional technocratic justice and is what the parties in an alleged offense require has much in common with contemporary restorative justice arguments about the benefits of informal justice.[69] The jury trial, properly understood, combines formal and informal to create a space of transformative public communication in which the meaning of an offense for victim and society and the offender's own status both as a wrongdoer and as a citizen deserving of respect can all be acknowledged.

The Jury vs. Penal Populism

Taking jury trials not individually but in the aggregate, we can see how they might shape the general contours of the justice system by educating jurors in the law and its effects, by encouraging the growth of responsibility for collective decisions, and by connecting individuals to the state apparatus that is authorized to protect them, thus in all these ways implicating individuals in the actions of the state. While the micro-level argument shows the normative gains for a particular case to have the public in the courtroom, the macro-level argument points to the normative advantages for the justice system if issues of law and order become part of public discourse and awareness outside the courtroom.

As we have seen, some argue that punishment is a matter for experts that should be de-politicized and taken out of the public realm. Such arguments are not without merit, especially as a response to the wave of arbitrary, punitive, inhumane, and costly "three strikes" mandatory minimum sentencing policy-making in the 1980s and 1990s. Prominent scholars otherwise friendly to democratic political action call for sentencing policy to be set by expert panels well-insulated from the political pressures that impact legislators and executive officials.[70] Though well-intentioned, I believe this strategy mistaken because it exacerbates one of the chief causes of three strikes legislation, namely the widespread distrust of experts and officials with discretionary authority agitated and capitalized upon by political parties, candidates, and other moral entrepreneurs seeking short-term political gains. It leaves the citizenry as no more than angry spectators "screaming from the sidelines" in Ian Loader's colorful imagery.[71] It assumes too quickly and without evidence that punitiveness is a fixed mass opinion that cannot be influenced by good reasons in constructive public dialogue.[72]

A neo-Tocquevillian account understands such so-called populist punitiveness not as a reaction to a state that is too timid and lenient toward violent offenders, but as a function of the kinds of social separation that isolate citizens from each other and from state officials acting in their name.[73] Studies attempting to gauge populist punitiveness have shown that the more a person knows about a particular case, the more context they have about why a violent act occurred, the more details they know about the individuals involved, the less punitive they are with regard to the case.[74] What is needed, therefore, is not exclusion but inclusion; not less participation but more participation within institutional settings that both empower citizen decision making and challenge it to be reasonable, responsible, and accountable.

Justice making in the micro-domain impacts larger collective views of justice in the macro-domain one juror at a time. In their famous study of the American jury, Harry Kalven and Hans Zeisel noticed that juries did not differ much in their verdicts from judges, but when they did differ it was in the direction of greater leniency. They speculated that one reason jurors were more lenient was that they, rather than judges, could more readily sympathize with the offender as a peer.[75] A neo-Tocquevillian approach would connect the leniency of jurors at the level of the trial to a greater critical awareness of the effects of criminal justice policy more generally, on neighborhoods, public budgets, not to mention on individuals and their families. The way to a less punitive and more restorative criminal justice system is not through de-politicizing justice, but the opposite, re-politicizing justice as a public deliberative practice.

The task for democratic court professionals is clear but difficult: restore the jury's place in the American criminal justice system. Three kinds of reform stand out, in order of increasing controversy. First, jury reforms already endorsed by many American judges and lawyers, like allowing note taking, deliberation during trial breaks, and questions for witnesses further the goals of communication and responsibility and can be easily implemented. Second, I think a more aggressive line can be taken on the necessity of jury trials without deviating from core strands of American legal practice and theory. At the time of Tocqueville's visit most criminal cases were heard in jury trials; now barely 5 percent move forward to this stage.[76] Constitutionally speaking, a return to the jury trial as the default mode of hearing alleged criminal offenses is easy. The jury is doctrinally well established, indeed holding such a prominent place in the debates over the framing and ratification of the Constitution and in the body of the fundamental law itself that the jury's contemporary emaciation should be more of a call to arms for Originalists than it has been. The difficulties are more prosaic: because of the hyperproceduralism of the American trial, with its multiplicity of rules of evidence and exclusion, the modern jury trial, as Alschuler has noted, "has become one of the most cumbersome and expensive fact-finding mechanisms that humankind has devised."[77] Prospective reformers on the left and right attuned to the human costs of the penal state will need to address procedural reforms, however knotty these prove to be, and seek to clarify and streamline court process. Third, other, more controversial changes should be debated, such as an increased role for juries in sentencing. Oddly, since the Supreme Court has mandated that for states with the death penalty juries must have a role in determining the sentence, all but a handful of states leave juries out of the decision in noncapital cases. Part of the general professionalization of American law in the twentieth century, it is time to question this restriction in noncapital cases.[78]

At a more fundamental level, reformers seeking to engage the penal state will organize public support for decriminalization, where possible, to keep some offensive acts out of the formal justice system, and for more serious experiments with restorative justice programs, especially for nonviolent and youth offenders. In this way, rebuilding the civic schoolhouse of the jury can be a core part of a long-term effort of democratic court professionals and criminal justice reformers to responsibilize citizens and encourage greater sobriety in the public discourse of crime and punishment.

Notes

1. Thanks are due to the Scottish Centre for Crime and Justice Research and to the School of Law at the University of Edinburgh, where I completed work on this chapter.

2. For Tocqueville's contribution to penal policy analysis, see Gustave de Beaumont and Alexis de Tocqueville, *On the Penitentiary System of the United States and its Application in France* (1833), trans. Francis Lieber (New York: A.M. Kelley, 1970). Tocqueville uses inconsistencies in penal policy, disparities in prison conditions in particular, to illustrate administrative instability and short-term legislative decisionmaking in American democracy. Alexis de Tocqueville, *Democracy in America*, ed. Olivier Zunz, trans. Arthur Goldhammer (New York: The Library of America, 2004), 287-88.

3. See John Pratt, *Penal Populism* (London: Routledge, 2007).

4. See Nicola Lacey, *The Prisoners' Dilemma: Political Economy and Punishment in Contemporary Democracies* (Cambridge: Cambridge University Press, 2008), 191-92; Franklin E. Zimring, "Populism, Democratic Government, and the Decline of Expert Authority: Some Reflections on 'Three Strikes' in California," *Pacific Law Journal* 28 (1996): 243–56; Franklin E. Zimring, Gordon Hawkins, and Sam Kamin, *Punishment and Democracy: Three Strikes and You're Out in California* (New York: Oxford University Press, 2001). Philip Pettit, "Is Criminal Justice Politically Feasible?" *Buffalo Criminal Law Review* 5 (2002): 427–50, and "Depoliticizing Democracy," *Ratio Juris* 17 (2004): 52-65.

5. See John Doble, "Attitudes to Punishment in the US—Punitive and Liberal Opinions," in *Changing Attitudes to Punishment*, eds. J. Roberts and M. Hough (Portland, OR: Willan, 2002); J. Roberts, L. Stalans, D. Indermaur, and M. Hough, *Penal Populism and Public Opinion: Lessons from Five Counties* (Oxford: Oxford University Press, 2003).

6. A number of works stress Tocqueville's "strange" and "aristocratic" liberalism that embraced both a highly participatory and constrained democracy. See, for example, Roger Boesche, *The Strange Liberalism of Alexis de Tocqueville* (Ithaca, NY: Cornell University Press, 1987) and Alan S. Kahan, *Aristocratic Liberalism: The Social and Political Thought of Jacob Burckhardt, John Stuart Mill, and Alexis de Tocqueville* (Oxford: Oxford University Press, 1992). Sheldon Wolin writes that "Tocqueville could render American democracy as tolerable by depicting it as a democracy qualified by the equivalents of aristocratic institutions." *Tocqueville Between Two Worlds* (Princeton: Princeton University Press: 2001), 479. Cf. Seymour Drescher, "Who Needs Ancienneté? Tocqueville on Aristocracy and Modernity," *History of Political Thought* 24 (2003), 627.

7. Tocqueville calls the jury an *école gratuite*, a school that is free of charge. I use the term "civic schoolhouse," to draw attention to the kind of education Tocqueville believes jurors receive.

8. This section closely follows my discussion in "Democracy's 'Free School': Tocqueville and Lieber on the Value of the Jury," *Political Theory* (forthcoming).

9. Tocqueville, *Democracy in America*, 318.

10. Tocqueville, *Democracy in America*, 303. See also Jack Lively's discussion of juror education in *The Social and Political Thought of Alexis de Tocqueville* (Oxford: Clarendon Press, 1965), 181.

11. Tocqueville, *Democracy in America*, 315.

12. Informant Francis Calley Gray said American children "never turn to their masters" but "manage everything among themselves, and there is no one of fifteen years old who has not performed a juror's functions a hundred times." Tocqueville, *Journey to America*, ed. J. P. Mayer, trans. George Lawrence (New Haven, CT: Yale University Press, 1960), 57.

13. Tocqueville, *Democracy in America*, 316.

14. Robert P. Kraynak writes that Tocqueville shows how "democratic citizens who exercise liberty with a sense of moral responsibility attain a nobility of character that shines with the brightness of virtue." "Tocqueville's Constitutionalism," *American Political Science Review* 81 (1987), 1193.

15. Tocqueville, *Democracy in America*, 316.

16. Ibid.

17. Tocqueville compares French and American ideas in *Democracy in America*, 351. See James Ceaser for a discussion of legalism as a traditionalist counterweight to rationalism in Tocqueville. "Alexis de Tocqueville on Political Science, Political Culture, and the Role of the Intellectual," *American Political Science Review* 79 (1985), 665.

18. Tocqueville, *Democracy in America*, 316.

19. This is a "peculiar pedagogy" indeed, in Bruce James Smith's words. The jury is a "free institution" that jars the individual out of the private sphere into the public, but also seems to encourage something less than "mature" political liberty. See "A Liberal of a New Kind," in *Interpreting Tocqueville's Democracy in America*, ed. Ken Masugi (Savage, MD: Rowman and Littlefield, 1991), 92-4.

20. Tocqueville, *Democracy in America*, 303.

21. Tocqueville, *Democracy in America*, 309.

22. Tocqueville, *Democracy in America*, 306. His account of the bar is a rare point of agreement with another keen nineteenth century ethnographer, James Bryce, who found the legal profession a "guiding and restraining power, tempering the crudity or haste of democracy by its attachment to rule and precedent," though less powerful a social force in the 1880s than it had been a half-century before. *American Commonwealth* (1888-) (Indianapolis, IN: Liberty Fund, 1995), 490.

23. Tocqueville, *Journey to America*, 297.

24. Tocqueville held the criminal law to be more straightforwardly a translation of public morality into law; for this reason, the public had traditionally viewed the judge's role in criminal cases as merely "a passive instrument of social power." *Democracy in America*, 318. In his view, it is only after being socialized though experiences being directed by the judge in civil trials that citizens had come to tacitly agree to being directed in criminal trials.

25. Tocqueville, *Democracy in America*, 318.

26. John Stuart Mill, *Considerations on Representative Government,* in *The Collected Works of John Stuart Mill* Vol. XIX, ed. John M. Robson (Toronto: University of Toronto Press, 1977), 390-1.

27. Mill, *Representative Government*, 391.

28. Mill, *Representative Government*, 385.

29. Mill, *Representative Government*, 404.

30. Mill, *Representative Government*, 411-412.

31. Mill, *Representative Government*, 412.

32. Mill, *Representative Government*, 412. Cf. Mill, "M. de Tocqueville on Democracy in America," *The Edinburgh Review* LXXII (Oct. 1840) (Reprinted in *Collected Works* Vol. XVIII: 1-83).

33. Richard Abel calls the jury a symbol of democracy that serves as a "reminder that an essential element in the legitimacy of our legal system is direct democracy." "Redirecting Social Studies of Law," *Law and Society Review* 14 (1980), 812. Yet the term "symbolic" dodges the question of what work the jury does that is valuable, implying that the fact of 1 or 1000 jury trials a week across the country, or the fact of maximal or minimal procedural restrictions on jury deliberations, would not impact the jury's power, which is constant and stems from what it could do and what it represents not what it is.

34. Mill, "Tocqueville on Democracy in America," 24-25.

35. Mill, *Representative Government*, 404

36. Mill, *Representative Government*, 404.

37. Mill, "Tocqueville on Democracy in America," 22-23.

38. Mill, *Representative Government*, 391.

39. Patrick Devlin, *Trial by Jury* (London: Methuen, 1966), 24-25.

40. Joel Feinberg, "Voluntary Euthanasia and the Inalienable Right to Life," *Philosophy & Public Affairs* 7 (1978): 93-123.

41. Lynn Sanders, "Against Deliberation," *Political Theory* 25 (1997): 347-376.

42. Mark E. Warren, "What Should We Expect from More Democracy? Radical Democratic Responses to Politics," *Political Theory* 24 (1996), 257.

43. I borrow the term "responsibilize," from criminal justice theorist Pat O'Malley, who uses it to describe the shedding of security tasks from the state to the citizenry. See his "Risk and Responsibility," in *Foucault and Political Reason: Liberalism, Neo-Liberalism and Rationalities of Government*, eds. A. Barry, T. Osbourne, and N. Rose (Chicago: University of Chicago Press, 1996). I use the term less ironically than O'Malley.

44. See my *Democratic Professionalism: Citizen Participation and the Reconstruction of Professional Ethics, Identity, and Practice* (University Park: Penn State University Press, 2008) for a critical discussion of trustee professionalism.

45. Livingston is the only informant Tocqueville mentions by name in *Democracy*, noting that he "is one of those rare men whom one likes from having read their writings" (p. 16).

46. Livingston, *Project of a New Penal Code for the State of Louisiana* (London: Baldwin, Cradock, and Joy, 1824), 15-16.

47. See Thomas Andrew Green, *Verdict According to Conscience: Perspectives on the English Criminal Trial Jury, 1200-1800* (Chicago: University of Chicago Press, 1985).

48. See Shannon C. Stimson, *The American Revolution in the Law: Anglo-American Jurisprudence before John Marshall* (Princeton: Princeton University Press, 1990).

49. See Jeffrey Abramson, *We, the Jury: The Jury System and the Ideal of Democracy* (Cambridge, MA: Harvard University Press, 2000).

50. See Aristotle's *Politics*, Book III, chapter 11. For a fine discussion, see Jeremy Waldron, "The Wisdom of the Multitude: Some Reflections on Book 3, Chapter 11 of Aristotle's *Politics*," *Political Theory* 23 (1995): 563-584.

51. See, for example, Reid Hastie, Steven D. Penrod, and Nancy Pennington, *Inside the Jury* (Cambridge, MA: Harvard University Press, 1983), 236.

52. Randolph N. Jonacrit, *The American Jury System* (New Haven, CT: Yale University Press, 2003), 49.

53. Neil Vidmar and Valerie P. Hans, *American Juries: The Verdict* (New York: Prometheus Books, 2007), 340.

54. See Devlin, *Trial by Jury*, 149; 158-62

55. Aristotle may have ignored the epistemic value of consensus because Greek juries did not deliberate but just dropped their verdict ballots off on their way out of the courtroom.

56. Jonacrit, *The American Jury System*, 61-3.

57. John Gastil, E. Pierre Deess, and Phil Weiser, "Civic Awakening in the Jury Room: A Test of the Connection between Jury Deliberation and Political Participation," *Journal of Politics* 64 (2002): 585-595; Gastil et al., "Jury Service and Electoral Participation: A Test of the Participation Hypothesis," *Journal of Politics* 70 (2008): 351-367.

58. *Trial By Jury*, 164.

59. It should be noted that American juries have also resisted change, as did Southern juries with respect to civil rights law. For a discussion, see Peter Bachrach "The Senate Debate on the Right to Jury Trial Versus the Right to Vote Controversy: A Case Study in Liberal Thought," *Ethics* 68 (1958): 210-216.

60. James P. Levine, *Juries and Politics* (Belmont, CA: Wadsworth, 1992), 116.

61. James P. Levine, "The Legislative Role of Juries," *American Bar Foundation Research Journal* 9 (1984), 627.

62. Levine, "Legislative Role of Juries," 633.

63. Gary J. Jacobsohn, "Citizen Participation in Policy-Making: The Role of the Jury," *Journal of Politics* 39 (1977), 76.

64. Harry Kalven, Jr., and Hans Zeisel note anonymity as one of the jury's historically touted virtues. *The American Jury* (Chicago: University of Chicago Press, 1966), 3-11.

65. See, for example, Tocqueville's encomium to township democracy, "On the Town Spirit in New England," which praises the "community spirit," and "strength and independence" of residents who are "citizens" and not "mere subjects of an administration." *Democracy in America*, 75.

66. R. A. Duff, *Trials and Punishments* (Cambridge: Cambridge University Press, 1986), 144.

67. Antony Duff et al., *The Trial on Trial Volume 3: Towards a Normative Theory of the Criminal Trial* (Oxford: Hart, 2007), 211.

68. Robert B. Burns, "The History and Theory of the American Jury," *California Law Review* 83 (1995), 1490.

69. Restorative justice is a movement within criminal justice that calls for improved communication and more opportunities for reconciliation between victim and offender, and for greater community involvement in the process. See Howard Zehr, *Changing Lenses: A New Focus for Crime and Justice* (Scottdale, PA: Herald Press, 1990); and John Braithwaite, *Restorative Justice and Responsive Regulation* (New York: Oxford University Press, 2002).

70. See the works cited in note 4 above.

71. Ian Loader, "Playing with Fire? Democracy and the Emotions of Crime and Punishment," in *Emotions, Crime and Justice*, eds. S. Karstedt, I. Loader, and H. Strang (Oxford: Hart, 2006).

72. See Albert W. Dzur and Rekha Mirchandani: "Punishment and Democracy: The Role of Public Deliberation," *Punishment & Society* 9 (2007), 151-175. The mass opinion blamed for three-strikes legislation in the US was influenced by a highly charged political environment and an exceptionally narrow media perspective on criminal justice issues. In short, "public opinion" was non-reflective and manipulated.

73. Indeed, though their overarching narrative frame insists the public is punitive, evidence offered by scholars such as Pratt and Zimring points to social fragmentation, neoliberal state policies, manipulative mass politics, and commercialized media as forces that distort rather than represent public views. Under circumstances that are not politicized, fragmented, and made into entertainment, public views are more sober and humane.

74. See the works cited in note 3 above.

75. Kalven and Zeisel, *The American Jury*, chapter 15.

76. In antebellum Indianapolis, for example, 92 percent of all criminal cases went to jury in the 1820s and 1830s. David J. Bodenhamer, "The Democratic Impulse and Legal Change in the Age of Jackson: The Example of Criminal Juries in Antebellum Indiana," *The Historian* 45 (1983), 218. Today, the most recent Bureau of Justice Statistics report finds that juries heard 4 percent of all alleged criminal offenses brought before federal courts. State courts report similar numbers.

77. Albert W. Alschuler, "Mediation with a Mugger: The Shortage of Adjudicative Services and the Need for a Two-Tier Trial System in Civil Cases," *Harvard Law Review* 99 (1986), 1824.

78. Until the 1930s more than a quarter of American states allowed juries a role in sentencing in noncapital cases. See Jenia Iontcheva, "Jury Sentencing as Democratic Practice," *Virginia Law Review* 89 (2003), 319.

Part III
Statesmanship Outside of Government

Chapter 10

From Associations to Organizations: Tocqueville, NGOs, and the Colonization of Civic Leadership

Derek Barker

When Alexis de Tocqueville visited the United States in 1832, he was struck by the vitality of its civic sphere: "Americans of all ages, all conditions, all minds constantly unite. . . . Everywhere that, at the head of a new undertaking, you see the government in France . . . count on it that you will perceive an association in the United States" (II.2.5, 489).[1] For Tocqueville, the key features of democracy in America were not institutional structures, but rather the associations through which citizens developed habits and mores of citizenship. Whether Tocqueville is considering juries, churches, or temperance groups, he is not interested in their success in the discrete tasks of administering justice, fostering spirituality, or advocating sobriety. Instead, Tocqueville attempts to theorize their broader civic role in cultivating habits and mores conducive to democracy. If Tocqueville returned to the United States today, he might be surprised by recent developments in our civil society. In place of Tocqueville's civic associations, different structures have emerged to dominate the civic landscape: non-governmental organizations, commonly referred to as NGOs. NGOs accomplish a wide variety of social tasks, such as grant making, service delivery, and political advocacy, and they address all kinds of social and public needs, from alleviating poverty to supporting the arts. At the same time, they are becoming highly professionalized, hierarchical, and bureaucratic, not unlike their government counterparts. This raises the question of whether NGOs are currently addressing the distinct political functions once performed by civic associations. Although formal organizations may be more efficient than ever in accomplishing their *technical* tasks, this essay considers whether they are cultivating *civic* work to strengthen democracy.

Tocqueville himself does not use the language of "leadership" or "statesmanship" to describe the democratic role of civic associations. However, if leadership, broadly defined, means the ability to facilitate.collective action, the role of civic associations in democracy must be an important component of a complete theory of civic leadership. At the same time, the concept of leadership may be useful for understanding new applications of Tocqueville's thought to current challenges in democracy. This essay raises the question of whether any entities in contemporary civil society currently play the leadership functions that Tocqueville observed in American civic associations during the nineteenth century. To do so, I identify several leadership qualities of civic associations in Tocqueville's political thought, and apply this framework to current trends in the NGO sector. My intent is not to present a comprehensive "theory" or new "definition" of civic leadership, but rather to identify a few important leadership qualities of civic associations and the most important challenges that contemporary civil society organizations face in fulfilling their leadership potential. This does not require a new interpretation of Tocqueville's thought, but rather an effort, in the spirit of applied political theory, to bring Tocqueville's thought to bear on specific problems in contemporary civil society.

Contrary to the received wisdom of civil society theory, I argue, whether organizations are located in the government, corporate, or civic sector is much less important than the degree to which they incorporate an organizational ethos that threatens to "colonize" society as a whole.[2] This colonization is neither intentional nor violent, but it points toward a single system in which civil society and government have the same underlying institutional challenges and professional culture, leaving civil society organizations equally disconnected from, and unable to command the confidence of, citizens. I do not claim that this colonization has been completed. Indeed, my intention is to suggest that alternative forms of civic leadership are beginning to emerge, and may be able to fulfill the democratic role once played by Tocquevillian associations.

Tocqueville, Civic Leadership, and the Politics of Association

Although Tocqueville accepted the inevitability of democracy as a "providential fact" (I, 6), his attitude toward this revolutionary change was cautious and critical. Tocqueville, who came from an aristocratic background, celebrated the fragile accomplishments of democracy in America, but he observed negative consequences of the attempt to establish democratic institutions in France, without the corresponding norms and habits necessary to sustain them. Tocqueville acknowledged that aristocracy was premised on a sense of radical inequality that was no longer socially or morally acceptable. However, in his famous chapter on individualism in democracies, Tocqueville also worried that democracy would undermine the social cohesion and stability once provided by feudal relationships:

> Aristocratic institutions have the effect of binding each man tightly to several of his fellow citizens. . . . As in aristocratic societies all citizens are placed at a fixed post, some above the others, it results also that each of them always perceived higher than himself a man whose protection is necessary to him, and below he finds another whom he can call upon for cooperation. . . . In democratic peoples . . . the fabric of time is torn at every moment and the trace of generations is effaced (II.2.2, 483).

Although Tocqueville's individualism thesis has influenced contemporary studies of community and social capital, it has received relatively little attention for its implications for concepts of leadership. However, from this perspective, individualism can be understood as a kind of leadership vacuum. The fundamental problem of democracy is that, without the leadership of royalty, the individual would become radically isolated from others: democracy "constantly leads him back toward himself alone and threatens finally to confine him wholly in the solitude of his own heart" (484). This isolation would in turn have several political consequences. Without aspiration to aristocratic distinction, citizens would begin to see themselves as part of a homogeneous mass. Lacking any sense of a higher community, citizens' moral capacities would degenerate into narrow self-interest. And isolated from one another, they would begin to view themselves as powerless to engage in collective action: "Despotism, which in its nature is fearful, sees the most certain guarantee of its own duration in the isolation of men" (II.2.4, 485).[3] The cumulative result would leave citizens vulnerable to a tyranny of majority opinion that, while free of coercive government power, would exercise a stultifying and oppressive power over citizens' souls, leaving little room for genuine freedom of thought and discussion (I.2.7).

Aristocratic leadership, through a rigidly hierarchical system of organization, thus served at least three important political functions: first, *integration*, connecting each member of the community to a larger entity through bonds of loyalty; second, *differentiation*, providing citizens with a sense of honor and distinct identity based on their unique station within a larger hierarchy; and third, *capacity-building*, a means for the weaker members of society to contribute to society through the works of great men. This system worked for a time, but it was based in relationships of radical inequality and dependency that had, for good reason, given way to a new system with political equality and class mobility.

According to Tocqueville, democracy requires some kind of substitute for aristocratic leadership, capable of mediating its disintegrating and leveling tendencies, yet in a way that is consistent with democratic norms. Immediately after laying out his individualism thesis, Tocqueville describes the associational life in the United States as a possible remedy. As Tocqueville writes, "In democratic peoples, associations must take the place of the powerful particular person whom equality of conditions has made disappear" (II.2.5, 492). In fact, each of the aristocratic leadership functions has a counterpart in Tocqueville's description of associational life. First, as Tocqueville elaborates, associations have an *integrating* role, as they provide citizens an opportunity to develop norms of enlightened self-interest, and the skills and habits of cooperation.[4] However, in contrast to aristocracy, the method of integration is horizontal, working through social networks among equals rather than relationships of dependency. Second, associations play a *differentiating* role, as they provide spaces for individuals to form groups with distinct interests and identities.[5] Most important, they provide a sense of community even for those who hold beliefs that are not accepted by the majority, thus mediating the tyranny of majority opinion. This differentiation, however, is again horizontal rather than vertical, creating diversity among equal groups rather than inequality between lords and vassals. Finally, associations enable *capacity-building*, as citizens learn the skills and habits of collective action and organize themselves to accomplish great deeds. Through the "reciprocal action of men upon one another," citizens in democracies can experience social and political power that they could not have as isolated individuals (II.2.5, 491). But at the same time, associations connect and maximize the power of equal citizens rather than rely upon the power of great individuals. In this way, civic associations provide a potential model of democratic leadership that is at least functionally equivalent to aristocracy: "I firmly believe that one cannot found an aristocracy anew in the world; but I think that when plain citizens associate, they can constitute very opulent, very influential, very strong beings—in a word, aristocratic persons" (II.4.7, 668).

Because leadership for Tocqueville depended upon a combination of socially accepted norms and habitual practices in daily life, however, he feared that democratic government alone would be unable to accomplish these leadership functions. Although Tocqueville recognized the necessity of government and praised its decentralized form in America, he also viewed it as insufficient on its own to produce the relational connections necessary for social trust and norms of cooperation.[6] Rule-driven and bureaucratic, government tends toward standardization and routine, in contrast to the dynamism and differentiation required of the civic sphere (II.2.5, 492). Finally, Tocqueville feared the development of a large administrative state that would displace citizen-based collective action: "The more it puts itself in place of associations, the more particular persons, losing the idea of associating with each other, will need it to come to their aid. . . . Will the public administration in the end direct all the industries for which an isolated citizen cannot suffice?" (II.2.5, 491). The civic leadership functions necessary in a democracy, Tocqueville suggests, depend critically upon a civic sphere that is distinct from government, not only in its voluntary character, but, more importantly, in its civic leadership qualities.

What has happened to the integration, differentiation, and capacity-building functions of civic associations? As the civic sphere has become increasingly dominated by specialization, efficiency, and above all, organization, we can apply each aspect of Tocqueville's theory to identify the most important challenges to civic leadership in democracy today.

Civil Society and NGOs: Neo-Tocquevillian Theories of Civic Leadership

Following the Eastern European democratic revolutions that began with the fall of the Berlin Wall in 1989, a concept with a long history in political philosophy re-emerged throughout academic scholarship, political journalism, and democratic activism around the world in the 1990s: "civil society," or the vast range of voluntary organizations and associations, as distinct from government and for-profit corporations. Political theorists, many directly influenced by Tocqueville, characterized this overlooked realm as "between government and market," a social space for voluntary collective action that could combine the virtues of each while avoiding their weaknesses.[7] In liberal democracies, civil society offered the potential to mediate the excesses of market economies in a non-coercive way independent of government. In the failed communist regimes, civil society made sense of how common citizens had managed to organize and even assert themselves against repressive governments in a way that maintained social solidarity. Robert Bellah and colleagues had written of the social importance of "habits of the heart," and a rich literature on "social capital" now began to emerge to describe the political importance of the civil society sector.[8] Lester Salamon captured the sense of excitement around the civil society concept in the early 1990s, describing an "associational revolution" in the civil sector, comparable in importance to the development of the nation-state in the government sector.[9]

Although NGOs lack the coercive power of government, they are distinct from other civic associations, for better or for worse, in that they are *organizations*, corporate entities with hierarchical structures, specialized tasks, and professional staff, potentially allowing them to play a privileged leadership role. Of course, the vast majority of NGOs have specific tasks unrelated to democracy, from alleviating third world poverty to supporting the arts. There may thus have been little reason to expect that any particular NGO would have greater legitimacy than government or produce any democratic benefits. Still, the role of the NGO sector in democracy may be greater than the sum of its parts, the theory suggested, because it suggests a shift in power away from government and toward organizations that are just as public in their mission, but potentially less bureaucratic in their administration. Although NGOs had no inherent democratic role, many advocates thought that they were ideally positioned as potential instruments through which citizens could act collectively. As management theorist Peter Drucker wrote, "The right answer to the question Who takes care of the social challenges of the knowledge society? is neither the government nor the employing organization. The answer is a separate and new social sector."[10] As the most organized entities in civil society, NGOs were thought to be able to apply large-scale financial resources toward social tasks without expanding government or depending on the whims of individual charity. They should have the potential for entrepreneurial risk-taking and innovation similar to for-profit corporations, but directed toward public-serving missions, leading to a dynamic and differentiated public sector. They could enlist everyday citizens as volunteers in collective action, while maintaining the knowledge and specialization necessary to address the most complex and pressing social problems. At least in the early 1990s, the assumption was that an active and engaged citizenry was ready to assert itself and fill this new space that was apparently opening in civil society. Recent scholarship continues to affirm this logic. For example, a recent task force of the American Political Science Association framed its discussion of nonprofit organizations as a potential remedy to the "general downward drift of associational life."[11] According to civil society theory, NGOs might allow democracy to have its cake and eat it too: technical expertise without government bureaucracy, vast financial resources without burdening taxpayers, collective power brought to bear on public problems without the use of legislation.

A decade later, NGOs have continued to proliferate, amass vast resources, and bring technical expertise to bear on a wide range of social problems. However, there is little evidence that they have made a meaningful dent in the challenges of civic integration, differentiation, and capacity that Tocqueville described as confronting democracy as a whole. If Tocqueville's theory of civic leadership is correct, the crucial problem for advocates of NGOs as democratic actors is that civic organizations must be clearly distinct from government institutions and for-profit corporations, especially in the way that they relate to citizens. In the following sections, I identify three inter-related trends across the NGO sphere, each of which limits organizations' possible civic leadership functions of integration, differentiation, and capacity-building.

Integration: Organizations and the Problem of Inwardness

The first leadership quality that Tocqueville saw in the rich associational life of nineteenth century America was its role in social integration and resisting the democratic tendency toward social isolation. One might think that perhaps their location in the civic rather than government sphere would enable NGOs to perform these integrative functions. Indeed, the rhetoric of "community building" and "civic engagement" is prevalent in the NGO sphere. However, similar to bureaucratic agencies in the government sphere, organizations have specific tasks that they must accomplish in order to ensure their survival. Significantly, NGOs are defined not by what they are, but rather what they are *not*—hence, "nongovernmental." This means that no particular NGO has any necessary connection to democracy, except to the extent that government is assumed to be inherently less democratic than alternative actors in the civic sphere. Instead of the civic work needed to improve democracy, their primary concerns are specific tasks such as grant-making, fundraising, service delivery, advocacy, or education. The civic associations described by Tocqueville had their own particular tasks, but they were also structured in ways that inclined them to produce critical civic benefits of integration, differentiation, and capacity-building. Contemporary NGOs, however, do not appear to have the same sorts of structural features. Instead, their overwhelming imperative is to accomplish their discrete tasks with maximum efficiency.

According to recent focus group research by Richard Harwood and John Creighton, executives from a range of community-based organizations display a pattern of "inwardness," a preoccupation with their primary tasks at the expense of their possible community-building role.[12] Consistent with the principles of NGO proponents, the organizations have recognizable community-serving missions, such as strengthening local schools and serving vulnerable children. One might expect that such place-based organizations would have an incentive to devote resources toward the integrative, community-building civic leadership that Tocqueville observed in historical civic associations. However, to accomplish their missions, organizations must have a disciplined and savvy focus on their core priorities. When asked about their possible civic role, organization executives were quite clear about their limitations, and instead see their work in strikingly narrow terms, with their immediate attention directed to specific projects and programs. As one executive remarks, "We're a program organization. . . . We have a very specific goal. We work with communities that want to adopt our programs!" (p. 11). This makes sense in the context of organizations' strategic environment. With their year-to-year survival often in doubt, securing funding for their programs takes on an overwhelming urgency. Short-term funding cycles, however, mean that organizations face pressures to execute projects quickly and demonstrate results. Even community-based organizations that might have an interest in developing the civic life of their community cannot do so. As one executive remarked, "We're not really in a position to play a broader community building role. . . . No one wants to fund us to do that" (p. 13). Organizations thus have no structural incentive to play a distinct civic leadership role beyond carrying out their discrete tasks.

Even when organizations claim to engage citizens or employ rhetoric of civic leadership, the *Organization-First* report suggests that they do so in largely self-serving ways. Organizations may, for example, use language of civic engagement to refer to outreach and public relations efforts such as panel presentations to bring about greater awareness of and build support for their programs. They might convene citizen advisory panels that appear to be receptive to community input, but in reality have little decision-making opportunity. Rather than serving to connect citizens with one another, boards of non-profit organizations tend to consist of elites with connections to funding organizations. As Harwood and Creighton write, when they asked organization staff to describe their community engagement work, "almost any activity an organization undertook involving convening leaders, facilitating discussions or gathering input was considered an apt example" (p. 5). Again, in view of their central imperatives, organizations have more incentive to equate civic leadership with self-serving public relations rather than sustained and authentic relationships with citizens.

The *Organization-First* study thus raises important theoretical challenges for the integrative role of NGOs, revealing that organizations have little structural incentive to engage in community-building work. In contrast to the associations described by Tocqueville, their primary tasks are largely technical in nature, with discrete programs or projects as the unit of analysis. Their location in the civic rather than government sphere does not appear to offer any distinct advantages for allowing citizens to experience cooperation or build trust with one another.

Differentiation: Organizations and the Politics of Accountability

Related to their integrative role, the second function of civic associations that Tocqueville observed was their differentiating role in civil society, in the midst of impersonal bureaucratic institutions taking on more and more social tasks. Tocqueville's fear of the stultifying and homogenizing tendencies of democratic government has perhaps been realized most starkly in the contemporary politics of accountability. With large government bureaucracies struggling to maintain the confidence of citizens, in the last few decades a movement for greater accountability has swept the field of public administration. One of the most common methods employed by government agencies to cope with the lack of confidence in their programs is to provide objective data that demonstrates their effectiveness. Thus the idea of "performance measurement" using standardized metrics has recently gained popularity.[13] Nowhere are the unintended consequences of performance measurement more evident than in public education, especially the No Child Left Behind (NCLB) legislation, which mandates that states develop standardized testing and implement harsh punishments for school systems that do not meet the standards. Critics have argued, however, that rather than improve school quality, NCLB constrains teachers' ability to innovate in the classroom. Instead, the standardized criteria create incentives to "game the system," for example, by encouraging problem students to drop out of school rather than bring down test scores.[14] Although such data are accurate in a strict sense, they tell citizens very little about the overall quality of the schools. Ironically, accountability systems may have negative consequences as agencies attempt to meet standardized statistical targets or comply with inflexible bureaucratic rules. Although Tocqueville could not have anticipated the precise form of postmodern political institutions, NCLB appears to bear out his fears that monolithic government bureaucracies would displace local civic experimentation.

If the assumptions about NGOs as democratic actors are correct, organizations in civil society should be able to play a differentiation role by acting with the scale and expertise of government, but with greater flexibility and additional opportunities for innovation. With independence from government and the voluntary nature of civil society, one might expect a robust diversity in the NGO sphere. Although NGOs exist to accomplish a wide variety of social tasks, however, they do not appear to be immune from the politics of accountability. Just like government agencies, NGOs have structural incentives to demonstrate visible successes in accomplishing their discrete tasks. For understandable reasons of efficiency and rational administration in a complex society, the NGO sphere is, like government, more specialized than ever before. This means that by necessity, as organizations take on more and more important social tasks, what they do and how they are doing it must also become obscure to citizens. In such circumstances, citizens can have little reason to view organizations with trust or confidence. To cope with this problem, as in government, one of the most important trends in the nonprofit sector has been the rise of metrics-based performance measurement to demonstrate effectiveness. The use of performance measurement in the civil sector has been evident, for example, in the shift toward "strategic" philanthropy, the dominant approach of most large-scale grant-making entities.[15] Strategic philanthropy is defined in principle by setting clear goals to guide multiple programs and evaluating programs in terms of these goals. However, in practice it typically entails the use of metrics. In response to pressure from funders and public supporters, such metrics are appealing because they provide a "scientific" way to quantify successes, compare programs, and eliminate inefficiencies.

Yet despite the best of intentions, performance measurement in the nonprofit sphere creates the same tendencies toward standardization in the civic sphere that have been associated with NCLB in the government sphere. While the "innumerable multitude of small undertakings" (II.2.5, 491) of civic associations provided a crucial realm in Tocqueville's theory for democratic differentiation and experimentation, perhaps the most important effects of the accountability movement concern the homogenization of the organization sphere. Unfortunately, performance measurement gives organizations incentives to direct their activities toward standardized, pre-determined outcomes. Sievers has argued that the use of metrics discourages organizations from pursuing outcomes that may be difficult to quantify, such as building social capital or addressing complex political conflicts.[16] Instead, with little incentive to take on difficult or intractable problems, the need for measurement inclines organizations toward short-term projects and quick fixes. As with NCLB, the need for measurement to demonstrate success rather than the interests of communities appears to be driving the non-profit agenda. Although non-profit organizations make up a complex and diverse universe, with important differences of mission, size, and stage of development, Kevin Kearns has described the typical use of metrics as reflecting a "one size fits all" mentality.[17] For example, organizations often use standardized criteria easily recognizable to peers outside of the organization, such as administrative or fundraising budget ratios, rather than metrics tailored to their unique goals. The demand for performance measurement ironically could undermine performance by encouraging organizations to shift scarce resources from program development to evaluation when they can least afford it. As Kearns writes, "Perhaps the most disturbing feature of these quantitative metrics, applied universally to all nonprofits, is that they do not accommodate the notion of organizational *learning* and growth." Performance measurement still begs the question of who decides what to measure. Rather than solve the accountability problem, it merely shifts it; now the question is not the effectiveness of each program, but the legitimacy of the system itself.

The constant comparison among competing organizations further exacerbates the stultifying and homogenizing consequences of standardized metrics. George Frederickson's recent report, *Easy Innovation and the Iron Cage*, documents these tendencies in the discourse of "best practices," "benchmarking," rankings, and the like.[18] What is the metrics phenomenon but the current "best practice" recognized across government, the corporate world, and civil society? The appeals to best practices and rankings give organizations a common language to account to funders, public supporters, and one another for what they are doing, a shorthand to demonstrate their effectiveness when the impact of a program is in doubt or difficult to quantify. Such practices implicitly define accountability according to status and reputation relative to competing organizations. However, there is no necessary connection between an organization's reputation and its true capacity for innovation. Rather, as Frederickson argues, "There is every possibility that the impetus to best practices and benchmarking is driven as much by the desire to increase an institution's reputational capital as it is by a genuine desire to innovate."

The dominant approach to performance measurement reflects a larger attitude described by Frederickson as "managed innovation." Rather than seeing innovation as inherently unpredictable, managed innovation assumes that organizational creativity occurs through a rational process that is consciously planned, executed in an orderly fashion, and evaluated through precise measurements. The most efficient way to accomplish this goal is by copying the practices of leading peers. As paradoxical as it seems, managed innovation suggests that organizational learning occurs not as a result of experimentation, but rather through adopting the management practices of other organizations. As Frederickson concludes:

> Nonprofits are highly varied, ranging from rather stable institutions such as foundations and universities, to highly volatile human service contract organizations. . . . But nonprofits and even foundations appear to be homogenizing, converging, and entering the iron cage because rewards in the form of reputational capital go to the highly ranked, not the deviant.

In contrast to the differentiation function of civic associations in Tocqueville's thought, the attempt to manage innovation within organizations ironically may reduce creativity. Instead of encouraging organizations to adopt cutting edge methods and outdo their peers, the NGO sector is dominated by an overwhelming homogeneity, as best practices become orthodoxy. Not only do these common accountability practices contribute to a homogenization of the civic sphere, they are largely unsuccessful in addressing problems of confidence and legitimacy. The most sophisticated accountability measures cannot restore public confidence, as metrics-based performance measurement often results in a cadre of experts manipulating data and undermining true accountability. As public administration scholar Christopher Pollitt argues, "the process of measurement inevitably becomes a domain of experts, and a deep asymmetry of knowledge between these 'insiders' and the citizen and politician 'outsiders' is unavoidable. Ultimately, the strenuous efforts of these experts [have] the paradoxical effect of *increasing* citizen distrust."[19] The data itself is no guarantee of legitimacy, and may in fact—for good reason—undermine public confidence in organizations.

Performance measurement and managed innovation demonstrate the complex dynamics of the colonization of the NGO sphere. First, the politics of accountability is compounded by the inward focus of organizations. Not only are NGOs caught in short term funding cycles, their funding needs sometimes force them into dependency upon larger and more bureaucratic external entities. This means that they must define themselves in terms of the agendas of their external funders, especially government, the primary funder of the nonprofit sector, along with a handful of large-scale grantmaking foundations. While the civic leadership potential of NGOs hinges on their autonomy from government and large institutional bureaucracies, in an era of public-private "partnerships" and funding scarcity, the operating reality of organizations is complex. Second, although these accountability devices are common in government, they may have originated in the corporate sphere. Originally employed by companies like Xerox, Frederickson argues that managed innovation demonstrates the complex interdependencies of business, government, and NGOs. Even if an organization is not directly funded by these entities, it may nevertheless have an incentive to follow the best practices set by other institutions. In this sense, NGOs are not so much colonized by government, as both are by the private sector. Or to be more precise, the politics of accountability subjects all complex organizations to similar bureaucratizing pressures. Whether the organization is public, private, or civic, its responses to problems of legitimacy and public confidence tend to follow a single underlying logic. The civil, corporate, and government spheres are best represented not so much by separate circles, as a Venn diagram with various overlaps and interdependencies, and NGOs at the center. The politics of accountability threatens the potential of NGOs to play a distinct role as innovative and participatory civic actors.

Capacity-Building: The Professionalization of Civil Society

Finally, Tocqueville saw civic associations as having a capacity-building role, helping citizens move beyond the debilitating passivity that comes from conditions of social isolation. While Tocqueville describes historical associations as primarily made up of citizens themselves, most organizations in the non-government sphere today consist of trained, specialized, and credentialed professionals. The professional culture of many organizations is thus dominated by a technocratic ideal—implicitly a theory of leadership—with a deep history, rooted in the specialization required to accomplish social tasks in a large scale and complex world. Its most forceful articulation was perhaps by the intellectual Walter Lippmann, in his famous exchange with the philosopher John Dewey, in the early twentieth century.[20] Elite theorists like Lippmann had little hope for the ability of everyday citizens to rule themselves in the way that Tocqueville described, and instead saw promise only in the development of a new cadre of public-spirited elites, with citizens left to be passive consumers of information and services. Although a degree of division of labor is necessary to accomplish difficult social tasks in a large-scale and complex society, the growing role of expertise across society may undermine the culture of participation in the civic sphere that, as Tocqueville explained, is necessary for democracy. While civic associations may at one time have presented unique opportunities for citizens to engage in collective action, the professionalization and specialization of civil society limit the potential of non-government organizations to play a comparable role.

The colonization of civic capacities by technocratic expertise begins with the naming of civic problems in technical terms. In the classic book, *Seeing Like a State*, James L. Scott describes the paradigmatic approach to social planning around the world as a "high modernist" ideology, an optimistic faith in top-down scientific planning.[21] This ideology holds that public problems are best identified according to standardized data, and addressed through the efficient administration of resources. According to Scott, the worst planning disasters in world history, such as the planned economies of the communist era, occurred when high modernist ideology was combined with the political power of authoritarian governments. This expert naming of social problems contrasts to a more humanistic approach that could see social problems as largely complex and political in nature, involving conflicts over deeply held values—what Rittel and Horst refer to as "wicked" problems—so that expert knowledge alone cannot hope to solve them.[22] Rather, in a democracy, citizens would play an active role in reaching collective decisions before experts could hope to discover the best means of administering them. Although Scott focused his critique on authoritarian states, organizations in the civil sphere may be similarly problematic to the extent that they come to resemble government institutions in their combination of social power and their professional cultures.

Top-down approaches to social problems are reflected in the most common self-understandings of expert professionals, especially how they see themselves in relation to citizens. For example, an especially common theme in the self-understandings of expert professions is discourse referring to a "serving" capacity, with citizens implicitly in a receptive role. The service ideal reflects the best of intentions and a sincere effort to connect expertise to urgent social problems. However, it also implies a focus on discrete services to be delivered, rather than on building the civic capacities of communities to organize themselves and solve their own problems. It is usually framed in apolitical terms, for example as an effort to do charity for others, rather than as addressing any distinctly political goals. Perhaps most important, service discourse may reflect a paternalistic impulse to care for others that can often result in relationships of dependency and clientelism.

Professionals identifying with a service role may be appropriate in the agencies of the modern welfare state, but it has become the dominant tendency across the expert-dominated professions, in both the government and NGO sectors. Although talk of civic engagement is currently widespread in higher education, for example, the mode of engagement is typically service-oriented. Since the 1980s, "service-learning" has been a popular mode of so-called "partnerships" between universities and their local communities. Yet service-learning in critical ways reaffirms typical expert relationships with communities. As Peggy Shaffer, director of a community partnership program at Miami University, explains: "Volunteerism, service, and charity force public agency and civic engagement into an individualistic frame where the beneficent individual or institution bestows its knowledge and resources on needy communities as an act of love and concern, rather than as an integral part of building and sustaining democratic communities."[23] Many campuses are starting to embrace richer language of "civic engagement," but much of these efforts have remained at the level of mission statements, without fundamentally moving beyond their historical roots in the service paradigm.

In philanthropy, the service role is reflected in the emphasis on financial resources and technical assistance rather than the civic capacities central to Tocqueville's analysis. In the 1990s, "civil society" and "NGOs" were buzzwords in the field of international development, yet financial assistance and service delivery have remained the dominant paradigms. To illustrate this larger trend, Ramon E. Daubon describes a project to assist the indigenous Guarani people in Argentina, in which agricultural training and equipment initially appeared to be successful in increasing production, and the project was closed. Years later, the machinery provided by the grants was no longer being used. The program had misunderstood the real needs of the community and created a relationship of dependency, due in part to the service role of the NGO: "To compound the error, the support teams literally fell in love with the experience. In their desire to alleviate the poverty of their subjects, they assumed them as their wards."[24] The community eventually achieved a degree of sustainability by returning to its traditional subsistence agriculture, but mostly in spite of the assistance it had received.

Another important variant of technocratic professionalism is the dissemination model of expertise. According to this view, experts understand themselves as serving the public by acting as impartial authorities in their fields and sharing their knowledge with policymakers and lay citizens. Citizens play a largely passive role in receiving or applying information. For example, the dominant approach to journalism is a dissemination model. Journalists feel a deep responsibility to discover the truth and communicate their knowledge to a mass audience. The late journalist Cole Campbell describes the typical mode of professional journalism in these terms: "This model casts journalists in the role of trustees—a kinder, gentler word for guardians—who transmit knowledge from other guardians to citizens, whose lives may expect to be affected by it. Traditional journalism thus assumes a professional practice, based on trained reporters and editors, who find authoritative information and communicate it authoritatively to the public."[25] According to this model, journalists are not experts in specialized fields, but rather meta-experts, trained to identify authorities and communicate their knowledge to a wider lay audience. Implicit in this practice is an assumption that the citizens are passive vessels to be filled, with no knowledge of their own. In higher education, Harry Boyte describes the core elements of mainstream academic work as limited to gathering, analyzing, and disseminating information.[26] The dissemination model of expertise is also implicit in the dominant outreach practices, described by Scott Peters as, "consisting only of one-way transfers and applications of technical knowledge and expertise that are made in response to demands for help by external constituencies."[27] The very ideas of "outreach" and "extension" assume that authoritative knowledge is a possession of universities that must be disseminated outward, rather than something that is co-created in dialogue between experts and citizens. Although the dissemination model might add a dimension of publicity to expert knowledge, it still places experts in the position of defining what counts as knowledge.

Just as it discounts the potential role of citizens in democracy, the logic of expertise ironically constricts the public role of professionals, restricting expert work to highly specialized tasks that are irrelevant to and disconnected from the needs of their communities. Hannah Arendt describes a distinct loss of "public happiness," from the active and engaged *hommes des letters* of the eighteenth century, to the "class of professional scribes and writers whose labours are needed by the ever-expanding bureaucracies" of contemporary organizations.[28] Academics, journalists, and philanthropists are talking in similar terms as their professions become defined in increasingly specialized and detached terms. Cole Campbell describes a sense of impotence or paralysis in the "warn and scorn" reporting in advance of Hurricane Katrina, when journalists predicted that New Orleans was at risk but did not have the political skills or power to affect the outcome.[29] In academia, the professional culture and institutional reward structures all favor research based on the traditional positivist paradigm of detachment, objectivity, and measureable data.[30] Harry Boyte describes a sense of frustration with the loss of civic purpose throughout academia: academics "feel increasingly cut off from local communities. . . . Their discontents take shape in a silent politics whose authority comes from hiding interests and suppressing attachment to living communities."[31] Across the expert-dominated professions, measurability has become an end in itself rather than a means to address social problems, preventing many of the most pressing human problems from being addressed. For example, the reward structures in academia cause measurability to set the research agenda. A group of political scientists, recently interviewed in the *New York Times*, admitted that their field had become irrelevant to the most pressing problems in democracy because they could only research phenomena that could be easily measured.[32] Across civil society, professionals experience a disconnect between their desire for greater social relevance and norms that leave them isolated from public life.

Again, on the dimension of building a capacity for civic action, civil society organizations have no distinct structural advantage, and instead appear to be part of a growing professionalization occurring across all sectors of modern society.

Conclusion: Toward a Decolonization of Civil Society

Tocqueville's primary fear was that without civic leadership, democracy would degenerate into a distinct and benevolent form of despotism, as government would come to replace associations of citizens as the primary agent of collective action, leading to "a herd of timid and industrious animals of which government is the shepherd" (II.4.6, p. 663). Although contemporary society continues to delegate social tasks to non-government actors, as these actors become increasingly organized they appear to have taken on many of the characteristics of government that Tocqueville feared. To say that the integration, differentiation, and capacity-building functions of civil society have been colonized by the inwardness of organizations, the politics of accountability, and the specialization of professions, however, does not mean that this colonization is absolute or irreversible. When an invasive plant is introduced into an ecosystem, its spread can be minimized and native species can be nurtured. This raises the question of what might be required for the decolonization of civil society.

Organizations and professionals within them can do only so much to produce a trusting and engaged citizenry, or to manufacture their own legitimacy. Instead, the most important change will surely occur—if it does—within the sphere of the informal associations that struck Tocqueville as critical in American democracy. Still, organizations can play an important role by *realigning* their identities and routines with the civic norms and habits of communities. In fact, even as the colonization of civil society appears to be reaching a new stage, a growing set of organizations and professionals is beginning to challenge the inwardness of NGOs. In various ways, these countervailing groups move beyond the paradigms of service delivery, technical assistance, and dissemination, to treat citizens as partners, co-producers, and civic actors.

Perhaps the most promising countervailing trend is the emergence of new forms of NGOs that are explicit in their attempt to strengthen the civic capacities of communities. For example, a growing set of organizations and networks associated with the idea of "deliberative democracy" create spaces for citizens to play a more active role in reaching collective decisions on controversial issues.[33] Even when they are concerned with particular issues or government policies, these organizations may have capacity-building effects as they strengthen citizens' habits of collective judgment and decision making. The most advanced of these organizations have been sustained over time and have influenced various levels of government policy.[34]

Similarly, organizations in the community organizing tradition, which develop local campaigns to maximize the political power of disadvantaged groups, offer an important form of grassroots collective action in a Tocquevillian spirit.[35] In contrast to the mobilization techniques of conventional advocacy work, this tradition is distinguished by its strategic sensibility and its disciplined commitment to grassroots democratic principles. Community organizing has a rich history, including its development in Chicago in the 1940s by Saul Alinsky, founder of the Industrial Areas Foundation (IAF); extensive use by groups such as Student Nonviolent Coordinating Committee (SNCC) in the civil rights movement; and recent popularity in the wake of the historic 2008 presidential election. Community organizing is integrative in that it works by connecting groups across their differences, and differentiating, in that it produces distinct local coalitions with which individuals might identify. Perhaps most important, community organizing leads to bottom-up collective action as coalitions assert their political power. Although critical of groups that have at times acted inconsistently with their democratic principles, Andrew Sabl writes, "the most distinctively Tocquevillian politics is the politics of community organizing."[36]

Opposition to the colonization of civil society also takes the form of professionals who are critically aware of the limitations of their expertise, and see an ethical responsibility or calling to align their profession with self-ruling citizens. Using a framework based on Tocqueville's political theory and Dewey's attempt to reconcile expertise with participatory democracy, Albert Dzur refers to a shift toward "democratic professionalism" occurring across fields as diverse as criminal justice, journalism, and bioethics.[37] Terms such as "scholarship of engagement" and "public scholarship" in academia are now being used to describe collaboration with community partners in advancing cutting edge knowledge.[38] Similar groups have emerged in philanthropy and journalism to experiment with ways to collaborate with citizens in their work as civic actors rather than passive recipients or spectators.[39] The common thread among these groups is a recognition that their professional work benefits from interaction and collaboration with citizens, giving them a structural incentive to move beyond the conventional narrow task or program focus. For example, they may see civic leadership work as a means to rebuild public confidence in their profession, or receive input or feedback from stakeholders to increase their effectiveness. In such cases, rather than create wholly new organizations, isolated individuals or small groups are attempting to carve out niches for civic work within established institutions. These civic professionals typically do not reflect the dominant paradigm within their fields, and sometimes may even be marginalized within their own institutions, but they have successfully formed peer networks across organizations to advance their work.

Consisting of organizations on the margins of their fields, or isolated individuals challenging the dominant culture of their institutions, this may be more of an inchoate stirring than a mature movement. However, taken together, they constitute an important countervailing force, and a reminder that the colonization of civil society is far from absolute. In creating an Open Government Initiative to make government agencies more participatory and collaborative, President Obama recently declared, "Knowledge is widely dispersed in society. . . . Executive departments and agencies should offer Americans increased opportunities to participate in policymaking and to provide their Government with the benefits of their collective expertise and information."[40] Similarly, Tocqueville had a high estimation of a democratic citizenry, at least provided that it has the opportunities to develop its civic capacities. In a Tocquevillian spirit, organizations and professionals in the non-government sector are beginning to recognize the extent of their inwardness, take a more capacious view of citizens, and engage in the hard work of civic leadership.

Notes

1. Alexis de Tocqueville, *Democracy in America*, trans. Harvey C. Mansfield and Delba Winthrop (Chicago: University of Chicago Press, 2000; reprint, 2002).

2. The concept of "colonization" derives from Habermas's account of the colonization of the "lifeworld" by state and market "systems." Similar to Tocqueville's concept of democratic mores, Habermas defines the lifeworld as the totality of shared norms and customs in which "communicative action" produces cultural knowledge, social solidarity, and personal identities. According to Habermas, the lifeworld is under constant threat of colonization by the market and the state, as money and power, rather than communicative action, come to dominate social interaction. I will describe a more specific colonization of civic associations—a critical component of the lifeworld—that is deeply informed by and part of the larger process that Habermas describes. Jurgen Habermas, *The Theory of Communicative Action, Volume 2: Lifeworld and System: A Critique of Functionalist Reason*, trans. Thomas McCarthy (Boston, MA: Beacon Press, 1985).

3. See especially the sections on individualism, II.2.2 and II.2.3.

4. II.2.8, "How Americans Combat Individualism by the Doctrine of Self-Interest Well Understood."

5. I.2.4, "On Political Association in the United States."

6. See also Robert Putnam, *Bowling Alone: The Collapse and Revival of American Community* (New York: Simon & Schuster, 2000).

7. Benjamin Barber, *A Place for Us: How to Make Society Civil and Democracy Strong* (New York: Hill and Wang, 1998).

8. Robert Bellah et al., *Habits of the Heart: Individualism and Commitment in American Life*, 1996 ed. (Berkeley, CA: University of California Press, 1985); Robert Putnam, *Bowling Alone*; Putnam, *Making Democracy Work: Civic Traditions in Modern Italy* (Princeton, NJ: Princeton University Press, 1993).

9. Lester M. Salamon, "The Rise of the Nonprofit Sector," *Foreign Affairs* (July-August 1994): 109-17.

10. Peter F. Drucker, "The Age of Social Transformation," *Atlantic Monthly* (May 1994): 53-80.

11. Stephen Macedo et al., *Democracy at Risk: How Political Choices Undermine Citizen Participation, and What We Can Do About It* (Washington, D.C.: Brookings Institution Press, 2005). See also Mark Warren, *Democracy and Associations* (Princeton, NJ: Princeton University Press, 2001).

12. Richard C. Harwood and John A. Creighton, *The Organization-First Approach: How Programs Crowd Out Community* (Bethesda, MD: Harwood Institute for Public Innovation, 2008).

13. Despite an initial commitment to broad principles of "openness, participation, and collaboration" that may have suggested a strongly democratic notion of accountability, the overwhelming focus of the Obama administration's Open Government initiative is the availability of data on government programs. Peter R. Orszag, *Memorandum for the Heads of Executive Departments and Agencies: Open Government Directive* (Washington, DC: 2009). For an overview of the performance measurement movement, see Robert D. Behn, "Why Measure Performance? Different Purposes Require Different Measures," *Public Administration Review* 63, no. 5 (2003): 586-606.

14. David Hursh, "The Growth of High-Stakes Testing in the USA: Accountability, Markets, and the Decline in Educational Equality," *British Educational Research Journal* 31, no. 5 (2005): 605-22.

15. Paul Brest, "In Defense of Strategic Philanthropy," *Proceedings of the American Philosophical Society* 149, no. 2 (2005): 132-40.

16. Bruce Sievers, "Civil Investing and Civic Engagement," *Kettering Review* (2005): 36-41.

17. Kevin Kearns, "Accountability in the Nonprofit Sector: Abandoning the 'One Size Fits All' Approach" (Dayton, OH: Symposium on Accountability, Kettering Foundation, 2008).

18. George Frederickson, "Easy Innovation and the Iron Cage: Best Practice, Benchmarking, Ranking, and the Management of Organizational Creativity," (Dayton, OH: Kettering Foundation, 2003).

19. Christopher Pollitt, "Performance Blight and the Tyranny of Light," in *Symposium on Accountability* (Dayton, OH: Kettering Foundation, 2008), 7.

20. Robert Westbrook, *John Dewey and American Democracy* (Ithaca, NY: Cornell University Press, 1991).

21. James C. Scott, *Seeing Like a State: How Certain Schemes to Improve the Human Condition Have Failed* (New Haven: Yale University Press, 1998).

22. Horst W. Rittel and Melvin M. Webber, "Dilemmas in a General Theory of Planning," *Policy Sciences* 4 (1973): 155-69.

23. Derek W. M. Barker and David W. Brown, eds., *A Different Kind of Politics: Readings on the Role of Higher Education in Democracy* (Dayton, OH: Kettering Foundation Press, 2009), 73.

24. Ramon Daubon, "A Civil Investing Strategy for Putting Communities in Charge," (Dayton, OH: Kettering Foundation, 2007).

25. Cole Campbell, "Journalism and Public Knowledge," *Kettering Review* (2007): 39-49.

26. Harry C. Boyte, "Public Work: Civic Populism Versus Technocracy in Higher Education," in *Agent of Democracy: Higher Education and the Hex Journey*, ed. David W. Brown and Deborah Witte (Dayton, OH: Kettering Foundation Press, 2008), 79-102.

27. Scott Peters, "Reconstructing a Democratic Tradition of Public Scholarship in the Land Grant System," in *Agent of Democracy: Higher Education and the Hex Journey*, ed. David W. Brown and Deborah Witte (Dayton, OH: Kettering Foundation Press, 2008), 121-48.

28. Hannah Arendt, *On Revolution* (New York: Penguin, 1963; reprint, 1990).

29. Campbell, "Journalism and Public Knowledge."

30. Barry Checkoway, "Renewing the Civic Mission of the American Research University," *Journal of Higher Education* 72, no. 2 (2000): 125-47.

31. Boyte, "Public Work: Civic Populism Versus Technocracy in Higher Education," 84-85.

32. Patricia Cohen, "Field Study: Just How Relevant Is Political Science," *New York Times*, October 19, 2009.

33. Mark Button and Kevin Mattson, "Deliberative Democracy in Practice: Challenges and Prospects for Civic Deliberation," *Polity* 31, no. 4 (1999): 609-37. Michael X. Delli Carpini, Fay Lomax Cook, and Lawrence R. Jacobs, "Public Deliberation, Discursive Participation, and Citizen Engagement: A Review of the Empirical Literature," *Annual Review of Political Science* 7 (2004): 315-44.

34. Elena Fagotto and Archon Fung, "Sustaining Public Engagement: Embedded Deliberation in Local Communities," (East Hartford, CT: Everyday Democracy and the Kettering Foundation, 2009).

35. Harry Boyte, *Everyday Politics: Reconnecting Citizens and Public Life* (Philadelphia: University of Pennsylvania Press, 2004), John L. McKnight, "Regenerating Community: The Recovery of a Space for Citizens," in *IPR Distinguished Public Policy Lecture Series* (Chicago, IL: Northwestern University, 2003), Mark Warren, *Dry Bones Rattling: Community Building to Revitalize American Democracy* (Princeton, NJ: Princeton University Press, 2001).

36. Andrew Sabl, "Community Organizing as Tocquevillean Politics: The Art, Practices, and Ethos of Association," *American Journal of Political Science* 46, no. 1 (2002): 1-19.

37. Albert Dzur, *Democratic Professionalism: Citizen Participation and the Reconstruction of Professional Ethics, Identity, and Practice* (University Park: Pennsylvania State University Press, 2008).

38. Barker and Brown, eds., *A Different Kind of Politics: Readings on the Role of Higher Education in Democracy*, John Saltmarsh, Matt Hartley, and Patti Clayton, "Democratic Engagement White Paper" (Boston, MA: New England Resource Center for Higher Education, 2009).

39. Campbell, "Journalism and Public Knowledge"; Scott London, "Investing in Public Life: A Report from the 2003-2004 Dialogues on Civil Investing" (Dayton, OH: Kettering Foundation/Pew Partnership for Civic Change, 2005).

40. Barack Obama, "Memorandum for the Heads of Executive Departments and Agencies/Subject: Transparency and Open Government," ed. The White House (Washington, DC: 2009).

Chapter 11

The Tragedy of American Progress: Alexis de Tocqueville and Willa Cather's *My Àntonia*

Jon D. Schaff

From the beginning of the American republic there has existed a tension between progress, usually defined in materialist terms, and some concept of stability in virtue. While the notion of progress typically has been dominant, periodic reactions against progress have arisen in particular conceptions of religion, history, and literature. Just beneath the surface of America's liberal commitment to material and technological progress has been a desire for stability and a yearning for a simpler way of life.[1] For example, underlying the Anti-Federalist concern for virtue and the Jeffersonian critique of industrialization and defense of the yeoman farmer is the understanding that materialism and technology represent incomplete pictures of the good life.[2] Further, the tendency of liberalism, especially in modern variants, to judge human choice simply on its status as uncompelled has been less than satisfying for those who seek some good outside of or in addition to the will. These questions remain current. Whether it is concern over jobs lost to outsourcing or the manipulation of human life by modern medical science, the problem of progress becomes more relevant as the speed of progress seems only to accelerate.

The problem of progress is a theme that is explored in profound ways by both Alexis de Tocqueville in *Democracy in America*, and by Willa Cather in her novel *My Àntonia*. This chapter turns to a novelist, as Tocqueville saw purpose in the poet as an instructor of the statesman. The "social and political construction" of a state, argues Tocqueville, inclines a people to certain habits. The statesman must decide whether those habits are humanizing or brutalizing. "The whole art of the legislator," Tocqueville writes, "is correctly to discern beforehand these natural inclinations of communities of men, in order to know whether they should be assisted or whether it may not be necessary to check them."[3] The statesman must strive to "raise the souls" of fellow citizens and "keep them lifted up towards heaven."[4] In his discussion of the usefulness of the literature of antiquity for democratic man, Tocqueville admits that for most democratic citizens, their education should be "scientific, commercial, and industrial, rather than literary." Ancient literature, though, may be of especial use for those who aspire to "literary excellence." Those who are particularly gifted, such as a potential statesman, will want to delve into the ancient literature, as Tocqueville believes it was created with particular care and therefore is generally of a superior quality. Tocqueville believes that this literature serves to "counterbalance some of our defects," concluding, "They are a prop on the side on which we are in most danger of falling."[5] While Tocqueville generally does not have high hopes for democratic literature, it is possible that a democracy could develop a writer with the attention to detail and a love of beauty and history that matches that of the classical writers Tocqueville so evidently admires. Such a writer would serve as an educator of statesmen, warning democratic statesmen about the excesses of the democratic spirit and determined to "prop-up" democracy precisely where it is weakest. Such an author is Willa Cather, whose work *My Àntonia* is a cautionary tale about excessive love of material progress.

My Àntonia investigates the competing claims of progress and traditionalism, and by favoring the life of country simplicity and family ties over liberating commerce and individualism, the novel suggests a conflict between the two that defies easy resolution. Indeed, the uneasy answer to the conflict between the unsettling dynamism of progress and the stability of the simple traditional life may be that there is no answer. While Americans may be attracted to the simplicity of a traditional agrarian life, few are willing to accept the poverty and stagnation incumbent in such a life. At the same time, Americans intuitively recognize that commercialism and technology ultimately cannot satisfy the higher longings of the human soul. The wanton creativity of dynamic progress leaves things of intrinsic worth in its wake, while giving us the commodious lifestyle moderns enjoy. At the heart of the American experience lie various contradictions: irreconcilable desires for both progress and stability; material betterment and traditionalism; efficient allocation of resources through the market and a desire for the calm of family life. Part and parcel of the American experiment is the tragedy of progress. This tragic situation is revealed in Cather's *My Àntonia*, in which the dramatic conflict of the narrator, Jim Burden, is the desire to escape his small Nebraska hometown while yearning to keep alive his memory of the pioneer West.

The Problem of Progress

Alexis de Tocqueville thoroughly develops this American idea of progress in his two volumes of *Democracy in America*. This most perceptive of observers of the

American character sees an unsettledness in the American soul that gives Americans their unique character but also presents dangers. This variability is best explained in the chapter "The Principle of Equality Suggests to Americans the Idea of the Indefinite Perfectibility of Man." Conspicuously located at the end of a discussion of the democratic nature of American religion, Tocqueville suggests in this chapter that democratic man has an almost religious-like zeal for progress. Tocqueville notes, "Although man has many points of resemblance with the brute creatures, one characteristic is peculiar to himself—he improves; they are incapable of improvement."[6] Man is a kind of animal who does not simply use nature, as do the lower animals, but manipulates it to his own ends through the invention of technology.

This desire and ability to improve are part of man's nature, not something that is unique to democratic man; however. democracy has given this human attribute a "novel character." In aristocracy each class has its appropriate place in a great chain of being, limiting the range of choices for any given individual. In an aristocracy "everyone thinks that the utmost limits of human power are to be discerned in proximity to himself, and none seeks any longer to resist the inevitable law of destiny."[7] But in democracies, "as manners, customs, and laws vary, from the tumultuous intercourse of men—as new facts arise—as news truths are brought to light—as ancient opinions are dissipated, and others take their place—the image of an ideal perfection, forever on the wing, presents itself to the human mind."[8] In democracies some individuals fail while others succeed, often success and failure taking place multiple times in the life of one individual. Each learns that "no people and no individual, how enlightened soever they may be, can lay claim to infallibility."[9] With each failure, one tries once more to succeed, learning from the previous mistakes and trying new strategies. An individual's successes teach him that triumph is attainable, so he goes after it anew. "His reverses teach him that none may hope to have discovered absolute good— his success stimulates him to the never ending pursuit of it. . . . He tends unceasingly towards that unmeasured greatness so indistinctly visible at the end of the long track which humanity has yet to tread." It is as if Tocqueville has discovered the philosophical origins of "if at first you don't succeed, try, try again!" An insatiable desire for perfection is of momentous import. Tocqueville argues, "It can hardly be believed how many facts naturally flow from the philosophical theory of the indefinite perfectibility of man, or how strong an influence it exercises even on men who, living entirely for the purposes of action and not of thought, seem to conform their actions to it, without knowing anything about it."[10]

By way of illustration, Tocqueville passes along the story of a conversation he had with a sailor. Tocqueville asked the sailor why Americans build their ships to last for only a short time. The sailor replied "that the art of navigation is every day making such rapid progress that the finest vessel would become almost useless if it lasted beyond a certain number of years."[11] This discussion reveals the potential problems in the belief in indefinite perfection. The art of shipbuilding is totally subsumed under the art (or science) of navigation. Ameri-

cans build ships purely for utility, not for beauty, for example. All other considerations are subordinated to this one factor. The sailor himself speaks of the
"useless" ships that quickly become obsolete. The desire for progress has little
patience for that which cannot defend itself on the grounds of immediate utility.
And what is the purpose of the ship? In Tocqueville's time a sea vessel served as
a tool of war and of commerce. The success and failure that Tocqueville discussed immediately before the story of the sailor is of a material nature. Desiring
riches and comfort, the American is overcome with a religious belief that his
deepest wants can be solved by commerce and technology.[12]

Part of Tocqueville's project is to warn democrats of the potential excesses
of the democratic passion, and thus he suggests limits on the desire for perfectibility. Tocqueville argues that the blank slate that was America at its foundation
indicated that "a path without a turn and a field without an horizon were opened
to the exploring and ardent curiosity of man." But due to the influence of the
Christian religion, "he discretely lays aside the use of his most formidable faculties, he no longer consents to doubt or to innovate, but carefully abstaining from
raising the curtain of the sanctuary, he yields with submissive respect to truths
which he will not discuss."[13] Because of religious sentiment, "the human mind is
never left to wander across a boundless field." Even "the boldest conceptions of
human device are subjected to certain forms which retard and stop their comple-
tion." For Tocqueville's fear is "[i]f the mind of the Americans were free from
all trammels, they would very shortly become the most daring innovators and
the most implacable disputants in the world."[14] The influence of Christianity
means that "no one in the United States has dared to advance the maxim, that
everything is permissible, with a view to the interests of society; an impious
adage which seems to have been invented in an age of freedom to shelter all the
tyrants of future ages. Thus, whilst the law permits the Americans to do whatever they please, religion prevents them from conceiving, and forbids them to
commit, what is rash or unjust."[15]

Yet Tocqueville describes competing notions that are at odds with one
another. "Thus, in the moral world everything is classed, adapted, decided, and
foreseen; in the political world everything is agitated, uncertain, and disputed; in
the one is a passive, though a voluntary, obedience; in the other an independence, scornful of experience and jealous of authority."[16] While Tocqueville
suggests that "the spirit of Religion" and "the spirit of Freedom" have in America sometimes worked together in a harmonious fashion, he also suggests that the
modes of religion and politics in democracy are often in relentless competition
with one another.[17] The result, Tocqueville worries, is the conquering of Christian religious principles by some other principles based on democratic political
assumptions.

"The two great dangers which threaten the existence of religions," Tocqueville writes, "are schism and indifference." One possibility is schism, the transfer of religious passion from one object to another. "In ages of fervent devotion,
men sometimes abandon their religion, but they only shake it off to adopt another. . . . The old religion then excites enthusiastic attachment or bitter enmity in

either party; some leave it with anger, others cling to it with increased devotedness, and although persuasions differ, irreligion is unknown."[18] The other condition to be feared is that of indifference. In this condition "Prodigious revolutions then take place in the human mind, without the apparent cooperation of the passions of man, and almost without his knowledge." The result is "[m]en lose the objects of their fondest hopes, as if through forgetfulness. They are carried away by an imperceptible current which they have not the courage to stem, but which they follow with regret, since it bears them from a faith they love to a skepticism that plunges them into despair."[19] The concern here is the possibility of replacing faith in Christianity, which serves as a harness on the desire for progress on the part of democratic man, with the religious belief in perfectibility. We see that Tocqueville's placing of the discussion of perfectibility in the milieu of democratic religion takes on greater importance. Progress seems to be a rival with Christianity for the allegiance of Americans. It may supplant Christianity in a kind of competition, or given the death of religious feeling and the victory of rationalist skepticism, the love of science that is central to the American concept of progress might be the only thing that retains its meaning to the man in despair.

Family also works with religion to temper the love of progress. Tocqueville states, "Religion is often unable to restrain man from the numberless temptations of fortune; nor can it check that passion for gain which every incident of his life contributes to arouse." It is religion mediated through women that leads Tocqueville to posit "women are the protectors of morals." The uneasy home life of Europeans does nothing to temper "the tumultuous passions which frequently disturb the dwelling." On the other hand "when the American retires from the turmoil of public life to the bosom of his family he finds order and peace. There his pleasures are simple and natural, his joys are innocent and calm."[20] Tocqueville writes that trading nations such as the United States regard the morality of women "as the highest security for order and prosperity of the household."[21] Praising the division of labor in the American household, Tocqueville contests the notion that "would make of man and woman beings not only equal but alike . . . they would mix them in all things—their occupations, their pleasures, their business." Tocqueville vigorously defends the effects of the division of labor, or, as he calls it, "the great principle of political economy," between men and women. Arguing that women actually gain power under this arrangement, Tocqueville notes that women are much better treated in America than in Europe. While women do not take part in the "outward concerns of the family," they are the guardians of the domestic realm. The strict morality of American women means that if a man wants to gain the favor of a woman, he must conform to her wishes. He must treat her well if she is to join him in marriage. Thus in America a young unmarried woman can "alone and without fear, undertake a long journey." Working with religion, female morals domesticate and limit the ambitions of men. He must direct his desire for material comfort to the needs of domestic life.[22]

A final danger of democratic times that we must note is that of individualism. Individualism, in this context, is not the same as egotism or selfishness and is not precisely akin to what Americans often refer to "rugged individualism." Tocqueville distinguishes individualism from these other phenomena. Individualism, Tocqueville suggests, "saps the virtues of public life." Individualism leads one to forget the past and neglect the future and to ignore one's duties as a citizen. Instead, "the interest" of the democratic individualist "is confined to those in close propinquity to himself" and finally citizens "become indifferent and as strangers to one another."[23] In this sense individualism is similar to what we might today call apathy or identify as a decline in civil society. One concerns oneself with friends and family, but does not follow public affairs or actively participate in government.

"[A] despot easily forgives his subjects for not loving him," writes Tocqueville, "provided they do not love each other." The despot "applauds as good citizens those who have no sympathy for any but themselves." Individualism, a leading characteristic of democratic times, thus poses an existential threat to democratic liberty.[24] The problem of individualism is for Tocqueville very much linked to the problem of progress, for Tocqueville thinks that individualism arises once the links that bound people together under feudalism are broken by the liberating and equalizing forces of modernity. While modernity brings great benefits, Tocqueville also fears that the individualism which it engenders poses a threat to political liberty.

Tocqueville, identifying a democratic disease, then offers various cures. Notably, these cures do not involve a reactionary attempt to return to the fixed hierarchies that existed in the feudal era. Indeed, one of the most important cures suggested by Tocqueville is what he calls "free institutions." By this Tocqueville largely means the proliferation in America of public offices and elections to fill those offices. Elections, Tocqueville argues, get people thinking about public affairs. Even if elections are characterized by the low arts of electioneering and engender a kind of partisan bitterness, nonetheless these vices are worth the virtue of getting people involved in their own governance. As Tocqueville puts it, "Freedom engenders private animosities, but despotism gives birth to a general indifference."[25]

The virtues of "free institutions" are particularly noticeable in local government. "It is difficult to draw a man out of his own circle to interest him in the destiny of the State," writes Tocqueville, "because he does not clearly understand what influence the destiny of the State can have upon his own lot." The centralized authority of the nation state is too distant and too abstract to lift the average citizen off his couch. Local government, however, touches upon immediate needs of citizens, causing them to take notice and inspire them to action. As Tocqueville puts it, "But if it be proposed to make a road cross the end of [a citizen's] estate, he will see at a glance that there is a connection between this small public affair and his greatest private affairs."[26] In short, it is far easier to get people excited about things next door than things in a distant national capitol. Tocqueville believes a certain commitment to localism helps create the public spiritedness that helps combat the effects of individualism. A lack of "central administration" is one of the principle variables in mitigating the effects of the tyranny of the majority.[27] Tocqueville concludes, "The free institutions which the inhabitants of the United States possess, and the political rights of which they make so much use, remind every citizen, and in a thousand ways, that he lives in society."[28]

The notion of progress remains a live topic today, with some cheerleading for unlimited progress while others take a more sober view.[29] Perhaps the most searching recent critique of the idea of progress has come from the iconoclastic leftist Christopher Lasch. Lasch writes that the foundations of liberalism in the eighteenth century posited that "human wants, being insatiable, required indefinite expansion of productive forces necessary to satisfy them. Insatiable desires, formerly condemned as a source of frustration, unhappiness, and spiritual instability, came to be seen as a powerful stimulus to economic expansion."[30] This insatiability, it was assumed, "could drive the economic machine—just as insatiable curiosity drove the scientific project—and thus ensure a never ending expansion of productive forces."[31] Lasch's study of the idea of progress taps into the idea of infinite perfectibility, in this case under the guise of endless productivity and material gain. The progressive ideology, Lasch notes, "rejects a heroic conception of life. The concept of progress can be defended against intelligent criticism only by postulating an indefinite expansion of desires, a steady rise in the general standard of comfort, and the incorporation of the masses into the culture of abundance."[32] The progressive ideology can have no limitations.

Nineteenth century reformers had, like Tocqueville, suggested the family as a possible remedy to the problem of progress. "The obligation to support a wife and children . . . would discipline possessive individualism and transform the potential gambler, speculator, dandy or confidence man into a conscientious provider."[33] Yet the love of progress is hegemonic, ultimately overtaking the family. "The passion to get ahead," laments Lasch, "had begun to imply the right to make a fresh start whenever earlier commitments," including those of family, "became unduly burdensome."[34] In the name of progress, we must overcome the family through innovations such as birth control, abortion, easy divorce, and the ideology of feminism. Lasch notes, "The dream of universal brotherhood, because it rests on the sentimental fiction that men and women are all the same, cannot survive the discovery that they differ."[35]

We can see that the idea of progress is problematic in the American experience. While the desire for material comfort is understandable, the common tendency is to see material progress as an unambiguous good and to suggest that the process of improvement is more important than the decisions actually made by individuals or society at large. Progress, devoid of any teleology outside of materialism, leaves us open to reducing all estimations of value to the level of comfort. Tocqueville and Lasch worry that this reductionism deadens the soul to higher considerations of the good. As society caters to man's lower desires, he loses any concept of the noble and self-sacrifice. Further, other institutions, such as church and the family, are reconstituted on the grounds of individual material desires. As we shall see, these themes are explored in Willa Cather's *My Àntonia*.

My Àntonia and the Tragedy of American Progress

Near the beginning of *My Àntonia* we are told that we are reading a work of Romanticism. Set in pioneer Nebraska, the novel opens with an unidentified narrator telling us of meeting one James Quayle Burden, an old friend from Nebraska, on the train in Iowa. Here we learn that Jim Burden is legal counsel for "one of the great Western railways" and now lives in New York City. The narrator also informs us that Jim has a "naturally romantic and ardent disposition." A middle-aged man,

> Jim is still able to lose himself in those big Western dreams. Though he is over forty now, he meets new people and new enterprises with the impulsiveness by which his boyhood friends remember him. He never seems to me to grow older. His fresh color and sandy hair and quick-changing blue eyes are those of a young man, and his sympathetic, solicitous interest in women is as youthful as it is Western and American.[36]

The discussion between Jim and the narrator turns to a girl they knew when they were young in Nebraska, a Bohemian named Àntonia Shimerda. They agree to write down their thoughts about Àntonia and compare notes at a later date. Jim writes an extensive essay and later shows it to his friend. He has titled his work "Àntonia." Yet as he presents his work, he is unhappy with the title. "He frowned at this moment, then prefixed another word, making it 'My Àntonia.' That seemed to satisfy him." The rest of the novel is presented as a reproduction of Jim's essay, with Jim serving as the narrator. Thus the novel is not necessarily an accurate portrayal of an "authentic" Àntonia, but the impressions of a romantic who is writing of *his* Àntonia.[37]

The themes of nation building permeate the novel. Indeed, as a railway employee, in some sense Jim is responsible for building the West. Jim's story opens with him arriving in Nebraska from Virginia, a young orphan being sent west to live with his grandparents. Two books Jim reads early in the novel clue the reader into the theme of nation building. On the train Jim is reading a dime store novel of the life of Jesse James. The Western genre presented in this cheap novel often plays on the theme of civilization building. More obvious is Jim's reading of *Swiss Family Robinson*, a novel about a family, not unlike Jim's, fighting to create a community in harsh nature.[38] Jim describes Nebraska as "not a country at all, but the material out of which countries are made."[39] Jim relates the fictional story of Mormons marking the trail west with sunflowers, which he recognizes as likely untrue, but still concedes, "Nevertheless, that legend has stuck in my mind, and sunflower-bordered roads always seem to me the roads to freedom." The road to the West is the road to an open country ready to be made as man sees fit. Later in the story as an older Jim prepares to head off for university, while on a country picnic he spots a plough in the distance. "On some upland farm, a plough had been left standing in the field. The sun was sinking just behind it. Magnified across the distance by the horizontal light, it stood out against the sun, was exactly contained with the circle of the disk; the handles, the tongue, the share—black against the molten red. There it was, heroic in size, a picture writing on the sun."[40] Here Jim sees the tool that turned the raw material of West into a country that could support a community of people. Cather asks us to identify with the pioneers who sought to better themselves by improving the land and controlling nature for their own ends. This is a view of progress, but a mitigated one as Cather warns us of some of the dangers of progress.

The depiction of commerce in the novel is almost wholly negative, which should give us pause as we consider the fact that adult Jim works for a major railroad interest. The first businessman we meet in the novel (except Jim himself) is Peter Krajiek, a Bohemian who takes advantage of the ignorance of the immigrant Shimerda family recently arrived in Nebraska. With their limited English, "Krajiek was their only interpreter, and could tell them anything he chose." The Shimerdas buy a homestead from Krajiek, "and had paid him more than it was worth." Jim's Grandmother protests of their actual dwelling, "It's no better than a badger hole; no proper dugout at all. And I hear he's made them pay twenty dollars for his old cookstove that ain't worth ten." Krajiek has also had financial dealings with two Russians, Pavel and Peter, "but he had cheated them in trade, so they avoided him."[41]

There is an innocence about the Shimerdas that makes them a particular target of cheats and scoundrels. They stick to Krajiek because they do not know any better way. "They hated Krajiek, but they clung to him because he was the only human being with whom they could talk or from whom they could get information. . . . They kept him in their hole and fed him for the same reason that the prairie dogs and brown owls housed the rattlesnakes—because they did not know how to get rid of him."[42] This prairie dog analogy carries over to an adventure Jim and Àntonia have at a prairie dog town near Peter and Pavel's homestead. While observing these prairie dogs, they are waylaid by an enormous rattlesnake, described by Jim as "the ancient, oldest Evil." Jim courageously fells this gargantuan reptile. Attempting to account for its size and relative ease of killing, Jim theorizes, "My rattler was old, and had led too easy a life; there was not much fight in him. He had probably lived there for years, with a fat prairie dog for breakfast whenever he felt like it, a sheltered home, even an owl feathered bed, and he had forgot that the world doesn't owe rattlers a living."[43] Cather clearly wants us to see a relationship between the Shmiredas and the mindless prairie dogs; easy prey for snakes, real or metaphorical, like Krajeik. Later, when Mr. Shimerda, Àntonia's father, commits suicide, there are some indications that Krajeik may actually be responsible for the death, but this is never completely resolved and we are left believing Mr. Shimerda took his own

life. Certainly Cather indicates that Krajeik is a man capable of murder, if not
actually guilty in this instance.[44]

It is no coincidence that the snake story leads into the introduction of the
second notorious commercial figure of the novel, the "merciless Black Hawk
money-lender," Wick Cutter. Cather describes this notorious figure, who is
owed substantial amounts of money by Pavel and Peter among others, as "a man
of evil name throughout the county."[45] Jim says of Cutter, "In every frontier
settlement there are men who have come there to escape restraint. Cutter was
one of the 'fast set' of Black Hawk business men. He was an inveterate gambler,
and a poor loser." Cutter is a man who knows no limitations, either in earning
money or with people. It is made clear that the unhappily married Cutter is notorious for affairs with his young Swedish house girls. As Jim describes, "He was
notoriously dissolute with women. Two Swedish girls who had lived in his
house were the worse for the experience. One of them he had taken to Omaha
and established in the business for which he had fitted her. He still visited her."[46]
When Àntonia gains employment with the Cutters, she becomes the object of
Cutter's advances, but is violently thwarted by Jim.[47] In the end, Cutter, unlike
Krajeik, actually commits a murder, with money as his motive. Long convinced
that his hated wife would survive him and give his fortune to her relations, Cutter murders her and then mortally wounds himself, keeping himself alive long
enough for witnesses to arrive so Cutter can show them that he has outlived her,
so her relatives will not inherit his money.[48]

The most powerful argument against selfish individualism comes from the
Russians, Peter and Pavel. In a harrowing tale, they relate what caused them to
leave Russia for America. While still in Russia, Peter and Pavel are commis-
sioned to drive one of a number of sleighs bearing a wedding party. In their
narrative, the Russians describe how they were beset upon by howling wolves
that began spooking the horses. Bolting in panic, the horses tipped their sleighs,
leaving the wedding guests helpless as the wolf packs descended upon them.
Before long Peter and Pavel were driving the last upright sleigh, coincidently
carrying the bride and the groom. Knowing that carrying four people they could
not hope to outrun the wolves, they tried to get the groom to throw off the bride.
When the groom naturally resisted, the two friends threw off both the bride and
the groom, literally throwing them to the wolves. This left their sleigh light
enough to gain the speed necessary to outrun the wolves. This act of selfishness
became known and haunted them from town to town, driving them out of Russia
altogether, finally making their way to America. They were bedeviled by bad
luck in America as well. This tragic story carries the lesson that those who look
out merely for themselves will find themselves cursed by fate.[49]

The Burdens' ultimate move into town shows instances of the supremacy of
human decency over commerce. With the move, the Burdens' hired hands, Otto
and Jake, decide to head out on their own and seek their fortune elsewhere. Jim
laments their leaving, saying of them, "Those two fellows had been faithful to us
through sun and storm, had given us things that could not be bought in any market in the world." We also see the one positive description of a businessman

(with the exception of Jim himself) in the person of the Burdens' neighbor Mr. Harling and his resourceful eldest daughter, Frances. Jim counts Mr. Harling as "the most enterprising business man in our county." With his daughter he had "more than once put their wits together to rescue some unfortunate farmer from the clutches of Wick Cutter, the Black Hawk money-lender." Frances in particular takes an interest in her customers as people, not simply as commodities from whom she can earn a profit. "She knew every farmer for miles about; how much land he had under cultivation, how many cattle he was feeding, what his liabilities were. Her interest in these people was for more than a business interest. She carried them all in her mind as if they were characters in a book or a play." Frances would go out of her way to visit the old people, "or to see the women who seldom got into town." In addition, "She went to the country funerals and weddings in all weathers. A farmer's daughter who was to be married could count on a wedding present from Frances Harling."[50] While the Harlings experience great financial success, Jim's estimation of them calculates their humanity far more than their ability to make money. There is a standard above profit by which to judge businessmen; it is the way they treat their fellow man. Profit appears to be secondary to the Harlings, below the service they can offer their neighbors. They do not simply look at their occupation through the lens of materialism.

Cather and her narrator Jim draw a substantially negative picture of commerce. She condemns the turning of all aspects of life into commodities. The danger of the market is precisely that it reworks everything in its image, making the worth of everything the economic worth it has to particular individuals. While one cannot deny the material benefits of free markets, Cather warns us that the market is amoral, making it a poor standard of ultimate worth. The market might give us material wealth, but with other non-monetary costs to humanity. There is, though, an ambiguity here because our narrator, Jim Burden, is himself an employee of a major corporation that brings economic progress to the West through the railroads. He "has helped young men [in the West] to do remarkable things in mines and timber and oil."[51] Is Jim involved in the same kind of operation that he condemns, or is he like the Harlings in that he conducts his business for reasons other than merely profit? At the very least the reader should be aware that Jim's own role as a corporate lawyer renders his condemnation of commerce somewhat ambiguous.

In addition to the problems of commerce, Cather directs us to the dehumanizing forces of urban life. Cather leaves this estimation unstated in the first section of the novel that deals with Jim's childhood on the rural farm. Jim's preference for rural life and condemnation of city life is more noticeable when the Burdens leave the farm for the city of Black Hawk. While Jim describes Black Hawk as a "clean, well-planted little prairie town, with white fences and good green yards about the dwellings," in almost the same breath he notes that the local river "was to be my compensation for the lost freedom of the farming country."[52] Jim immediately recognizes that his family's move into town will entail sacrifices. Later Jim begins to feel oppressed by a stifled mode of existence, lamenting the stolid nature of town life. "The life that went on in [the city] seemed to me made up of evasions and negations; shifts to save cooking, to save washing and cleaning, devices to propitiate the tongue of gossip. This guarded mode of existence was like living under a tyranny. People's speech, their voices, their very glances, became furtive and repressed."[53] Oddly, those who demand ease of living, seeking liberation from the toil of such mundane tasks as cooking and cleaning, actually find themselves trapped by that very desire, giving up freedom in the name of gaining comfort. The ultimate verdict on urban life is rendered by Àntonia, whose opinion on these matters can be considered definitive. She says to Jim, "I'd always be miserable in a city. I'd die of lonesomeness. I'd like to be where I know every stack and tree, and where all the ground is friendly. I want to live and die here."[54]

Cather perhaps best explains the divergence between rural life and city life in Jim's description of the disparity between the city bred girls and the "hired girls," the daughters of immigrant farmers who have moved into town to earn money working for the wealthier city dwellers. Jim admires the nature of these vivacious immigrant country girls while casting aspersions on the lifeless young women born and bred in Black Hawk. Jim laments the physical inferiority of the city girls. "Some of the High School girls were jolly and pretty, but they stayed indoors in the winter because of the cold, and in the summer because of the heat. When one danced with them their bodies never moved inside their clothes; their muscles seemed to ask but one thing—not be disturbed." These girls left no lasting impression on Jim; he remembers them as "merely faces in the schoolroom, gay and rosy, or listless and dull, cut off below the shoulders." To the contrary, the hired girls gave off an aura of physical and sexual power. "Physically they were almost a race apart, and out-of-door work had given them a vigor which, when they got over their first shyness on coming to town, developed into a positive carriage and freedom of movement, and made them conspicuous among Black Hawk women." These hired girls and their raw sexuality were often a cause for scandal in Black Hawk:

The Black Hawk boys looked forward to marrying Black Hawk girls, and living in a brand new little house with best chairs that must not be sat upon, and hand-painted china that must not be used. But sometimes a young fellow would look up from his ledger, or out through the grating of his father's bank, and let his eyes follow Lena Lindgard, as she passed by the window with her slow, undulating walk, or Tiny Soderball, tripping by in her short skirt and striped stockings.[55] While some of these girls found themselves "in trouble" after seducing a man, Jim prefers them to the lifeless and boring city girls. There seems to be a judgment on the city in deadening the characters of those born and raised in its milieu. The city is incapable of producing the type of woman that interests Jim's romantic soul.

The effect of city life on individuals is expressed in the difference between Lena Lindgard and Anton Cuzak, Àntonia's eventual husband whom we meet late in the novel. Adult Lena, living in the larger city of Lincoln, learns to loathe rural life. As described by Jim, "Usually, when Lena referred to her life in the country at all, she dismissed it with a single remark, humorous or mildly cyni-cal." Even Lincoln is not big enough for Lena, who ends up in San Francisco later in life. She ends up living with fellow immigrant Tiny Soderball, who says of Lena, "Lincoln was never any place for her. In a town that size Lena would always be gossiped about. Frisco's the right field for her." Jim's estimation of the older Tiny seems to sum up the effect of the city on a person. "She was satis-fied with her success, but not elated. She was like someone in whom the faculty of becoming interested is worn out."[56] In contrast, Anton Cuzak learns to adapt to the country life. "He was still, as Àntonia said, a city man. He liked theaters and lighted streets music and a game of dominoes after the day's work was over. His sociability was stronger than his acquisitive instinct. He liked to live day by day and night by night, sharing the excitement of the crowd. Yet his wife had managed to hold him here on a farm, in one of the loneliest countries in the world."[57]

If the choices of these immigrant girls and, more importantly, Jim and his own family are of any indication, this city life that thrives on manipulative commercialism and soul deadening conformity might be the future of the West. The desire for material progress and physical comfort will produce more men like Krajiek and more women like the unerotic Black Hawk girls. The liberation that urban life represents attracts those like Lena Lindgard who grow tired of the struggle and effort of life on the farm. While the Anton Cuzaks have the au-thor's admiration, if Jim and Lena are any indication, the comfort, freedom and isolation offered by commerce and the city will be attractive to those committed to acquisitive individualism. So how might we overcome the deficiencies of progressive materialism?

Like Tocqueville, Cather puts forward religion as a possible solution, al-though Jim's seeming lack of strong religious convictions might make us cau-tious in this conclusion.[58] While it is not clear religion gives Jim any particular comfort, he appreciates its influence on others. He does mention the intonations of prayers and Scripture by his soft-spoken grandfather as one of his particular childhood memories.[59] The strongest portrayal of religious conviction comes after the death of Mr. Shimerda and in the person of a Bohemian, Anton Jelinek, a young man Jim clearly admires. Jelinek, a Catholic, arrives to help organize the affairs of the Shimerdas, and relates a story of the power of the Eucharist. As a child still in Bohemia, during a time of war with the Austrians, Jelinek went with a priest to administer the Eucharist to dying soldiers in the midst of a chole-ra epidemic. Neither Jelinek nor the priest got sick, their immunity only ex-plained through the miraculous intervention of Christ through the Eucharist, says Jelinek. "But we have no sickness, we have no fear, because we carry the body and blood of Christ, and it preserve us." Jim's grandfather, a Baptist who does not share Jelinek's theology of the Eucharist, tolerates the difference and graciously intones, "I am always glad to meet a young man who thinks seriously about such things, and would never be the one to say you were not in God's care when you were among the soldiers."[60] At Mr. Shimerda's funeral Mr. Burden utters a prayer and then Mrs. Burden asks her hired man, Otto Fuchs, to lead the small group in a hymn. He sings "Jesus, Lover of My Soul," and Jim reflects, "Whenever I have heard the hymn since, it has made me remember that white waste and the little group of people, and the bluish air, full of fine, eddying snow, like long veils flying—'While the nearest waters roll/While the tempest still is high.'"[61] This tells us that Jim still hears Christian hymns, although we aren't told where Jim hears them and whether he believes the message. What is clear is that other sympathetic characters in the novel see religion as a refuge and as something that guides their lives, perhaps setting limits on what is acceptable and what is not.

With less ambiguity Cather suggests family, and specifically children, as a way to overcome the individualism of progressive materialism. Jim himself treats his grandparents with respect and is an obedient grandson.[62] But Cather attempts to show that by linking oneself to the future through children one can escape the meaninglessness of acquisitive materialism, living outside the desires of the moment and finding meaning in living for another rather than one's self. The summer before he leaves Black Hawk for university, Jim goes on a picnic with a set of the immigrant girls, including Àntonia. The discussion turns to caring for their numerous younger siblings and the sacrifices made to that end. One of the immigrant girls, Anna, says, "Yes, the babies came along pretty fast, to be sure. But I never minded. I was fond of them all. The youngest one, that we didn't any of us want, is the one we love best now."[63] Anna recognizes that even though much had to be sacrificed materially for the prodigious number of children, the joy gained from the welcoming of new life and the relationship of family more than makes up for the material loss. Only a people with hope for the future continue to produce children at the rate of these immigrant families. Babies, in a very real sense, equal hope.

This concept of the worth of family is most vividly expressed in the person of Àntonia. Àntonia gets engaged to a scoundrel named Larry Donovan (who happens to be an "up and comer" with the railroad). They travel to Denver to get married, but before they are married Donovan is fired from the railroad for knocking down fares (yet another example of the perils of commerce) and then jilts Àntonia, running off to Mexico. Unmarried Àntonia is left single but with child, a horrible scandal at the time. Even though Àntonia's older brother advises her to kill the baby, she decides to raise the child on her own. She is described by a neighbor, Widow Steavens, as "a natural born mother."[64]

After falling out of contact for twenty years, Jim finally returns to Black Hawk, a middle-aged man in search of Àntonia. He returns to find Àntonia married and now a mother of a dozen children. She asks Jim how many children he has. "When I told her I had no children she seemed embarrassed. 'Oh, ain't that too bad!'" Being a mother has changed Àntonia, softening her. She expresses to Jim a newfound fear of guns, saying, "Ever since I had children, I don't like to kill anything. It makes me feel faint to have to wring a goose's neck. Ain't that strange, Jim?" When the well-traveled Jim says the Queen of Italy once said the same thing to a friend of his, Àntonia responds, "Then I'm sure she's a good mother." Being married and a mother, Àntonia no longer has spells of depression that bothered her when she was younger.[65]

Àntonia's life stands in stark contrast to her alter ego, Lena Lindgard. She epitomizes individualism in contrast to Àntonia's selflessness. The difference between Àntonia and Lena is exhibited in a seemingly mundane occurrence during the summer picnic mentioned above. Jim has gone swimming and has sand in his hair. Lena offers to get it out. As Jim puts it, "She began to run her hands slowly through my hair." This is not exactly how one gets sand out of hair, although it is a good way to flirt. On the other hand, "Àntonia pushed her away. 'You'll never get it out like that,' she said sharply. She gave my head a rough touzling and finished me off with something like a box to the ear."[66] Lena attempts to get the sand out like a lover, while Àntonia does it like a mother. Lena is uninterested in marriage and children. When immigrant Anna speaks of loving her youngest sibling the best, Lena responds, "Oh, the babies are all right; if only they don't come in the winter. Ours nearly always did. I don't see how mother stood it."[67] Later, beginning a prosperous career in dress design, she declares, "Why, I'm not going to marry anyone." She says to Jim, "Men are all right for friends, but as soon as you marry them they turn into cranky old fathers, even the wild ones. They begin to tell you what's sensible and what's foolish, and want you to stick at home all the time. I prefer to be foolish when I feel like it, and be accountable to nobody." She is cynical about family, saying, "You can't tell me anything about family life. I've had plenty." For Lena, family is "like being under somebody's thumb."[68] She wants to be liberated from caring for anyone. The attachments of family keep her from individual fulfillment. Lena has the attitude toward family of the liberated modern described by Lasch.

As noted here and above, Àntonia and her husband have made particular choices about the life they wish to lead. She has chosen a life devoted to family more than comfort. She and her husband live a modest life away from the bright lights and big city. They chose to be bound by children and the inevitable material sacrifices children represent rather than be liberated by wealth and a lack of family ties. Cather suggests that Àntonia lives the most content and happy life of any of the characters, including Jim (whom we know to be rather unhappily married and childless). An agrarian life tied to land and family seems to be at the heart of Cather's solution to the problem of progress.

The Costs of the Solutions

There is a definite sense of place in Cather's *My Àntonia*. The novel reads as a love letter to the pioneer West. In the all-important summer before he leaves for college, Jim finds himself reading Virgil, an author who created a myth of place for the Romans. The morning of the picnic with the immigrant girls Jim goes for a swim. He reminisces, "For the first time it occurred to me that I would be homesick for that river after I left it. The sandbars, with their clean white beaches and their little groves of willows and cottonwood seedlings, were a sort of No Man's Land, little newly created worlds that belonged to the Black Hawk boys." Soon after, he stumbles across Àntonia, whom he finds crying by the riverbank. He asks her what is the matter, and she replies, "It makes me homesick, Jimmy, this flower, this smell." She tells Jim of the vivid memories of her home village, and insists, "Jim, if I was put down there in the middle of the night, I could find my way all over that little town; and along the river to the next town, where my grandmother lived. My feet remember all the little paths through the woods, and where the big roots stick out to trip you. I ain't never forgot my own country."[69] Off at college Jim decides to dedicate himself to telling the tale of his country. Reading Virgil once again, he reads the words that serve as the epigraph to the novel, "Optima dies . . . prima fugit," or, "The best days are the first to flee." Like Virgil, Jim is motivated by the idea, "for I shall be first, if I live, to bring the Muse into my country." Jim's professor, Gaston Cleric, informs Jim that by "country" Virgil meant not a nation, but a small local community, "to his father's fields, 'sloping down to the river and to the old beech trees with broken tops.'" Jim's ode to Àntonia that makes up the novel can be seen as his attempt to finally declare his allegiance to his country. The novel represents Jim's effort to put into words the "precious, incommunicable past" that he shares with Àntonia.[70]

Why does Jim wait twenty years to finally bring his country to life in words? This brings into question that portion of Jim's life that is not recorded in the novel. As far as the reader knows, Jim goes to the University of Nebraska and then to Harvard Law School. He becomes a lawyer for the railroad industry and marries a wealthy New York socialite. Jim is apparently wealthy himself and has traveled the nation and Europe. Other than these bits of information we know nothing of Jim's life between college and middle age, so we are left to surmise. The novel's epigraph, "the best days are the first to flee," suggests that the world that Jim lauds in *My Àntonia* will soon pass away. What will replace it? Jim's life and those of Lena Lindgard and Tiny Soderball give an indication. The future is one dominated by corporations, urban life, and pursuit of individual material comfort to the detriment of family connections. All three of these characters, cosmopolitan citizens of the world, desert the land that raised them (and that their parents and grandparents helped build) to pursue individual gratification elsewhere. The pursuit of this gratification has left all three of these characters, to one extent or another, unsatisfied.

Jim's romantic nature gives him insight into what he has given up in the name of material progress. He realizes that as an unencumbered individual he has lost meaning in his life. Jim knows that he has given up things of value (family, community) in the name of progress and economic gain. Perhaps Jim returns to Black Hawk and to Àntonia after many years away in recognition of the emptiness of his own life. While Jim has status, wealth, and a bevy of cosmopolitan experiences, he seems to believe that the poor and simple Àntonia has decided better. Her family and connectedness to the place of her youth define her life as an adult. It seems clear that Jim and Cather herself want the reader to see Àntonia as making the best choice of all the characters. She has chosen to limit herself by the bonds of family and place and yet is happier and more content than those who have seen more and have more material wealth than she has. Cather would later more thoroughly reject progressive modernity, but *My Àntonia* suggests that an escape from the dehumanizing effects of progressive modernity can be achieved within modernity.[71]

The fictional world of *My Àntonia*, encapsulated in the life of Àntonia herself, contains many of the elements that Tocqueville suggests will alleviate the worst tendencies of democratic life. Tocqueville suggests religion, family and connection to local community as remedies for excessive love of material progress. We see nothing of Àntonia's religion, but as discussed above the religious experience is treated reverently throughout the novel. Further, Àntonia has chosen to be limited by family and motherhood rather than live the rootless life of the childless. Finally, Àntonia has chosen a life devoted to her country, narrowly defined, over one of the anonymity of mass man. We get no picture of the political life of the Cuzaks, so we don't know if their commitment to their native land of the Nebraska plains includes political activity, but that faithfulness to their place is not in question. A love of the plains is deeply ingrained within them. Especially when contrasted with Jim and Lena, deracinated cosmopolitans both, Àntonia has, in a manner resonant with Tocqueville, escaped enslavement to progressive materialism.

But Àntonia's choices are not without cost. Perhaps Jim's romantic nature blinds him to the realities of what he sees when he returns to the middle-aged Àntonia. Even Jim recognizes that she is a bit haggard, time having been harsh on her. Àntonia herself points out that she hasn't many of her own teeth left.[72] This gives us some indication of the costs of Àntonia's choice. While one can look back with fondness at Àntonia's quaint rural lifestyle, her poverty has meant physical hardship most would prefer not to endure. Simply put, most people would like to keep their teeth, and modern dentistry does not arise amongst simple rural folk. The wealth created by the commercialism and technological advances that make Tocqueville, Lasch, and seemingly Cather so anxious also frees us from drudgery and privation. One can be disgusted by the crass commercialism of American culture, but that materialism has produced wealth that has liberated Americans from physical labor, disease, pain, and untold number of hardships great and small. Technological advances, spurred by the desire for profit, have made the transfer of information and wealth easier than we could have imagined only a generation ago. Tocqueville suggests that utility drives American ingenuity, as is suggested by the conversation Tocqueville has with the American sailor concerning American ship-making. It is hard to argue with the results of that ingenuity.

There is a very natural human desire to make the lives of our loved ones, to say nothing of ourselves, easier and free of pain. To cite one possible example, one may yearn for the simply rustic country lifestyle such as led by Àntonia, but when one's child is diagnosed with childhood leukemia one wants to live in a society blessed with untold wealth so that one's child can receive the treatment, and possibly the cure, that may save that child's life. One can lament the vulgarity of American culture, the cult of fashion and celebrity, and the use of technology in ethically questionable manipulations of human life. Cather seems to be suggesting that in pursuit of physical comforts one might gain the material world at the cost of one's soul, but at the same time one cannot deny the amazing results of modern economics, medicine, and science.

What Cather seems to be indicating is that, indeed, the best days are the first to flee. There is in the American experience an inherent contradiction. There is the desire for stability, for family, and something at least approximating the agrarian life. These desires are undermined, though, by a yearning for comfort and material well-being. This necessitates a dedication to the free market to efficiently allocate resources and to technology to master the natural world. Yet markets and technology have no respect for traditional religion or family. In *My Àntonia*, characters such as Jim and Lena must abandon family and community to gain the kind of economic and (in Jim's case) intellectual freedom that they desire. Many Americans intuit this contradiction, enjoying the ease of life provided by labor saving devices and modern medicine while simultaneously questioning the technological and economic system that creates what we desire.[73] The characteristically American desire for progress destroys things we value: family and community.

Tocqueville suggests much the same thing. While arguing that religion, family and localism all help mitigate against the materialism and individualism of democracy, the democratic ethos tends to rework these institutions in a manner unfavorable to democracy's survival. Regarding religion, Tocqueville finally admits that it will have to cater to democracy's love of well-being. Preachers, he concludes, "will not succeed in curing men of the love of riches, but they may still persuade men to enrich themselves by none but honest means." It is important for religion to refrain from running "counter to the ideas which generally prevail, and the permanent interests which exist in the mass of the people."[74] Tocqueville has taken great pains to inform us in other parts of *Democracy in America* that a devotion to material progress is one of the "ideas which generally prevail" in democracy, as well as being a perceived "permanent interest."

A similar phenomenon exists regarding the family. Tocqueville can be described as agnostic regarding the democratic family. While he has much positive to say about the democratic family (namely that it enhances natural affection), he concludes "I know not, upon the whole, whether society loses by the change [from aristocratic to democratic family], but I am inclined to believe man individually is a gainer by it."[75] So while individuals might benefit from the looser arrangement of the democratic family, Tocqueville refuses to tell us whether society is ultimately better off. We can, though, make some connections that suggest his assessment of the democratic family might be negative. He finishes his chapter on the democratic family by saying, "Democracy loosens social ties, but it draws the ties of nature more tight; it brings kindred more closely together, whilst it places the various member of the community more widely apart."[76] It seems the ability of the family to counter the evils of individualism is severely hampered in democracy. If anything, the democratic family, by drawing persons closer to the home yet further from fellow citizens, contributes to individualism's vices.

Local self-government is also threatened by tendencies inherent in democracy. Recall that Tocqueville suggests vibrant local government as one remedy for the problem of individualism. Tocqueville argues that those "who live in ages of equality are naturally fond of central power" and if they find that the central power serves their interests, "the confidence they place in it knows no bounds."[77] The consequence of that centralization is the famous soft despotism, "an immense and tutelary power, which takes upon itself alone to secure their gratifications and to watch over their fate."[78] Weakened individuals look to the state to provide the security they once gained from religious faith and the family. Liberty is thereby threatened.

Jim Burden is implicated in this tragedy. He loves the West and the pioneers like Àntonia who built it. But as a representative of the corporate East it is his job to transfer wealth and technology to the West. Inevitably the railroads that Jim helps build will bring people and wealth to the West and threaten the rural and pioneering way of life that he values. The best days are indeed the first to flee, and it is Jim Burden's job to drive them away. Jim's own life stands as a marker for the tragedy of American progress: seeking liberation through wealth and technology and then lamenting the lost social structures that progress leaves in its wake. There does not seem to be any solution to this problem. One may have tradition and community, at the price of higher poverty and physical suffering. One may have progress, at the cost of deadening the soul to beauty, nature, and the goods of family and community. There are some, including many libertarian theorists. who have learned to love progress and see any attempt to defend other goods as a threat to the dynamism that is the sum of all that is good. These libertarians typically suggest that market forces will inevitably produce what we desire, and what we desire is by definition good for us. Others wish to limit progress in some manner in the name of competing goods such as equality, a clean environment, localism, or other goods.[79] Yet few of these advocates are willing to admit that by opting for these other goods in the place of progress they are limiting the wealth and health of their fellow citizens. Usually it is those at the margins, the poor and sick, who pay the highest cost of the economic inefficiency caused by limiting progress.

The task of the democratic statesman is to defend goods higher than mere comfort. To do so he must defend particular institutions, namely religion, the family and local government, that limit desire for material goods while pointing citizens toward superior goods. Both Tocqueville and Cather suggest that given certain assumptions built into democratic life, this task will prove difficult. But that statesman, armed with the poetry of a Cather, might be able to defend reasonable limits on acquisitiveness so that the good and beautiful do not simply become part of our precious, incommunicable past.

Notes

1. This is not the place for a comprehensive history of the idea of progress in American history. One might look to Thomas Paine's statement in 1776 in *Common Sense*, "We have it in our power to begin the world over again" or the phrase *novus ordo seclorum*, "new order of the ages," that appears on the Great Seal of the United States as indications of what I have in mind. See Thomas Paine, *Common Sense and The Crisis* (Garden City, NY: Anchor Press, 1973), 59. In a literary light, consider the writings of Mark Twain such as *A Connecticut Yankee in King Arthur's Court* and *Innocents Abroad*, both of which transport scientific and materialist Americans to a traditional aristocratic society, with comedic results. By contrast, one could consider Henry David Thoreau's defense of simplicity in his book *Walden* or more recently the rise of "crunchy conservatism," exemplified by Rod Dreher's *Crunchy Cons* (New York: Crown Forum, 2006).

2. See Herbert Storing, *What the Anti-Federalists Were For* (Chicago: University of Chicago Press, 1981), especially 71-76, and Thomas Jefferson, "Notes on the State of Virginia: Query XIX Manufactures" in *The Portable Thomas Jefferson*, ed. Merrill Peterson (New York: Penguin Books, 1975). One should note, though, that Storing, in his study of the Anti-Federalists, concludes that "The Anti-Federalists are liberals . . . in the decisive sense that they see the end of government as the security of individual liberty, not the promotion of virtue or the fostering of some organic common good." See *What the Anti-Federalists Were For*, 83 n7.

3. Alexis de Tocqueville, *Democracy in America*, trans. Henry Reeve (New York: Bantam Classics, 2000), 671.

4. Ibid., 672.

5. Ibid., 578-580.

6. Ibid., 544.

7. Ibid.

8. Ibid., 545.

9. Ibid.

10. Ibid.

11. Ibid., 545-546.

12. For a more complete discussion of Tocqueville on the religious passion for perfection, see Scott Yenor, "Natural Religion and Human Perfectibility: Tocqueville's Account of Religion in Modern Democracy," in *Perspectives on Political Science* (Winter 2004): 10-17.

13. Tocqueville, *Democracy*, 48.

14. Ibid., 352

15. Ibid., 352-353.

16. Ibid., 48

17. Ibid.

18. Ibid., 360-361

19. Ibid., 361.

20. Ibid., 351.

21. Ibid., 736.

22. Ibid., 747-751.

23. Ibid., 620-621.

24. Ibid., 625.

25. Ibid., 626.

26. Ibid., 627.

27. Ibid., 313-314.

28. Ibid., 629.

29. For some examples, see Virginia Postrel, *The Future and Its Enemies* (New York: Touchstone, 1998) and Gregg Easterbrook, *The Progress Paradox* (New York: Random House, 2003).

30. Christopher Lasch, *The True and Only Heaven* (New York: WW Norton Company, 1991), 13.

31. Ibid., 52.

32. Ibid., 78.

33. Ibid., 59.

34. Ibid., 63.

35. Ibid., 36.

36. Willa Cather, *My Àntonia* (Mineola, NY: Dover Publications, 1994), 1-2.

37. Ibid., 3.

38. Ibid., 5, 34. A reader of *My Àntonia* will want to pay attention to the various works Jim reads throughout the novel, as they give insight into his character and frame of mind at various junctures.

39. Ibid., 17.

40. Ibid., 118.

41. Ibid., 13, 19.

42. Ibid., 18.

43. Ibid., 24-27.

44. Ibid., 49.

45. Ibid., 27.

46. Ibid., 102.

47. Ibid., 119-122.

48. Ibid., 170-172.

49. Ibid., 30-32.

50. Ibid., 71-74.

51. Ibid., 2.

52. Ibid., 72.

53. Ibid., 106-107.

54. Ibid., 152.

55. Ibid., 96-99.

56. Ibid., 139, 143.

57. Ibid., 173.

58. For a more thorough depiction of religion by Cather one should investigate her novels *Death Comes for the Archbishop* and *Shadows on the Rock*.

59. Cather, *My Àntonia*, 10.

60. Ibid., 52-53.

61. Ibid., 58.

62. For example, even though Jim defies what he knows would be his grandparent's prohibition on him going to the local dance hall, once he is asked by his grandmother to stop attending, he respects her wishes. See Cather, *My Àntonia*, 111.

63. Cather, *My Àntonia*, 116.

64. Ibid., 147-151.

65. Ibid., 159, 162.

66. Ibid., 116.

67. Ibid., 117.

68. Ibid., 138-139.

69. Ibid., 112-115.

70. Ibid., 175.

71. Like many authors of her time, Cather found her faith in modern life seriously wounded, perhaps fatally, by the first World War. This can be seen in later Cather novels such as *A Lost Lady*, *Lucy Gayheart*, and *One of Ours*. Interestingly, unlike Àntonia, none of the heroes of these novels produce any children. Cather's novels about Catholicism (*Death Comes for the Archbishop* and *Shadows on the Rock*) suggest that she too was attracted to religious orthodoxy as a response to soulless modernity. It might be said that Cather was an appreciator of orthodox Christianity, while not being an explicit defender.

72. Cather, *My Àntonia*, 159.

73. One need only look to the anger aroused by a corporation, Wal-Mart, that gives quality merchandise at a low price and creates a great deal of jobs and wealth. But because Wal-Mart causes economic dislocation and is corporate rather than local, it becomes controversial.

74. Tocqueville, *Democracy*, 538.

75. Ibid., 729.

76. Ibid., 725.

77. Ibid., 851.

78. Ibid., 869.

79. Examples abound, but one might reference E.F. Schumacher, *Small Is Beautiful: Economics as if People Mattered* (New York: Harper Perennial, 1989). For an environmentalist approach, see Al Gore, *Earth in The Balance: Ecology and the Human Spirit* (New York: Penguin, 1993). For a brief defense of localism, see Patrick Deneen, "A Republic of Front Porches," March 2, 2009, www.frontporchrepublic.com/2009/03/front-porch-republic/. For an insightful look at how the modern economy influences our approach to work and technology, see Matthew Crawford, *Shop Class as Soulcraft: An Inquiry into the Value of Work* (New York: Penguin, 2009).

Væ enim mihi est, si non evangelizavero.

Chapter 12

The Catholic Church in the Modern World: A Tocquevillian Analysis of Vatican II[1]

L. Joseph Hebert, Jr.

Alexis de Tocqueville stands out as one of the greatest political liberals to defend religion, not in the sense of amorphous spirituality, but in the form of organized worship and dogmatic authority. Contrary to those "philosophers of the
eighteenth century"—and beyond—who anticipated the displacement of religious zeal by "freedom and enlightenment," Tocqueville saw faith as both compatible with genuine democratic liberty and essential to the formation and preservation of the mores that allow liberal democracy to flourish. In his seminal
work *Democracy in America*, Tocqueville remarks that "in America one sees
one of the freest and most enlightened peoples in the world *eagerly* fulfill all the
external duties of religion" (emphasis added), and he repeatedly encourages the
democratic peoples of Europe to emulate the American marriage of the spirits of
religion and liberty. In this and many other passages, Tocqueville appears confident that America's "first political institution"—Christianity—can survive and
even flourish in modern times, and that, with effort, it can serve as a leaven for
liberal democracy throughout "the Christian universe" (280-82, 27ff, 517ff, 6).[2]

Upon closer inspection, one finds that Tocqueville's confidence in Christianity was not unqualified. Though he repeatedly insisted that religious impulses are natural to the heart of man, Tocqueville also acknowledged that these
desires, and other sublime instincts of the human soul, are in constant need of
cultivation if they are to bear fruit. For the majority of men, Tocqueville held,
individual reason is an insufficient guide to the moral and intellectual problems
riddling human life. Religious dogma is needed to provide clear, intelligible, and

certain answers to the fundamental questions of existence, and religious worship is necessary to communicate these answers and instill the corresponding habits of thought and action. In the absence of religious authority, Tocqueville feared, minds would become paralyzed and souls would become degraded, susceptible to the blandishments of materialism and radical individualism, and vulnerable to the pressures of majority opinion and administrative despotism. Were such authority to disappear, religious impulses would remain, but they would become divorced from the essential lessons about God and human nature conveyed by traditional religion, and attached instead to vague and dangerous pseudo-religious systems such as pantheism and materialistic progressivism (417ff, 517ff, 180, 615, 639ff).

Yet Tocqueville frequently observes that, even in America, religious authority *is* weakening in modern times, and with it the entire moral order—including beliefs and habits—it defines (228, 403-26). The above-mentioned pathologies are a serious threat to democratic societies; in fact, they represent the *natural* development of the democratic social state unless extraordinary steps are taken to guide it in a healthier direction. The purpose of Tocqueville's work, and of the "new political science" for which he calls, is to combat these tendencies so corrosive of human flourishing (643-45). Tocqueville's political science seeks both to explain the deepest causes of these dangers, and to indicate the best available means for their mitigation (13). Religious authority comes to light in Tocqueville's thought as both a means of combating the erosion of individual and civic virtue and an institution that must be preserved from the effects of such erosion as cannot be prevented. A proper understanding of Tocqueville's art of democratic statesmanship therefore entails an examination of the ways in which that art can and ought to be employed both in the defense of religion, and in the application of religious beliefs and habits to modern society.

Though Tocqueville calls upon politicians and "all honest and enlightened men" to join him in "raising up souls and keeping them turned toward Heaven" (519), the success or failure of his strategy for preserving and promoting religion in democratic times rests on the willingness and ability of religious authorities themselves to grasp and apply the lessons Tocqueville is teaching. It is therefore necessary for the student of Tocqueville to follow him in considering how these lessons might relate to and be integrated with the perspective of religious leaders attempting to navigate the troubled waters of the modern world. Here it is vital to note that Tocqueville himself does not write as a believer: he twice protests that he regards "religions only from a purely human point of view," and eschews any knowledge of or even interest in "the supernatural means God uses to make a religious belief reach the heart of man" (284, 419). Needless to say, what Tocqueville disregards in his account is precisely what counts most for those he seeks to advise. Though a false religion might conceivably be of genuine use to the order and justice of political society, and even to the psychological strength of its members, it cannot lead souls to eternal happiness (278, 417ff, 517ff). If Tocqueville is ambivalent toward divine grace and the ultimate good it promises, believers are not, and one therefore has to question whether Tocqueville's political art can be palatable to, much less applicable by, the religious authorities he courts.

The applicability of Tocqueville's thought to religious authority can ultimately be measured only by a sincere attempt to apply it. This chapter represents the initial stages of one such attempt. Two considerations may serve to indicate why this effort is worthwhile. First, though Tocqueville acknowledges his skepticism concerning the truth of key religious dogmas, his appreciation of the indispensable role such beliefs play not only in the maintenance of civic order, but also in the elevation of souls (517ff), renders him as genuine a friend of Christianity as a nonbeliever could be.[3] By the standards of his own day as well as ours, Tocqueville possessed a comparatively profound understanding of the Christian faith (see, e.g., 504-505), a superlative grasp of the character of modern times, and a sincere desire to advance the interests of the former in light of the latter. Second, Christians have long recognized the divine provenance of both nature and the reason through which man examines it, and have therefore acknowledged the necessity of studying nature—including the nature of man and its implications for the fields of ethics and politics—alongside the ways and means of supernatural grace.[4] To the extent that they are grounded in nature, Tocqueville's account of modern democracy's promise and perils and his advice for managing them can provide valuable insights even to those who see more causes than nature at play.

Tocqueville's advice to religious leaders is meant to apply to Christians of all denominations, and, *mutatis mutandis*, to other religions. This chapter focuses on the applications of Tocqueville's insights to the Roman Catholic Church, and especially to the intentions and effects of its Second Vatican Council (Vatican II, or "the Council"), held between 1962 and 1965. This focus, though limiting in a sense, is not arbitrary. As we shall see, Tocqueville's advice to religious leaders consists largely in urging them to strike the proper balance between the accommodation of modern democratic penchants and the maintenance of enduring beliefs and principles. Though he was impressed by many of the accomplishments of Protestant Christianity in America, Tocqueville ultimately placed more hope in the ability of the Catholic Church—with is hierarchical structure, ancient lineage, changeless doctrine, and majestic forms—to withstand the pressures of extreme democratic individualism, if she could only come to terms with the existence of modern democracy, and hence the need to apply the art of democratic statesmanship. An evaluation of Tocqueville's political art as it pertains to religion ought therefore to pay special attention to the light it can shed on the course of relations between the Catholic Church and liberal democracy. Since Vatican II represents the most discrete and perhaps the most consequential attempt by the Catholic Church to respond to the special challenges of the modern world, this chapter will seek to analyze both the goals and the effects of that Council with reference to Tocqueville's political thought.[5] In doing so, we shall find a remarkable resemblance between the aims of Vatican II and the advice Tocqueville gives to modern religious leaders, combined with an initially puzzling discrepancy between the aims and effects of the Council. Our concluding analysis will seek out a Tocquevillian explanation of and remedy for these post-conciliar difficulties.

Tocqueville on Political Science and Political Art

For Tocqueville, political science is the study of human action on the societal level. It is therefore intimately connected with, and even grounded upon, morality or ethics, which directs the actions of individuals. Tocqueville treats the nature of morality and its relation to political society in the second volume of *Democracy*:

> There is almost no human action, however particular one supposes it, that does not take its birth (*prenne naissance*) from a very general idea that men have conceived of God, of his relations with the human race, of the nature of their souls, and of their duties toward their fellows. One cannot keep these ideas from being the common source from which all the rest flow (417).

Whether he acts alone or in association with others, man, as a rational being, cannot help but act in light of a general idea we might call *moral order*: a conception of the good grounded in the structure of reality, including the hierarchy of beings into which man himself fits. Moreover, man desires that the general idea in light of which he acts be true, or correspond with reality itself, and his soul is degraded to the extent that he succumbs to forces that appear to contradict the true moral order (435-37, 8-11, 456). Since the truth about moral order is sought either through philosophy, through religion, or both, we can say that man as rational animal is also—in aspiration, if not actually—a *philosophic* and *religious* animal. Since the idea of moral order encompasses a multiplicity of beings, including God and any other higher causes, as well as the individual and his fellows, man as a rational animal is also a *social* and *political* animal. The moral order in which he believes will guide not only his own actions but also his interactions with others; to the extent that others hold to a different moral order, common action becomes difficult or impossible, and society itself is threatened (407). Political society therefore depends upon, and political leaders must foster, the maintenance of a common idea of moral order that is both open to reality and capable of supporting the harmonious interaction of society's members. The skillful and knowledgeable practice by which these goals are sought is what Tocqueville calls the legislative or political art.[6]

In an ideal world, the political art Tocqueville describes would not be necessary. If all men, through philosophy, divine revelation, or both, were able to apprehend and live by the true moral order, politics could be limited to the provision of rules directed toward the realization of universally held ends. In practice, however, the majority of men lack the leisure, capacity, or desire for genuine philosophizing—and even "philosophers themselves are almost always surrounded by uncertainties" about key moral problems (417). A similar dynamic affects religion, where divine revelation is initially entrusted to certain historical figures, and theologians subsequently debate the meaning or application of revealed truths. Both the discovery of true moral order, then, and its communication to political society in the form of a shared general idea, are fraught with difficulty. Properly speaking, it is the task of political science—including a political theology, which might be either open or closed to divine revelation, but which in any case must appreciate the interdependency of politics and religion—to formulate as well as possible answers to the great problems of human destiny, such as God and human nature. It is then the challenge of political art to apply these formulations to societies that may or may not be cognizant of or receptive to the insights gleaned through the higher sciences. In this latter task especially, politics requires the support of religious authority, which is supremely able "to furnish a solution for each of these primordial questions that is clear, precise, intelligible to the crowd, and very lasting" (418). For the good of both religion and political society, Tocqueville suggests, religious leaders ought to be students of political science and practitioners of political art.

In Tocqueville's view, political science can, with difficulty, apprehend the unmoving goal toward which the human race ought to tend (518). Otherwise put, it can discover a "general law" governing the "universal society" of human beings—a law Tocqueville calls "justice"—which every political society is bound to apply as a jury is bound by positive law. Every society can and ought to be measured according to this standard, which represents both "the sovereignty of the human race" and the rule of reason.[7] Yet every society, when measured by this standard, will be found wanting (240). Human nature is characterized not only by a longing to associate ourselves, in thought and deed, with "the admirable order of all things" (504); it is also beset by weaknesses that render it "incapable of firmly grasping the true and the just, [and] most often reduced to choosing between two excesses" (39). The sublime potentialities and needs of the human soul make it imperative—indeed a matter of justice—that political societies strive for the grandeur and happiness of which we are capable. Yet the infirmities of human nature demand that such higher goals be pursued with prudence, in the awareness that genuine notions of moral order will often be ignored or distorted by societies if they are proclaimed or applied artlessly. Political science, then, must study human nature in its strengths and its weaknesses, so as to bring to light both the goal humanity must seek and the various obstacles that thwart its realization. It is then the task of political art, looking to both this goal and these obstacles, to work out the means of most closely approximating that goal and avoiding or mitigating those obstacles.

In *Democracy*, Tocqueville calls for a "new political science for a world wholly new." The new world of which he speaks is that of democracy, by which he refers to a certain "social state" or set of conditions of moral, political, and economic equality, which he sees as transforming "the Christian universe" unstoppably and irreversibly (3-7). The social state—whether it be "aristocratic" or "democratic"—is for Tocqueville one of the chief intervening causes between the individual soul and the order of things with which it seeks to associate; it is

therefore, everywhere and always, one of the greatest aids and obstacles to realizing the goals of universal society (45ff). Prior to the modern period, all political societies existed in a milieu that was significantly shaped by fundamental
conventional inequalities among human beings. Political science therefore focused on fostering the harmony and mitigating the tension between the demands
of human nature and the particular species of inequality that dominated various
political regimes, whether they were governed by the one, the few, or what was
then deemed "the many." Only in modern times, however, has there been a real
and decisive shift in the direction of political societies dominated by the actual
majority of their living members. This revolution in the social state itself transforms virtually everything in human affairs, including the basic character of
governmental forms. Modern democracy is not the same as classical democracy,
and modern despotism is in crucial respects much more "democratic" than its
ancient precursors (450ff, 661ff). It is therefore the central task of Tocqueville's
political science to describe this new social state and the unique ways it furthers
or frustrates the realization of justice. Corresponding to this new political
science is a new political art capable of promoting what is good and mitigating
what is bad in modern democracy: the art of democratic statesmanship.

It is vital to note that the newness of the new political science and new political art correspond strictly to the newness of the promise made and perils
posed by modern social conditions. Human nature and its goal remain unmoved
in modern times, even if dominant opinions about them change. What changes
are the specific helps and hindrances to human happiness—including opinions
and mores—characteristic of democratic times, to be identified by political
scientists and fostered or minimized respectively by practitioners of the political
art (518). Tocqueville stands opposed to those who insist that the conditions of
modern life demand a wholesale revision of the fundamental aims of political
life, as well as to those who deny that modern conditions require a systematic
modification of the means by which to secure those unmoving aims.[8]

Democracy, Individualism, and Self-Interest Well Understood

The primary meaning of democracy, for Tocqueville, is equality of social conditions. The democratic social state is characterized by the absence or weakness of
conventional barriers, such as social class or caste, to the success or influence of
individuals. In its truest and greatest sense, then, democracy promises to liberate
nature—including the natural *inequalities* of mind and heart—from social arti-
fice. Democracy so understood is founded on what we often call meritocracy,
and what Tocqueville (with Edmund Burke and Thomas Jefferson) called "natural aristocracy" (5, 50). Insofar as democracy realizes this promise, it is a great
force for justice, understood as that which promotes the natural greatness and
happiness of human beings. The danger of democracy stems from a different

interpretation of its central feature, equality: one that is conventional rather than natural. At the core of democratic tyranny is the rejection of natural moral and intellectual inequalities and the subjection of all souls to a common and dehumanizing rule, so that seekers of truth and justice dare not speak against the errors of the democratic majority, and come to doubt even their right to disagree with erring public opinion (235ff, 613-15, 661ff). A key task of Tocqueville's political science, and one of its central contributions to modern political art, is to determine what conditions cause one or the other version of democracy to prevail, so that statesmen and citizens may artfully pursue equality in liberty rather than equality in servitude.

The range of factors affecting democracy's course is broad, and *Democracy* is therefore a lengthy tome. Yet among the many strategies Tocqueville offers for enhancing the health of modern democracy, two stand out: political participation and religious authority. At first glance these strategies would seem to be opposite in nature, one advocating the independence of citizens and the other recommending their voluntary obedience to higher authority. Tocqueville himself accentuates this contrast, as if inviting us to find the explanation for it (43, 276-77, 406). Only an examination of the core problem of democracy Tocqueville is attempting to solve can explain his recourse to these seemingly diverging remedies. That core problem is what he famously calls *individualism* (482ff, 643).[9]

Properly speaking, Tocqueville defines individualism as a sentiment: "a reflective and peaceable sentiment that disposes each citizen to isolate himself from the mass of his fellows and . . . willingly abandon[] society to itself." Even in so defining it, however, Tocqueville makes clear that individualism "proceeds from an erroneous judgment rather than a depraved sentiment" and "has its source in the defects of the mind as much as in the vices of the heart" (482). In a broader sense, then, individualism is a more (*moeur*), or habit of the mind and heart (275), and proceeds from a disorder of the human soul, which tends to combine ideas and sentiments as the hub of a wheel unites its spokes.[10]

The erroneous judgment with which individualism begins concerns the relationship of man to the moral order described above. With the loss of conventional authority man is no longer disposed to accept the word of others concerning "the greatest problems of human destiny": "God and human nature." As a consequence, each man is induced—without having read or intending to follow René Descartes—to employ a "Cartesian" philosophic method: "to seek the reason for things by [himself] and in [himself] alone." Though men in this position of doubt would do well, Tocqueville thinks, to turn to the guidance of the natural aristocracy in their midst, many or most modern souls will lack sufficient experience to know who belongs to this aristocracy; also, a sort of petty but powerful pride will dissuade them from acknowledging moral or intellectual superiority even where it is evident. Hence democratic society will be marked by a growing disdain of the extraordinary (talents and virtue) as well as the supernatural as a basis of authority. Otherwise put, democratic man will tend to reject or sharply limit the bounds of meritocracy. Wrongly judging that he is left to his own resources in dealing with problems that perplex even the greatest minds, the individualistic citizen will become intellectually paralyzed and tempted to give up entirely on the search for truth about God and human nature (403ff).

Since it is not possible to live without some notion of moral order, the confused democratic soul will seek answers from one or a combination of three sources: prior habit, personal experience, and majority opinion (179-80, 403ff). These sources are attractive to the individualist because none of them requires him to accept the superiority of another's intellect over his own. Each of these pseudo-authorities also exacerbates individualism because none of them requires—or even permits—the individual's participation in *deliberation* about matters of higher concern. Religion, which at its best depicts that "admirable order of things" every soul longs to contemplate (504-5), is reduced to a habit maintained because changing it would be painful (282ff, 417ff). Religion as habit will inevitably exert a weaker influence than personal experience, however, and the personal experience of democratic man is shaped by both the opportunity and the necessity of making his own way in the world (506ff). The practical centrality of material concerns leads to a kind of pragmatism whereby general ideas are measured by their ability to assist with immediate material exigencies, rendering the notions of virtue, beauty, and happiness seemingly inapplicable to one's own life as well as offensively inegalitarian when applied to others' (433ff, 500ff). Finally, the intellectual and practical limitations of each individual foster a dependency on both the opinion of the majority and the material assistance of its institutional representative: the state (640ff). The result, Tocqueville fears, will be a "herd of timid and industrious animals" too proud to accept guidance or aid from virtuous neighbors, but too weak to notice or escape their growing servitude to the tyranny of a materialistic majority and its bureaucratic masters (661ff).[11]

One remedy for this democratic sickness, a remedy for which Tocqueville is justly famous, is that of political decentralization combined with civic participation. Nineteenth century Americans, Tocqueville observes, were able to defeat individualism with liberty itself, because they interpreted democratic liberty as mandating the maximum possible involvement of individuals and communities in matters of public concern. Anticipating the notion of subsidiarity later to be formulated by the Catholic Church, Tocqueville insisted that social problems be dealt with by affected communities—especially through local government and voluntary civic associations—to the greatest extent possible.[12] For Tocqueville, decentralization was worth the cost (real or apparent) of diminished administrative efficiency and uniformity because of its effect on the human soul. By drawing individuals into the practical handling of problems larger than themselves, self-government expands both the minds and hearts of citizens. The experience of civic participation requires democratic man to deepen his understanding of complex issues, and allows him to see that his own soul is naturally satisfied by acting disinterestedly for the common good. It also makes him more aware of, and less likely to disdain, the intellectual and moral leadership of the natural aristocracy (82ff, 485ff; compare 50). It encourages democratic citizens to see

that genuine liberty is defined in relation to membership in a community governed in light of principles of moral order, and not in relation to the individual's ability to do as he pleases regardless of this community (42). In other words,
Tocqueville seeks to combat the false and passive independence of individualism with a genuine and active independence that strengthens the bonds linking
individuals to their communities and, through their communities, to a more robust idea of moral order.

For these reasons and more, Tocqueville regards decentralization as a crucial means to be employed by statesmen for the benefit of modern democratic
peoples. Teaching these peoples the art of association nonetheless poses a dras-
tic challenge to statesmen. Associations of the kind Tocqueville recommends
demand significant personal sacrifices of time, effort, material resources, and
pride. They frustrate the development of systems of uniformity and efficiency
that seem promising to the democratic soul (639ff). What will induce modern
man to make such sacrifices and forego such apparent advantages? Tocqueville's advice to democratic statesman on this score comprises his teaching on
self-interest well understood.

The doctrine of self-interest well understood is a means of bringing democratic man to recognize the error of the judgment on which individualism is
founded. As a device tailored for modern man, it does not appeal to the beauties
of virtue and greatness, which he is not inclined to appreciate. Rather, it seeks to
persuade each citizen that the exclusive pursuit of his individual well-being will
lead to his own ruin, "that man, in serving his fellows, serves himself, and that
his particular interest is to do good." In advocating this doctrine, Tocqueville
makes it abundantly clear that he considers self-interest well understood deficient as a moral theory, since virtue motivated by the "disinterested" love of
moral order is in fact a genuine and higher "interest" of human beings.[13] Tocqueville in no way abandons the pursuit of virtue as the natural good of man, but
he does deem it necessary, in democratic times, to bring citizens "insensibly"
nearer to virtue "through habits," rather than leading them directly to it through
high-sounding speeches. The democratic political art must rely on elevating *experience* as much as or more than sound *doctrine* to cultivate the sublime faculties of modern souls, "turn[ing] personal interest against itself" only after seeming to embrace it, and leading citizens to do good "at first by necessity and then
by choice" (500ff, 488).

As Tocqueville's treatment of self-interest well understood attests, however,
the experiences of self-government alone are generally insufficient for bringing
virtue to fruition. For most citizens, the efforts demanded by civic virtue are too
severe, and its sublime rewards too fleeting, to sustain the ascent to virtue without further motive. The challenge here is great, for "it will always be hard to
make a man who does not wish to die"—or, we may add, to make lesser but real
sacrifices—to "live well." This is why Tocqueville considers it indispensible to
apply the doctrine of self-interest well understood to matters of religion. Even
the skeptical mind, he argues, can be brought to "wager" that risking some of the
goods of this world is wise in light of "the immense inheritance that he has been

promised in the other"—though he may harbor doubts about that promise (504ff).

It does not escape Tocqueville that wagering on the afterlife falls short of genuine religion, just as self-interested civic duty falls short of true virtue. In one of his most telling passages, Tocqueville outlines the "magnificent expression" of "true Christianity," which grounds the love of neighbor in the love of God and defines the happiness of Heaven as the contemplation of "the admirable order of all things." As with civic virtue, the idea of self-interest well understood applied to religion is to correct the intellectual error behind individualism—the error of absolute independence—and draw democratic citizens into an experience that points to a higher order. In associational life, the citizen is made to approach virtue through habit, without necessarily being conscious of it.[14] Religion, by contrast, is uniquely able to draw men out of the realm of everyday habit, and to convey to them "general ideas relative to God and human nature" with precision and certainty (418). Religion's chief virtue, from the perspective of Tocqueville's political art, is to excel at bringing the human soul back into contemplation of itself, in order to make democratic man aware of his higher needs and potentialities. Through the periodic encounter with "sublime or moving depictions of the greatness and goodness of the Creator" and of "the lofty destiny reserved for men," democratic souls become conscious—despite their contrary proclivities—of "the delicate enjoyments attached to virtue alone, and of the true happiness that accompanies it" (517). What they practice insensibly in the political sphere begins to make sense in their minds only in light of what they are brought to contemplate in the realm of religion.

Democracy, Religion, and the Political Art

We have seen that religion comes to light for Tocqueville as an indispensible means for grounding and making conscious the quest for virtue that democratic individualism threatens to obscure. As noted, however, religion is not only a weapon to be wielded against individualism, but also an inheritance that must be protected against the corrosive effects of individualism. Religion therefore occupies a delicate though vital position in Tocqueville's thought. To begin with, religion could not succeed at checking the tyrannical ambitions and strengthening the virtue of democratic citizens were it not founded on a degree of independence from the forces that shape the daily life of democracies, and so religion must remain "strange" to the democratic ear if it is to be helpful to the democratic soul (517). A major part of this fruitful strangeness comes from religion's basis in the transcendent authority of God Himself, a doctrine that can be either attractive (420-21) or offensive (425-26) to the democratic mind, depending on the latter's degree of extremism. Though the democratic soul feels at home with the idea of uniformity suggested by monotheism, democratic citizens are loath to relinquish the autonomy they enjoy in their daily pursuits, or to admit the existence of any authority over the course of their lives, save that of the majority of individuals like themselves, or their representatives in the state. As a result, the natural tendency of democratic minds in religion is pantheism, a doctrine that rejects any God transcending things in the world and reduces both God and the universe to a ceaseless flux of unordered parts. Though the task of preserving human virtue demands that modern statesmen "unite and do combat against" pantheism, if such combat is to be effective its means and extent must be measured carefully in light of the conditions that "naturally" attract democratic souls to this mode of thought, lest such combat succeed only at further alienating democratic man from religious authority.

Pantheism's appeal is deeply paradoxical: "although it destroys human individuality, or rather because it destroys it, [pantheism] will have secret charms for men" dominated by individualism. For Tocqueville, pantheism destroys *genuine* individuality because it eradicates the concept of moral order by which "the genuine greatness of man" is measured; on its terms, neither individual achievement nor human dignity itself can be grounded. Yet this very betrayal of legitimate individuality "nourishes the pride and flatters the laziness of [democratic] minds" (426). By denying the cosmic principles on which virtue is based, pantheism liberates individuals from the responsibility of conforming to objective standards of excellence, and frees them to devote their lives to petty egoistic pleasures. At the same time, it condemns them to a life in which such pleasures are the only cognizable goal. The result is a populace easily molded and cowed by the forces of materialism, majority tyranny, and administrative despotism that threaten to rob democratic citizens of the greatness and happiness at which human nature truly aims (410, 509, 663ff).

A key question for democratic statesmanship is therefore how to present religion to democratic souls in a manner that preserves religion's authoritative character without needlessly offending democratic sensibilities. Of course, it is difficult to give any precise formula for such a task of political art. Nonetheless, in *Democracy* Tocqueville attempts to provide the strategic building blocks for succeeding at this task. His first foundation is the observation, twice repeated, that democratic man—given his skeptical frame of mind—will accept no fundamentally new source of religious authority (408, 519). Hence, although mere habit is not enough to sustain genuine religious faith, the cultivation of virtue through religion will best take place within the protective shelter of a given people's religious heritage. In the France or America of Tocqueville's day, this meant Christianity. Moreover, though Tocqueville's account does not assume the revealed truth of Christianity, and is therefore open in principle to the salutary effects of other faiths, Tocqueville does not fail to note that Christianity gave birth to modern democracy and is essentially compatible with it, while he judges other religions to be less so, or even wholly incompatible (419-20). His advice on religion is therefore primarily directed toward those who would promote Christianity in modern times, and it focuses on three areas in which a delicate balance must be struck if religion is to retain any significant influence over the souls of democratic citizens.

The first area for balance is Church-state relations. Tocqueville sees that the moral teachings of Christianity have definite consequences for political life, and he celebrates the power of religion to check and regulate the actions of citizens and governmental authorities. Yet he warns that democratic peoples expect to wield unlimited—even Godlike—authority in public affairs, and will not tolerate the intrusion of clerics into that realm. His famous solution is for religion to gain real but indirect power over politics by ceding *direct* authority in the political sphere. By first gaining the trust of democratic individuals in this fashion and then building on its influence over human hearts, religion can preserve and strengthen those mores capable of regulating political society through the free choices of citizens and leaders. In Tocqueville's analysis, the "complete separation of church and state" adopted by Jacksonian Americans actually permitted Christianity to become "the *first* of their *political* institutions" (278-88, 419, emphasis added).

The second and third areas Tocqueville addresses concern moral doctrine and worship. In both cases, Tocqueville advises adaptation to democratic penchants, but with caution. As we have seen, democratic souls are rarely responsive to talk of the beauty of virtue or the sublimity of the cosmic order. Tocqueville also emphasizes the impatience of the democratic mind with forms, signs, symbols, or anything else that stands in the way of the direct apprehension of cold, calculating, individualistic reason. Much of the content of true Christianity and many of the modes in which that content is traditionally expressed are foreign to modern sensibilities—though not, it is vital to stress, to the human soul itself, which both longs for the things Christianity teaches, and requires the assistance of forms, signs, and symbols to grasp them. Tocqueville therefore recommends a delicate balancing act between the relaxation of those offending elements that are "accessory" to religious faith, and the preservation of those "principal" opinions and practices without which the "eternal truths" of Christianity could not be conveyed (421-22).

Just what is principal in Christianity, and what sort of accessory changes can better convey this essence in modern times? Tocqueville treats these questions very seriously but very cautiously in *Democracy*. Two considerations loom especially large in his account: Christianity is influential because it is authoritative and because it is incarnational. Both of these qualities can be seen at work in the influence Tocqueville attributes to Christianity over the development of modern democracy itself. Though it is possible, in principle, to grasp the natural equality and liberty of all men by use of reason alone, Tocqueville observes that human societies were blinded to this fact until "Jesus Christ came to earth to make it understood" (413). In all of human history, only the conviction that God Himself "became flesh and dwelt among us" (John 1.14) was capable of bringing men to see themselves as they naturally are,[15] a revelation which in turn led to the democratic revolution Tocqueville describes. The doctrine of the Incarnation has this power because it renders the natural source of all human action—God, the author of the moral order in light of which we long to live, and hence the highest possible authority for us—accessible to us in human form. Rather than simply preaching that God, our invisible Creator, created us in His image and loves us equally, Christianity shows us a God who was willing to adopt human nature and all of the sufferings to which it is subject, confirming the universal dignity of man and offering a model of virtue capable of being imitated by all.[16] This unique quality of Christianity is disturbed to the extent that Christ's humanity is allowed to eclipse His divinity, or in the degree that His divinity is divorced from His earthly presence. It follows that, other things being equal, the influence of Christianity over mores will be preserved to the extent that religion is able to cultivate a sense of both divine authority and divine presence in the world.

By these standards, many sects of Christianity could be deemed salutary, insofar as they strive to integrate these central features; yet not all meet these standards equally.[17] Though he is reticent to weigh the various types of Christianity in *Democracy*, Tocqueville is quite ready to do so in his correspondence, and it is therefore possible to describe his views as follows. The essence of Christianity, in both its authoritative and incarnational character, is for Tocqueville found in the Roman Catholic Church. Various Protestant sects approach this essence more or less closely, but all are founded to some degree on the contrary principle of religious individualism. Though many Protestant sects retain traditional elements of doctrine, morality, and a sense of God's presence in the Church—especially in Scripture as God's Word and in the Holy Spirit, who guides the faithful in knowing and applying that Word—Protestantism as a whole tends to emphasize the freedom of individuals to interpret the faith for themselves, and to treat modes of religious worship, association, and governance as symbolic, ancillary, or elective. Though these tendencies render Protestantism more immediately attractive to democratic souls—given that the human soul likes to regulate earth and Heaven in the same manner (275)—they may also compromise Christianity's ability to stand firm against the individualistic excesses of modern democracy. For this reason Tocqueville anticipates a gradual slide of Protestant faith into latitudinarianism, deism, and worse.[18]

In the future, Tocqueville predicts, democratic souls longing for genuine Christianity will be increasingly attracted to the Catholic Church, despite their initial astonishment at her robust doctrines and skepticism about her claims to authority (424-25). In fact, the very features of Catholicism which initially repulse modern men render its potential long-term influence over them greater. If the task of religion is to provide certainty on doubtful but crucial questions, what can appear more certain than an authority that has not changed its fundamental doctrines in over two millennia (compare 418 with 422)? If the presence of God must be felt in order to make doctrines understood, what presence could be more palpable than that of Christ truly present in the Eucharist, bestowing grace through seven sacraments, and continuously teaching, governing, and sanctifying the world through His chosen ministers and people?[19] Though each of these beliefs requires great faith, and many even run contrary to certain strong democratic proclivities, Tocqueville is at pains to show that none of these beliefs is wholly incompatible with modern democracy, and suggests that together they fulfill most powerfully the promises religion makes to the human soul.

For Tocqueville, then, Catholicism is the form of Christianity most in need of assistance from the democratic political art, given its stark opposition to the spirit of individualism, but also—and for the very same reason—the one best capable of turning souls toward Heaven through the proper use of that art. Though it may be an exaggeration to say that Tocqueville places all of his hopes for religion's influence on modern life in Catholicism, it is no stretch to say that his analysis points to a decisive role for the Catholic Church in modern times. In general, Tocqueville predicts that Christianity as a whole will lose adherents in the modern age, while Catholicism will gain the allegiance of a growing proportion of genuinely religious souls (425). Yet Tocqueville's predictions cannot be understood outside of the encouragement and direction he seeks to provide to those practicing democratic statesmanship. In principle, then, the Catholic Church could wield a stronger or weaker influence over modern man depending on her response to the pitfalls and promises outlined above.

The application of democratic statesmanship to Catholicism is a delicate matter indeed. While recommending that religions adapt accessory beliefs and practices to suit democratic mores, Tocqueville is careful to note—citing America as an example—that Catholicism can thrive in democratic times without altering any of its core features. In *Democracy* and his other writings, Tocqueville identifies three moves the Church might make in order to lead modern men more effectively. First, without abandoning her moral authority and indirect influence over the political realm, she ought to disentangle herself from feudal-era political arrangements and accept modern democracy, including its doctrine of church-state separation, as a legitimate, if imperfect, form of political society (282ff). Next, Tocqueville believed, she could do more to foster civic and practical virtues in her lay members, without losing sight of the value of more contemplative virtues (275-77, 422-24, 504-506). Finally, though she dare not change her traditional modes of worship, "in which the form and the foundation are often so tightly united that they are one," the Church could take more pains to ensure that the faithful grasp the meaning contained in those forms, and that they observe "the doctrine of the Church that forbids [diluting] the worship that is reserved only for God" (421-23).[20]

In all three cases, the adaptations Tocqueville recommends fall within the traditional bounds of the Catholic faith, which has always acknowledged the equal dignity of all human beings, the responsibility of government to the governed, the dignity of all honest professions, the sacred duty to obey and assist the political sovereign, and the necessity of active participation in worship uniquely directed to God.[21] In all three cases, Tocqueville's modern democratic political art suggests a certain re-balancing of elements within the faith: political equality and liberty must be embraced without weakening the Church's authority in moral and religious matters; political and social activity must be specially honored without detracting from the intrinsic superiority of contemplation and worship; and finally, the focus and purpose of worship should be made clearer without destroying the powerful symbolism of its traditional modes. In all three cases, Tocqueville cites nineteenth century American Catholicism as proof that such a balance is possible. In the remainder of this chapter, we shall explore that possibility further by considering the development of the Catholic Church's relationship to modernity in the century and a half since Tocqueville wrote *Democracy*. That development is best seen by examining the intentions and the effects of the Second Vatican Council.

Modern Democracy and the Teaching of Vatican II

In 1962 the bishops of the world, along with other Catholic leaders, were called to gather in Rome. With the pope (first John XXIII, then Paul VI), these "Church Fathers" comprised the Second Vatican Ecumenical Council, which issued a series of documents covering virtually every aspect of the Church's inner life and its relation to the world at large.[22] By its own account, the chief aims of the Council were "to impart an ever-increasing *vigor to the Christian life* of the faithful; to *adapt more closely to the needs of our age* those institutions which are subject to change; to foster whatever can promote union among all who believe in Christ; to strengthen whatever can help to *call all mankind into the Church's fold*" (*SC* 1, emphasis added). Otherwise put, the Council sought to reaffirm the essential teachings and practices of Christianity, and even to expand their influence on society at large, by giving careful attention to two factors: first, the unique features of the modern age as they concern religious belief and practice; second, the degree to which religion can accommodate modernity without compromising itself. It is no distortion, then, to look at the Council as the Catholic Church's most concerted attempt to engage in what we have called democratic statesmanship. Though we can only glance briefly at its documents here, even a quick sketch will demonstrate the strong interest of the Council in addressing all three areas in which Tocqueville thought the Church could profitably modify her stance: relations between church and state; the connection between religious and civil or civic duty; and the efficacy of religious worship.

Prior to the Council, the Church had never simply repudiated modern democracy. In her repeated denunciations of those forms of rationalism and moral relativism characteristic of contemporary ideologies, however, the Church had placed tremendous emphasis on her own moral authority and the obligations it imposes on men, whether individually or in political society. Though she regarded civil power as distinct from ecclesial, as supported by its own divine mandate, and as supreme within its sphere, the Church also held that the superiority of her own charge—the eternal salvation of souls—gave her primacy over the state whenever the latter's charge—temporal affairs—affected that supreme goal of man. Though no citizen could rightfully be forced to embrace Catholicism against his will, under ideal conditions governments could and ought to declare the truth of Catholicism, foster it as far as possible, and restrict actions or statements tending to undermine the faith of citizens. When social conditions rendered this ideal policy impracticable, governments could decline to favor the Catholic faith, so long as the Church was given full liberty to exercise moral authority over her members and Catholic citizens were given full scope to promote the common good as illuminated by Church teaching. Thus Pope Leo XIII praised the separation of church and state in America for allowing Catholicism to flourish in a Protestant land, while noting that a government promoting Catholicism would be preferable in itself.[23]

Views of this kind led Tocqueville to describe Catholicism as inconsistently tolerant, and to speculate that American Catholics would forget about religious liberty were they in the majority (275-76).[24] Despite his reservations, however, Tocqueville concluded that a degree of "intolerance" was inseparable from belief and a necessary price to pay for the benefits of religious conviction in a democratic citizenry.[25] As we have seen, Tocqueville anticipated far greater danger in modern times from a religious indifferentism leaving the souls of citizens exposed to the moral and intellectual doubt, paralysis, and errors described above. Nonetheless, Tocqueville did see religious toleration and freedom of speech as essential modern doctrines (39, 172ff), and he therefore deemed it necessary for the Church in democratic times to withdraw her claims to direct authority in the political sphere, and to focus on maintaining and strengthening her authority over the free consciences of men.

As it happens, this is precisely what Vatican II sought to do in its *Declaration on Religious Liberty* (1965). Noting the prominence in modernity of the sense that man's dignity entitles him to act on his own judgment, free from coercion—though not, it hopefully adds, from moral duty—the Council sought to delineate limits to the governmental regulation of religious practice or expression. Having searched the Sacred Tradition of Christianity, it declared the historically new doctrine of religious liberty to be greatly in accord with truth and justice, and—within "due limits" defined by the common good of man— harmonious with traditional Church teachings. While reaffirming the objective moral duty of each person to seek the truth, and therefore ultimately to embrace the Catholic faith, and while maintaining the duty of governments to respect the liberty of the Catholic Church in honor of her divine mission and the revealed truth of her doctrines, the Council placed sharp limits on the promotion of religion by government. Government must favor religion in a general sense, and it is acceptable for "one religious community" (unspecified in the text) to be given "civil recognition" "in the constitutional organization of the state." Yet the right of individuals and associations to follow their consciences—even if erroneous— must be respected by political authority, unless intervention is necessary to promote a public order grounded in morality and justice (*DH* 1, 3, 6-8).

In this *Declaration* the Council leaves significant room for ecclesial influence in political affairs. Since the Church is the final interpreter of the idea of moral order, she is able to determine, however indirectly, the theoretical and prudential limits of religious liberty.[26] As this position implies, the *Declaration* by no means concedes the ultimate equality of non-Catholic religions, whose rights are based on limits to state power declared by the Church, while the Church's freedom is divinely ordained and not subject to any limitation by the state (*DH* 12). Nonetheless, with this *Declaration* the Council decisively recasts religious liberty: what was once presented as a reluctant concession to imperfect conditions now appears as an ideal to be limited only so far as is necessary. In a similar vein, in its *Pastoral Constitution on the Church in the Modern World* (1965), the Council both formally disavows ties between the Church and any particular political system or culture, and embraces the idea of government limited by civil liberties and personal rights—so long as the latter are grounded in duties deriving from God and the objective moral order. Echoing Tocqueville's advice to religious leaders, the Church declares that she cannot depend on privileges granted by earthly authority, but will even forego her legitimate rights when they compromise her mission; and she asks for nothing more than the liberty to pursue that mission by preaching truths that have the (indirect) power to transform political society as well as to save souls (*GS* 58, 73-6).

The Council's embrace of limited "secular"[27] government is accompanied by a repeated emphasis on the role of the laity in furthering the Church's mission. Without repudiating the hierarchical structure of the Church, the prerogatives of her ordained ministers, or the virtues of a life specially devoted to prayer and ecclesial service, the Council's *Dogmatic Constitution on the Church* (1964) and *Decree on the Apostolate of Lay People* (1965) stress the possibility of and need for holiness in all walks of life. As members of the People of God, all Christians are priests of a sort, offering spiritual sacrifices and proclaiming Christ to the world. Individually and in associations of various kinds, the laity are to study the doctrine of the Church, examine the conditions of their own sphere of life—be it family, work, culture, or politics—and employ their own prudence in applying the former to the latter. Though they must always exercise this "common priesthood" in obedience to the Magisterium of the Church—the teaching authority of the Pope and of the bishops in union with him—and though Church authorities must therefore test lay initiatives and judge their fidelity to Church doctrine, the free association of the faithful to further their unique divine calling is to be encouraged by the hierarchy (*LG* 10, 30-38; *AA* 3, 23-25, 28-32).

Though the laity may be asked to assist with Church affairs, their special calling is to sanctify the world from within (*AA* 9-14). They are therefore on the front lines of the Church's encounter with modernity. As our metaphor suggests, Christianity has always regarded its encounter with the world to be one fraught with conflict. The Council reaffirms this perception. In fulfilling their divine mandate, the laity are to wrestle against the ruling darkness and iniquity of the world (*LG* 35). Lest this sound like a denigration of the realm to which laity are consigned, however, the Council stresses the intrinsic worth of created goods, and therefore the genuine worthiness of attempts to achieve progress in the things of this life. Nonetheless, the Council warns that our relationship to created goods is all too easily corrupted by the darkness in every human heart, which—due to the effects of original sin—tends to place the creature before its

Creator, thus distorting the hierarchy of goods that ought to inform our every action. In particular, the Council warns that advances in technology, communications, education, and civil and personal rights, though beneficial in themselves, are readily vitiated by divorcing them from a greater wisdom that can only be supplied by knowledge of and adherence to moral order. Just as Tocqueville advised, the Council combines an emphasis on civic duty and openness to worldly progress with the teaching that the true common good can only be achieved by the proper cultivation of each soul, a process rooted in personal conversion, self-sacrifice, and the practice of the virtues (*GS* 11, 13, 15, 26, 37-38, 53-76).

The Council also recognizes, like Tocqueville, that the transmission of moral order and its accompanying virtues to the faithful takes place most powerfully through religious worship. The very first Council document, its *Constitution on the Sacred Liturgy* (1963), describes liturgy (the Church's official modes of worship) as the source and summit of the Christian faith (*SC* 10). Here the Council echoes Tocqueville's insight into the incarnational character of Christianity. In Jesus Christ, God reveals to us both His divine nature in human form, and the perfection and hence the meaning of our own humanity (*GS* 22). Christ's divine power, His brotherhood with us, His sacrifice for us, and His resurrected body are rendered visible and remain present to us symbolically, spiritually, and even substantially in the sacraments or efficacious signs around which worship centers. The Church's success in shaping the mores of men—upon which both their salvation and the betterment of the world depends—is directly proportionate to her ability to draw them into the worship of God and to make them fully aware of the meaning of the rites through which they worship. The chief goal of the liturgical reform for which the Council calls is therefore full and active participation of the people in the sacred rites (*SC* 5-14).

How can modern man be brought to understand the profound significance of ancient sacraments? The Council seems to fear, as Tocqueville warned, that modern man will be alienated by forms that are not transparent to his reason. It also seems to recognize, at least in most passages, that the form and substance of Catholic worship are often inextricably combined, and that the sense of permanence religion must convey renders excessive changes in outward forms dangerous. *Sacrosanctum Concilium* therefore attempts to articulate a standard for a systematic yet cautious revision of liturgy. Yet even a brief overview of this document reveals the difficulty the Council apparently had in reconciling the demand for liturgical change with the need to preserve key traditions of worship.

The chief goal of the Council's plan for liturgical reform is to express more clearly the holy things the Church's rituals signify and effect, so that the people may understand them with ease. Although some emphasis is placed on better training the faithful to understand the traditional forms of worship—to learn the meaning of Latin prayers, to receive instruction on the history and meaning of ancient practices, and to join in the simpler Gregorian chants—stress is also given to the elimination of "duplications," "accretions," and other complexities of prayer and action, so that the reformed liturgy might "normally" require "little explanation." Though some parts of the liturgy are divine and therefore unchangeable, the Council proclaims, other elements can and must be changed to suit the times. No clear principle is given for distinguishing one from the other, however. Though innovations must never be made without careful consideration and proof that the good of the Church genuinely and certainly requires them, the Council cautions, liturgical books are to be revised "as soon as possible" and in all of their parts. Though the treasury of sacred music and art is to be preserved, new forms of both are also to be welcomed, so long as they promote the reverence and honor due to sacred things. Again, no definite principle is provided for how simplicity and sacrality are to be combined. These general demands and cautions, combined with a list of specific suggestions, complete the Council's seemingly Tocquevillian recipe for renewing the faith of modern man and giving added vigor to the life of the Church in the modern world (*SC* 2, 13-14, 21-25, 33-35, 50-54, 106, 116, 123-126; *LG* 52-69).

The Effects of Vatican II

On the fortieth anniversary of the close of the Second Vatican Council, the newly elected Pope Benedict XVI gave an address to the Cardinals of Rome in which he boldly asked the following questions: "What has been the result of the Council? Was it well received? What, in the acceptance of the Council, was good and what was inadequate or mistaken? What remains to be done?" The pope immediately conceded that "in vast areas of the Church the implementation of the Council has been somewhat difficult," offering as only a slight exaggeration the image of "a naval battle in the darkness of the storm," with "the confused din of uninterrupted clamoring . . . now fill[ing] almost the whole of the Church."[28] As has been widely observed, a Council that sought to reinvigorate the life of faith, better convey it to modern man, foster unity among Christians, and call all of mankind into the Church's fold, has frequently been associated with effects that are the opposite of those intended, sometimes drastically so. Externally, the Church has displayed a shrinking figure as the number of priests, monks, nuns, and laypeople consistently practicing their Catholic faith has plummeted. Internally, she has suffered not only from widespread hostility or indifference to her teachings,[29] but also from continuous clashes among her members about the meaning of the Council and of the faith itself.[30]

While the very bitterness of these clashes makes an objective assessment of the Council's effects difficult, it is nonetheless necessary, after forty years, for the next generation of Catholics—and all democratic citizens interested in the influence of religion on modern life—to begin a systematic analysis of this new era of relations between the Catholic Church and the modern world. Fortunately, a growing wealth of scholarship, spiritual writings, and magisterial documents provides us with ample materials and direction in this endeavor. Utilizing a few of these resources, our brief review will focus on the gulf between Tocqueville's advice to the Roman Catholic Church and the similar intentions of the Second Vatican Council, on the one hand, and the practical effects of the Council within the typical Catholic diocese, parish, and conscience, on the other hand. We shall then turn to a Tocquevillian analysis of the possible causes of and remedies for these discrepancies.

In the aforementioned address, Pope Benedict traces the difficulties in implementing the Council to the question of how to interpret it. A correct reading of the Council shares the Tocquevillian view that religion can adapt to times and places, but must retain a clear connection to the eternal and unchanging. Such a reading employs a "hermeneutic of reform," recognizing the Council's quest for "renewal in the continuity of the one-subject Church which the Lord has given to us." This reading acknowledges that differences of historical context may require the Church to make certain changes in policy, even some that are quite significant. At the same time, it stresses that the fundamental principles of the faith are revealed by God, constituting a treasure of which the Church is the guardian, rightly possessing neither the authority nor the desire to change them. By contrast, "a hermeneutic of discontinuity and rupture" sees the Council as opening the faith to an inherently limitless innovation and radical modernization. Claiming to adhere to the Council's "spirit" as opposed to its letter, this approach sees Vatican II as the reconstitution of Catholicism by modern man, rejecting prior revelations of God's will and two millennia of inspired development of doctrine and practice, and subjecting religion to the contemporary world's "every whim." Though it is important to remember that these contrary hermeneutics represent clashing forces within the Church, and that neither simply holds sway, even a brief synopsis of Catholic life since the Council will reveal the powerful influence the spirit of discontinuity has had on the religious experiences of the average Catholic.

In conducting a review of this change in spirit it is fitting to begin with the Church's liturgy. As we have seen, Tocqueville stresses the incarnational character of Christianity, the necessity of forms for proper religious formation, and the unity of form and content in Catholic worship. We have also seen Vatican II's contention that liturgy, in which the faithful encounter the incarnated Christ in the Eucharist, is central to the practice of the Christian life. In a 2007 exhortation expounding on this very theme, Pope Benedict—whose writings as Cardinal Ratzinger reveal his profound grasp of the liturgy as the source and summit of Christian faith—stressed that the hermeneutic of continuity must be applied to "the changes which the Council called for" in the liturgy.[31] Later that year, in a letter to bishops accompanying legislation allowing for broad access to the liturgical forms used in 1962—essentially the same liturgy known to countless generations of Catholics before the Council—the pope noted the extent to which a hermeneutic of rupture had in fact been applied to the postconciliar liturgy. "Speaking from experience," he remarked that the emphasis on human "creativity" in post-Vatican II Catholic worship "frequently led to deformations of the liturgy which were hard to bear," and which "caused deep pain to individuals totally rooted in the faith of the Church." The rehabilitation of the traditional liturgy had become necessary, he implied, in order to recover both "the [more powerful] sacrality which attracts many people to the former usage," and a sense of continuity with "earlier generations."[32]

The pope's emphasis on ceremonial continuity may seem quaint to those who miss the connection between forms of worship and other elements of faith. For those seeking to understand this connection, however, the writings of then-Cardinal Ratzinger, as well as scholars whose work he has endorsed, such as Klaus Gamber, is highly illuminating.[33] In brief, we may say that, prior to the Council, Catholic liturgy had its share of difficulties, mostly centered on the need for greater participation (i.e., understanding involvement) among the laity. Yet the liturgy was possessed of a tremendous power acknowledged by Catholics and non-Catholics alike. This power stemmed precisely from the artful expression of the incarnational character identified by Tocqueville and the Council as essential to Christianity. The priest, consecrated by a bishop who traced his authority through an earthly succession to Christ through the Apostles, played a liturgical role that was simultaneously central and humble. Standing for Christ in the sanctuary at the head of the faithful and acting *in persona Christi*, he also prayed as part of the congregation who together faced the liturgical east, which simultaneously signified Christ's sacrificial presence on the altar, the second coming of the resurrected Christ, and the heavenly kingdom into which the faithful seek entrance through Christ. While the authority of the Church and her priesthood were emphasized by this arrangement, it was made still clearer that all Christians were equally subordinate to the action of the divine. Given minimal preparation and appreciation, this liturgy—whose every prayer and symbolic gesture had developed organically over two millennia of Christian worship—was eminently capable of embodying and communicating the idea of a cosmic order connecting God to human society through the Church, and thereby assisting in the Tocquevillian goal of counteracting the individualistic excesses to which modern man is susceptible.

"After the Council," writes then-Cardinal Ratzinger, came "something else entirely": "we abandoned the organic, living process of growth and development over centuries, and replaced it—as in a manufacturing process—with a fabrication, a banal on-the-spot product."[34] It is crucial to note that this abandonment of liturgical tradition was not mandated by the Council itself, but emerged gradually yet swiftly *after* its conclusion, if ostensibly in its name. In 1965 a new *Ordo* (official text) of the Mass was published containing modifications to the traditional rite; every indication was given that this revision satisfied the demands of *Sacrosanctum Concilium*. In the years that followed, however, a special commission went to work on what can best be described as a complete overhaul of the Church's prayer life. Giving the broadest scope to the revisions required by the Council, and seeming to ignore its insistence that all changes be carefully weighed, this committee made sweeping changes to the calendar of feasts, to the cycle of Scripture readings, and to key portions of the Mass itself. On grounds of continuity as well as content, even a firm supporter of the Council's call for liturgical reform such as Gamber could describe these changes as a "needless destruction" of Catholic tradition, and a 1967 synod of the world's bishops failed to approve them. Despite this and other indications of disfavor, what is now commonly known as the *Novus Ordo Missae* was promulgated by Pope Paul VI in 1969, and implemented under the assumption (definitively repudiated only in 2007) that the older form of the rite was generally forbidden.[35]

The manner and scope of this further liturgical reform—largely superfluous, from the Council's perspective—already signified a certain spirit of rupture with the past. What followed exacerbated this problem immeasurably. In addition to official changes that noticeably deemphasized the verbal and symbolic reminders of the incarnational and hierarchical elements of Christianity that had pervaded traditional worship, the new liturgical books were suffused with countless options and allowances for "suitable" alternatives, a situation that quickly led on a worldwide basis to the promotion—as if they were dictates of the Council—of a range of practices not in fact mandated, authorized, or (in some cases) even permitted by actual Church authority. The substance of these changes frequently tended to deemphasize the real presence of Christ in the Eucharist or the dependence of the faithful upon the Church—through the ministry of her bishops and priests—to achieve full communion with God.[36] Continuity with the Church's past was also attenuated, often severely, with everything from prayers and postures to architecture and music suddenly changing, as if "what earlier generations held as sacred" was now "considered harmful."[37]

As a result of these changes, a false message was sent to the Catholic faithful concerning both the nature of liturgy and the meaning of Vatican II itself. Many Catholics, who would never read the Council documents, or read them carefully, were struck in their weekly or daily experience of worship by a manifest and seemingly comprehensive rejection of the traditional, incarnational, and authoritative elements of their religion. As the changes described above were made, the priest turned to face the people and began to act less *in persona Christi* and more as "an actor, totally dependent on his audience."[38] In response to this "newly created role" of the priest came the "assigning of all kinds of liturgical functions to different individuals and entrusting the 'creative' planning of the liturgy to groups of people," radically diminishing the sense that "what is done by the human beings who meet" in the liturgy is or must be directed to a transcendent God. Instead of perceiving themselves to be part of a "Church Militant" marching toward heaven and under divine command, many or most Catholics came to experience worship as a "self-enclosed circle," "a feast that the community gives itself, a festival of self-affirmation."[39] This distortion of the incarnational and cosmic character of worship simultaneously weakened its authoritative dimension, by radically diminishing the people's connection to a religious order capable of directing them toward an objective conception of God and moral order. In Tocquevillian terms, these changes encouraged democratic souls to entertain the pantheistic belief that God is subject to their whims as much or more as they to His admirable order.

Given the centrality of liturgy to the "political art" by which religion reorients souls, it is not surprising that such a radical disorientation of liturgy would be accompanied by a weakening of the Catholic faith in general. As worship seemed to change from "a procession toward the Lord"[40] to a self-expression—for better or for worse—on the part of the faithful, the popular image of the Church also changed, from the transmitter and guardian of divine truths by which all souls must be guided, to yet another medium through which human efforts could be channeled. Rather than elevating the thoughts and sentiments of democratic citizens through a "strange" encounter with another realm, worship was increasingly used to promote a notion of progress only vaguely and selectively rooted—if at all—in the actual moral order outlined by Christianity. The harmful effects of this change in attitude have become particularly evident in two areas of chief concern to both Tocqueville and the Second Vatican Council: the fostering of civic virtue in the laity and the preservation or enhancement of Christianity's indirect influence over politics.

For both Tocqueville and the Council, Christianity holds great promise in the modern world. Its contribution depends upon the achievement of a delicate balancing act: the dignity and importance of the duties lay people perform in the world must be articulated and honored without compromising the transcendent, permanent, and hierarchical elements so essential to religion itself; these latter regime-balancing elements can then be carried by the laity into familial, commercial, and political life, thereby moderating the extremes into which modern democratic life is apt to fall. As commentators have noted, however, the implementation of Vatican II has tended toward a far different dynamic in these matters than the one the Council intended. Rather than emphasizing the vocation of the laity *in the world*, and seeking to prepare them for this vocation through sound Catholic formation, the dominant strand of postconciliar reform has focused on drastically increasing the involvement of the laity *in the Church*, especially in her liturgy and catechesis (instruction of members in the faith).[41] Though many lay Catholics filling these offices are well intentioned and solidly grounded in the faith, the general trend has been toward an atmosphere—in faith and morals as well as in liturgy—of capitulation to contemporary fashions and indifference or hostility to the traditions and doctrines of the Church. Rather than preparing the faithful to bring religion into the world, such reforms tend to subject religion to the whims of the world.

A telling example of this dynamic can be seen in the misapplication of Vatican II's teaching on religious liberty. For both Tocqueville and the Council, this modern doctrine, properly understood, allows the Church to focus on influencing the consciences of citizens, who then act accordingly in society and politics. Yet after the Council, a growing number of Catholics—even apparently the majority—have come to believe that the Church has no right to direct the formation of consciences, and that good Catholics can dissent from Church teachings on sexuality, marriage, the sanctity of human life, and other matters of faith and morals. This attitude apparently reflects the convictions of many of those charged with teaching the faith today.[42] As a result of this situation, numerous American politicians are able publicly to flaunt their Catholicism while simultaneously promoting policies facilitating what the Church—in the very documents of the Council (*GS* 47, 51)—describes as grave crimes. When called to account, even by their own bishops, such politicians invariably justify their actions by specious reference to freedom of conscience, church-state separation, and the spirit of Vatican II. One can only speculate how much more powerful the Church's influence on modern liberal democracy would be were her membership not so frequently misled on these points.

It would be a gross exaggeration to suggest that the Catholic Church has seen nothing but decline since Vatican II. As noted in our next section, many profound and beautiful articulations and applications of the faith have emerged since the Council, from the Church's Magisterium and from diverse sectors of the Church's membership. Many of these teachings are promoted and carried out by steadily growing lay and religious associations, and some have beneficially influenced parish and diocesan life. Significantly, much that is good in these movements is drawn from the actual words and genuine spirit of Vatican II. Yet it must be observed that these trends as yet represent a force that is counter-cultural, not only within the world at large, but also within the lived experience of Catholic life today. It remains to be seen, then, what Tocqueville's political science and art might teach us about the causes of these postconciliar difficulties and what, if anything, might be done to enhance the potentially moderating influence of Catholicism on the trajectory of modern democracy.

A Tocquevillian Analysis of Vatican II

Accounts of the Second Vatican Council have filled volumes. The following initial analysis will pay special attention to its relation to that element of modernity upon which Tocqueville is likely to shed the most light: individualism understood as a moral and intellectual error. In brief, we shall see that Vatican II, though it shared Tocqueville's general intention to combat modern errors through a refocusing of religious worship and doctrine in light of modern conditions, failed to draw sufficient attention, through explicit and detailed warnings, to the deadly power wielded by individualism in modern times. This oversight helps to explain why the Church's governance in the postconciliar era has in crucial respects fallen short of that level of political art whose necessity and possibility are articulated in Tocqueville's political science.

As noted, Tocqueville famously described nineteenth century Americans as Cartesians who had not read Descartes—though adding, importantly, that they continued to exempt key religious teachings from the litmus test of individual reason (403-407). Tocqueville's advice to religious leaders, comprising the art of democratic statesmanship applied to their field, aims primarily at continuing to shield religion from this Cartesian spirit, so that Christianity may remain in a position to moderate the individualism of modern democratic society as a whole. This is why Tocqueville stresses the need for caution and continuity even as he recommends that certain adjustments be made to religion in modern times. As we have seen, the documents of the Second Vatican Council express a similar desire to balance reasonable adaptation with the preservation of what is true and essential in Christianity. In this sense they can be said to accord with Tocqueville's art of democratic statesmanship. Upon closer inspection, however, there are omissions in the documents indicating points on which the contemporary Church might profit from a more thorough appropriation of Tocqueville's insights.

Certain lacunae that might have seemed small when the Council documents were published, and which might have had little to no effect had those documents been read in the proper spirit, were in fact misconstrued by those who interpreted the Council in a spirit of rupture. The Church's new policy concerning religious liberty, for example, is presented with extreme brevity; the reasons for the new policy and its precise relation to the old are referenced but not expounded (*DH* 2-6). This has made it all too easy for interpreters to assert a discontinuity between *Dignitatis Humanae* and prior Church teachings on the subject, and to assume a harmony between that document and typical modern accounts of religious liberty grounded in religious indifferentism.[43] Under the assumption that there is no moral obligation to seek and practice the true faith—an assumption contrary to explicit texts of the Council—contemporary Catholics often act as if the Church were obligated to adapt to their individual preferences, which in turn are shaped by the imperious influence of mass society. In effect, the Church becomes subordinated to the political society she wishes to guide.

Underlying specific cases such as this one is a general problem stemming from the Council's effort to qualify its critique of the moral and intellectual ills of modern society with the assurance that modern culture itself is not inherently corrupt, and with expressions of enthusiasm for embracing what is good in modern life (*GS* 44, 57). Though it is true, from Tocqueville's perspective, that modern democracy is characterized by both good and bad developments, and that what is good in democracy must be fostered even as what is bad in it must be combated, these attitudes are neither exhaustive nor sufficient as guides to an artful confrontation with modernity. Rather, it is crucial to remember that all socio-political systems are prone to certain injustices, as is human nature, and that modern democratic souls are powerfully impelled toward identifiable errors and wrongs. Naming these dangers and cultivating a "salutary fear" of their realization is a vital part of the firm friendship that the Tocquevillian statesman is called to practice toward democratic societies.

In his aforementioned address to the Roman Curia, Pope Benedict XVI insisted that the Second Vatican Council, in pronouncing a "fundamental 'yes' to the modern era," "could not have intended to abolish the Gospel's opposition to human dangers and errors," or to ignore "the inner tensions as well as the contradictions" and consequent threats "*inherent* in the modern epoch" (emphasis added). Yet one cannot help noting the rather unsystematic attention paid to such concerns in the Council documents. Though they identify in passing a number of specific errors and injustices characteristic of modern man (see, e.g., *GS* 30), the documents never present a critique of modernity itself that would

demonstrate and accentuate its fundamental need for moral guidance. Previously, the Church had been emphatic in her denunciation of the arch-heresy of
"modernism," a term encompassing any tendency to abandon essential Christian
doctrines or practices out of sympathy for rationalist ideologies such as "liberalism, socialism, communism, anarchism, nihilism, naturalism, materialism, rationalism, and Free Masonry."[44] Even if this preconciliar concept was in need of
further development, it is easy to see how Vatican II's omission of any general
theory or detailed exposure of modern errors could be misconstrued as signaling
a radically new and indefinitely open stance toward modernity, rather than a
prudent refinement of the Church's approach to it.[45]

Finally, in light of Tocqueville's characterization of religious worship as a
place for souls to hear about "the delicate enjoyments attached to virtue alone,
and of the true happiness that accompanies it" (517), it is striking that the Council offers no extended discussion of virtue and happiness. As the 1994 *Catechism of the Catholic Church* makes clear, the Church interprets the Beatitudes
(Mt. 5, 1-12) in terms of man's natural and supernatural calling to achieve happiness through the cultivation of moral and theological virtues.[46] Notions emphasized by the Council, such as human rights, dignity, and development, must
be understood in light of a moral order confirming the centrality of virtue if they
are not to be misinterpreted in ways the Council itself condemns. Yet, though
the logic of its documents is perfectly in line with this classical understanding,
the Council makes only passing references to the virtues,[47] seeming to assume—
contrary to the actual tendencies of modern society—that the faithful are likely
to hear about them and be encouraged to learn them elsewhere.

The above criticisms of the Council must be qualified in two ways. First, a
fair reading of the Council documents will identify numerous (if terse) warnings
against errors and injustices that have since been promoted or minimized in the
Council's name, as well as a consistent reliance on the notion of virtue referenced above. Even if more emphasis on and elaboration of these points was
(and is) advisable, the chief fault for missing or falsifying the Council's teachings must lie elsewhere.

Second, the efforts of the Church's Magisterium have since filled many of
the lacunae that might be found in Vatican II itself. Pope Paul VI warned against
the temptation "to reduce [the Church's] mission to the dimensions of a simply
temporal project," "to a man-centered goal," or to "material well-being."[48] Pope
John Paul II's warnings about "the culture of death" seemed aimed at countering
any naiveté about modern culture found in *Gaudium et Spes*,[49] while the *Catechism* produced under his direction has made it possible for Catholics throughout
the world conveniently to identify and correct misrepresentations of Catholic
doctrine. Additionally, the Polish pontiff's strong stance against communism
and critical friendship toward liberal democracy demonstrate the possibility of
striking a genuinely Tocquevillian balance between church-state separation, on
the one hand, and the influence of religion over political life, on the other. For
his part, Benedict XVI virtually began his papacy by denouncing "the dictatorship of relativism,"[50] a phrase aptly capturing the tendency of individualism to

veer toward both intellectual stultification and political despotism. As our prior citations suggest, Benedict's efforts against the spirit of rupture in Catholic culture generally, and on behalf of a restoration of liturgical continuity in particular, are very carefully aimed at strengthening the genuine spirit of the Council in the daily life of the Church. To this extent, we can say that many (if not most) post-conciliar Church leaders have demonstrated a consistent grasp of key elements of Tocquevillian statesmanship.

From the perspective of both Tocqueville and the goals of the Second Vatican Council, however, there remains much work to be done in correcting the misuse that has been made of Vatican II. As commentators such as Msgr. George Kelly have attested—and as facts referenced in our previous section confirm—the Catholic Church has become and remains in many places mired in a culture of disobedience to Church teaching and conformity to worldly standards.[51] Though much progress has been made at recovering the riches of the faith in certain quarters, and though the grip of dissenters has slackened somewhat on the whole, Church historian Joseph Veracalli concludes that, even as the "first wave" of open rebellion fades away, a "second wave of decomposition," characterized by rancorous disputes among the would-be orthodox, has been fostered by a "continual failure on the part of ecclesiastical leadership" to articulate "clearly the legitimate parameters of Catholic thought and activity." Despite noble attempts to apply the Gospel to modern conditions, Church authorities have not yet succeeded at eliminating the "dissonance between what the Church espouses as an ideal and what is operationally embodied in too many of her organizations."[52]

What insight can Tocqueville's thought provide into the causes and possible remedies of this failure? Space does not permit a detailed analysis of the problems and possibilities of contemporary Church governance. Yet the following points should serve as a basis for future analysis. First, Tocqueville teaches us that modern man's disinclination to accept moral authority is closely connected to a fear of confronting the fundamental problems of human existence. Americans are Cartesians without reading Descartes because Cartesianism allows them to escape from the burden of carefully examining God and human nature; and Americans—whether Catholic or not—will remain Cartesians unless they are actively drawn out of individualism's soothing if debilitating embrace. As Dietrich von Hildebrand points out, the pretence that modern man has reached a point of such maturity that he longer needs discipline to put him on the right path is a grievous error.[53] One cannot expect modern souls to discover the truths and beauties of Christianity on their own, or even with the assistance of documents most of them will never read or ponder. Instead, the Church must carefully cultivate the *experiences* of her members at the level of local worship, instruction, and social-political participation, so that they consistently see and hear the faith being lived and spelled out in no uncertain terms. While the Church's theory of modernity might benefit from further development, the key to her success will be a willingness and ability to master the "art of association," which Tocqueville identifies as the "mother science" of modern times (492).

What would such a mastery of associational art look like? This question entails an examination of both the locus and manner of democratic statesmanship in the Church today. Here two further points will complete our initial analysis. First, the art of association clearly implies the necessity of a bottom-up or "grass roots" element in any viable Church renewal. Although one cannot expect modern souls in general to study Church teachings and apply them without strong direction, part of that direction can and must come from leaders among the people who, as Tocqueville counsels, use associations to lead one another just as the nobility once used their hereditary status to influence society (489-92). It greatly accords with both Tocqueville's political art and the teachings of the Council for Catholics outside of the Church's hierarchy to appropriate what they can of both the faith and political science and to put them to immediate work in all areas under their influence.

At the same time, it must be noted—as Tocqueville himself stresses—that the essence of religion is revelation from above, and the strength of the Catholic Church remains bound to that of her features which is most awkward in modern times: the superlatively authoritative and hierarchical character of her teaching and structure. Though Tocqueville favors religious teachings that leave citizens as free as possible in matters not essential to faith and morals, and though the Catholic faith also emphasizes liberty in doubtful things, both are energetic in emphasizing the value of religious doctrines and practice that lend stability and clarity to the realm of ideas centering on "God and human nature" (*Democracy* 43, 417ff; *GS* 92). Though the postconciliar Church has largely held firm to her role as *Mater et Magistra* of the faithful when it comes to official teachings on fundamental issues, she has been far less diligent in ensuring that her authority is honored or even felt in the daily experiences of her flock. As Kelly, Veracalli, and von Hildebrand suggest, the efforts of local Catholic associations will achieve limited success at best until Church authorities become willing to distinguish much more clearly and practically between those individuals, groups, ideas, and practices compatible with the Catholic faith and those that are not. In many cases, this will require a radical rethinking of present approaches to applying the perennial truths of Christianity to the exigencies of modern life. If Tocqueville is correct, however, making bold but prudent improvements in ecclesial discipline would help the Church not only strengthen the faith of her members, but also render her greatest contribution to the good governance of liberal democratic society today.

Notes

1. I am grateful to Devin Schadt, Brian Danoff, and Elena Hebert for their invaluable feedback on prior drafts of this chapter. An earlier version was presented at the 2009 meeting of the Society of Catholic Social Scientists.

2. Unless otherwise noted, parenthetical references are to Alexis de Tocqueville, *Democracy in America*, trans., ed., and with an introduction by Harvey C. Mansfield and

Delba Winthrop (Chicago: The University of Chicago Press, 2000). I have occasionally made slight alterations to the translation.

3. Similarly, Tocqueville was a friend to democracy without being its partisan. For a discussion of this point, see the introduction to *Democracy and Its Friendly Critics: Tocqueville and Political Life Today*, ed. Peter Augustine Lawler (Lanham, MD: Lexington Books, 2004).

4. See *Catechism of the Catholic Church, Popular and Definitive Edition* (U.S. Conference of Catholic Bishops, 2000),1954-1960 (references are to paragraph number).

5. A more thorough account of the Church and modernity would examine in depth the series of papal letters addressing the conditions of modern society—the "social encyclicals"—beginning with the pontificate of Pope Leo XIII (1878-1903). See *Catholic Social Thought: The Documentary Heritage*, ed. David J O'Brien and Thomas Shannon (Maryknoll, NY: Orbis Books, 1992); and *Compendium of the Social Doctrine of the Church* (Washington, D.C.: USCCB Publishing, 2005).

6. In *Democracy* (518), Tocqueville refers to "the art of the legislator"; in his "Speech to the Academy of Moral and Political Sciences" (included as chapter 1 of this volume), he speaks of "the art of politics." These phrases appear to be synonymous.

7. See Tocqueville's "Speech to the Academy." On the basis of Tocqueville's metaphysical uncertainties and narrow focus on democratic times, Catherine Zuckert contends that he is less interested in truth than in the practical effects of what is believed to be true. See "Political Sociology Versus Speculative Philosophy," in *Interpreting Tocqueville's Democracy in America*, ed. Ken Masugi (Savage, MD: Rowman and Littlefield Publishers, 1991), 121-152. Sanford Kessler responds, on the basis of Tocqueville's speech as well as his stated aims in *Democracy*, that Tocqueville is in fact "a political philosopher of the first rank." See *Tocqueville's Civil Religion: American Christianity and the Prospects for Freedom* (Albany, NY: State University of New York Press, 1994), 38-41.

8. Examples from Tocqueville's day would include most Enlightenment thinkers, on the one hand, and reactionaries such as Joseph de Maistre, on the other.

9. For a more extensive discussion of this theme, see L. Joseph Hebert, Jr., *More than Kings and Less than Men: Tocqueville on the Promise and Perils of Democratic Individualism* (Lanham, MD: Lexington Books, 2010).

10. For this description of the soul, see Alexis de Tocqueville, *De La Démocratie en Amerique, Première edition historico-critique revue et augmentée par Eduardo Nolla, Tome II* (Paris: Librairie Philosophique J. Vrin, 1990), 8nj.

11. For a more detailed account of this danger, see Hebert, *More than Kings*, chapter 3.

12. See *Catechism*, 1878-1885, especially the emphasis on association in 1882, and the resemblance of 1884 to Tocqueville's note in *Democracy* (703n24).

13. For an excellent treatment of the limits of the doctrine of self-interest well understood, see Brian Danoff, "Asking of Freedom Something Other Than Itself: Tocqueville, Putnam, and the Vocation of the Democratic Moralist," in *Politics & Policy* 35, no. 2 (2007): 165-90.

14. Tocqueville admires the way statesmen are at liberty to reflect on human nature in democratic assemblies, but he is skeptical of the chances that democracy will elevate leaders capable of speaking well on this most crucial of subjects (472ff, compare 411ff, 246ff, 187ff). The greatest opportunity for a "higher education" in politics appears to come from the interaction of citizens with the legal classes (251ff). Here, as with religion, the maintenance of respect for expertise in a higher realm of knowledge is crucial to the moderation of democratic excesses.

15. Compare the famous line from the Second Vatican Council's "Pastoral Constitution on the Church in the Modern World" (*Gaudium et Spes*), no. 22: "Christ the Lord . . . fully reveals man to himself and brings to light his most high calling." All Vatican II citations are from *Vatican Council II, Volume I: The Conciliar and Post-Conciliar Documents, New Revised Edition*, ed. Austin Flannery, O.P. (Northport, New York: Costello Publishing Company, Inc., 1975-1996).

16. Thus Nietzsche's quip that Christianity is "Platonism for the people."

17. Compare Vatican II's "Dogmatic Constitution on the Church" (*Lumen Gentium*), no. 15, and its "Decree on Ecumenism" (*Unitatis Redintegratio*), especially no. 3.

18. Alexis de Tocqueville, "Letter to Louis de Kergorlay, 29 June, 1831," in *Selected Letters on Politics and Society,* ed. Roger Boesche, trans. James Toupin and Roger Boesche (Berkeley: University of California Press, 1985), 46-53.

19. See *Catechism*, 1088-89, 1373-77, 888-96.

20. For an example of a reform Tocqueville would support, see his letter to Paul Clamorgan of January 1, 1839 (*Selected Letters*, 131ff), in which he deplores the special place sometimes given to landed nobility in religious ceremonies.

21. See *Catechism*, 1897-1942, 2426-2436, 1136-1162, 2097, 2132.

22. The documents cited below are "The Constitution on the Sacred Liturgy," *Sacrosanctum Concilium* (*SC*); "Dogmatic Constitution on the Church," *Lumen Gentium* (*LG*); "Decree on Ecumenism," *Unitatis Redintegratio* (*UR*); "Decree on the Apostolate of Lay People," *Apostolicam Actuositatem* (*AA*); "Declaration on Religious Liberty," *Dignitatis Humanae* (*DH*); and "Pastoral Constitution on the Church in the Modern World," *Gaudium et Spes* (*GS*).

23. See Pope Leo XIII, "On the Christian Constitution of States," *Immortale Dei* (1885), and "Catholicism in the United States," *Longinqua* (1895), available on www.vatican.va. For an excellent overview of this topic, see *Catholicism and Religious Freedom: Contemporary Reflections on Vatican II's* Declaration on Religious Liberty, ed. Kenneth Grasso and Robert P. Hunt (Lanham, MD: Rowman and Littlefield Publishers, 2006). Also of great assistance are Ernest Fortin, "The Regime of Separation: Theoretical Considerations on the Separation of Church and State," in *Human Rights, Virtue, and the Common Good: Untimely Meditations on Religion and Politics*, ed. Brian Benestad (Lanham, MD: Rowman and Littlefield Publishers, 1996); Kenneth Craycraft, "Religion as Moral Duty and Civic Right: *Dignitatis Humanae* on Religious Liberty," in *Catholicism, Liberalism, and Communitarianism*, ed. Kenneth L. Grasso, Gerard V. Bradley, and Robert P. Hunt (Lanham, MD: Rowman and Littlefield Publishers, 1995); and Russell Hittinger, "*Dignitatis Humanae*, Religious Liberty, and Ecclesiastical Self-Government," in *The First Grace* (Wilmington, DE: ISI Books, 2003).

24. See also Tocqueville's letter to Kergorlay, cited above.

25. See the abovementioned letter to Kergorlay, and Tocqueville's Letter to Arthur de Gobineau of October 2, 1843, in *The European Revolution & Correspondence with Gobineau,* ed., trans., and with an introduction by John Lukacs (Westport, CT: Greenwood Press, 1959), 204-210.

26. This is strongly implied in *Catechism*, 2109.

27. As the prior paragraph indicates, the Council does not approve of a government wholly indifferent or hostile to religious truth.

28. "Address of His Holiness Pope Benedict XVI to the Roman Curia" (www.vatican.va, 2005).

29. For a thorough documentation of numerical and doctrinal decline, see *Index of Leading Catholic Indicators: The Church Since Vatican II*, Kenneth C. Jones (Fort Collins, CO: Roman Catholic Books, 2003).

30. See *After 40 Years: Vatican Council II's Diverse Legacy: Proceedings from the 28th Annual Convention of the Fellowship of Catholic Scholars*, ed. Kenneth D. Whitehead (South Bend, IN: St. Augustine's Press, 2007), especially "Vatican II Today: Forty Years Later: Struggles and Initiatives," Rev. Thomas G. Winandy, O.F.M. cap., and "*Lumen Gentium*: The Once and Future Constitution," Rev. John McDermott, S.J.

31. "Post-Synodal Apostolic Exhortation *Sacramentum Caritatis*, of the Holy Father Pope Benedict XVI to the Bishops, Clergy, Consecrated Persons, and the Lay Faithful, on the Eucharist as the Source and Summit of the Church's Life and Mission" (www.vatican.va, 2007).

32. "Letter of His Holiness Pope Benedict XVI to the bishops on the occasion of the publication of the Apostolic Letter 'Motu Proprio data' *Summorum Pontificum* on the use of the Roman Liturgy prior to the reform of 1970" (www.vatican.va, 2007).

33. What follows in the text is largely based on Joseph Cardinal Ratzinger (now Pope Benedict XVI), *The Spirit of the Liturgy* (San Francisco: Ignatius Press, 2000); Monsignor Klaus Gamber, *The Reform of the Roman Liturgy: Its Problems and Background* (Fort Collins, CO: Roman Catholic Books, 1993); David Berger, *Thomas Aquinas and the Liturgy* (Naples, FL: Sapientia Press of Ave Maria University, 2004); Dietrich von Hildebrand, "The Case for the Latin Mass," in *The Charitable Anathema* (Harrison, NY: Roman Catholic Books, 1993), 35-44; and Sacrosanctum Concilium *and the Reform of the Liturgy: Proceedings from the 29th Annual Convention of the Fellowship of Catholic Scholars*, ed. Kenneth D. Whitehead (Chicago: University of Scranton Press, 2009); as well as on personal and anecdotal experiences. I am also indebted to the information and analysis provided by Fr. John Zuhlsdorf of *What Does the Prayer Really Say?* (www.wdtprs.com), and contributors to *The New Liturgical Movement* (www.newliturgicalmovement.org).

34. From his preface to the French edition of Gamber's work, cited above, and quoted on the back cover of the English edition. The account that follows is mostly drawn from Gamber's text.

35. Similar revisions were eventually made to most other rituals of the Church in the name of Vatican II, though we cannot enter into an evaluation of their relative merits here.

36. The most important of such changes are the reception of Holy Communion in the hand, the unnecessary distribution of the Holy Eucharist by lay people, and the insistence that the priest always pray "toward the people"—all of which contravene Church tradition, tend to undermine essential dogmas, and were only reluctantly permitted (if at all) by Rome in the years following the Council.

37. See Pope Benedict XVI's letter accompanying *Summorum Pontificum*.

38. Gamber, *The Reform of the Roman Liturgy*, 88.

39. See Ratzinger, *The Spirit of the Liturgy*, 23, 80.

40. *The Spirit of the Liturgy*, 80.

41. See Russel Shaw, *Catholic Laity in the Mission of the Church* (Bethune, SC: Requiem Press, 2005).

42. See *Index*, 63-81.

43. See Grasso and Hunt's introduction to *Catholicism and Religious Freedom*.

44. Quoted from Robert Kraynak, "Pope Leo XIII and the Catholic Response to Modernity" (*Modern Age*, Fall 2007). For the Church's condemnation of modernism, see,

e.g., *Pascendi Dominici Gregis*, "Encyclical of Pope Pius X on the Doctrines of the Modernists," (www.vatican.va, 1907).

45. Along the same lines, scholars such as Dietrich von Hildebrand have noted the importance of anathemas (condemnations of specific errors), in the development and implementing of Church doctrines and disciplines throughout history, and the absence or near absence of such denouncements in Vatican-II or in postconciliar magisterial documents. See *The Charitable Anathema*. The Council does repeat St. Paul's exclamation, "Woe to me if I do not preach the Gospel" (1 Cor. 9:16, cited in *LG* 17), which may be read as an implicit, general, and advance anathema against any attempt to dilute doctrine and discipline in its name.

46. See *Catechism*, 1699-1845.

47. The closest the Council comes to an articulation of virtue is found in *GS* 14-22. In fact, the practice of "freely choosing what is good," referenced in *GS* 17, captures almost verbatim Tocqueville's own definition of virtue: "the free choice of what is good." See *Journey to England and Ireland*, trans. George Lawrence, ed. J. P. Mayer (London: Faber and Faber Ltd., 1957), 117. See also *Catechism*, 1804: "The virtuous man is he who freely practices the good."

48. *Evangelii Nuntiandi*, "On Evangelization in the Modern World" (Boston: Pauline Books and Media, 1975).

49. See Rev. Paul DeLadurantaye, "At the Service of the Human Person," in *After 40 Years*.

50. "Homily of His Eminence Cardinal Joseph Ratzinger, Dean of the College of Cardinals, 18 April 2005" (www.vatican.va). Ratzinger's election as pope, which some thought impossible after such a blunt address, instead followed swiftly.

51. Msgr. George Kelly, *Battle for the American Church (Revisited)* (San Francisco: Ignatius Press, 1995).

52. Joseph Varacalli, "A Catholic House in Repair or Further Dividing?" in *The Catholic Social Science Review* 14 (2009), 150-152.

53. *The Charitable Anathema*, 11-18.

Chapter 13

Tocqueville on How to Praise the Puritans Today

Peter Augustine Lawler

What statesmen or "legislators" should talk up or encourage, Tocqueville explains, varies with the circumstances they encounter. The enduring truth is that we're beasts with angels in us—an endlessly wonderful, elusive, and mysterious mixture of soul and body.[1] People almost always tend to simplify the truth about who we are by confusing one part of the mixture with whole human being, and both characteristically aristocratic and characteristically democratic science distort the truth about who we are in either a proudly "sterile" or a merely utilitarian direction (DA.2.1.10). In aristocratic times, where people are too fatalistic about misery and injustice and too lost in a soulful "contemplation of another world," the task is to arouse people in the direction of the satisfaction of bodily desires. The legislator assists in "turning the greatest effort of the human mind toward physical studies," even toward exciting the mind "with the search for well-being" (DA.2.2.15).

Tocqueville would have joined Descartes and his students—such as John Locke—in deploying our reason and freedom to make our lives more wealthy, enjoyable, and secure, and he would have joined them in exaggerating how free in that physical sense we can or should be. He would have joined them in talking up one part of who we are and slighting the others. He would even have encouraged Americans to be what they became—restless even in the midst of unprecedented prosperity—at least for a while.

But once a democratic people has achieved a certain amount of "enlightenment and freedom" that encouragement is no longer necessary or even beneficial. All that remains is to "leave them alone" for them to continue to make their lives more and more easy and comfortable. The danger then becomes that "this honest and legitimate search for well-being" loses all sense of appropriately human limits. Democrats too readily come "to believe all is nothing but matter," and that untrue theoretical materialism—a theory that distorts or denies the existence of human soul—leads them to pursue "enjoyments with an insane ardor" (DA.2.2.15). The insanity, of course, is the result of futilely denying who we really are as beings with souls. It's the insanity of people believing they have no choice but to attempt to satisfy what are really their spiritual needs through material acquisitions (DA.2.2.13).

Tocqueville even observes that "madness is more common" in America "than anywhere else." He describes democratic, American behavior that no materialist could explain: "the singular melancholy that the inhabitants of democratic lands often display amid their abundance, and the disgust with life that sometimes seizes them in the midst of an easy and tranquil existence" (DA.2.2.13). "Alone among all the beings," he adds, "man shows a natural disgust for existence and an immense desire to exist: he scorns life and fears nothingness" (DA.1.2.9). The restless democratic materialist, most of all, fears nothingness. He fears that his proud desire to distinguish himself as a being with a soul can have no real satisfaction, that he is nothing but a momentary, meaningless speck that exists between abysses, that he in no way can transcend the biological destiny he shares with all the other physical beings.

This madness Tocqueville views as a likely prelude to self-brutalization. By not employing "his most sublime faculties" for their proper purposes, the democratic person can finally lose the ability to use them at all. His utilitarian theoretical materialism works well, of course, "to improve everything around him" with his needs in mind. But by gradually surrendering what's required to exempt himself from his impersonal theory, he "finally degrade[s] himself" (DA.2.2.15). The angel, Tocqueville explains, is even the source of the inexhaustible needs that drive him relentlessly even in the midst of prosperity, and the angel might be surrendered as nothing more than a source of restlessly miserable dissatisfaction (DA.2.2.16). So the loss of his sublime or angelic qualities, Tocqueville concludes, is *the* democratic "peril." If the democratic person believes his soul is nothing, it might well in fact become nothing. The soul has to be understood as a proud source of true greatness and true happiness to be sustainable over the long term.

So democratic statesmen, legislators, and enlightened people in general "must . . . apply themselves relentlessly to raising up souls and keep them turned to Heaven." Against especially the vain and pernicious theoretical materialists (such as, we can say, today's "new atheists"), "continuous efforts" must be made in democracies "to spread . . . a taste for the infinite, a sentiment of greatness, and a love of immaterial pleasures" (DA.2.2.15). As part of that effort, Tocqueville calls attention in meticulous detail to the enduring greatness of the immaterial idealism of our Puritan Founders, and he shows us why we should continue to do so today.

The Puritans were, in fact, strong where our Lockean or more materialistic Founders were weak. They are the source of our egalitarian duties which are as indispensable for our self-understanding as are our natural, individualistic rights. My task here is to show how we need to praise the Puritan contribution to who we are today, supplementing Tocqueville with the path breaking work of our theologian/novelist Marilynne Robinson.

There's little less fashionable today than praising the Puritans, especially for their egalitarian political idealism, their promotion of genuinely humane and liberating learning, and their capacity for enjoyment and human happiness. Praising the Puritans is especially difficult for us because even most of our Protestants have abandoned them. When a European calls us Puritanical we don't say, "yes, thanks a lot, you're right." Instead, we either deny it, saying we're way beyond those days. Or we admit it, saying, "yes, we should be less capitalistic, less repressed, and more free thinking, just like you." But the truth is that the Puritans remain the chief source of *the* American difference—our ability to live freely and prosperously without unduly slighting the longings of our souls. It's the Puritans' idealism that made and even makes Americans civilized.

Virginia and New England

Tocqueville's *Democracy in America* almost begins by showing us how much our democracy owes the Puritans. He calls attention to two quite different English foundings, two quite different displays of democratic freedom—the one in the South and the other in the North. Virginia was founded by "gold seekers," "restless and turbulent spirits," solitary adventurers out to get rich quick. They were England's "lower classes," people "without resources" or virtuous habits, people incapable of being animated by "noble thought" or some "immaterial scheme." They had no sense of home and no sense of having the paternalistic, magnanimous responsibilities of class. They weren't even ennobled by any bourgeois devotion to the virtue of worthwhile work well done. They, like the middle-class Americans Tocqueville elsewhere describes, loved money, but, unlike the properly middle class, they weren't at all devoted to the just principle that it should be the reward of one's own honest industry. The Virginians were in every crucial respect *uncivilized* (DA.1.2.2; all other references to and quotes about the founding in Virginia and New England—including the Puritans—are from this section unless otherwise noted).

So the Virginians readily accepted the introduction of slavery—or extreme stratification based on the introduction of a separate class of men who work and do nothing but—into the colony. That racist institution further contributed to their combination of "ignorance" and "haughtiness," enervating their minds and heightening their propensity to dishonor work. It diverted them further from useful activity.

The English of Virginia, Tocqueville wants us to see, had all of the vices but none of the virtues of hereditary aristocrats, as well as, of course, all the vices but none of the virtues of the American middle-class. Their laziness was un-compensated for—as, Tocqueville reports, aristocratic leisure sometimes was—by souls soaring above ordinary vulgarity in the direction of immaterial ideals. Everything ignoble about modern liberty in America Tocqueville, in effect, traces to the South's founding in Virginia.

He goes on to tell us that the Puritans established colonies without lords or masters—without, in fact, economic classes. They weren't out to get rich or even improve their economic condition; they were in no way driven by material necessity. They "belonged to the well-to-do-classes of the mother country" and would have been better off in the most obvious ways staying home. Their lives were structured by resources and by morality; they came to America as family men, bringing their wives and children. They were models of social virtue. They were also extremely educated men—on the cutting edge, in many ways, of European enlightenment. They were, Tocqueville observes, animated by "a purely intellectual need." They aimed "to make an *idea* triumph" in this world.

The Puritanical Idealism of Pilgrims

The Puritans were, in fact, singularly distinguished by the nobility of their idealistic, intellectual goal. They willingly imposed themselves to "the inevitable miseries of exile" to live and pray freely as they believed God intended. Those called "the pilgrims," Tocqueville observes, were that way because their "austere principles" caused them to be called Puritans. Their pure standards—their excessive claims for freedom from the alleged corruption of bodily need and pleasure—caused them to be insufferable to all the governments and societies now in existence. The Puritans always seem to others to be "enemies of pleasures" (DA.2.3.19).

Puritan principles could become real only in a new world carved out of the wilderness, where they are the founders of "a great people" of God. They had no choice, they thought, but to be "pious adventurers," combining the spirits of religion, morality, family, and education with something like the restlessness that drove other "small troop[s] of adventurers going to seek fortune beyond the seas." Unlike the Americans Tocqueville observed himself, their restlessness led them to their true home and didn't leave them isolated or disoriented.

The first Americans of the North chose exile in America not for prosperity or physical liberty, but to satisfy an intellectual need that has nothing to do with their bodies. The Virginians, by contrast, were extremely moved by singularly materialistic—really, criminal—pursuits. (Most colonies, Tocqueville notices, originate in the lawless greed characteristic of pirates.) But that's not to say the men of New England thought of themselves as too good or too pure for this world.

Their *idea* was fundamentally biblical. And they found in it radical political consequences. It supported "the most absolute democratic and republican theories." And it was most of all the "rigor" of their adherence to these principles that so "offended . . . the daily workings" of established society that their "mother country" thought it had no choice but to persecute them. Tocqueville even says that one aspect of the Puritan rigor in thought was they were completely free from the political prejudices that governed their and almost every other age. The result was that a democracy more perfect than the wildest dreams of the ancients emerged "fully grown and fully armed from the midst of the old feudal society."

The Rigor of Puritanical Egalitarianism

Puritan practice was even better than the Platonic city in speech, because the "air of antiquity" was improved by "a sort of biblical perfume." What most distinguished Puritan New England from the democracies of Greece and Rome was the absence of slavery. Theirs was the first government in theory or practice rigorously based on the general, egalitarian idea of the equal liberty of all human beings under God. Tocqueville claims that "it was necessary that Jesus Christ come down to earth to make it understood that all members of the human species were naturally alike and equal." That's why even "[t]he most profound and vast geniuses of Greece and Rome . . . did their utmost to prove that slavery was natural and that it would always exist." And that's why even ancient democracies were really aristocracies; the freedom of a small number of citizens really depended on the work of a large number of slaves (DA.2.1.3).

The philosophers of Greece and Rome were all "a part of the aristocracy of masters," and their thought was always distorted enough by the proud particularity of aristocrats to stop short of grasping the most simple and general principle of human equality. They, despite their great philosophy, had prejudices the Puritans didn't share. It was, strangely, because the Puritans were "ardent [Christian] sectarians" that they were "exalted [egalitarian political] innovators." And it was by being bound tightly to "certain religious beliefs" that they were free from political prejudice. The classical philosophers, by contrast, proudly thought of themselves as letting their minds roam free from all dogma or prejudice or belief in anything more than the high and pleasurable pursuit of the mind in the free discovery of the truth about all things. But their political ideas (just like their science) were nonetheless conditioned by their social state.

We can add, of course, that even in the *Republic*'s just city in speech the principle of, say, the equality of men and women applied only to the ruling class. And it was assumed that most citizens are always enslaved to the poetic manipulations of "the cave" or the comprehensive process of political socialization that constitutes the "regime." But the Puritan ideal was based on the idea that equality and liberty go, so to speak, all the way down. All human beings are equally free to know the truth about God and the good for themselves.

That's why the Puritans were as radically opposed to the injustice of slavery as the Virginians were indifferent to it. And Puritan society not only displayed political equality but "more and more offered the new spectacle of a society homogeneous in all its parts." The Greek and Roman philosophers, of course, didn't even offer the imaginary possibility of the combination of social homogeneity and political and intellectual sophistication. The Puritanical achievement of "perfect equality in fortunes and still more in intelligence" can't be confused with either middle-class bourgeois mediocrity or the aimless relativism of the democracy Socrates describes.

Another difference between Puritanical and Platonic or ancient idealism, of course, is that the Puritan's idea of justice was intended to become real. The result was that audacious theories actually directed real political communities. For the Puritans, the biblical view of our radical equality under God was the source of real political duties that correspond to the truth about who we are. It transcended, so to speak, the choice between tyrant and philosopher that animates the idealistic men who founded Plato's city. The Puritans didn't revel in the control they could exert over others, but neither did they find the responsibilities of political leadership merely drudgery. And they were dead serious that real cities could be built according to a universal standard of justice based on the insight that all men are created equal. They were so serious that they found abominable diversions—such as the theatre—that diverted people from their true purposes (DA.2.3.19).

Puritanical Political Freedom

That meant, Tocqueville explains, that the Puritans had "a more elevated and complete view" of both political freedom and social duties than did their time's "European legislators." They were, in both those respects, ahead of their time. Citizens in New England were ahead of those even in Great Britain in their full and equal involvement in public affairs and in taking responsibility for their country's defense. They were emphatic in tying taxation to popular consent, electing public officials and otherwise holding them democratically accountable, and in trial by jury.

All those democratic political freedoms that we Americans often trace to the social contract theory of the philosopher Locke the Puritans adopted "without discussion and in fact." Being clearly derived from biblical principle, they didn't depend on or exist merely in the speculative dialogue of the philosophers. Even the Americans Tocqueville saw for himself in his visit understood that accepting some religious dogma "without discussion" turns out to be an indispensable foundation of the effective exercise of political freedom.

Because the Puritan conception of political freedom wasn't based on the apolitical, selfish, rights-obsessed, and duty negligent Lockean individual, it both not only demanded virtuous civic participation but also connected political freedom with the creature's charitable duty to the unfortunate. It set a high or virtuous standard for political competence and incorruptibility, and it didn't seem to need to rely on institutions with teeth in them to restrain the spirit of faction and boundless ambition of leaders.

Whatever Puritan government was, it was not another name for a band of robbers, just as Puritan freedom could never be confused with another name for nothing left to lose. The Virginians' view of freedom was finally merely useful or materialistic; it is the liberty of beings with interests and nothing more. The Puritans distinguished themselves by their "beautiful definition of freedom," "a civil, a moral, a federal *liberty*," "a *liberty* for that only which is *just* and *good*." That's the liberty for which it makes sense "to stand with the hazard of your very *lives*" (emphasis added). Only if liberty is beautiful or for the display of the most admirable and virtuous human characteristics can it really be worth the courageous risk of life.

The citizens of New England took care of the poor, maintained the highways, kept careful records and registries, secured law and order, and, most of all, provided public education for everyone—through high school when possible. The justification of universal education was that everyone should be able to read the Bible to know the truth about God and his duties to Him for himself. Nobody should be deceived by having to rely on the word of others; they had the democratic or Cartesian distrust of authority without the paralyzing and disorienting rejection of all authority (DA.2.1.1) That egalitarian religious understanding, of course, was the source of the American popular enlightenment that had so many practical benefits.

Middle-class Americans, Tocqueville explains, later achieved a universal level of mediocre literacy as what's required for making money for oneself. For the middle class, education's justification was wholly practical or applied, and not at all for the cultivation of the mind or soul. But it's the Puritans who provided us the genuinely ennobling justification for universal education. For them, democratic education *is* liberal education, for discovering the liberating truth about who we are. The degrading theory that universal education must be primarily technical education dissolves for us Americans once we remember that the democratic view that education is for everyone has two justifications—one directed toward the body and the other toward the soul.

Tocqueville's Puritans, we might even add, were more for democratic liberal education than Tocqueville himself. He recommended the study of the Greek and Roman authors in their original language for the few Americans with the talent and passion to pursue literary careers and so to assume responsibility for the ennobling of democratic language. Most Americans, he thought, would just become dangerously dissatisfied with the banality of their industrious middle-class routine if infused with such aristocratic longing (DA.2.1.15). But the Puritans believed that the soul's longings exist in us all and deserved to be educated in every case.

"Puritan civilization in North America," Marilynne Robinson observes in her collection of essays *The Death of Adam*, "quickly achieved unprecedented levels of literacy, longevity, and mass prosperity, or happiness, as it was called in those days."[2] What's good for the soul, the Puritans showed, can also be good for the body, and the spirit of religion is what reconciles the pursuit of prosperity and human happiness (as opposed to the endlessly restless pursuit of happiness Locke described). It's most instructive to see the early Americans "seeking with an almost equal ardor material wealth and moral satisfactions." Just as it's instructive to see the marvelous combination of "the *spirit of religion*" with "the *spirit of freedom.*" In this respect, the Puritans look less like extremists than evidence of the fact that, as Tocqueville says, "[t]he human heart is vaster than one supposes; it can at once contain a taste for the goods of earth and a love of those of Heaven" (DA.2.2.15, emphasis in original).

Puritanical Tyranny

Although Puritans' egalitarian political institutions were remarkably free from prejudice, that wasn't true, Tocqueville observes, of many of the laws they freely and democratically enacted. "Nothing is more singular and instructive," he even claims, "than the legislation of this period." The enigma he displays for our reflection is that "bizarre or tyrannical laws were not imposed," but "they were voted in by the free concurrence of all interested persons." Their egalitarianism—their civic-minded extremely small republicanism—produced not only a tyranny of the majority, but a bizarre tyranny of a majority that approached unanimity. Tyranny characteristically flows from the mere willfulness or selfishness of the ruling group. But this one came from a whole people who were genuinely puritanical or, from one view, repressively idealistic; the undeniable evidence is their own "mores were still more austere and more puritanical than their laws."

Another Puritan enigma is how "the legislation of a rude and half-civilized people," that is, the people portrayed in "the texts of Deuteronomy, Exodus, and Leviticus," could have found its way "into the heart of a society whose spirit was enlightened and mores mild." The people of those books weren't much like the highly educated and civilized Puritans. That contradiction resulted in laws full of death as the penalty for violating all sorts of moral lapses, and severe penalties even for kissing, laziness, and the use of tobacco. But those barbarous penalties were, in fact, rarely enforced against the guilty, and the truth is that such legislation couldn't hope to be made effective for long among an enlightened and peaceful people.

The error of the Puritans, Tocqueville observed, was to be so overly concerned with "maintaining moral order and good mores" that they turned every sin into a crime. The Puritan legislator was so "full of the ardor for regulation" that he became preoccupied with politically purifying every moment of social, religious, and political life. That meant, of course, regularly invading "the domain of conscience" through legislation that commanded detailed conformity in the worship of God. The Puritan's schoolmarmish meddlesomeness was despotic, but it differed from the soft despotism that Tocqueville feared for the democratic future by being genuinely concerned with the souls of citizens and creatures (DA.2.4.6). The Puritans certainly didn't aim to free people from taking careful responsibility for their personal destinies. They were just far more serious than is reasonable for beings with bodies that people not be diverted from the needs of their souls.

It's even possible, as Tocqueville suggests, to call Puritanical politics both egalitarian and aristocratic. Everyone is held to a high moral standard, and everyone is to be raised and educated well enough to participate in political life with wisdom and virtue. The great project was to make the many as good as aristocrats imagined the few to be, and to integrate in particular human beings the aristocratic love of learning and the biblical insight that nobody, even Jesus himself, is above work or engaging in manual labor. The Puritan ideal of democracy didn't include the self-obsessed, materialistic, and petty characteristics Tocqueville attributed to democracy in general, and it had nothing of the apathetic indifference that Socrates described when displaying what pure democracy would be like.

When Tocqueville says that there is, in fact "a manly and legitimate passion for equality" that aims "to elevate the small to the rank of the great," it seems that he had the Puritans in mind. And that elevating passion— for an aristocracy of everyone—is surely a feature of democracy at its best. Tocqueville criticizes those who would prefer "reduc[ing] men to preferring equality in servitude to inequality in freedom" (DA.1.1.3). That's what atheistic or pantheistic democratic or materialistic theorists do by either denying or attempting to destroy souls or what genuinely elevates particular men. Aristocrats, meanwhile, tend to think that the choice is between democratic servitude or aristocratic freedom. The Puritans provided the insight and considerable evidence that we're not stuck with that extreme choice.

From a true or genuinely comprehensive view of human liberty, Tocqueville concludes, the Puritans were both behind and ahead of their times. Their egalitarian political innovations, we might say, were still ahead of the America Tocqueville described, ahead of governments that were administratively incompetent, somewhat negligent when it comes to the unfortunate, weak on instructing citizens on their duties, and basically unconcerned with education.

But the Puritans could have learned even from the Virginians and the Europeans of their time a lot about respecting the liberty of conscience, surely an indispensable element of even Christian liberty. Jesus, in Tocqueville's view, showed little interest in enforcing religious morality through political legislation, and that's why Christianity, in fact, has been compatible with a variety of political regimes. It's not the Gospels—which "speak only of the general relations of men to God and among themselves"—that was the inspiration of the Puritan dedication to criminalizing every sin (DA.2.1.5). But it was the Gospels—more than anything the Books of the Old Testament—that devoted them so extremely to the equality of all moral creatures. The bizarre and tyrannical aspects of Puritan government might not be attributed so much to their being Christian as their being not Christian enough. Tocqueville's criticism of the Puritans is less a criticism of Christianity's true influence on politics than of their excessive politicization of their very extreme religious idealism.

The American Compromise Between Virginia and New England

Both the North and the South—New England and Virginia—began with extreme views of what human liberty is. Neither Tocqueville could affirm as what's "true and just," although both have elements of truth and justice. The Americans, with their subtle and unprecedented statesmanship, haven't found it necessary to choose, as Tocqueville says people are often stuck with doing, between the excesses of one extreme or another. America at its political best is a compromise between colonial North and South, between New England and Virginia, between meddlesome, intrusive idealists and vulgarly self-indulgent and morally indifferent pirates.

The Puritans can be criticized as hyper-moralistic despots in some ways, but the Virginians were amoral despots in others. For the Virginian, in effect, every man is the despot, and his point of living is to make himself wealthy and powerful, even at the expense of others. That view, truth to tell, is even present in the Lockeanism of our Founding Virginians, who regarded every man as a sovereign who consents to government only for his personal convenience. And it's the individualism or emotional solitude that is the product of that Lockeanism that paves the way to the soft despotism he feared far more than any Puritan excess. The American religious and political, localist way of combating individualism, Tocqueville makes it quite clear, are our most fortunate Puritanical legacies, ones indispensable for combating individualism.

We see this spirit of compromise in our Declaration and Constitution, in which the influence of the Virginians Jefferson and Madison was as much as prudent statesmen as principled theorists. The theoretical core of the Declaration is all about inalienable rights and not about the personal God of the Bible. "Nature's God" is a past-tense Creator, and the guidance he provides men now is questionable, insofar as they institute government and many other inventions to move as far away from being governed by nature as possible. But thanks to the insistence of members of Congress who were more under the influence of Christian Calvinism than, say, Jefferson and Franklin, God also became, near the Declaration's end, providential and judgmental, or present-tense and personal.

Probably the most nuanced or balanced judgment on the significance of our Declaration comes from R. L. Bruckberger in *Images of America* (1959). Bruckberger, another of our friendly French critics, took what Tocqueville said about our Puritans about as seriously as anyone, and maybe surpassed Tocqueville in seeing more clearly the connection between the Puritans and the Calvinist believers who helped to shape our founding documents. "The greatest luck of all for the Declaration," Bruckberger explains, "was precisely the divergence and the compromise between the Puritan tradition and what Jefferson wrote." A "strictly Puritan" Declaration, of course, "would probably not have managed to avoid an aftertaste of theocracy and religious fanaticism." But if it had "been written from the standpoint of the . . . philosophy of that day, it would have been a-religious, if not actually offensive to Christians."[3]

The Declaration as a whole, Bruckberger concludes, might even be viewed "as a more profound accomplishment," one of "the great masterpieces of art, in which luck is strangely fused with genius."[4] The combination of American Lockeanism and American Puritanism/Calvinism produced something like an accidental American Thomism. It's that fact that led the American Catholic John Courtney Murray in *We Hold These Truths* (1960) to praise our political Fathers for "building better than they knew," although even Murray didn't acknowledge properly the Puritan contribution to what our political Fathers built.[5]

Arguably the Declaration as compromise is a better guidance for Americans than the intentions of either of the parties to the compromise. God is personal, but that fact supports rather than negates the equal right to freedom all human beings have. Properly understood, in Tocqueville's eyes, that understanding of equality unites the teaching of Jesus and the teaching of Locke, while both Locke and Jesus distance religious idealism from the requirements of good government. But it's still the idealism of Jesus that turns equality into more than a principle of calculation or self-interested consent, into a beautiful idea or an undeniable moral proposition that leads us to do good even at the risk of our lives.

It's Christianity, as Tocqueville explains, that invigorates Americans with moral duties they share in common and so limits the apathetic indifference of individualism (DA.2.1.15;2.2.9). But it's also because they're Christians that Americans don't imagine for a moment that anything—such as extreme, bizarre, tyrannical violation of rights—might be done in the service of egalitarian reform (DA.1.2.10). The deeper danger of excessively politicized Puritanical idealism was, of course, its hyper-serious or "radically historicist" secularization into socialism, communism, hyper-progressivism, and so forth. But that danger in America was actually countered by a Christianity purged of the bizarre Puritanical insistence that sin be criminalized.

We can speculate that one reason among many Tocqueville doesn't discuss the Declaration as America's "creed" is that he regarded it as more Lockean and less Christian than it really is. Certainly Tocqueville joins Lincoln and actually goes further in regarding all men as equal, finally, as creatures; it's the Creator's perspective that taught him the justice and even greatness of political egalitarianism. It's "the creator and preserver of men," Tocqueville contends, "who sees distinctly, though at once, the whole human race and each man" (DA.2.4.8). He sees each of us perfectly in how he or she is similar to and different from others, overcoming the aristocratic weakness of thinking too particularly and the democratic weakness of thinking too generally (DA.2.1.3).

Human equality depends on a personal Creator who knows and cares about who particular men are, and not the impersonal reductionism of materialism or its religious equivalent pantheism which abolishes the very existence of the greatness of human individuality (DA.2.1.7). We can speculate that Tocqueville would have affirmed Bruckberger's Declaration as a profound display of the compromise that characterizes American at its best.

One way among many of seeing the residual difference between the idealistic New Englanders and the selfish Virginians among the leading Founders is by thinking about what separated the two friends Thomas Jefferson and John Adams (not a Puritan, of course). Jefferson, of course, opposed slavery in principle for basically Lockean reasons. But Locke taught him less why people born into slavery should abolish it than why those who don't have slaves shouldn't acquire them. And he readily developed a rather serene, Epicurean, fatalistic indifference to being stuck with that peculiar, unjust institution. And Jefferson was also all too open to emerging forms of fanatical, revolutionary idealism in France, being too ready to spill blood today for a more perfect future. The spirit of religion, from Adams' view, didn't properly chasten Jefferson's idealistic imagination.

Adams, of course, was unwavering in his opposition to slavery, and he and his great son never developed any indifference to that evil institution. Not only that, he saw from the beginning the anti-Christian impetus of the French Revolution and what it would do to the ideas of equality and genuine self-government. The French denied that God or nature gave particular persons any real content, and so they could be radically reconstructed according to a merely political or civil theology. The French idealism was different from the Puritans in its denial that people were, in truth, anything more than citizens, just as the Lockean moralism of the doctrine of self-interest rightly understood is based on the denial that people are anything more than beings with interests.

Neo-Puritanical Idealism

Tocqueville's general view was that, by 1830, the passionate religious intensity of the Puritans had just about disappeared in America, including the religious motivation for egalitarian political reform. But he also noticed that "One finds here and there in the heart of American society souls altogether filled with an exalted and almost fierce spiritualism that one scarcely encounters in Europe." Although that ferocity seemed to be the exception to the rule, America, he saw, was undeniably the land of religious revivals or, as we say, "Great Awakenings." Tocqueville took that fact as evidence that the soul has needs that can be distorted and denied, but never destroyed (DA.2.2.12).

That the Puritan contribution to our egalitarian idealism endured far after the founding generation Tocqueville couldn't have known. But the outstanding Calvinist novelist Marilynne Robinson has worked hard to tell some of the rest of the story. She reminds us that there was a revival of something like Puritan (or Calvinist) enthusiasm in the East as a result of the Second Great Awakening. The radically egalitarian political idealism—particularly the insistent abolitionism—that sprang from that mysteriously revived piety made these neo-Puritans (mostly Congregationalists) so hated in their native states that the Puritans once again had to become pilgrims. They relocated in the Middle West, where they started a good number of racially and gender integrated colleges (like Oberlin). At these colleges, everyone did manual labor, including the faculty. That way, the educated class would be more useful, and there would be no economic barriers to higher education. The goal was to create the classless, humanely and spiritually educated world of the original Puritans. Those new colleges, Robinson claims, were "real liberal arts colleges," where "the humanities in the very broad sense" were generously studied.[6] They didn't have what Tocqueville called the middle-class purpose of learning a trade or skill; they were educating beings with souls, who only incidentally had interests. Liberal education—beginning but not ending with the Bible—is a vehicle for liberation for every human being.

Liberal education, Robinson contends, was understood as liberating education by these new Puritans in a more immediate sense. They were often founded as stations on the underground railroad. They were structured "as centers of humane learning that would make their graduates and those influenced by them resistant to the spread of slavery." (Robinson shows in *The Death of Adam* how scholars associated with those institutions turned the hugely influential McGuffey reader into a vehicle for forming anti-slavery opinion.) The abolition of slavery was only one feature of this project for political liberation. Its aim was "near utopian," to reform American society "by practicing as well as pointing to standards of justice and freedom to which the nation had not yet risen."[7]

For neo-Puritans, maybe even more than the original Puritans, religious enthusiasm was the source of boldly innovative egalitarian idealism—the theory and practice of generous and transformational change "of the whole of society," and not just "the suppression of slavery in the states of the South." Because their view of equality was wholly "uncondescending," they really were about the creation of an aristocracy of everyone.[8]

The Puritans, Robinson claims, are the foundation of the humane, egalitarian left for much of the history of our country. Their idealism was indispensable for spurring the American Revolution; the theory of Locke was not generous enough to inspire the honorable risk of everything in pursuit of liberation for prejudice and patriarchy. The theory of Locke also wasn't genuinely liberal enough to cause men to risk everything to abolish slavery. Mr. Jefferson wouldn't have thought much of integrated Oberlin, the underground railroad, or providing support to the radical John Brown. Puritan abolitionism was the real provocation for the Civil War, as southern apologists have always claimed. Even the natural lawyer Mr. Lincoln knew well enough that Jefferson's abstract principles, by themselves, couldn't be what would inspire men to die to make men free, to eradicate the key difference between New England and Virginia by banishing slavery from our country.

The second wave of Puritan enthusiasm in America was, in fact, decimated by the war. There are, Robinson explains, a lot of reasons for the end of that

Great Awakening. One is the near utopians were, incoherently, both near pacifists and embraced and encouraged far too readily the liberation violence that was the war. They supported the near-insanity of John Brown, fervently preached their congregations into joining in the sacred struggle against slavery, and then recoiled from the massively bloody facts of the war. Whole Congregationalist towns were traumatized to virtual extinction by the loss of most of their men. And then there was disappointment by the real results of the war. Slavery in the South was displaced by a softer but largely uneducated form of servitude for most blacks. The idealism faded with the thought that the war may not have been worth it.

The new utopianism was, in fact, incompatible with the intensification of the division of labor required by the newly emerging industrial economy. It increasingly seemed quaint and irrelevant. Once again, we can say, the idealism of the Puritans was indispensable but excessive, and it was too extreme to be sustainable by being compatible with the ordinary requirements of personal liberty.

The last significant product of these second wave neo-Puritans, Robinson suggests in one place, was the anti-imperialist Calvinist progressive William Jennings Bryan. He was educated at one of those abolitionist institutions—Illinois College, and he was correct, morally and politically, in his basically leftist polemic against Darrow's Nietzschean Darwin for sundering America's relationship with the Puritan tradition of egalitarian idealism and social reform. Nothing, of course, seems more quaint and irrelevant to us than Bryan's lost cause, which, of course, seems to have been fatally flawed on the level of science. But Bryan was right, after all, that Darrow's pernicious or materialistic use of Darwin was serving to undermine our country's dedication to the proposition that all men should be treated with the significance of beings with souls.

Overcoming Anti-Puritanical Amnesia

There are good reasons why Americans suffer from amnesia when it comes to their indebtedness to the extremism of Puritan idealism. But the most important one, Robinson claims, is that we're not generous enough to want to remember it. Americans have been caught for a long time in the survivalist theories of Darwin and Hobbes and the economists. Our modest purpose is survival or "nonfailure," and we have to do what's required to win the struggle for survival. Whatever the differences between Darwin and the Hobbesian economists, they agree that the true virtues are the survivalist ones. Even our freedom is for working hard to avoid nonbeing and nothing more, and so being generous or loyal or even genuinely civilized is unnatural.

Robinson's goal is to ennoble the American left—to make it once again humanely liberal or generous—by restoring the Puritan/Calvinist foundation of its criticisms of the excesses of capitalism and individualism. Her standard is an integrated vision of *who* we are informed by "the highest levels of thought and learning" and "in which everyone has a part."[9] The standard of primitive Puritanism is offered as an antidote to that view of our natural condition described by Hobbes and Darwin, with its crudely one-dimensional view of human nature as preached by the primitive economists and primitive capitalists. It's more reasonable and ennobling—truer to who we really are—to see ourselves as children of Adam and not as really, really clever chimps or as miserable accidents futilely obsessed with fending off the inevitable.

It's intellectually fashionable, Robinson observes, to talk about some antagonism today between religion and humanism. But religion and humanism have, through most of our history, shared certain crucial areas of agreement: People have souls and so have been given distinctive obligations and certain distinctive pleasures—both of which require time, teaching, and discipline to cultivate. Our true believers and our true humanists—who, like Socrates, may not be believers—need to restore the Puritan's Sunday against the economists and the Darwinians who want to reduce us to less than who we really are. Tocqueville, of course, also singled out for special praise the primary legal legacy he saw remaining from what might seem to have been Puritanical repression—the more or less compulsory cessation of all commercial activity on Sunday (DA.2.2.15).

That alleged repression Tocqueville regarded as liberation—from the insane ardor of the incessantly restless pursuit of an always fugitive happiness (understood as material pleasure) for the secure and serene pleasures of the soul. The Americans, on Sunday, stopped working in order to hear and think about the "delicate enjoyments" and "true happiness" that come from acting virtuously as beings made in the image of the great and eternal God. Even when they heard Christian sermons that enjoined them to be humble, they were exalted. They were always told that, as beings with souls destined for immortality, they were more than merely beings with interests (DA.2.2.15).

Tocqueville, in his defense of Sunday's celebration of the greatness of the personal soul, actually calls attention not to any distinctively Christian teaching, but to Socrates and Plato, who taught that "the soul has nothing in common with the body and survives it." The doctrine that we are in some sense immortal is indispensable to genuinely liberal education and great individuality, and it persists in America as a Puritan inheritance, although it isn't really distinctively Puritan at all. That doctrine is indispensable for understanding our genuine greatness, our singular existence above the other animals but less than God. It preserves the truth about ourselves that's the source of our most sublime faculties and our noblest, more enduring deeds, the ones with which we resist degradation (DA.2.2.15).

The neo-Puritanical Robinson actually disagrees with Tocqueville on the purpose of Sunday as preserving a certain Platonism for the people—a doctrine of the soul's immortality. For Tocqueville, Sunday celebrates our immortality or connection with eternity; it is about our transcendence of our merely temporal being. For Robinson, "the concept of transcendence is based on a misreading of creation." The miracle we celebrate on Sunday is time, which is much more improbable or even "preposterous" than eternity. Or, more precisely, the miracle is about the being open enough to the reality around him to know he lives in time: "Nothing could be more miraculous," Robinson observes, "than the fact that we have a consciousness that makes the world intelligible to us and are moved by what is beautiful."[10] For Robinson, it's the temporal being who exhibits the Socratic openness to the intelligibility and beauty of the world he inhabits.

But to be fair Tocqueville himself claims that "I have no need to travel through heaven and earth to discover a marvelous object, full of contrasts, of infinite greatness and pettiness, of profound obscurities and singular clarity, capable of giving birth at one to pity, admiration, scorn, and terror." That "marvelous object," he says, is "myself: man comes from nothing, traverses time, and is going to disappear forever in the bosom of God." Tocqueville himself understands something of himself, but far from everything. As the being who lives between complete self-knowledge and "impenetrable darkness," the human being, Tocqueville and Robinson agree, is an inexhaustible source of poetry. Nothing, Tocqueville himself admits, is more wonderful than the being with time with him, existing miraculously in this world for a moment between "two abysses" (DA.2.1.17) There's no need to look beyond this world, as Robinson claims, to honor the "great mystery," which, Robinson reports, "is plainly before my eyes."[11]

Anything eternal must be complete and uncreated, and God, mysteriously, must be both "in and beyond time."[12] "So it is possible to imagine," Robinson observes, "that time was created in order that there might be narrative—event, sequence and causation, ignorance and error, retribution and atonement." Time is the cause of our "strangely mixed natures" and so why "we scarcely know ourselves."[13] From this view, Sunday celebrates the greatness of the temporal being with a narrative, stuck between knowledge and ignorance and with the responsibility of living well with what he can know. Robinson and Tocqueville agree, more or less, that Sunday is for celebrating the singular, mysterious, wonderful dignity of being human.

Robinson's Puritanical defense of the greatness of human individuality in democratic times is far less condescending than Tocqueville's. For Tocqueville, we are great and wonderful beings because we're conscious that we live for a very contingent moment between two abysses. But to face that truth straight on makes us too miserably anxious to think or act or be happy. And so we need to be diverted in practice through political action and in theory through religious dogma of some kind from what we really know in order to display our greatness in thought and deed. But for Puritanical Robinson, what we really know is good enough on its own. For Tocqueville, Sunday celebrates the truth insofar as it preserves a contemplative image required for us to use our most sublime faculties. For Robinson, the genuinely Puritanical view is that what we can see for ourselves in time is good enough—when understood in terms of Creator and creatures—to sustain our generosity and nobility.

For Robinson and the Puritans against Tocqueville's aristocrats, leisure couldn't possibly be the basis of culture. The foundations of culture are personal responsibility—including the responsibilities of citizens and creatures—and moral agency, and there should be no leisure class exempt from acting generously or charitably on behalf of others. But culture does, as aristocrats claim, depend on us thinking highly enough of ourselves that we have time enough to do a lot more than survive. For Tocqueville, the choice often seems to be the high-mindedness connected with unjust aristocratic leisure class or the vulgar, self-interested utility of the democratic middle class. But the Puritans, as he himself showed, presented a third alternative.

Anyone who looks at our country from outside right now, Robinson insists, should wonder "why we make so little of so much." As the outside observer Tocqueville wondered, why is there so little intellectual enjoyment, artistic excellence, personal greatness, and genuine happiness among the most free and prosperous people ever? One reason is we're not nearly as Puritanical as we used to and should be. "[J]ust for the pleasure of it," Robinson complains, "I miss civilization, and I want it back."[14] Compared, ironically, to today's American middle-pursuit of materialistic enjoyments, the Puritans are hardly the enemies of the actual enjoyment of pleasures.

Praising the Puritans Today

Now more than ever is the time for our statesmen, legislators, and enlightened writers to talk up the Puritans in the name of the most sublime faculties, those with which we can be happy as human beings. The justice of the middle-class American, as Tocqueville says, is that nobody is above or below being a being with interests—someone who is free and who works for himself (DA.2.2.8). But the Christians provide the indispensable addition that each of us is more than a being with interests, and so each of us share in a kind of greatness the aristocrats reserved only for themselves. So each of us was made to enjoy civilization and liberal education and the leisurely, social, conversational contemplation of who we are under God. Truth to tell, we're much more repressed and unhappy these days than the Puritans ever were, at least at their best.

It's fashionable today to identify our Puritanical legacy chiefly with the moralism of our "religious right" and so to identify it with illiberal and prejudiced fundamentalism. We tend to contrast that moralism with leftism defined as the mixture of moral libertarianism and egalitarian political progressivism than characterizes our liberalism. That contrast is most misleading. Most of our enduring egalitarian, "leftist" (if you want) criticisms of individualistic indifference both personal and political, Tocqueville and Robinson show us, come from the Puritans. To the extent that we remain egalitarian idealists and believe that our liberty is for doing good for all our fellow citizens and creatures we remain Puritanical.

So our Calvinism, contrary to Weber, is most deeply less about our spirit of capitalism than one of our main ways of curbing its selfish excesses. Our religion, as Tocqueville observes, saves us from degrading self-absorption and for the free and dignified performance of our common moral duties (DA.2.1.5). The spirit of political liberty—the ennobling activity of citizens—depends, the Puritans taught us, on the spirit of religion. And they also showed that egalitarian citizenship depends on the truth that each of us is more than merely a citizen.

Notes

1. Alexis de Tocqueville, *Democracy in America*, ed. Harvey Mansfield and Delba Winthrop (University of Chicago Press, 2000), volume 2, part 1, chapter 17; volume 2, part 2, chapter 16. Hereafter I refer in the text to *Democracy in America* as DA, followed by volume, part, and chapter numbers.

2. Marilynne Robinson, *The Death of Adam: Essays on Modern Thought* (New York: Mariner Books, 2000), 150-51.

3. R. L. Bruckberger, *Images of America: A Political, Industrial, and Social Portrait*, trans. C. G. Paulding and Virgilia Peterson (New Brunswick, NJ: Transaction, 2009), 93.

4. Ibid.

5. John Courtney Murray, *We Hold These Truths: Catholic Reflections on the American Proposition* (Lanham, MD: Rowman & Littlefield, 2005), 77.

6. Marilynne Robinson, "A Great Amnesia," *Harper's Magazine* (May 2008): 17-21.

7. Ibid.

8. Ibid.

9. Ibid.

10. Marilynne Robinson, "The Art of Fiction No. 198", *The Paris Review* (Fall 2008), 65.

11. Robinson, *The Death of Adam*, 243.

12. Marilynne Robinson, "No Other Gods," *Theology Today* 63 (2007).

13. Robinson, *The Death of Adam*, 243-44.

14. Ibid., 4.

Part IV
Statesmanship Abroad

Chapter 14

Tocqueville's Foreign Policy of Moderation and Democracy Expansion

Paul Carrese[1]

Amid the renewed appreciation for Tocqueville's philosophy in this era of globalization and democracy expansion stands the black mark of his support for European colonialism and imperialism. Doesn't he contradict his liberal principles by encouraging, in his French political career of the 1830s and 1840s, French colonialism in Algeria—and the British venture in India as well? While he is applauded for his moderate liberal stance in advocating gradual abolition of slavery in France's colonies, his actions in the national legislature as a leading member on foreign affairs, and especially Algeria policy, seem to evince nationalism and European chauvinism.[2] Some even find the germ of an illiberal, dark, and "Eurocentric" side to his democratic theory in his earlier analysis, in *Democracy in America*, of the Anglo-American policies toward Amerindians and African slaves. While Tocqueville the philosopher condemns the brutal conduct of the Anglo-Americans he fails to condemn American continental expansion at the expense of Amerindians; and while he severely criticizes American slavery he does not endorse its immediate abolition.[3] Most scholars explain the contradiction by arguing that Tocqueville allowed French nationalism and his own political ambitions to trump his liberal principles, in both his philosophizing and his statesmanship. Equal natural rights for individuals and political freedom for self-governing communities may be universal truths in theory, but when French—or more broadly, white Christian—interests required limiting or abandoning these principles, he sacrificed his ideals. In this view, there is little constructive to learn, only a puzzle or a failing to be pondered, regarding Tocqueville's views on international affairs and foreign policy for liberal democracies.

As instructive as these studies are for understanding Tocqueville and modern liberal thought, the portrait they paint is incomplete for overlooking several complexities to his philosophy and his difficult attempt to be both philosopher and statesman. Moreover, these complexities are similar to those still facing the liberal democracies of the West and now also the East, such as India. Reconsideration of Tocqueville's dilemmas thus should be fruitful for understanding our own foreign policy debates and choices. The fundamental complexity to address is his conception of liberalism, but this also points to the continuing debates about what liberal democratic principles require for international relations and foreign policy. Tocqueville sought to moderate the rationalism and idealism of earlier liberalism as he studied and advised the new liberal democracies. He revived an approach to political philosophy that appreciated the naturally recurring strengths, failings, and dilemmas of both rulers and citizens in their search for liberty and equal rights amid the fog of politics. He dissented from the Enlightenment tendency to claim absolute wisdom and impartiality that entitles a philosopher to impose a single standard of justice on diverse political situations, even though he believed a philosopher can discern universal principles of justice and see the limits of particular parties, schools, or decisions.[4]

Tocqueville announced this approach at the close of his introduction to *Democracy in America*: "This book is not precisely in anyone's camp; in writing it I did not mean either to serve or to contest any party. I undertook to see, not differently, but further than the parties; and while they are occupied with the next day, I wanted to ponder the future."[5] *Democracy* thus does not deny the practical realities of peoples and nation states struggling to either achieve or spread liberal principles. It does not reflexively condemn liberal rulers who failed while trying to make the best of the bad situations that politics, especially international affairs, always poses. This is not to say that he adopted the realist school in international relations, championed by Machiavelli, Hobbes, and Morgenthau, that calculations of power and interest by states trump all other standards for politics. Rather, the difficulty in assessing the consistency of Tocqueville's thinking is the one posed to Western political philosophy since its inception with Socrates and Plato, that of negotiating the gap between philosophy and action. Tocqueville's earliest philosophical statement, in *Democracy*, tried to bridge that gap by affirming liberal principles but also appreciating the practical difficulties of implementing them, to include the problem of expanding the writ of liberalism in a just way. In this he followed the philosophic attempt by Montesquieu, a century earlier, to moderate the realist view of power politics and conquest by balancing it with more humane, Christian, and liberal principles to guide international affairs.

In deciding to confront "the Algeria Question" when he entered political office in the years after the French conquest of 1830, Tocqueville shifted from philosopher to statesman and therefore did what most scholars never have to do. He confronted the brutal realities of international affairs by making stark choices, and was held accountable in his day for the actual consequences of those choices—and knew he would be held accountable in historical judgment also.

Given the multiplicity of competing actors, principles, and interests in international affairs and the omnipresent threat of war, the statesmanlike task often is to achieve the least-worst outcome among options that range from bad to awful to catastrophic. This is especially true given that one can invite war either by commission or omission, depending upon how one's acts are perceived by other international actors. At the very least, these sober views about international affairs were held by most theorists of and actors in international affairs in Tocqueville's day and for millennia before, including among nineteenth century liberals—and even among many liberal critics of imperialism from Smith to Burke and Bentham. The exception arises in Kant's philosophy and among some other liberal critics of war or imperialism, including Diderot and Condorcet. That said, it is not obviously sound to judge Tocqueville's philosophical or practical consistency by the standard of Kantian liberal theory and its cousin, liberal-internationalism in international relations theory. To begin with, he never endorsed and in fact obliquely criticized such views as extreme given their impractical and therefore dangerous idealism. Moreover, subsequent history gives reasons to argue that the effort to implement major tenets of this theory under the League of Nations concept—such as an international treaty regime that outlawed war and reduced armaments among certain states—produced unanticipated and disastrous consequences. While there are theoretical and historical defenses made about how liberal internationalism was implemented in the twentieth century, Tocqueville's doubts about such idealism at least can be seen as reasonable.[6] The perpetual debates among committed liberals, for over two centuries, between the realist and liberal-internationalist schools further cast doubt upon the branding of a philosopher or statesman as illiberal for failing to accept the Kantian conception of international relations. Indeed, a full consideration of Tocqueville's philosophy and statesmanship allows us to recall that a third liberal alternative, with a pedigree older than Kant's, is a worthy option for both theorists and practitioners of international politics.

This alternative is evident from his analyses of foreign policy issues in *Democracy in America* and in his more practical writings and deeds regarding Algeria, Europe, and Eurasian crises in mid-nineteenth century affairs. Throughout, Tocqueville largely held to the principles of liberal moderation and prudence about international affairs as broadly sketched in *Democracy*. Drawing on the complex, moderate conception of liberalism developed by Montesquieu he sought to apply a blend of realism and liberal idealism in global affairs—that is, balancing interest and power politics with universal principles of justice. In contrast to Kant, he also insisted that practical judgment must supplement principle when a liberal democracy makes foreign policy. In *Democracy* he emphatically praises George Washington as a model for the practice of such principles. Indeed, his praise for how Washington proposed to cope with an imperial problem not of his making—the fate of Amerindians who faced the continual expansion of American settlers—provides clues for Tocqueville's approach to an imperial problem that he, too, inherited. He held no elective office in 1830 when France invaded Algiers, and had not advocated invasion or conquest, but once it was achieved what should France do? Should it withdraw on grounds of the injustice of remaining as an imperial power? Or, should France bring as much justice from the situation as possible, given that the likely consequences of withdrawal would be just neither to the conquered, nor to France, nor to political stability in Europe and beyond? Given the conventions or understandings of international politics dominant in nineteenth century Europe, Africa, and Asia, was it even plausible to unilaterally withdraw from a conquest without inviting, in the near or long term, decline in international prestige and power—even to the point of inviting either alliances against it or attack? If France withdrew what political order would take its place—indigenous rule, or (as in the case of Algiers) a return of the former conquering power (the Ottoman regency), or conquest by some other power, European or African or Asian? Tocqueville as statesman needed to consider these cascading levels of questions and consequences, down to a degree of perplexity that few philosophers entertain. True, to Kant's school of philosophy it would be un-philosophical and illiberal to consider consequences in this way. His conception of categorical, *a priori* moral principles argued that to do so is to allow partial interest and power to infect or trump moral principle.[7] Yet the theoretical merits of Kantian philosophy do not so clearly outweigh its paucity of actual success in international affairs to suggest that Tocqueville can simply be branded illiberal for developing and implementing a rival conception of liberal foreign policy principles. In American politics, Abraham Lincoln's efforts to steer a middle course between abolitionism and acquiescence in the expansion of slavery provides a helpful analogue. Frederick Douglass, freed slave and abolitionist, condemned compromisers such as Lincoln at an early date, yet after the Civil War Douglass fully endorsed Lincoln's strategy to first save the Union and Constitution—and gradually educate the white majority in the justice of fighting to limit and eventually abolish the moral evil of slavery—rather than risk losing white support by grasping for too much too quickly.[8]

The fundamental issue about Tocqueville's theory and practice is not, then, consistency but the adequacy of rival theories about international relations, including his own third way. Tocqueville followed Montesquieu, who in turn adapted a legacy dating to Aristotle, Plutarch, and medieval theories of just war and prudence, in arguing that the statesman's perennial challenge is to heed liberal principles while also making the necessary prudential judgments about how to achieve them—or find the least-worst departure from them—in difficult circumstances. One example of the prudential concerns that most scholars have overlooked or rarely mentioned is Tocqueville's prescient warnings, shared by some other observers of international affairs, about the decline of the Ottoman empire and the concomitant rise of an autocratic Russia in the east that would expand to the west and south. This "Eastern Question" was the context for debates about the Algeria Question, since Tocqueville feared that Ottoman decline (as had occurred in Algiers) would lead to a global contest between Euro-American forces of democracy expansion and Russia's newly emboldened autocratic rule. What justice required for the Algerians (more precisely, the several peoples ruled under the Ottoman regency of Algiers) could not be separated from what Algeria meant for European and Eurasian politics, and for the principles that maintained some stability and justice in international affairs.

Analysis of these facets of Tocqueville's views on liberal foreign policy, and Algeria in particular, might give us a grudging admiration for the dilemmas of statesmanship he faced given his complex theory of liberalism and his practical circumstances. He had not advocated the conquest of Algiers, but he thought it would be dangerous for France and the global liberal-democratic movement to withdraw without achieving a non-despotic and proto-liberal state there, both for Frenchmen and Algerians. He was among few observers to notice both Arab and Berber (or Kabyle) nationalism in Algeria opposing European colonialism, or to advocate ideas for winning hearts and minds (as counter-insurgency strategy phrases it today). Nonetheless, he thought it likely that if France withdrew after ejecting the Ottomans then Algeria would be conquered by yet another power rather than enjoy the liberal ideal of self-determination. Most scholars have noted these ambivalent, complex views, as well as his severe criticisms of the brutality and myopia of French military and colonial policy.[9] Most nonetheless conclude that he abandoned liberal principles by trying to salvage the conquest to serve France's international status and the spread of liberalism, not to mention by his odious language about civilizing the Algerians. To argue to the contrary—that his judgments did not clearly betray his principles for a moderate liberal foreign policy—does not establish the justice of his judgments, or of his philosophy of moderation in international affairs. Indeed, in light of Montesquieu's criticisms of English subjugation of Ireland, and also Tocqueville's admiration for Washington's call to limit Anglo-American settlements in adherence to treaties with Amerindians, Tocqueville's support for French colonialism suggests some departure from the liberal moderation enunciated by these forebears. Particularly difficult is his view that a grand colonial project would shake the French from their democratic apathy and materialism, since this seems to exploit another people. A policy of democracy expansion need not be immoderate or imperial, on Tocqueville's own terms, but interest would seem to trump justice if French nation-building was his primary rationale for a project of Algerian nation-building. Still, reconsideration of Tocqueville's theory and practice does permit re-assessment of the adequacy of either realism or liberal idealism as the sole philosophy of international affairs and war, and this in turn points to rediscovery of the alternative view, liberal moderation, that Montesquieu, Washington, and Tocqueville developed.

Montesquieu and Washington on Moderation in International Relations

In *Democracy in America* Tocqueville argues that America's first foreign policy, forged by George Washington, was a principled blend of realist and liberal idealist concepts. Elements of his analysis suggest that Tocqueville draws upon Montesquieu's philosophy of moderation to formulate these views.[10] This lineage is not much noticed by scholars of Tocqueville or of American foreign policy, but it is another instance of the French visitor discerning a fundamental and enduring trait. America has always incorporated both realism and liberalism in its foreign policy and in debates about it, although she has at times veered toward one extreme or the other, and at other times found policies in a middle ground.[11] During the last century the discipline of political science has obscured this tradition of complexity and balance by dividing into schools of liberal-internationalism and realism (the latter in either assertive or isolationist variants), insisting that one or the other school must be the exclusive rational paradigm for understanding and practicing international relations. A few scholars have noted Montesquieu's importance in providing fundamental principles for American thinking about international relations, but the broader literature of international relations confines his contribution to his advocacy of commerce. This view largely casts him as a forerunner of democratic peace theory—the view that modern republics or democracies will not make war on other democracies given a mutual concern for peaceful pursuit of prosperity and stability.[12]

Montesquieu's philosophy arguably was more comprehensive and sober than liberal idealism, and laid the conceptual foundation for a constitutional democracy that would pursue tranquility at home and both commercial expansion and power abroad. His conception has guided America and influenced other leading liberal democracies in recent centuries, although he gets little credit for this now. He developed a "right of nations" theory in *The Spirit of Laws* (1748) within a comprehensive philosophy of moderation in domestic and international affairs. A philosophy of moderation in the theory and practice of politics argued that a humane policy would blend realist concerns about power, interest, and security with liberal and Christian principles about natural right and peace as the higher aims of human affairs.[13] Montesquieu's complex blend of liberal idealism with realist views of necessity borrows a disposition from the effort by the medieval just war theory to blend idealism and pragmatism.[14] Montesquieu also drew on the modern international jurists Grotius, Pufendorf, and Vattel to formulate guidance for statesmen that balanced the necessity of power with limits to war found in rights of individuals and basic international right.[15] Montesquieu is known as the great authority for the American founders on principles of constitutionalism, including the theory of pluralism or competing interests in politics, but his contribution to international relations theory or the foreign policy of America's founders is largely neglected—perhaps because his theory was too complex, and, not as idealistically liberal as those of Rousseau and Kant. His innovation was to argue that the principles of domestic constitutionalism and the rule of law point to principles of international affairs that should govern, as much as is possible, the claims of interest and security. Rational efforts to moderate the human tendency to conflict can extend from the domestic sphere to international affairs, and are bolstered by a dose of Christian humanism, while recognizing the anarchy or lack of world government to enforce any international law. Montesquieu found this blend or balance of principles arising from our nature and political condition:

> Considered as inhabitants of a planet so large that different peoples are necessary, they have laws bearing on the relation that these peoples have with one another, and this is the RIGHT OF NATIONS. . . . The *right of nations* is by nature founded on the principle that the various nations should do to one another in times of peace the most good possible, and in times of war the least ill possible, without harming their true interests.[16]

One of the few extensive analyses of Montesquieu's theory of international relations, by Pangle and Ahrensdorf, treats him as a realist derivative of Machiavelli, Hobbes, and Locke, who offers merely prudential counsels to limit power and interest.[17] This overlooks Montesquieu's clear statement that the right of nations is "the political law of nations considered in their relation with each other," and that offensive force must be "regulated" by it (*Spirit*, 10.1, p. 138). It also neglects his declaration that conquest and force must follow that "law of natural enlightenment, which wants us to do to others what we would want to have done to us" (10.3, p. 139). Thus, Pangle and Ahrensdorf cite but minimize Montesquieu's summation of his philosophy of international affairs, pronounced when assessing modern Europe's principles as an improvement over those of the Romans. He argued that the right of nations is now marked by a spirit of preservation and justice rather than of subjugation, and for this progress "homage" is owed to "our modern times, to contemporary reasoning, to the religion of the present day, to our philosophy, and to our mores" (10.3, p.139). Indeed, this reference to Christianity indicates that his advocacy of commerce as softening international affairs and promoting peace does not aim to undermine religion, as Pangle and Ahrensdorf argue. Rather, the great theme of his right of nations, from international law to commerce, is that "it is moderation which governs men, and not excesses" (*Spirit*, 21.22, p. 426; see also 29.1). One of his final remarks on the topic seems idealistic in crediting Christianity for humane principles to moderate politics, "for which human nature can never be sufficiently grateful." Ever the moderate, he also warns of religious fanaticism: the victor now "leaves to the vanquished these great things: life, liberty, laws, goods, and always religion, when one does not blind oneself" (*Spirit*, 24.3, p. 462).

Montesquieu's philosophical commitment to moderation is Aristotelian in some ways, identifying the extremes largely or permanently present in both the theory and practice of politics and seeking the right point of balance between them—even if his ultimate aims are more modern and liberal than Aristotle's. Another link to Aristotle that many scholars overlook is that Montesquieu conceives of prudence in pre-Machiavellian and pre-realist terms. Prudence is not calculation of self-interest apart from moral principle but rather the awareness that principle is not self-enacting and therefore requires the judgment of astute leaders in particular situations. Conversely, Montesquieu affirms a prudent recognition of the practical limits to how much a particular leader or state can do, or sacrifice, in any given situation to defend high moral ideals at the expense of other political and moral principles. This prudential spirit directly informs the conception of democracy promotion in Tocqueville's philosophy and also in American foreign policy, which tries to balance liberal ideals with the limits that come from necessity, varied circumstances, and the promoter's national interest and other obligations.

Moderation of course informs the principles for which Montesquieu is better known, separation of powers and federalism, each prescribing a balance between multiple centers of power as best for securing rights, liberty, and stability in politics. Moreover, the American constitutional order is the showcase of Montesquieu's moderation put into practice. His less-noted influence on the foreign policy of America's founders is most evident, paradoxically, in the most famous foreign policy document of the era—the principles announced by Washington when retiring as president in 1796. Tocqueville subsequently praised these ideas of the Farewell Address as still directing the policy of the Americans four decades later, and he particularly praised their moderation or balance. Washington urged America to be "prepared for war" but more fundamentally to "observe good faith and justice toward all nations" so as to be able to "choose peace or war, as our interest guided by our justice shall counsel."[18] His maxim "to steer clear of permanent alliances" often is confused with Jefferson's later warning that all alliances are entangling, but the difference makes clear that Washington was no isolationist. Indeed, Washington argued that America would be "at no distant period, a great nation," and it would need "temporary alliances" as well as engagement with foreign nations, political and commercial. Still, it should "cultivate peace and harmony with all" because "[r]eligion and morality enjoin this conduct; and can it be that good policy does not equally enjoin it?" He cites the prudential maxim that "honesty is always the best policy," but also urges America in more idealistic terms to "give to mankind the magnanimous and too novel example of a people always guided by an exalted justice and benevolence." This is the spirit of Montesquieu's right of nations philosophy translated to the situation of a young but promising American republic.

Democracy in America on Enlightened Self-Interest as Liberal Moderation

Tocqueville described in *Democracy in America* the adoption of these principles when he observed that Washington's Address still guided American policy in the 1830s. He endorsed Washington's maxims as "beautiful and just," and as "succeed[ing] in keeping his country at peace when all the rest of the universe was at war." Moreover, Tocqueville used one of his signature concepts about modern democracy to assess this proper balance of justice and interest in foreign affairs, praising Washington for "establishing as a point of doctrine that the self-interest well understood of Americans" was to avoid Europe's great power quarrels.[19] Tocqueville also noted, however, America's difficulties in holding to enlightened self-interest given the temptation to veer to two opposing extremes, of idealism and imperial conquest.

Idealism led many Americans to favor war in the 1790s against Britain, however unprepared America might be, to support newly republican France. Tocqueville notes that public opinion denounced Washington for resisting that urge, but that forty years later "now the entire people approves" Washington's policy. What he omits, perhaps in deference to Jefferson and his protégé Madison, is that this same temptation eventually did lead America into the disastrous War of 1812 in the interval—in which America sought to defend its rights without having invested in land or naval forces that could deter or cope with threats (such as the British invasion and burning of the nation's capital city in 1814).[20] Tocqueville's fundamental point is that if the Constitution had not given firm powers to an executive and if not for Washington holding that office, "it is certain that the nation would have done then [1790s] precisely what it condemns today [1830s]." The lesson he draws is that democracies must candidly confront the harsh fact that in international affairs they will be "decidedly inferior" to non-democratic states in matters of war and foreign policy unless they can incorporate sufficient balance in their constitutional orders to compensate. The "everyday practical wisdom" of individuals and groups fostered by "democratic freedom" is perfect for domestic politics, but relations between states always will require constitutional democracies, like all states, to "coordinate the details of a great undertaking, fix on a design, and afterwards follow it with determination through obstacles." The new democracies also must be capable of formulating measures "in secret" and of "patiently awaiting their result," as all states must. Tocqueville worries, however, about the democratic tendency "to obey sentiment rather than reasoning in politics, and to abandon a long matured design to satisfy a momentary passion" (*Democracy*, I.2.5, 219). In the 1790s and the War of 1812 this extreme of idealism or naiveté involved a reckless rush to war, but in the second volume of *Democracy* Tocqueville will warn about the converse—an idealistic pacifism that dictates isolationism. This view simply dismisses war as a wasteful diversion from pursuit of material prosperity, but Tocqueville discerns a refusal to recognize what may be necessary.

Tocqueville discerns another extreme, opposite to these versions of naïve idealism, that tempts America to eschew Washington's moderate policy for other reasons. This opposite extreme comes to light through his indictment of the cold-blooded realism that marks the brutal treatment of African slaves and Amerindians. He attributes this brutal expediency to America's restless desire for prosperity and power. In both volumes of *Democracy* he analyzes great power politics and America's rise to global prominence as a natural consequence of its geographic position, its political principles, and it economic dynamism.[21] He is ambivalent about America's nationalism and the power politics it has undertaken and, he foresees, inevitably will amplify. He respects the realities of "great states" and "force" in world affairs given that happiness requires freedom and conquered peoples are miserable (1.1.8, 151-54). On the other hand, Americans

have not followed Washington's "noble and virtuous policy" of benign treatment of the Amerindians and a halt to westward expansion, instead constantly
invading Indian territory and violating treaties (1.2.10, 320; see 320-35). The
Americans soon will cover "almost all of North America" and "become one of
the greatest peoples of the world." However, they therefore risk civil war over
slavery, and tolerate inhumane conduct by the greediest Anglo-Americans toward slaves and Indians (I.2.10, 363-68, 391-94).[22] For all of the reliance upon
Tocqueville in the recent scholarship about democratization—the editors of the
Journal of Democracy declared a few years ago "We are all Tocquevilleans
now"—there is not much scholarly discussion of his warnings about the misery
caused by this kind of democratization by force.[23] Echoing Montesquieu's analysis of the English, he observes that commerce gives rise to naval power and
thus to national greatness, to which the Americans add a restlessness that will
lead them to surpass the English. In this section, entitled "Some Considerations
on the Causes of the Commercial Greatness of the United States," Tocqueville
observes that the Americans are destined to "become the first maritime power on
the globe"—indeed, they are "driven to gain control of the seas, as the Romans
were to conquer the world" (I.2.10, 390; see 384-390). The phrasing of these
observations seems intended to remind readers of Montesquieu's *Considerations
on the Causes of the Greatness of the Romans and Their Decline* (1734), which
warns modern republics about Rome's loss of liberty and slide into empire due
to expansion and a spirit of conquest.[24]

Nonetheless, Tocqueville does not shrink from forecasting the role he sees
America called to play as a great power. "Reason indicates and experience
proves that there is no lasting commercial greatness if it cannot unite in case of
need with military power," a truth he thinks is understood in America "as everywhere else." Already Americans makes their flag respected on the high seas,
but "soon they will be able to make it feared" (I.2.10, 390). Whether by treaties
or in violation of them the Americans will dominate, before long, the entire
temperate part of North America from sea to sea (I.2.10, "Conclusion," 391-94).
He concludes the first volume of *Democracy* by placing these insights into a
context that seems to assuage his moral concerns about the American westward
expansion and its continuing trend. Tocqueville perceives the dawning of what
we now call globalization—a reality "entirely new in the world" in which no
one any longer is a stranger to "what is taking place in any corner of the globe
whatsoever." This places democratic expansion in a new light. America's new
"greatness" and stature in "the first rank of nations" cannot be viewed in isolation from the tides of global affairs. He predicts it will become one of the two
great powers of the world, opposite Russia, one representing liberty and the other autocracy. They stand for diametrically opposed principles, but "nonetheless,
each of them seems called by a secret design of Providence to hold the destiny
of half the world in its hands one day" (395-96). Whatever one's views on the
Cold War that marked the latter half of the twentieth century, Tocqueville's
prescience about the contrast of principles points to the possible clash of states,
and he leaves no doubt as to which principle—liberty or servitude—he wishes to

see defended or advanced. A tendency toward expansion that is partly English and Anglo-American thus exemplifies the providential march of democracy across the history of Europe, then the Americas, and beyond. In the centuries ahead Tocqueville foresees a global struggle in which the enlightened self-interest of the Americans, their effort to balance justice and interest, will make democratic expansion the better alternative to autocratic expansion. This strategic judgment by Tocqueville would explain why, as the volume closes, he tempers his earlier criticism of America's power-politics and its injustice toward slaves and Amerindians.

In volume two of *Democracy in America* (1840), published after he had written two public letters on Algeria (1837) and been elected to France's national legislature (1839), Tocqueville more explicitly addresses war and liberal democracy but continues his ambivalent tone and search for moderation. He sees a narrowed political awareness in America and other modern democracies given their focus on material prosperity. He pointedly warns that if the habit of "eagerly coveting petty objects" does not give way at times to honorable ambitions, then democratic humanity will lose its "spark and greatness." In such an era he fears "the mediocrity of desires" much less than any "audacity," and worries that leaders will "want to put citizens to sleep in a happiness too even and peaceful." He thus concludes that "it is good to give them difficult and perilous affairs sometimes in order to elevate ambition and to open a theater for it" (II.3.19, on "So Few Great Ambitions," 601, 604). He also analyzes democratic armies and attitudes to war, and recognizes that the commercial, materialist spirit means that "warlike passions will become more rare and less lively." He admires the rejection of the spirit of military conquest that had dominated in aristocratic times, and also admires the principle of civilian control of the military that ensures such anti-militarism. Nonetheless, war is "an accident to which all peoples are subject" and democracies "must keep themselves ready to repel war." On the one hand, once war occurs, it cannot be denied that it "almost always enlarges the thought of a people and elevates its heart," and at times only war can "arrest the excessive development of certain penchants" and "deep-seated maladies to which democratic societies are subject." On the other hand, war is also "the surest and shortest means" to "destroy freedom within a democratic nation." It enormously expands "the prerogatives of civil government" and "centralizes the direction of all men and the employment of all things in its hands" (II.3.22, "Why Democratic Peoples Naturally Desire Peace," 617, 620-21).

In this discussion and its sequels Tocqueville urges democracies to strike a balance. Their aversion to militarism and war is both just and civilized, but given the endemic reality of war in human affairs a democracy must plan for it and educate armies and citizens to avoid both pacifism and militarism (II.3, chs. 22-26). An earlier observation in this section of *Democracy*, regarding both political ambition and war in the egalitarian age, captures the spirit of his search for a democratic greatness lying between pusillanimity and conquest. Democracies typically display a "multitude of small, very sensible ambitions in the midst of which some badly regulated great desires burst out from time to time," but unfortunately a "proportionate ambition, moderate yet vast, is scarcely ever encountered" (II.3.19, 603). Tocqueville argues that enlightened self-interest in liberal foreign policy must counsel against a self-absorbed and petty isolationism as much as against the more typical political temptation of conquest.

Tocqueville's Search for Moderation on Algeria

Tocqueville may have had in mind his own country's growing dilemmas in Algeria when, in this later section of *Democracy in America* (1840), he offered a very Montesquieuan observation about the moderation that should characterize war in democratic societies—marked by neither pacifism nor Roman-esque conquest: "According to the law of nations adopted by civilized nations, wars do not have the goal of appropriating the goods of particular persons, but only of taking possession of political power. They destroy private property only occasionally in order to attain the second object" (II.3.26, 633). Regardless of how much the French conquest of Algeria crossed his mind when writing either volume of *Democracy*, we know that in his writings and speeches on Algeria he referred to his earlier observations about American foreign policy. In an 1846 debate in the Chamber of Deputies Tocqueville severely criticized the ministry of King Louis Philippe for a passive foreign policy that, among other failings, did not coordinate with Britain—let alone match the boldness of the British government. He recommended to the ministry his study of the strengths and weakness of American foreign policy and the principles that would lead to success, to include discerning the national interest of a liberal polity and persevering in the execution of strategies despite obstacles or delays.[25] In 1847, in the first of two reports on Algeria that Tocqueville drafted for a special committee of the Chamber, he obliquely recalled his criticisms in *Democracy* of the Spanish treatment of the Amerindians; the phrasing does not suggest criticism of the Anglo-Americans per se. He raised the case of the Americas to persuade the French ministry that a more humane, liberal policy of "good government" would genuinely pacify the Algerians and allow for the further demilitarizing of French policy. The current tendency to suppress the insurgency by force and seek military pacification would yield disaster for Algeria and for France's liberal standing in the world:

> [If] in our eyes the old inhabitants of Algeria are merely an obstacle to be
> pushed aside or trampled underfoot, if we surrounded their populations, not to
> lift them in our arms toward well-being and enlightenment but to destroy and
> smother them, the question between the two races would be that of life and
> death. Sooner or later, Algeria would become a closed field, a walled arena,
> where the two peoples would have to fight without mercy, and where one of the
> two would have to die. May God save us, gentlemen, from such a destiny! Let
> us not, in the middle of the nineteenth century, begin the history of the conquest
> of America over again. Let us not imitate the bloody examples that the opinion

of the human race has stigmatized. Let us bear in mind that we would be a thousand times less excusable . . . for we are less fanatical, and we have the principles and the enlightenment the French Revolution spread throughout the world.[26]

Tocqueville's efforts to direct French foreign policy toward liberal moderation began with his first speeches in the Chamber in 1839, on "the Eastern Question"—namely, what the western European powers should do as the Ottoman empire and Islamic civilization fractured. Mary Lawlor's study suggests that he advocated a grand strategy for France that would provide the ends or aims to guide assessment of particular issues. This was indispensable for making sound choices about means and ways to best achieve those ends—or, to minimize any necessary departures from them. Tocqueville assessed issues of the eastern Mediterranean, of Egypt and Syria and the Ottomans, with reference to the interests and dispositions of Russia, Britain, Austria, and other great powers. He sought a balance of powers that would manage the Ottoman decline, in which France would be neither imperial and opportunistic nor merely passive as a new alignment took shape between West and East, Christianity and Islam, Russian autocracy and Western liberalism.[27] In an 1843 speech, amid tensions but also partnership with Britain, Tocqueville berated French passivity in European and global affairs. He recommended instead a balance between partnership with other liberal states and a restoration of the "powerful and preponderant" influence France long had exercised in Europe.[28] His interest in colonial affairs, and particularly his leadership from 1839 onward regarding both abolition of slavery in France's colonies and Algeria policy, served the larger strategy he had suggested in *Democracy in America*. As globalization began to change the world, and as the crisis in the Muslim world pointed toward continued expansion by liberal European states but also by Russia at the head of other autocratic powers, France must have both the soft power or attractive prestige of liberal principle and the hard power of arms and credible threats in order to steer affairs toward liberal ends.[29] Tocqueville more fully articulated this analysis of international relations and a strategy to cope with it in an 1840 speech that praised France as the only egalitarian, republican power of the great five European powers—Britain, Austria, Prussia, and Russia being the others. France thus should take a leading role in the effort to manage the decline of the Ottoman empire, with "the ancient Asiatic world disappearing, and in its place the European world rising."[30]

Tocqueville's grand strategy drew upon his admiration for the moderate principles of Montesquieu and Washington as well as lessons he had learned from study of America's expansion. The capability to defend and perpetuate liberal democracy in a dangerous world required a capacity to spread liberal principle, if necessary, as tectonic plates shifted in global affairs—lest illiberal powers or other threatening developments filled any vacuum. This is the context for and larger rationale behind his public statements and writings on Algeria. Given several recent studies critical of his efforts, noted above—especially the excavation of statements that are particularly scandalous to more Kantian, liberal-idealist minds—a more complete portrait of Tocqueville's thought should assess the indications that he thought he was serving principles of liberal moderation through a policy of reluctant colonialism and imperialism.[31]

His early public letters on Algeria, published in 1837 during his first, failed run for office, suggest a moderate colonialism that would permit "the arms and arts of Europe" to permanently and peacefully settle among an Islamic people. Their faith had spread into north Africa when "the successors of Muhammad," fueled by their "great religious passion," invaded and "conquered everything" all the way to the borders of France.[32] Later the Spanish had "chased the Arabs from the Iberian peninsula" and sought to retake Algiers for Christianity, but when the Algerians "sought the aid of the Turks" the latter, "having beaten the Christians and seized Algiers, declared themselves masters of those they had come to defend" ("First Letter on Algeria," *Writings*, p. 10). The Turks established and held for three centuries not a genuine government but "a continuation of conquest, a violent exploitation of the conquered by the conquerors" (First Letter, p. 12). Whether one would argue today that Tocqueville holds an "Orientalist" chauvinism toward Islamic peoples or a reasonable perception of a clash of civilizations that had long marked the Mediterranean, he clearly grasps that after centuries of Muslim dominance the Christian (or secularized Christian) states of western Europe were now reversing the tide.[33] Historians debate the legitimacy of the rationales, or rationalizations, for European re-expansion into north Africa, which range from suppression of Muslim state-sponsored piracy to stopping the white slave trade and liberating existing slaves. The main European concern was the "Barbary" states—the Ottoman regencies of Algiers, Tunis, and Tripoli—which Americans would recognize from President Jefferson's war against the Barbary pirates from 1801 to 1805, in turn memorialized in the reference to Tripoli in the Marine Hymn.[34]

Tocqueville's second Letter, also from 1837, makes it difficult to believe he is merely a biased "Orientalist" given his insistence on the moral equality of the French and Algerians as to basic natural rights. He criticizes France's "profound ignorance" of anything about the Ottoman regency or the Algerian peoples. This led the French to violate both "law and rights" and to subject the Algerians to merely a different flavor of conquest instead of providing a government. Indeed, the French had blindly used "means far more Turkish than those the Turks ever used" ("Second Letter on Algeria," August 22, 1837, *Writings*, 15-16). He urges the right balance between hard power and soft power measures, and suggests that at the time of the conquest the French should have attempted "to put ourselves in the place of the defeated." Instead of replacing their administration and government with the French model, "we should for a time have bent to their ways" of government—hired its former officials, "accepted its traditions, and guarded its practices" ("Second Letter," *Writings*, 19). The French also should try to co-opt the Algerians with commerce, especially the Berbers or Kabyle residing in the Atlas mountains—subduing them "by our arts and not by our arms." The Berbers are "savages" but can be drawn "toward civilized man" in peaceful ways. As for the Arabs, the sole objective must be "to live in peace with those Arabs whom we cannot hope to govern at present, and to organize them in the manner least dangerous for our future progress" ("Second Letter," *Writings*, 20-21). In this optimistic and expansionist spirit, before his first journey to Algeria, Tocqueville urges that "with time, perseverance, ability, and justice, I have no doubt that we shall be able to raise a great monument to our country's glory on the African coast." This could only be achieved, however, by redressing mistakes and pursuing peaceful cohabitation under law, which in turn points to a blending of the European and Algerian peoples ("Second Letter," *Writings*, 24).

After his first journey to Algeria, in 1841, Tocqueville's views about the French project are less optimistic, but initially also more stridently nationalist, imperialist, and militarist. This is most evident in an 1841 essay he drafted, which scholars have mined for its "uncompromising" and "even cruel" remarks on the need for European domination.[35] However, while he circulated this "Essay on Algeria" privately to a few friends he never refined it for publication; it was not published until 1962. Both as a philosopher and a statesman it seems fair to judge Tocqueville primarily by writings and utterances he prepared for public examination. Indeed, the contrast between the occasional belligerence of the 1841 "Essay" and his final writings on Algeria in 1847 suggests that over time his judgment tempered both his earliest idealism (1837) and the stridency of his unrefined thoughts (1841).[36] For example, his remarks in *Democracy in America* about the stages of civilization evident in both the clash of the "three races" in America and the contrast between Spanish, French, and English civilizations probably inform his early emphasis on the "savages" of Algeria and the aim to draw them from "barbarism" (*Democracy*, I.2.10, 319 n. 19 and 1837 "Letters"). After two trips to Algeria (1841 and 1846), and further debate and writing, his final writings lower the aims for the colonial project but persist in urging corrections and long-term strategies, rather than withdrawal.

The first of his two parliamentary reports of 1847 scolds the government for reducing the Algerians to conditions worse than those under the Ottomans. He softens earlier boasts about civilizational superiority by conceding that "Muslim society in Africa was not uncivilized; it was merely a backward and imperfect civilization." The French, however, have destroyed the earlier order of schools, charities, and laws, thereby making "Muslim society much more miserable, more disordered, more ignorant, and more barbarous" than before ("First Report," *Writings*, 140-41). He now emphatically recommends learning about the Arab and Berber (Kabyle) peoples so as to learn how to govern rather than conquer them, by winning hearts and minds. He still insists that "civilized and Christian society" must dominate but the spirit must be moderate and the means must repudiate any semblance of Turkish oppression. Not only must military measures recede, but territorial expansion must cease—and the Report is severe in condemning any further expeditions against the Kabyle in the mountains ("First Report," *Writings*, 130-31, 134-35, 168-172). That said, the colonial government has regularly passed "from the extreme of benevolence to that of rigor" and now must avoid these "two excesses" (139, 141). Islam could adapt to "enlightenment" again, for "it has often admitted certain sciences or certain arts into itself," and so restoration of indigenous schools and religious education is indispensable (142).[37] The right balance will find the French "strong" and secure but the crucial issue now is "our manner of treating the indigenous population," at a minimum to accord with "the natural rights of humanity" (145, 146). Nonetheless Tocqueville closes the "First Report" by affirming the strategic importance for France and for liberal democracy of a successful colonial enterprise:

> The peaceful domination and rapid colonization of Algeria are assuredly the two greatest interests that France has in the world today; they are great in themselves, and in the direct and necessary relation that they have with all the others. Our preponderance in Europe, the order of our finances, the lives of part of our citizenry, and our national honor are engaged here in the most compelling manner ("First Report," *Writings*, 167-68).

The "Second Report" addresses a government plan for colonizing French soldiers in Algeria as farmers. It opens by acknowledging two members of the parliamentary committee who insist that "humanity and wisdom" repudiate any colonialism given the injustice it would inflict on the Algerians.[38] Tocqueville reports the majority view that these or other colonization measures are not categorically unjust given the partly nomadic and partly communal property laws under the Ottoman regency. Certainly the lands formerly owned by the Ottoman state can be distributed "without injuring anyone's rights," although any such plans must be undertaken "delicately, humanely, and competently" ("Second Report," *Writings*, 175-76). The committee nonetheless rejects the government proposal, and interestingly Tocqueville emphasizes its reliance on imperial rules for importing and regulating the French solider-farmers rather than on market-oriented incentives to attract French citizens. The government proposes the kind of measures that "Czar Alexander" of Russia and other autocratic powers have undertaken in central and eastern Europe, which Tocqueville summarily rejects: "Is this idea applicable to Frenchmen? Clearly not" ("Second Report," *Writings*, 187).

Welch notes that a model more acceptable to Tocqueville, and which informs these two reports, is the British colonial project in India. Tocqueville's unpublished notes from the 1840s reveal his studies of Indian culture and religion and even his hopes of traveling there to report on the British effort to bring liberal and Christian civilization to a mostly Hindu and Muslim people in Asia who had known only monarchical or rigidly aristocratic rule.[39] Critics insist, of course, that no model of colonialism accords with liberal principles, but debates about international relations and liberal-democratic foreign policy continue to this day to feature concerns similar to those that led Tocqueville to adopt an ambivalent colonialism. The historian Niall Ferguson recently has ventured the revisionist view, after much scholarship in the twentieth century condemning European colonialism as brutal imperialism, that British colonialism was more successful than any other because it spread such liberal principles as the rule of law, markets, and liberty. Ferguson acknowledges brutal and unjust elements but insists we must confront the question of whether modernity and the advantages of globalization would have spread so comprehensively in the world, and so relatively quickly, without colonialism. The Indian economist and political theorist Amartya Sen repudiates the historical and cultural paternalism of such a view, insisting that in India's case there were indigenous ingredients for modern and liberal civilization long percolating. Apart from questions of injustice and exploitation, European imperialism impeded rather than fostered the development of more enlightened and modern views in Asia.[40] Before adopting Sen's view on the basis of its intrinsic justice we might consider, forty years into the liberal policy of commercial engagement with the People's Republic of China, the current debate as to whether China has succeeded in resisting political liberalism while increasing the power of its autocratic state by exploiting commercial globalization. Similar questions arise about Russia's illiberal spirit two decades after the fall of autocratic communism in Europe. Tocqueville followed Montesquieu in advocating the liberalizing and civilizing effects of global commerce, but neither philosopher adopted the Kantian view that such transformations could occur in international affairs without recourse to elements of power, coercion, or credible threats.

Democracy Expansion and the Burdens of Liberal Statesmanship

Tocqueville's insight into the character of liberal democracy and a rising democratic people was so deep as to foresee not only the Mexican-American War, the total conquest of the Amerindians across the continent, and some kind of American civil war over slavery but also the kind of conflict between Russian and American coalitions that marked the Cold War a century hence. He characterizes the foreign policy proper to liberal democracy as enlightened self-interest—that a well-defended liberal democracy can best serve its long-term interests by being peaceful and doing good in the world. His concerns about America's capacity to abide by liberal principle while expanding democracy mirror Montesquieu's view of Britain a century earlier. Montesquieu praised an English constitutionalism of liberty and commerce but also criticized the hegemonic and illiberal tendencies in its commercial expansion, evident in its brutal treatment of Ireland.[41] Tocqueville carried his search for liberal moderation into his analysis of and recommendations for Algerian policy and global affairs. The balancing principle he found regarding the conduct of America in its western frontier, or of Britain in India, or of France in northern Africa was the concern that, amid the historic and global shifts of power in the nineteenth century, the liberal democracies had no reasonable choice but to expand liberalism to prevent or counter autocratic expansion.[42]

It is not hard to claim that Montesquieu and Washington more consistently hold to a philosophy of liberal moderation than Tocqueville did, given the gamble the latter made that the moral costs of continued military conflict and foreign domination in Algeria would be repaid by the great justice of protecting and expanding liberal principles in a dangerous world. To be fair to Tocqueville, Montesquieu never directly confronted these kinds of dilemmas of international statesmanship as a public official, while Washington's primary goal was to establish conditions for a young republic to mature toward power, not to steer a great power in the shifting currents of the world. Nonetheless, Tocqueville's statesmanship as well as the experience of American continental expansion raises a concern that liberal moderation in international affairs effectively slides toward realism and interest at the expense of liberal principle. The principle of democracy promotion, seemingly peaceful and passive or attractive, may contain an inherent tendency toward expansion as imposition, whether by diplomatic compellence or military force. Tocqueville's analysis of American power condemned its treatment of slaves and Indians, but could see no plausible or principled way out of those problems, and ultimately praised its power as a boon to the global progress of democratic liberty relative to illiberal powers. His ambivalent support for European colonialism in Africa and Asia, in his writings and his speeches, clearly draws on this complexity in his earlier views about America. It may be, then, that a liberal-democratic foreign policy is Tocquevillian as a matter of general principles or theory, but would not strictly follow Tocqueville's practice, since the latter's choices as a statesman need not define a broader theory of liberal moderation. Doubts about Tocqueville's prudence need not cast doubt, however, on the importance of practical judgment or prudence for a foreign policy of liberal moderation. Given its roots in Montesquieu's complex philosophy as well as Tocqueville's praise for the example of Washington, a Tocquevillean philosophy characteristically values the need for prudential judgment by particular statesmen, in particular situations, to discern how best to comply with or protect liberal principles.[43] Montesquieu's concerns about England and Ireland, as well as Washington's concern for the Amerindians and his eventual condemnation of slavery and emancipation of all his slaves, suggest that liberal moderation can hold a middle ground that balances justice and interest, and need not default to realism or amoral self-interest.

Tocquevillean principles for a foreign policy of liberal moderation, adapted to our more fully globalized era, therefore suggest at least three general points. The first is the fundamental principle to seek liberal-democratic peace over sheer power in international affairs, while also appreciating the need for power to promote liberal democracy and guarantee a system of globalized peace and commerce. The second is to prepare leaders to adjust to new circumstances and the moves of other global players while trying to adhere to principles, which requires a prudence that finds a middle ground between idealistic but impossible doctrine and low, amoral calculations about power, interests, alliances, and war. The third speaks more directly to America, but could apply to any hegemonic but benevolent power in such a globalized liberal order. This is to recognize the prevailing ambivalence about American and Western hegemony, both among Americans and globally—neither a repudiation of it nor pure admiration, but some blend. Liberal democracies therefore must always explain the moderation of their policies, including in democracy promotion, especially how their use of power ultimately serves humane principles of equality, freedom, and pluralism. This last point does not mean, of course, that to moderate leadership requires forsaking it. This distinctive foreign policy of liberal democracy seeks international peace and right neither through isolationism nor empire, nor by consulting only national interest, nor by adhering only to idealism apart from circumstances or experience. Of course, the leading liberal states of Britain and America have not perfectly held to these principles of liberal moderation during the past several centuries. America's experience suggests, however, that after excesses in one direction or another it typically pulls back toward this blend of liberalism and realism when assessing errors or what future course to chart.[44] Whether we would condemn Tocqueville's qualified and reluctant support for colonialism as illiberal or recognize it as a choice he deemed prudent if regrettable, in our post-colonialist era a policy of democracy promotion by a powerful liberal democracy falls in that middle ground. A moderate approach to democracy promotion can at once affirm its justice, recognize limits imposed by the interests and resources of the promoting state, and counsel great prudence in the tricky task of helping to develop a new political culture and institutions of liberal democracy.[45]

Tocqueville's encounters with the Algeria question, the Eastern question, and the balance of power among European states as globalization commenced, don't reveal a dark side to Tocqueville and a failure of principle as much as they indicate the inescapable dilemmas of statesmanship in international affairs. If some liberals find some of his judgments about how to salvage the Algeria project imprudent and unjust that does not necessarily reflect badly upon his philosophy, but it does remind us of the difficulty of descending from philosophy into the problematic, and at times wretched, choices that confront statesmen. Tocqueville's effort to see farther than the current parties, schools, or debates shows respect for the practical challenges of governing. It defends the principled compromises that likely will be necessary to achieve possible goods against the criticisms lodged by a utopian and morally satisfying view that may achieve, unintentionally of course, a worse result according to that moral standard itself.[46] Tocqueville's philosophy of moderation also reveals a sense of duty paired with ambition that prompted him to leave the study and serve as a national leader. By recording his views about his practical dilemmas he nonetheless served those of us who remain mostly in the study. His writings on Algeria, slavery, and global affairs prod us to reassess the adequacy of any doctrinaire theory of either pure interest or pure morality to help liberal democracies navigate the realities of politics, and offer us an opportunity to rediscover the neglected approach of liberal moderation in international affairs.

Notes

1. Professor, Political Science, U.S. Air Force Academy. The views expressed are those solely of the author, and not of the Air Force Academy or the U.S. government. I am grateful to Brian Danoff and Joseph Hebert for helpful comments.

2. See, among other works, Melvin Richter, "Tocqueville on Algeria," *Review of Politics* 25 (1963): 362-98; Jennifer Pitts, "Empire and Democracy: Tocqueville and the Algeria Question," *The Journal of Political Philosophy* 8 (2000): 295-318; Cheryl B. Welch, "Colonial Violence and the Rhetoric of Evasion: Tocqueville on Algeria," *Political Theory* 31 (2003): 235-64; and Roger Boesche, "The Dark Side of Tocqueville: On War and Empire," *Review of Politics* 67 (2005): 737-52. See also Pitts, ed., *Alexis de Tocqueville: Writings on Empire and Slavery* (Baltimore, MD: Johns Hopkins University Press, 2001), introduction, ix-xxxviii; Pitts, *A Turn to Empire: The Rise of Imperial Liberalism in Britain and France* (Princeton, NJ: Princeton University Press, 2006), Introduction, 1-22, and chapter 7, "Tocqueville and the Algeria Question," 204-39; and Pitts, "Liberalism, Democracy, and Empire: Tocqueville on Algeria," in *Reading Tocqueville: From Oracle to Actor*, ed. Raf Greenens and Annelian De Dijn (London: Palgrave Macmillan, 2007), 12-30.

3. Pitts criticizes the views in *Democracy in America* in, e.g., introduction to *Empire and Slavery*, xiv-xvi; Boesche criticizes his "Eurocentric" views in "The Dark Side of Tocqueville," 745.

4. On the complexity of Tocqueville's philosophy see, among other recent works, "Editors' Introduction" in *Democracy*, ed. Harvey C. Mansfield and Delba Winthrop, xvii-lxxxi, especially at xxx-xxxix; Cheryl B. Welch, *De Tocqueville* (Oxford: Oxford University Press, 2001); and L. Joseph Hebert, Jr., *More Than Kings and Less Than Men: Tocqueville on the Promise and Perils of Democratic Individualism* (Lanham, MD: Lexington Books, 2010). Sheldon Wolin takes a more critical stance in *Tocqueville Between Two Worlds: The Making of a Political and Theoretical Life* (Princeton: Princeton University Press, 2001), 38-45, 84-86, 89-90, 177-82; see also the range of views in *The Cambridge Companion to Tocqueville*, ed. Cheryl B. Welch (Cambridge: Cambridge University Press, 2006). Tocque-ville's more thematic criticism of the radical Enlightenment and some *philosophes* is in *The Old Regime and the Revolution* (volume 1), trans. Alan Kahan, ed. François Furet and Françoise Mélonio (Chicago: University of Chicago Press, 1998), esp. book 1, chapter 1, and book 3.

5. Tocqueville, *Democracy in America*, ed. Mansfield and Winthrop, Introduction, 15. I have checked this translation by consulting Tocqueville, *Œuvres complètes*, ed. J. Mayer (Paris: Gallimard, 1951-), Tome I, 2 vols., and *Democracy in America*, ed. J.P Mayer, trans. George Lawrence (Garden City, NY: Doubleday, Anchor Books, 1969). Robert Eden provides a distinctive interpretation to this passage in "Tocqueville and the Problem of Natural Right," *Interpretation* 17 (1990), 379-387.

6. See E. H. Carr, *The Twenty Years' Crisis, 1919-1939: An Introduction to the Study of International Relations* (New York: Harper & Row, 1964 [1939]); one need not accept all the realist tenets of Carr's approach to appreciate the weight of his critique of liberal idealism.

7. Immanuel Kant, "Perpetual Peace: A Philosophical Sketch" (1795), in *Kant: Political Writings*, ed. H.S. Reiss, second edition (New York: Cambridge University Press, 1991), 93-130; see also John Rawls, *The Law of Peoples* (Cambridge, MA: Harvard University Press, 2001).

8. Lincoln states his compromise view most succinctly in his letter to the abolitionist Horace Greely: "My paramount object in this struggle *is* to save the Union, and is *not* either to save or to destroy slavery" (emphases in original); August 22, 1862, in *Collected Works of Abraham Lincoln*, ed. Roy Basler, 9 vols. (New Brunswick, NJ: Rutgers University Press, 1953), 5: 388-89; for Douglass, see "Oration in Memory of Abraham Lincoln," April 14, 1876, in *The Life and Writings of Frederick Douglass*, ed. Philip Foner, 4 volumes (New York: International Publishers, 1950-1955), 4: 309ff. In general see Steven Kautz, "Abraham Lincoln: The Moderation of a Democratic Statesman," in *The History of American Political Thought*, ed. Bryan-Paul Frost and Jeffrey Sikkenga (Lanham, MD: Lexington Books, 2003) 395-415.

9. Two studies that are less severely critical of Tocqueville's judgments about Algeria are Mary Lawlor, *Alexis de Tocqueville in the Chamber of Deputies: His Views on Foreign and Colonial Policy* (Washington, DC: Catholic University of America Press, 1959), and Cheryl B. Welch, "Tocqueville on Fraternity and Fratricide," in *The Cambridge Companion to Tocqueville*, 303-336.

10. I discuss Washington and Tocqueville in "American Power and the Legacy of Washington: Enduring Principles for Foreign and Security Policy," in Paul Bolt, Damon Coletta, and Collins Shackelford, eds., *American Defense Policy*, 8th ed. (Baltimore, MD: Johns Hopkins Press, 2005), 6-16. Among the sources on Washington cited there, see, e.g., Felix Gilbert, *To the Farewell Address: Ideas of Early American Foreign Policy* (Princeton, NJ: Princeton University Press, 1961); 4-6, 16-18, 135-136.

11. On the complexity of American thinking and the relevance of early debates, see Walter A. McDougall, *Promised Land, Crusader State: The American Encounter with the World Since 1776* (New York: Houghton Mifflin, 1997), and Walter Russell Mead, *Special Providence: American Foreign Policy and How It Changed the World* (New York: Century/Knopf, 2001).

12. See Michael Doyle, "Liberalism and World Politics," *American Political Science Review* 80 (1986): 1151-69, and Spencer R. Weart, *Never at War: Why Democracies Will Not Fight One Another* (New Haven, CT: Yale University Press, 1998). Doyle mischaracterizes Montesquieu as focusing only on commerce (at 1152), when in fact Montesquieu discerns the limits of liberal rationalism and the need for prudence of the sort that Doyle advocates (at 1162-63). More discerning discussions of Montesquieu include Nicholas G. Onuf, *The Republican Legacy in International Thought* (New York: Cambridge University Press, 1998), 233-246, 262; David C. Hendrickson, *Peace Pact: The Lost World of the American Founding* (Lawrence: University Press of Kansas, 2003), 29, 43-45, 53-54; and Daniel Deudney, *Bounding Power: Republican Security Theory From the Polis to the Global Village* (Princeton, NJ: Princeton University Press, 2007), 10-11, 126-28, 269-71; see also n. 17, below.

13. I discuss this philosophy of moderation, or balance and complexity, in "Montesquieu's Complex Natural Right and Moderate Liberalism: The Roots of American Moderation," *Polity* 36, no. 2 (January 2004): 227-50.

14. Against interpretations of Aquinas's natural law and just war philosophy as categorical, see Daniel Westberg, *Right Practical Reason: Aristotle, Action, and Prudence in Aquinas* (Oxford: Clarendon Press, 1994); Jeremy Catto, "Ideas and Experience in the Political Thought of Aquinas," *Past and Present* 71 (May 1976): 3-21; and Marc D. Guerra, "Beyond Natural Law Talk: Politics and Prudence in St. Thomas Aquinas's *On Kingship*," *Perspectives on Political Science* 31 (2002): 9-14.

15. See Gerhard von Glahn, *Law Among Nations: An Introduction to Public International Law*, 5th ed. (New York: Macmillan, 1986), 3, 22-25, 27-35; and Hendrickson,

"Foundations of the New Diplomacy," in *Peace Pact: The Lost World of the American Founding*, 169-176.

16. Montesquieu, *The Spirit of the Laws*, ed. and trans. Anne Cohler, Basia Miller, and Harold Stone (New York: Cambridge University Press, 1989), Book 1, chapters 3, 7, emphases in the original. I have revised the translation as needed, consulting *De l'Esprit des Lois*, in *Œuvres complètes*, Pléiade edition, ed. Roger Caillois, 2 vols. (Paris: Gallimard, 1949-51), vol 2. Subsequent references cite book, chapter, and page number parenthetically in the body of the essay (e.g., 1.3, 7).

17. Thomas L. Pangle and Peter J. Ahrensdorf, *Justice Among Nations: On the Moral Basis of Power and Peace* (Lawrence, KS: University Press of Kansas, 1999), 157-61.

18. "Farewell Address," 1796, in *George Washington: Writings*, ed. John Rhodehamel (New York: Literary Classics of the United States, 1997), 962-977, especially at 972ff.

19. *Democracy in America*, ed. Mansfield and Winthrop, Vol. 1, pt. 2, ch. 5, 217-220. Subsequent references are made parenthetically, citing volume, part, chapter, page of this edition. Tocqueville elsewhere defines "self-interest well understood" or "enlightened love of themselves" as the belief "that man, in serving those like him, serves himself, and that his particular interest is to do good." *Democracy*, 2.2.8, 500-502.

20. Tocqueville earlier criticizes American conduct of the war, in *Democracy* 1.1.8, 159-61.

21. See 1.1.8, 149-61; 1.2.5, 217-220; and in the long chapter on "The Three Races" in America, 1.2.10, at 319-22, 368, 391-96. In volume 2, see 3.1 on "the right of nations" (539), and 3.22-26 on war and armies (617-35).

22. For criticism that Tocqueville mistakenly viewed this kind of racism and imperialism as alien to liberalism, when in fact American liberalism blended itself with such "inegalitarian ideologies," see, e.g., Rogers Smith, "Beyond Tocqueville, Myrdal, and Hartz: The Multiple Traditions in America," *American Political Science Review* 87 (1993): 549-66.

23. Marc F. Plattner and Larry Diamond, "Introduction," *Journal of Democracy* 11 (2000): 5-10; see, however, the essays in that issue by Nathan Glazer, "Race and Ethnicity in America," 95-102—which views Tocqueville quite differently than Smith (n22)—and Zbigniew Brezinski, "War and Foreign Policy, American-Style," 172-78, and also Welch, "Tocqueville on Fraternity and Fratricide."

24. Montesquieu, *Considerations on the Causes of the Greatness of the Romans and Their Decline*, ed. and trans. David Lowenthal (Indianapolis, IN: Hackett, 1999 [1965]). Paul Rahe discusses the larger significance of this work for Montesquieu's philosophy in *Soft Despotism, Democracy's Drift: Montesquieu, Rousseau, Tocqueville & The Modern Prospect* (New Haven & London: Yale University Press, 2009), especially 4-10.

25. June 17, 1846, discussed in Lawlor, *Tocqueville in the Chamber of Deputies*, 10-12. Few of Tocqueville's writings on international affairs or grand strategy are translated into English; a helpful example, also from 1846, is in *The Tocqueville Reader*, ed. Olivier Zunz and Alan Kahan (Oxford: Blackwell Publishing, 2002), 220-21 (addressing the strategic, military, and commercial importance of the port of Cherbourg).

26. "First Report on Algeria," 1847 ("Report by M. de Tocqueville on the Bill on Special Funding Requested for Algeria"), in Pitts, ed., *Writings on Empire and Slavery*, 129-173 at 146.

27. Lawlor, *Chamber of Deputies*, 8-9, 39-42.

28. Lawlor, *Chamber of Deputies*, 11; see 10-12.

29. Lawlor, *Chamber of Deputies*, 12-13. Joseph S. Nye, Jr., is credited with coining the terms soft and hard power; see, e.g., *Bound to Lead: The Changing Nature of American Power* (New York: Basic Books, 1991).

30. Lawlor, *Chamber of Deputies*, 54; see 52-59.

31. See notes 2 and 9 above. As noted, Lawlor is less severe and concludes that Tocqueville's "moderate, and at times critical views of the colonial situation in Algiers" indicate that he did not consider it "a glorious conquest" for France in terms of military domination as an end in itself; *Chamber of Deputies*, 134. Welch explicates "Tocqueville's hope to control and moderate European collisions with less-advanced civilizations"; "Fraternity and Fratricide," 316.

32. "First Letter on Algeria," June 23, 1837, in Pitts, ed., *Writings on Empire and Slavery*, 6, 8. Subsequent references to this collection will parenthetically cite the document and page number.

33. See Edward Said, *Orientalism: Western Conceptions of the Orient* (New York: Random House, 1978), but see also the great critic (and target) of the Orientalism thesis, Bernard Lewis, in *What Went Wrong? Western Impact and Middle Eastern Response* (Oxford University Press, 2001). In Samuel Huntington's important essay "The Clash of Civilizations," *Foreign Affairs* 72 (1993): 22-49, he cites Lewis for authoring the title phrase (32, n2); see Lewis, "The Roots of Muslim Rage," *The Atlantic Monthly* (September 1990): 47-60.

34. A skeptical view of the rationales about Muslim piracy and white slavery is found in Ann Thomson, "Arguments for the Conquest of Algiers in the Late Eighteenth and Early Nineteenth Centuries," *Maghreb Review* 14 (1989): 108-118; more sympathetic views are Gillian Weiss, "Imagining Europe Through Barbary Captivity," *Taiwan Journal of East Asian Studies* 4 (2007): 49-67 and Robert C. Davis, *Christian Slaves, Muslim Masters: White Slaves in the Mediterranean, the Barbary Coast, and Italy, 1500-1800* (New York: Palgrave Macmillan, 2003).

35. Pitts, "Introduction" to *Writings on Empire*, xxiv; "Tocqueville's readers have often been shocked at the ruthlessness of many of his recommendations for imperial conquest," xiii.

36. Pitts translates several writings never prepared for publication, including "Notes on the Koran" (1838), "Notes on the Voyage to Algeria" (1841), and "Essay on Algeria" (1841), in *Writings on Empire*. Boesche emphasizes Tocqueville's unpublished writings and letters in his argument about a "dark side," especially his 1841 letters with Mill.

37. Compare his concern in *Democracy in America* that the detailed direction of politics and society in the Qur'an makes Islam incompatible with liberal democracy (II.1.5, 419-20); a colonial policy emphasizing education would address this issue by gradual, peaceful means.

38. "Report by M. de Tocqueville on the Bill Requesting a Credit of Three Million Francs for Algerian Agricultural Camps" ("Second Report on Algeria") (1847), in Pitts, ed., *Writings on Empire and Slavery*, 174-98 at 174.

39. Welch, "Fraternity and Fratricide," 324. An excerpt of Tocqueville's India notes, from 1843, is translated in *The Tocqueville Reader*, 229-31. See also Seymour Drescher, "Tocqueville's Comparative Perspectives," in *The Cambridge Companion to Tocqueville*, 21-48, and other references to India in that volume.

40. See Niall Ferguson, *Empire: The Rise and Demise of the British World Order and the Lessons for Global Power* (New York: Basic Books, 2003) and Amartya Sen, *The Argumentative Indian: Writings on Indian History, Culture, and Identity* (New York: Farrar, Strauss, and Giroux, 2005).

41. Montesquieu, *Spirit of Laws*, book 19, ch. 27, 325-33.

42. A recent study of Tocqueville's advocacy of liberal activism in expanding democracy is David Clinton, *Tocqueville, Lieber, and Bagehot: Liberalism Confronts the World* (New York: Palgrave Macmillan, 2003).

43. In general, see Alberto Coll, "Normative Prudence as a Tradition of Statecraft," in *Ethics & International Affairs: A Reader*, ed. Joel Rosenthal (Washington, DC: Georgetown University Press, 1995), 58-77.

44. On complexity and moderation in American foreign policy see the works by McDougall and Mead in note 11 above, and also John Lewis Gaddis, *Surprise, Security, and the American Experience* (Cambridge, MA: Harvard University Press, 2005).

45. Two recent arguments are Larry Diamond, *The Spirit of Democracy: The Struggle to Build Free Societies Throughout the World* (New York: Times Books, 2008), and Marc F. Plattner, "Introduction," in *Is Democracy Exportable?*, edited by Zoltan Barany and Robert G. Moser (New York: Cambridge University Press, 2009), 1-12. In the latter volume see also Thomas L. Pangle, "The Morality of Exporting Democracy: An Historical-Philosophical Perspective," 15-34; Pangle explores the ideas provided by ancient Athens, Montesquieu, and the America founders, but not Tocqueville.

46. Jack Snyder summarizes these schools or policy camps of realism and liberal idealism, and advocates blending or balancing these discrete views in the practice of policy making, in "One World, Rival Theories," *Foreign Policy*, no. 145 (November/December 2004): 53-62; an earlier argument for synthesis is Joseph S. Nye, Jr., "Neorealism and Neoliberalism," *World Politics* 40 (1988): 235-51.

Chapter 15[1]

The Twofold Challenge for Democratic Culture in Our Time

Thomas L. Pangle

From the gathering of political and cultural leaders in the First European Cultural Summit there has emerged a heightened awareness of the need to strengthen, and to bring into more fruitful complementarity, two distinct and sometimes antagonistic domains of our common trans-Atlantic culture: the realm of democracy, or of republican civic spirit; and the realm of what is often called "high" culture—the life of the cultivated mind and heart, finding expression in literature and the arts, in religion and philosophy and philosophic science.

These two realms of human endeavor and aspiration may be said to constitute the heart of the great tradition of European humanism. This humanism is animated by the conviction that human beings can flourish only when they do not live in subservience to authority that is either outside their power to influence substantially, or beyond their power of comprehension.

The foundations of European humanism, thus conceived, were laid in ancient Greece. The Greek citizens spawned the idea of constitutional self-government; and in doing so they drew upon the previous achievement of the Greek poets, who had given to the world the proud independence of individually authored works laying claim to an immortally glorious, if tragic, human wisdom.

Our tradition of humanism so understood, in its essence and in its genealogy, by no means excludes piety, or obedience to, as well as reverence for, superhuman and even supra-rational divinity. But this tradition as *humanist* bows only to that divine instruction which makes itself intelligible to, and thereby shows respect for, humankind's rational capacity for reflection, deliberation, and judgment.

Humanism so understood is as much at the heart of the United States of America as it is at the core of the now maturing movement toward a United States of Europe. Yet our two fraternal versions of "United States" are differentiated even or precisely in their spiritual kinship. Today we are engaged in a trans-Atlantic conversation that struggles with the question, how do Europeans and Americans make distinct contributions to, and exhibit different versions of, this shared culture of humanism constituted by these two realms, the civic and the intellectual? And I submit that, while both these realms remain lively on both sides of the Atlantic, it is nevertheless the case that on each of our continents one of the two realms has fallen into a weaker condition than on the other continent. It follows that we have need of one another, that we need to hear from one another, even or especially in friendly criticism and admonition, if we are to maintain or to restore the spiritual balance that is essential to our shared civilizational health.

Democracy in Europe

I take my bearings on the goals, promises, and challenges of democratic leadership from Alexis de Tocqueville's classic analysis of democracy in America. It is appropriate that we turn to his great work of that name, and not only for inspiration, but above all for guidance. Tocqueville opened a dialogue at the highest level between Europeans and Americans, a dialogue focused on the reasonable aspirations and the fundamental problems of modern, liberal democracy in its essentials—essentials that he saw emerging most clearly in and through the United States. We are attempting to launch a dialogue that is, as it were, the antistrophe: a dialogue on the aspirations and problems of democracy as seen emerging in Europe.

How can we tell whether democracy is strengthening or weakening, in the West? By what ought we to measure the weakness or strength of democracy? Tocqueville gives us help in answering these questions.

Tocqueville's thought is dominated by the conviction that it is our fate—a fate prepared by the whole of western history—to live in an ever more egalitarian and hence democratic culture. But this fate he views as darkly ambiguous. Democracy has two radically opposed possible directions of development. Democracy can lead upward, to an unprecedentedly broad culture of human dignity and even nobility. But democracy can more easily—it is more naturally or spontaneously inclined to—drift downward, toward an unprecedentedly pervasive civic degradation.

What is Tocqueville's more specific vision of these two competing candidates for our destiny as democrats? The noble possibility Tocqueville limns in the introduction to his work:

I conceive a society, then, where all, regarding the law as their work, would love it and submit themselves to it without trouble; where the authority of government being respected as necessary and not as divine, the love that one would bear for the head of state would not be a passion, but a rational and tranquil feeling. Each possessing rights, and being assured of preserving his rights, there would be established among all the classes a manly confidence, and a sort of mutual condescension, as far removed from haughty pride as from baseness. . . . The free association of citizens would be able to take the place, then, of the individual power of the nobles, and the state would be sheltered from both tyranny and license. . . . In the absence of enthusiasm and of the passion of faiths, enlightenment and experience will sometimes elicit great sacrifices from the citizens; each person, being equally weak, will feel an equal need for those like him; and, recognizing that he cannot obtain their support except on the condition that he lend to them his cooperation, he will without trouble discover that for him the particular interest merges with the general interest.[2]

The threatened degradation Tocqueville articulates in the following disturbing passage, from his closing pages:

I think then that the kind of oppression with which democratic peoples are menaced will not resemble anything that has preceded it in the world; our contemporaries would scarcely find its image in their memories. . . . I see an innumerable crowd of human beings, similar and equal, who restlessly revolve around themselves in order to procure the petty and vulgar pleasures with which they glut their souls. Each of them, withdrawn apart, is as a stranger to the destiny of all the others: his children and his particular friends make up for him the entire human species; as for dwelling with his fellow citizens, he is beside them, but he does not see them; he touches them, and feels them not at all; he exists only in himself and for himself alone, and, if he still has a family, one can say that at least he has no longer a fatherland.

Above these, there rises up an immense and tutelary power, which takes upon itself alone the responsibility of assuring their enjoyment and watching over their fate. It is absolute, detailed, regular, foresightful, and soft. It would resemble paternal power if, like that, it had for its aim preparing human beings for the age of manhood; but it seeks, on the contrary, only to fix them irrevocably in childhood; it likes to have the citizens enjoying themselves, provided that they think only of enjoying themselves. It willingly works for their happiness; but it wishes to be the sole agent and the sole arbiter of it; it provides for their security, foresees and secures their needs, facilitates their pleasures, conducts their principal affairs, directs their industry, regulates their estates, divides their inheritances; can it not perhaps relieve them entirely of the trouble of thinking and the effort of living? . . .

After having thus taken in its powerful hands each individual in turn, and having kneaded him as it likes, the sovereign extends its arms over society as a whole; it covers the surface of it with a network of petty, complicated rules, minute and uniform, through which the most original spirits and the most vigorous souls cannot make way to surpass the crowd; it does not break the wills, but it softens them, bends them, and directs them; it rarely compels action, but constantly opposes itself to anyone's acting; it does not at all destroy, but it

prevents birth; it does not at all tyrannize, but it hinders, it compresses, it ener-
vates, it extinguishes, it dazes, and it finally reduces each nation to being nothing more than a herd of timid and industrious animals, of which the government
is the shepherd.

I have always believed that this sort of servitude—regulated, soft and
peaceful—of which I have just painted the picture, could combine itself more
readily than one imagines with some of the external forms of liberty, and that it
would not be impossible to establish it even under the wing of the sovereignty
of the people.[3]

Now what does Tocqueville teach to be the greatest forces that can be
summoned and deployed, by democrats, to resist the drift toward this new, soft
despotism? From Tocqueville's rich cabinet of remedies I select two that seem
especially worth pondering today.

From Passive to Participatory Democracy

First, Tocqueville implores enlightened democratic leaders of all kinds to strive
relentlessly to cultivate, not only in political life but throughout every part of
society, energetic, small-scale, voluntary associations that draw individuals out
of their cocoons of family and friends and jobs, into participation in deliberation,
decision, and action that make meaningful, or even crucial, differences in shaping life in the present and the future.

This requires a strenuous commitment to governmental decentralization
wherever possible—a devolution from vast and distant bureaucracies and courts,
to local and accessible citizen initiative and responsibility. In other words, government must be brought down to the level where it is not only more transparent
to the people, but more truly in the hands of the people.

This requires in addition an unceasing effort to foster, through legal and
governmental and policy incentives of all kinds, non-governmental associations
that assume some of the burdens and responsibilities of needed communal action. Through local voluntary clubs and groupings of all sorts, or through national and international fraternal associations with independent local chapters,
neighbors at close and long distance, who would otherwise remain strangers, can
discover the deep satisfactions of developing through mutual interaction the
political capacities of mature fellow citizens.

In remarking the success of this sort of process of informal democratic civic
education as it has developed in America, Tocqueville stresses the unique importance of organized religion. It is the churches, he observes, that are the oldest, the most successful, and the most inspiring wellsprings of American association. Nor has the contribution of institutional religion to American democracy
been exhausted by the critical role churches have played as matrices of association. Organized religion directly and massively contradicts materialism and narrow individualism; such religion comes to the support of embattled marital

bonds and family responsibilities; it places obstacles before the overweening authority of majoritarian public opinion, and champions minority rights; last but not least, organized religion serves as a counterweight to skepticism and moral relativism. It is true, of course, that the historical influence of traditional religion, especially in the Old and Third Worlds, has often been far from friendly or beneficial to democracy, toleration, or human rights. But here again the American tradition of church-state relations offers salutary lessons. For in America, it can be argued, organized religion—Catholic as well as Protestant—has remained relatively strong precisely because it has been compelled to suppress the ambition to become politically dominant or officially established. Precisely because no religious sect has become the national religion, religious sects in general have maintained the respect of the whole nation and the faith of a large proportion of the populace.

Following Tocqueville, we can imagine, and we need to work to realize, a democracy where citizens are aroused, not only by a sense of duty and dignity but also by enlightened self-interest, to more steady participation in local government; where the young are directed toward greater courage and patriotism by sharing the burdens of defense and emergency relief; where the commitments of spouses and the responsibilities of parents are more faithfully honored because more sternly enforced by public opinion, as much or more than by law; where parents, students, and teachers are more energetically cooperating in shaping local schools; where laborers are more fully involved in shaping, together with management, their workplace; where more widespread and active membership in churches and cultural or higher educational associations helps lift the human spirit from the anxious pursuit of short-lived gratifications.

A People Aroused to Collective Responsibilities

The second powerful counterforce to the drift toward soft democratic despotism upon which I wish to focus stands, paradoxically, in a healthy tension with the first. For it involves a movement in the direction opposite to decentralization and devolution. I have in mind Tocqueville's admonition that we welcome and exploit those often deeply troubling historical moments when a democratic people, as a whole nation or federation, is energized by vast crises that entail galvanizing responsibilities and that call forth grand projects of reform—in foreign as well as in domestic policy.

These calls to greatness arouse and energize the population as a whole, precisely because and insofar as they generate sharp controversy within the awakened citizenry as a whole. Deep division at such historical junctures is the healthy root of the vigorous party system—which for long periods may languish in desuetude, but which awakens, so to speak, at times of division caused by the confrontation with overwhelming challenges. At such times, the discord, the division, the national debate, is a sign and a source of seriousness, of vibrancy, of thoughtfulness, and of ambition sweeping up the mass of the people. The actual issues at stake can sometimes seem almost trivial to foreign eyes: Tocqueville takes as his leading example his own reaction to the mass conflict in America over the temperance movement (that is, the agitation to ban the sale, and thus to prevent the drinking, of alcoholic beverages). Tocqueville confesses that as a Frenchman, he found it utterly ridiculous, at first, to see a whole country convulsed over such a question. But then, he reports, it slowly dawned upon him that the great value of this controversy was not the issue itself, but the stimulus it gave to public debate: the way it led beyond the narrow issue, to include debate over other, more truly serious, and related questions—and to the whetting of public appetite for national debate as a regular part of civic life.

To lift citizens out the narrowness of individualism, out of the pettiness of materialism, out of the suffocation of egalitarian levelling, democratic leaders have a duty from time to time (in Tocqueville's words) "to give citizens difficult and dangerous problems to face, to rouse ambition and to give it a field of action." In a letter to John Stuart Mill (of March 18, 1841) reflecting on the threat of war in the Anglo-French crisis of 1840, Tocqueville wrote:

> I do not have to tell you, my dear Mill, that the greatest malady that threatens a people organized as we are is the gradual softening of mores, the abasement of the mind, the mediocrity of tastes; that is where the great dangers of the future lie. One cannot let a nation that is democratically constituted . . . take up easily the habit of sacrificing what it believes to be its grandeur to its repose, great matters to petty ones; it is not healthy to allow such a nation to believe that it must console itself by making railroads and by making prosper the well-being of each private individual in the bosom of peace, no matter how this peace is obtained.[4]

Retrieving the Concept of Leisure

Tocqueville would hardly have been surprised to learn that the life of the mind remains somewhat more in danger of becoming obscured in American life than it is in European. Certain it is that we Americans today, even more than in Tocqueville's time, are more and more at risk of losing ourselves in a too-exclusive immersion in the world of labor or business, supplemented, ever more exclusively, by nothing more than relaxation and entertainment. In other words, we are in danger of forgetting even the meaning of *leisure*.

The truly distinctive meaning and meaningfulness of leisure is given its classic expression in the last two books of Aristotle's *Politics*, taken together with the closing sections of his *Nicomachean Ethics*. In these pages Aristotle maps human existence as embracing three overlapping spheres: work, play, and leisure.

Work or business is the most basic and necessary of the three. Our existence is defined primarily by the needs of our mortal bodies, and by derivative requirements for power and security of all sorts: work or business comprises the activities by which we struggle to meet these gripping concerns. The temporary satisfaction of these needs is fleetingly pleasant and attractive; but what gives these demands, and the work they elicit, a compelling hold on us is something essentially unpleasant or threatening. When or insofar as these primary corporeal needs are not met, the consequent pain can soon eclipse everything else; what is more, we are haunted by the anxious foresight that warns us that our capacity to meet these basic needs may not persist, unless we work ever harder to accumulate ever more provisions of all kinds for and against the unchartable future. Work is therefore serious, both in the sense that its importance is indisputable, and in the sense that its challenge arouses and engrosses our dedicated and intense efforts of body and mind. But by the same token, work or business is not choiceworthy for its own sake. Work or business is essentially constrained and even servile: a clear sign of this is the fact that, when we perform work, we expect to be fully "compensated"—without which, we regard ourselves as enslaved.

Accordingly, we naturally seek relief, and even escape, from work or business—and we find this not merely in rest but in relaxation, in recreation, in play. Play seems pure pleasure, unconstrained and lighthearted; play seems to find its end in itself, and even whimsically creates ends as it goes. But by the same token, play is essentially lacking in seriousness. We can play "hard," or with intensity, but not with real dedication—or, when we do become dedicated to a game, it begins to cease to be mere play. Play as playful cannot engross our conscious being except partially or temporarily, and then always with an element of escapism, of shutting out and turning away from the serious world of work or business. For this is the "importance" of play: it is the recuperation, from the burden of work, that allows us to take up again that burden, to return to work as to what is serious and truly important. In other words, on close inspection, play transpires as not a sustainable end in itself, but rather as a supplement or even a means to work. The clear sign is that if we play for too long, play begins to be infected by the curse of *ennui*.

It is all too easy for modern humanity to be driven by *ennui* in only one direction—back to work. *Ennui* seems to teach the morbid lesson that work is all that really counts. In the grim words of Baudelaire's *Journal Intime*, "one must work, if not from taste then at least from despair. For, to reduce everything to a single truth: work is less boring than pleasure."[5] Yet this moment of *ennui* with its "single truth" has another, dialectical, potential—a potential of liberation from the spiritually unsatisfactory cycle of work and play. In this moment of *ennui*, we could be open to the saving significance of leisure.

Work is essentially serious but unpleasant; play is essentially pleasant but unserious. Leisure, in the classic sense, is essentially serious pleasure—seriously consuming pleasure. Leisure is constituted by activity that fully and unconstrainedly engages the very core of our conscious being, and thus ushers us into the experience of a felicity that is much more than mere contentment. Leisure at its fullest Aristotle identifies with philosophy, crowning what the Greeks called "music"—by which they meant all those activities that are presided over by the Muses, the goddesses of poetry, of drama and dance, of the fine arts, of history and theory. The classic conception of leisure is thus inextricably interwoven with divinity, and with sustained reflection on divinity or on the question as to what is divine. At the heart of Aristotle's outlook is his insistence that our being is above all our consciousness and self-consciousness, and that to exist fully is to become as awake as possible: awake to ourselves and to the question of our nature and our place in the scheme of things or in the whole. This is by no means to say that it is only or even mainly philosophy and theology that guide the public toward some participation in genuinely leisured study and reflection. The *"demiourgoi,"* the *"public craftsmen" par excellence,* are the artists, or at least those among the artists who take their civic-cultural educative responsibilities seriously. It is through these artists' sublime imitations and mimetic transfigurations of nature that we are most likely to become first aware of the entrancing joy of contemplation and meditation. It is through the poets' dramas of moral struggle that we are most likely to first discover the austere gratifications of critical scrutiny directed at the beauties that initially transfix us.

Today, this entire framework of life is slipping from sight in our workaday American world. The zeal for work and play in contemporary democracy threatens the atrophy of our soul's awareness of the music of life that is our highest and most authentic human vocation.

No doubt, there are truly beneficial and even ennobling cultural achievements that would be impossible without our zeal for hard work. The free enterprise system, animated by the profit motive and allied with technology, has secured unprecedented physical well-being for vast numbers. On the spiritual plane, the work ethic instills virtues of self-discipline, promotes education (if largely of a technical sort), inspires mutual respect and energetic cooperation among equals, and affords the deep satisfactions of professionalism—the self-respecting sense of a job well done.

But there is a constant danger that our preoccupations will become too exclusively centered on the ultimately ephemeral goods and esteem of the marketplace. The consequence is not only a loss of spirituality, but a kind of anxious, even frantic busyness that feeds on itself even while it alternates with lassitude, *ennui,* or despair. To paraphrase Tocqueville, in his still-pertinent observations on the feverish quality of so much of American society: for one whose heart is constricted to the quest solely for the material goods of this world, and for the prestige and self-respect that is won by possessing more and more such goods, the path and pace of life is always harried: the recollection of the brevity of existence goads him; apart from the goods and recognition that he already possesses, he vaguely imagines at every moment countless others that old age or death will prevent him from acquiring, if he doesn't hurry. A strange self-denial of the spirit steadily tightens its grip. The syndrome was articulated by Tocqueville's contemporary Karl Marx in these telling words:

Political economy, despite its worldly and wanton appearance—is a true moral science. This science of marvelous industry is the science of *asceticism* . . . Self-renunciation, the renunciation of life and of all human needs, is its principal thesis. . . . The less you go to the theater, to the dance, . . . the less you think, love, theorize, sing, paint, etc., the more you save!—the greater becomes your treasure which neither moths nor dust will devour: your *capital*. The less you are, the less that you express your life, the greater is your *alienated* life. . . . in everything that you can not do, your money can do *for* you: your money can support the dance, and the theater . . . your money can appropriate art, your money can acquire learning, your money can accumulate the treasures of the past—it can buy all this *for* you. . . . To be sure, the capitalist also takes his pleasures . . . but his pleasure is only a side-issue—it is *recreation*—something subordinated to production.[6]

Conclusion

This invocation of Karl Marx, and the attendant shadow of his dark legacy, suffices to remind us that that there is a terrible danger hidden in the concern for high culture, when or insofar as it induces a revulsion against "capitalism" or the "bourgeois." The history of Europe in the last two centuries has taught us (much more vividly than we have been taught by the history of the United States) how easily—even or especially in truly serious thinkers—the perceived threat to high culture posed by "the bourgeois way of life" can become a source of contempt for real-world democracy. This danger is as visible in great thinkers on the Right as it is among those on the Left. And the danger is (to employ a favorite Marxist locution) no accident. For modern democracy does bring with it an inevitable popularization, and thus to some extent a vulgarization, of culture. In the words of Winston Churchill (speaking in 1941), modern democracy requires us to resign ourselves to the recognition that what we have to expect from it is "a wider, if a simpler culture."[7] Disgust at this unavoidable consequence of modern democracy makes it all too easy for defenders of the life of the mind to forget the true value, the true virtues, of modern mass democracy. The virtues of this democracy at its best are surely not refined taste, love of the sublime, and Pascal's *esprit de finesse*. The virtues of democracy at its best are the spiritually ennobling and mentally invigorating civic virtues—virtues expressed in widespread active participation in, and acceptance of responsibility for, the argument and the action of genuine collective self-government.

We are permitted to hope that Europe—and not least "Old Europe"—can still teach, and America can still learn, not to allow the world of work and recreation to swallow up or to make us forget entirely the meaning and the experience of the life of leisure: the life of the mind seeking its own inherent satisfactions through un-productive reflection, receptivity, and spiritual generation.

At the same time, we may hopefully ask, regarding democracy in Europe: can and will the inevitable weakening of national governmental power and authority in the new European Union afford the opportunity for a strengthening of local government and the role of voluntary associations? Or will this opportunity be lost, or fail to materialize—with power flowing overwhelmingly to a paternalistic form of egalitarian administrative despotism?

And in the second place, can European public opinion find, in the current world, challenges that define for Europe, as a whole, an energizing European consciousness and civic conscience? Can the populace of Europe come alive to widespread, stirring debate that leads to resolute collective decision? Can Europe discover or recover the inner resources for debate that is strenuous without being poisonous, for argument that can antagonize but that does not demonize? Or is Europe still too haunted by the living ghosts of old quarrels that not so long ago divided her in a destructive way, quarrels that signaled bloody stasis rather than dialectical unity? If or insofar as Tocqueville teaches the truth about modern democracy, then the answers to these questions will go a long way in determining whether or not the idea of Europe promises a new birth of freedom for democracy in Europe and thus for mankind.

Notes

1. Previously published as "De Tweeledige uitdaging van een democratische cultuur in onze tijd," trans. Henny Vlot, *Nexus* 40 (2004): 73-85 (*Europa Realiseren/Realising Europe*: The Papers of the First European Cultural Summit, hosted by the Dutch Presidency of the European Union). Reprinted with kind permission of the publisher.

2. Alexis de Tocqueville, *Democracy in America*, volume I, "Introduction." My translation.

3. Tocqueville, *Democracy*, volume II, part IV, chapter 6. My translation.

4. Tocqueville, Letter to John Stuart Mill, March 18, 1841, in Alexis de Tocqueville, *Selected Letters on Politics and Society*, ed. Roger Boesche (Berkeley: University of California Press, 1985), 150-51. I have slightly altered the translation.

5. Charles Baudelaire quoted in Josef Pieper, *Leisure: The Basis of Culture*, trans. Alexander Dru (New York: Pantheon Books, 1952), 75.

6. Karl Marx, "The Meaning of Human Requirements," from *Economic and Philosophic Manuscripts of 1844*. My translation.

7. Winston Churchill, "The Choice for Europe," in *Blood, Sweat and Tears* (New York: G.P. Putnam's Sons, 1941), 18.

Index

About the Contributors

Derek Wai Ming Barker is program officer at the Kettering Foundation in Dayton, Ohio. His research focuses on democratic theory and the history of political thought. He is the author of *Tragedy and Citizenship: Conflict, Reconciliation, and Democracy from Haemon to Hegel* (State University of New York Press, 2008).

Richard Boyd is associate professor of government at Georgetown University. Previously he taught at the University of Chicago, University of Pennsylvania, University of Wisconsin-Madison, and Deep Springs College. He is author of *Uncivil Society: The Perils of Pluralism and the Making of Modern Liberalism* (2004); a forthcoming book *Liberalism, Capacities, and Citizenship*; and numerous journal articles and book chapters on the intellectual history of liberalism.

Paul Carrese is professor of political science at the U.S. Air Force Academy and former director of its honors program. He is co-editor of John Marshall's *The Life of George Washington: Special Edition* (2001), and is author of *The Cloaking of Power: Montesquieu, Blackstone, and the Rise of Judicial Activism* (2003); he has published articles and book chapters on constitutionalism, Montesquieu, Tocqueville, Washington's ideals and character, and the principles of American foreign policy.

Brian Danoff is assistant professor of political science at Miami University in Oxford, Ohio. He is the author of *Educating Democracy: Alexis de Tocqueville and Leadership in America* (2010). His articles on American political thought and modern political theory have appeared in such journals as *The Review of Politics, Perspectives on Political Science, Presidential Studies Quarterly*, and *Politics and Policy*.

Albert W. Dzur is associate professor of political science and philosophy at Bowling Green State University. He is the author of *Democratic Professionalism: Citizen Participation and the Reconstruction of Professional Ethics, Identi-*

ty, and Practice (2008). His current research explores the potential of democratic theory for imagining more participatory and reflective criminal justice institutions.

Khalil Habib is assistant professor of philosophy and director of the Pell Honors Program at Salve Regina University in Newport, Rhode Island. He specializes in classical and early modern political philosophy and ethics. His current research interest examines the origins of liberalism, the theoretical foundations of modernity, and Islamic and Christian political thought.

L. Joseph Hebert is associate professor and chair of political science and leadership studies and director of pre-law studies at St. Ambrose University in Davenport, Iowa. He is the author of *More than Kings and Less Than Men: Tocqueville on the Promise and Perils of Democratic Individualism* (2010) and of published works exploring Tocqueville's treatment of intellectual liberty and cosmopolitanism.

Peter Augustine Lawler is Dana Professor of Government at Berry College and editor of the acclaimed scholarly quarterly *Perspectives on Political Science.* He was a member of President Bush's Bioethics Council and a recipient of the 2007 Weaver Prize in Scholarly Letters. He has written or edited fourteen books and over two hundred articles and chapters in a wide variety of venues. His newest book is *Modern and American Dignity.*

Susan McWilliams is assistant professor of politics at Pomona College in Claremont, California. She is working on a book that explores the role of travel stories in the history of Western political thought. Her work has appeared in journals such as *The American Conservative, Boston Review, Commonweal, Perspectives on Political Science,* and *PS: Political Science and Politics.*

Thomas L. Pangle holds the Joe R. Long Endowed Chair in Democratic Studies in the Department of Government at the University of Texas at Austin. His latest book is *The Theological Basis of Liberal Modernity in Montesquieu's "Spirit of the Laws"* (University of Chicago Press).

William B. Parsons is assistant professor of political science at Carroll College in Helena, Montana. He teaches courses in ancient and modern political thought, as well as comparative politics. His research interests are American political thought and early modern political thought; his current project is a study of the political thought of Thomas Paine.

Jon D. Schaff is professor of political science at Northern State University in Aberdeen, South Dakota where he teaches courses on the American presidency and American political thought, among others. His articles on the presidency and Abraham Lincoln have appeared in such journals as *Political Research*

Quarterly, *White House Studies*, and *Perspectives on Political Science*. He also writes on the political culture of the Great Plains.

F. Flagg Taylor IV is assistant professor of government at Skidmore College. He is the editor of *Modern Tyranny: Ideology and Totalitarianism since 1917* (forthcoming, Spring 2011).

Aristide Tessitore is professor of political science at Furman University. He is author of *Reading Aristotle's Ethics: Virtue, Rhetoric and Political Philosophy* (1996) and editor of *Aristotle and Modern Politics: The Persistence of Political Philosophy* (2002). He has published numerous articles on classical political philosophy and more recently on the thought of Alexis de Tocqueville. His work has appeared in such journals as the *American Political Science Review*, *Political Theory*, *Journal of Politics*, *Polity*, *Review of Politics*, *Perspectives on Political Science*, and the *Southern Journal of Philosophy*.

Conor Williams is a PhD candidate in Georgetown University's government department. He is writing a dissertation on the effects of historicized politics on twentieth-century liberal pluralists, with an emphasis on John Dewey and Michael Oakeshott.

Thad Williamson is assistant professor in the Jepson School of Leadership Studies at the University of Richmond. His academic work engages political theory, public policy, urban politics, and theories of social change. He is author of *Sprawl, Justice and Citizenship: The Civic Costs of the American Way of Life* (2010) and co-author of *Making a Place for Community: Local Democracy in a Global Era* (2002), and co-editor of *Property-Owning Democracy: Rawls and Beyond* (2011). He is currently researching a study of power and decision making in contemporary Richmond, Virginia.

Breinigsville, PA USA
15 March 2011
257633BV00001B/3/P